Mormon Women's History

The Fairleigh Dickinson University Press Mormon Studies Series

The Fairleigh Dickinson University Press Mormon Studies Series is committed to the publication of scholarly works that explore Mormon history, literature, film, biography, and theology, as well as considering how Mormonism has interacted with society, culture, folklore, philosophy, politics, and the arts.

**General Editor: Dr. Rachel Cope, Department of
Church History and Doctrine, Brigham Young University**

Series Editors:

Dr. Andrew Hedges, Associate Professor, Church History and Doctrine, Brigham Young University

Dr. Susanna Morrill, Department Chair and Associate Professor of Religious Studies, Lewis and Clark College

Dr. Andrew Skinner, Professor, Ancient Scripture, Brigham Young University

Dr. John W. Welch, Robert K. Thomas University Professor of Law, Brigham Young University

Advisory Board:

Catherine Brekus (Harvard University Divinity School), Richard Bushman (Columbia University), David Campbell (University of Notre Dame), James H. Charlesworth (Princeton Theological Seminary), Terryl Givens (University of Richmond), David Holland (Harvard University Divinity School), Kate Holbrook (Church History Library), Laurie Maffly-Kipp (Washington University in St. Louis), Tom Mould (Elon University), and Stephen Webb (Independent Scholar).

On the Web at http://www.fdu.edu/fdupress

Publications in Mormon Studies

Rachel Cope, *Mormon Women's History: Beyond Biography* (2017)

Nicholas J. Frederick, *The Bible, Mormon Scripture, and the Rhetoric of Allusivity* (2016)

Ignacio M. García, *Chicano While Mormon: Activism, War, and Keeping the Faith* (2015)

Mauro Properzi, *Mormonism and the Emotions: An Analysis of LDS Scriptural Texts* (2015)

Adam J. Powell, *Irenaeus, Joseph Smith, and God-making Heresy* (2015)

Mormon Women's History

Beyond Biography

Edited by
Rachel Cope,
Amy Easton-Flake,
Keith A. Erekson, and Lisa Olsen Tait

FAIRLEIGH DICKINSON UNIVERSITY PRESS
Madison • Teaneck

Published by Fairleigh Dickinson University Press
Copublished by The Rowman & Littlefield Publishing Group, Inc.
4501 Forbes Boulevard, Suite 200, Lanham, Maryland 20706
www.rowman.com

Unit A, Whitacre Mews, 26-34 Stannary Street, London SE11 4AB

British Library Cataloguing in Publication Information Available

Library of Congress Cataloging-in-Publication Data

Names: Cope, Rachel, editor.
Title: Mormon women's history : beyond biography / edited by Rachel Cope.
Description: Madison ; Teaneck : Fairleigh Dickinson University Press, [2017]
   | Series: Fairleigh Dickinson University Press Mormon studies series |
   Includes bibliographical references and index.
Identifiers: LCCN 2017038052 (print) | LCCN 2017042056 (ebook) | ISBN
   9781611479652 (Electronic) | ISBN 9781611479645 (cloth : alk. paper)
Subjects: LCSH: Mormon women—History. | Mormon Church—Historiography.
Classification: LCC BX8643.W66 (ebook) | LCC BX8643.W66 M68 2017 (print) |
   DDC 289.3082—dc23
LC record available at https://lccn.loc.gov/2017038052

♾️™ The paper used in this publication meets the minimum requirements of
American National Standard for Information Sciences—Permanence of Paper
for Printed Library Materials, ANSI/NISO Z39.48-1992.

Printed in the United States of America

Contents

Introduction

Rachel Cope

This volume, the outgrowth of a symposium whose title and theme was "Beyond Biography: Sources in Context for Mormon Women's History," is part of a vibrant renaissance in the study of Mormon women. This renaissance has emerged on the heels of several recent volumes—including important biographies of Mormon female leaders like Amy Brown Lyman and Emmeline B. Wells; primary source collections like Joanna Brooks, et al.'s *Mormon Feminism*, Jill Derr et al.'s *The First Fifty Years of Relief Society*, and Jennifer Reeder and Kate Holbrook's *At the Pulpit*; edited collections like Kate Holbrook and Matthew Bowman's *Women and Mormonism*; and monographs like Laurel Thatcher Ulrich's recent book, *A House Full of Females: Plural Marriage and Women's Rights in Early Mormonism, 1835–1870*. Such works have advanced a number of themes illustrated in this volume, particularly, the importance of contextualizing the study of Mormon women in broader narratives of American religious and cultural history and the use of a wide range of scholarly tools in those efforts.[1]

In response to this scholarly renaissance, the authors whose works appear in this book have drawn upon both traditional and nontraditional primary sources in order to demonstrate how to engage in creative readings and interpretations of different types of source material and how to analyze and contextualize such sources so that a more complete and complex picture of Mormon women's history emerges. The stories that unfold in this book thus highlight the impact that Mormon women have had on their church's history and on American religious history as a whole, essentially spanning Mormon settlement in Utah through the early twentieth century—a formative and radical time period toward which scholars continue to gravitate, since it seems to speak to and resonate with modern changes and sensibilities. By emphasizing the time period and geographic space traditionally the focus of historians of Mormonism, this volume points out the many ways that new sources and creative methodological approaches can push and probe the boundaries of a historiography we thought we already knew. It is our hope that these examples will not only expand the scope of current historiography but also stimulate future scholarship that looks to and beyond Utah in the long nineteenth century.

As the compilation of this volume was underway, my grandmother, Florence Annetta Fairbanks (1919–2016), whose life story implicitly and explicitly encompasses the themes covered in this volume, passed away. Here, I use my grandmother's story, and the sources that contain that story, to suggest that there are many ways in which sources and contexts can help a woman's story shift from simple biography to complex and nuanced story—to reveal how a life that could easily be forgotten outside of the context of family history has the potential to shed light on larger historical themes and events.

At first glance, my grandmother's story echoes that of many Mormon women of her generation. She and her siblings were born to and raised by devout Latter-day Saints (LDS) parents. After graduating from Brigham Young University, Florence Cope married James Austin Cope Jr., in the Salt Lake Temple. She raised a large family on a budget. She canned fruit and vegetables from her immense garden, baked bread, made fantastic Christmas candy, and always had a meal for someone in need. She faithfully wove scripture reading and prayer into the fabric of her daily life and taught her children to do likewise. Cope served as Relief Society president, and her husband served as a bishop, stake president, and patriarch.[2] After raising their family, they served two LDS missions together, one in Kalamazoo, Michigan, and the other in San Antonio, Texas. They had a large posterity, and children, grandchildren, and great-grandchildren often filled their home.

This brief sketch suggests that Cope's story is rather normative—normative because it is common and because it echoes the brief biographical form found in LDS family history accounts and obituaries.[3] Indeed, it tells the story we might expect of a Mormon woman whose life spanned much of the twentieth century. And because this version of the story seems to meet preconceived assumptions, it is easy to conclude that her life sheds very little light on much of anything beyond her own family.

But careful contextualization—enabled by the extensive collection of diaries and journals, letters, scrapbooks, photo albums, photographs, cookbooks, cards, college notebooks and memorabilia, Relief Society lesson outlines, spiritual diaries, personal notes, family papers, books, and other items that Cope recorded and preserved over the course of her lifetime, which have recently been donated to the L. Tom Perry Special Collections Library in the

Figure Intro.1.   This is a photograph of Florence Fairbanks Cope and James Austin Cope Jr. just prior to serving their LDS mission in San Antonio, Texas, from 1990 to 1991.

Harold B. Lee Library at Brigham Young University—reveals that there is more to Cope's story than a simple biographical sketch implies. True, she was a wife and mother, a homemaker, a woman whose influence seemed confined to her own personal domestic sphere. But the significance of her story, preserved in the kinds of sources historians can use (sources similar to those used in the various articles throughout this book) has the potential to reach beyond Fairbanks and Cope family history. A study of Cope's life reveals the expansive and complex nature of family structures and relationships—the angle of her story that is the focus of this introduction—to demonstrate how one woman's experiences can shed light on a larger religious narrative. However, many readers will recognize that, in addition to explaining what Mormons believed about families and how they lived in them, Cope's story also advances other themes included in this volume: it captures the tensions and diverse tugs on Mormon women's minds and hearts from institutions and community; it highlights the strain of adaptation from the independent polygamous Mormon commonwealth to integration with the United States; it captures attempts to assimilate American Indians into "white" culture, as with Sally Exervier Ward; it underscores the importance of women's theological contributions, as with Hannah Tapfield King; it illustrates the many means through which women, such as members of the Browett family, enabled relationships with one another; it emphasizes the creation of the home and its theological influence; it exemplifies the use of divergent source materials, such as the correspondence of Mine Jorgensen, the artwork of Mary Teasdel, or the poetry of Emily Scott; and it covers the time frame on which this volume focuses—the "Utah" period, ranging from 1847 through the turn of the century. In *Beyond Biography*, we sound a call to move the study of Mormon (and American) women (and men) beyond simple life narration to incorporate the contextual significance of those lives and to grapple with a vast array of topics essential for understanding Mormon history and, by extension, the religious history of which Mormon history is a part.

Despite the seemingly narrow scope of Cope's biographical sketch, a contextualized reading of her papers reveals that she was not, in fact, born into a "typical" family, a detail that perhaps challenges the idea that family has always been defined in the same way. Cope's father, John B. Fairbanks, born in 1855, was nearly sixty-four years her senior.[4] Although Fairbanks had been raised in territorial Utah where many Mormons practiced polygamy, his own marriage to Lillie Annetta Huish, which took place over a decade prior to the LDS Church's announcement that it would no longer endorse the practice of plural marriage, was monogamous. Family legend suggests that LDS Church leaders asked Fairbanks to practice polygamy. Although John and Lillie agreed to take this difficult step, the Manifesto ending plural marriage was issued before they did so. A letter John wrote to Lillie in 1890 upon hearing about the Manifesto hints at their commitment to the principle and to their belief that it contained salvific elements.[5] For the Fairbanks family, news about the end of plural marriage did not seem to serve as a source of relief but, rather, as a shock, and even as a source of regret. John Fairbanks, it seems, may have felt some guilt for not immediately following the counsel to take a plural wife.

When John and Lillie's tenth son and eleventh child, Avard, was still an infant, Lillie had an accident that ultimately resulted in her untimely death.[6] At this tragic time, John Fairbanks drew upon the help of his eighteen-year-old daughter Nettie, who became a maternal figure as well as an elder sister to her younger siblings. After the Fairbanks children had reached adulthood, John, then age sixty-one, met Florence Gifford, a schoolteacher in her mid-twenties who was raising her young niece, Nellie Johnson.[7] The couple married on September 21, 1917. They would raise Nellie to adulthood and have five additional children. Florence Fairbanks Cope was the eldest of John Fairbanks's second family.

Although John Fairbanks had two monogamous marriages during his lifetime, his belief in the eternal nature of the Mormon marriage sealing meant that he ultimately did, indeed, have two wives. Therefore, even though Cope was born into a monogamous family in the post-Manifesto age, she grew up believing that her father's two families would eventually be joined together as one. Commitment to this union is, perhaps, best captured by her full name: Florence after her own mother, and Annetta after her father's deceased wife (Lillie Annetta). Such a complex familial experience demonstrates the Mormon belief that sequential families will become simultaneous families in a postmortal sphere.[8]

The Fairbanks family continued to be impacted by a diverse array of intricate familial ties that complicate and run counter to twenty-first-century notions of family. Cope grew up with an elderly father whose background was rooted in the age of Mormon pioneers, with eleven older half siblings who were twenty to forty-one years her senior, and with nieces and nephews who ranged from her own age to close to that of her mother. Her personal papers suggest that half siblings often assumed paternal and aunt- or uncle-like roles, while nieces and nephews acted as parents, cousins, or siblings. Additionally, Cope considered her cousin, Nellie, whom her parents raised, her older sister.[9] Clearly, the roles of grandparent, parent, aunt, uncle, cousin, and sibling were, in many ways, conflated in the context of Fairbanks family relationships—a network of ties that shed light on early Mormon conceptions of family and on the often-fluid nature of kinship throughout American history.[10]

During the first five years of Cope's life, the Fairbanks family lived in Salt Lake City, but they later moved to Springdale (near Zion's National Park in southern Utah) in order to live with Florence's grandmother, Alice Gifford. In Springdale, the meaning of kinship extended even further for Cope. Her Grandmother Gifford was a plural wife—Alice's husband, Oliver Gifford, married Emily Ann Hepworth in 1882, prior to the announcement of the Manifesto.[11] The division of Oliver's time between his two families meant that Alice needed extra help on the family farm and assistance in raising Nellie's sisters, Lanetta and Margie, following complications that resulted from her broken hip. In this context, Cope became a part of an extended polygamous family whose lives crossed multiple generational lines.[12] Alice, for example, was only eight months older than her son-in-law, John Fairbanks. Cousins, siblings, parents, and grandparents assumed a multiplicity of roles, and extended family members, neighbors, and friends became a central part of the Fairbanks family's fictive ties.[13] When Alice Gifford passed away in 1928, the Fairbanks family moved back to Salt Lake, while Grandfather Oliver Gifford remained in Springdale with his plural wife, Emily. In the first decade of Cope's life, the definition of family came to involve far more than mom, dad, and children. Her family, on both the Fairbanks and the Gifford sides, was centered in a vast network of complex relationships that enriched and complicated daily life, relationships that capture significant themes and ideas woven throughout history, theology, and culture.[14]

In 1941, Florence Fairbanks was sealed to James Austin Cope Jr. in the Salt Lake Temple. Over the course of nearly twenty-two years, she had thirteen children. But her broad sense of family relationships continued to shape her life. Participating in the LDS Church's Indian Student Placement Services— a program that placed American Indian students in Mormon (white) homes during the academic year so they could attend public schools—she became a foster parent to three American Indian teenagers.[15] The Cope family also "adopted" some individuals who were alone or struggling, making them a part of their own family. For example, a widowed and childless neighbor, Janet Oakerman, became like an aunt to the family.[16] (Even today, the Cope family continues to put flowers on her grave each Memorial Day.) Cope's service to the LDS Church also resulted in relationships that extended beyond the contours of her own home. While Cope was serving as president of the Relief Society in her local congregation, her infant daughter, Janet, passed away. The kinship Cope felt with the women in that organization—women who became her spiritual sisters—helped her through the mourning process.[17] This aspect of her story, recorded within her own personal diaries but also captured in correspondence, speaks to how women expressed themselves during trying times and hints at the ways in which a sense of sisterhood helped women endure and overcome those experiences.[18]

Cope's sense of spiritual community is further captured within and beyond the context of the Relief Society. When her husband served as bishop of the Spanish Fork Seventh Ward, he and Florence invited inactive couples (those less engaged in congregational worship) to participate in a scripture study group held in the Copes' home. In the context of this domestic setting, women as well as men engaged in significant and deeply personal theological discussions. Ultimately, those involved in the group reengaged with their Mormon faith, and the Copes built powerful bonds of spiritual kinship with them. Creating and nurturing a "ward family" was a very real part of the Copes' lived religious experience as they fostered the pragmatic effects of their doctrinal beliefs within the context of their own home. Such acts extended throughout their lives. Even in their eighties, the Copes opened their home to a struggling seventeen-year-old from Nigeria, Nnabuife, who lived in their basement for over a year and affectionately referred to them as "Grandma" and "Grandpa." As these examples demonstrate, Cope's story reveals the expansive and complex nature of Mormon families, specifically the importance of fictive ties that bring wards, church auxiliaries, neighbors, and even strangers together—an expansiveness that Mormons themselves sometimes overlook.

Cope's youngest son, Todd, was born a couple of weeks after her first grandchild, Davie, making her both mother and grandmother to infants simultaneously. Her personal writings show that she raised children with her eldest daughter, AnnEtta, and her grandchildren played with their aunts and uncles (just as Florence had grown up doing). As a grandma, she played multiple roles in the lives of her grandchildren, ever committed to creating a domestic space that reflected her religious beliefs.

In the final years of her life, Cope's husband and eldest daughter passed away. Her belief in the endless nature of familial and social ties was enriched as a result of these experiences. As she neared her own death, she looked forward to being reunited with her parents, her husband, and her eldest and youngest daughters, AnnEtta and Janet. She spoke most frequently of her reunion with Janet and anticipated the opportunity to finally raise her baby girl, a Mormon teaching that made Cope's motherhood as tangible after death as it was before.[19] At the time of her passing, Cope had 78 grandchildren, 247 great-grandchildren, and 9 great-great-grandchildren, but that vast number of people comprised only a portion of those she considered family.

As the daughter of a man born in 1855, Cope's life and the vast collection of documents she preserved, which span 161 years, offer a lens into Mormonism's complex past. Like all of women's history, Mormon women's history needs to be more than an acknowledgment that women existed; it needs to speak to broader issues, ideas, and events—and Cope's personal papers provide multiple means through which historians can do that. Florence Annetta Fairbanks Cope's story, when its details and sources are properly contextualized, reaches beyond biography, offering a glimpse into Mormonism's sense of kinship, community, and covenant, as well as countless other themes. And she is just one example of the kind of work that can be done when historians look at similar kinds of papers preserved by a vast array of other women.

* * *

This volume is composed of ten chapters that use Mormon women's experiences to grapple with and challenge various historiographical and/or methodological issues and to demonstrate how their experiences can make significant contributions to larger historical narratives and expand the scope of historiographical discussions. Specifically, these articles highlight a multiplicity of ways in which women's stories extend beyond simple biographical sketches and encapsulate the depth and breadth of Mormon history. These chapters place their subjects' lives into a myriad of contexts and ably demonstrate how the creative use of a variety of primary sources—including journals and diaries, letters, family histories, periodicals, art, poetry, material culture, genealogical records, and theological treatises—can shed light on history. By examining topics as varied as American Indian women, family and community ties, poetry, art, material culture, missionary wives, and theology, this collective work illustrates the many ways in which overlooked lives, and the sources that capture elements of those lives, can say new and interesting things about women, Mormonism, and religion in general. Consequently, the chapters in this book help us draw closer to understanding Ann Braude's insightful declaration that "women's history *is* American religious history."[20]

A detailed historiographical discussion, which responds, in part, to Braude's declaration, unfolds in the first chapter. The volume opens with Keith A. Erekson's review of the literature on Mormon women coupled with recommendations for advancing future inquiry to move beyond biography. The literary treatment of Mormon women began in the nineteenth century, with outsized external attention on the practice of polygamy and internally written defenses of the practice and practitioners. In the twentieth century, historians took on the important task of recovering the lives and voices of Mormon women, resulting most often in nuanced biographical treatments. Yet, as Erekson demonstrates, the field still struggles to understand women's agency, individuality, and integration within wider historical narratives. Moving beyond biography, he contends, requires an innovative use of sources created by and about Mormon women, careful attention to the functions they carried out (not just the formal positions they held within the church), conscientious discovery of their participation in institutions, thoughtful revisiting of the significance of their conversion experiences and narratives, and thorough historicization of their families and family experience within wider cultural analysis.

The challenges—and rewards—of meticulous historical source work are illustrated by Jenny Hale Pulsipher's masterful recovery and recontextualization of Sally Exervier Ward, a Shoshone Indian woman and convert to the Church of Jesus Christ of Latter-day Saints. In this case, the dearth of historical source material on women generally is exacerbated by the tendency to elevate the perspective of the "winners" in the struggle for literal and cultural dominance. Nevertheless, by listening closely to family legends and oral histories, Pulsipher deromanticizes and reconstructs the experience of obscure, illiterate, female, and non-white individuals. Mormons' unique beliefs about American Indians' Book of Mormon ancestry and the LDS practice of polygamy—a marriage system also practiced among Native peoples—makes an American Indian perspective valuable, even crucial, to understanding nineteenth-century LDS history. Along the way, Pulsipher demonstrates that, despite a theology that suggested a noble spiritual heritage for the American Indians, Mormons found it difficult to transcend the cultural prejudice against Indians and those of mixed blood prevalent in nineteenth-century America. The victory of prevailing cultural prejudice over professions of spiritual kinship tragically undermined relationships and triggered violence.

Andrea G. Radke-Moss carefully unravels the memories and meanings ascribed by Mormon women and men to their experiences of vigilante violence, sexual assault, and religious exile by considering the litany of injustices they faced during the Mormon-Missouri War of 1838. By training her eye on the reports and memories of rape, Radke-Moss exposes the gendered formation of Mormon collective memory and identity. In public and political speeches and writings, Mormon men crafted a narrative of religious persecution, idolized Mormon prophet Joseph Smith as a "defender of female virtue," and justified the use of violence in a massacre perpetrated by Mormons twenty years later. On the other hand, in private conversations and veiled references, Mormon women articulated a sense of shared sisterhood through suffering and survival. Radke-Moss traces both strains of memories through reminiscences, official Church publications, and twenty-first-century popular culture, commenting on the implications for understanding memory and identity through the lingering effects of war, violence, and trauma.

Drawing upon fragments of information scattered throughout church and government documents, as well as passing references found in diaries and correspondence located at various repositories throughout the United States and the United Kingdom, Amy Harris weaves together the stories of the Browett women—a mother, daughter, and two daughters-in-law who converted to Mormonism—in order to demonstrate how genealogical research makes it possible to uncover the stories of otherwise forgotten women. By contextualizing their biographical details, she also shows how individual stories are influenced by and shed light on culture, belief, and religious practice. Specifically, Harris contends that the flexibility of family and marriage structures inherent in the Browett women's English experience prepared them for Mormonism's comprehensive approach to family relationships. Notwithstanding widowhood, singleness, divorce, and childlessness, the Browett women participated fully in Mormon rituals that offered an inclusive and expansive network of family relationships to everyone. Together, Harris argues, the Browett women's stories illuminate how women combined their preexisting cultural beliefs and practices with Mormonism's startling combination of family, priesthood, and salvation—a combination that encompassed men and women in sacralized and potentially divine kinship networks.

Amy Easton-Flake turns our attention to the significance of poetry as historical source, using Mormon women's poems published in the pages of the *Woman's Exponent* between 1872 and 1914 to make her case. Easton-Flake notes that historians have been reluctant to use poetry as a historical source, due to modernist views of poems as ambiguous, apolitical, aesthetic objects as well as to the legacy of the "new critical" approach to poetry that casts literary critics as the only experts able to unlock the meaning of poetry. Easton-Flake draws on recent literary scholarship that has demonstrated the expansive and central role of poetry in nineteenth-century America to argue that this literary medium provides a unique window into Mormon women's interiority and how they constructed and promoted collective identity. Poetry reveals experiences left obscure in other contemporary sources, particularly as relating to topics that were personal, sacred, or socially transgressive. In this latter sense, poetry provided an approved entry into public discourse for women occupying a position on the boundary between private and public life. As Easton-Flake argues, in the process of embracing women's poems, we allow these women to define their own lives and society and to receive recognition for affecting ideas and social change through their writings.

In her chapter on Mormon women artists, Heather Belnap Jensen demonstrates how a select group of women, including Mary Teasdel, Rose Hartwell, and Alice Merrill Horne, formed an unofficial artistic sisterhood at home and abroad to become incarnations of what contemporary William C. Brownell termed "aesthetic evangelists." As Jensen explains, women in Mormon Utah's nascent art community infused their work with a sense of higher purpose, declaring it their spiritual calling to preside over the holy realms of art and culture, to consecrate their artistic capacities to the edification of the Saints, and to proselytize the Gospel of Beauty. Moving their stories beyond biography, Jensen considers these women's unofficial mission in the context of broader cultural developments, including the sacralization of art, the growth of women's social collectives, and the increasing professionalization of women in the art world. As Jensen argues, the study of this sisterhood further illuminates our understanding of the nexus of women, art, and religion at this historical juncture, as it demonstrates how women on the American frontier were critical to the cultivation of visual arts and how a religious institution such as the LDS Church could facilitate both the advancement of the arts as well as women's greater participation in the public sphere.

Examining a set of seemingly unremarkable articles in a women's magazine, Josh E. Probert reveals a profound reorientation of Mormon women's lives in the late nineteenth and early twentieth centuries. Probert contends that Leah Dunford Widtsoe and Alice Merrill Horne each drew on established discourses espoused by East Coast tastemakers to describe "artistic" and "rational" home design as a moral imperative, ascribing to household furnishings the power to mold the character of a home's inhabitants. However, the standards described by Widtsoe and Horne were materially unrealistic for many of their readers and ran contrary to the ethic of pioneer frugality and egalitarianism upon which the community had been built. Therefore, Probert suggests, Widtsoe and Horne sought to spiritualize the ideal even further by invoking unique Latter-day Saint theology, arguing that Mormon women needed to educate themselves in aesthetics in order to participate in building the Millennial New Jerusalem. This argument served to legitimize the aesthetic pleasure and social status that consumer society promised, but it also made Mormons' unique identity contingent upon the cultural codes of that society and signaled a new relationship of Mormon women to the world at large.

Julie K. Allen skillfully unravels the complex set of social relationships experienced by Mormon women who remained home while their husbands served missions. She takes as her documentary basis a cache of nearly two hundred letters—which she translated from the original Danish—between Mormon converts, a husband and wife, who immigrated to Utah. When Hans Jørgensen was called on a mission to return to their native Denmark, his wife, Mine, managed affairs at home for nearly three years. Allen teases out of the letters the emotional hardship of separation and loneliness and the necessity of Mine's assuming male gender roles of farming and contract negotiation. Having settled in a community composed predominantly of Danish converts, Mine had to navigate a world in which Danish, American, and Mormon values and norms competed and coalesced in shifting configurations of lived religion, gender dynamics, domesticity, acculturation, social class, and the tug and pull of center and periphery. As a "straw widow"—a woman operating singly within the community—she was both pulled into new roles and reminded of the limitations of her gender, language, geographic displacement, and convert status.

In his chapter on gendering the Mormon theological narrative, Benjamin E. Park takes up the question of why, historiographically and methodologically, the Mormon theological sphere has been a patriarchal space. He asks: Why have historians of LDS thought primarily focused on male voices, and why has the religious thought of women been relegated to a different sphere? What models could be employed not only to include women but to allow women's voices to shape the frameworks in which we understand their contributions? Looking at the theme of redemption in 1840s Nauvoo, Park provides an example of what this kind of history might look like. By using both familiar sources as well as sources that are often overlooked, he pieces together the intellectual climate of a community that challenged the boundaries of American society. In the process, Park demonstrates how historians of theological, intellectual, and religious history can integrate a wider array of voices and frameworks into broader synthetic narratives.

The book concludes with R. Marie Griffith's observation that the field of Mormon women's studies is ripe for a crossover book—a work of scholarship that transcends its immediate intellectual context to reshape wider historical narratives. She analyzes the work of Robert Orsi in depth and cites numerous examples from a variety of historical subfields to mount a compelling call for work on Mormon women that will reshape patterns of thinking and analysis and generate field-changing interpretations of gender and religion in US history. "We need a book that compels students to fall in love with Mormon women's lives," she states, "and really grasp these lives in larger historical context." What might such a crossover book look like? Griffith notes the rich themes of Mormon missionization and globalization, patriarchy and agency, friendship and solidarity. She reminds us of the need to think about both what is unique to Mormon women's experience and what is shared. A successful crossover work, she contends, touches on emotion that is not always comfortable to discuss, such as pain, frustration, or chafing within a tradition that prompts both devotion and loneliness. In short, Griffith implores, we need more studies of Mormon women that both penetrate the "deep truths embedded in" their social setting and resonate "with the deep truths embedded in others'."

As each of the chapter summaries indicate, the chapters in this book examine sources and contexts for Mormon women's history. The commitment to meeting the challenge to look at Mormon women's history from a variety of lenses may be seen in the contributors' choice of topics, their creative use of archival and cultural sources, and the insightful and innovative ways in which they contextualize their subjects. The endnotes to each chapter further reveal their engagement with and reliance on a vibrant and growing body of scholarship on Mormon studies, women's studies, and religious studies, thereby acknowledging that the insights gained in these fields bear wider implications for all who study women and religion in American history and culture. While the stories, experiences, and examples laced throughout the pages of *Beyond Biography* are neither comprehensive nor conclusive, they are suggestive of the many ways that Mormon women's history can move beyond the study of individual lives to enhance and inform larger historical narratives about Mormonism and the larger cultures in which it participates.

NOTES

1. Dave Hall, *A Faded Legacy: Amy Brown Lyman and Mormon Women's Activism, 1872–1959* (Salt Lake City: University of Utah Press, 2015); Carol Cornwall Madsen, *An Advocate for Women: The Public Life of Emmeline B. Wells, 1870–1920* (Provo, UT: Brigham Young University Press, 2005); Carol Cornwall Madsen, *Emmeline B. Wells: An Intimate History* (Salt Lake City: University of Utah Press, 2017); Joanna Brooks, Rachel Hunt Steenblik, and Hannah Wheelwright, eds., *Mormon Feminism: Essential Writings* (New York: Oxford University Press, 2016); Jill Derr et al., eds., *The First Fifty Years of Relief Society: Key Documents in Latter-day Saint Women's History* (Salt Lake City, UT: Church Historian's Press, 2016); Jennifer Reeder and Kate Holbrook, eds., *At the Pulpit: 185 Years of Discourses by Latter-day Saint Women* (Salt Lake City, UT: Church Historian's Press, 2017); Kate Holbrook and Matthew Bowman, eds., *Women and Mormonism: Historical and Contemporary Perspectives* (Salt Lake City: University of Utah Press, 2016).

2. The Relief Society is a philanthropic and educational women's organization and an official auxiliary of the Church of Jesus Christ of Latter-day Saints. Cope served as the president of this organization in her local ward (congregation). A bishop is the lay ecclesiastical leader of a ward, similar to a pastor. The stake president is the lay ecclesiastical leader of a stake, which is a geographic subdivision similar to a Catholic diocese. Patriarch is an office in the Melchizedek Priesthood. A stake patriarch is ordained to give special blessings, called patriarchal blessings, to members of his stake.

3. The overview of her life reads much like the sketches Mormons are urged to write of their parents or grandparents; it is laudatory, shows that Cope fulfilled multiple roles, and suggests that she was a "good and faithful servant."

4. John B. Fairbanks was one of the art missionaries sent by the LDS Church to study in Paris in the late nineteenth century. Rachel Cope, "John B. Fairbanks: The Man behind the Canvas" (master's thesis, Brigham Young University, 2003); Rachel Cope, "'With God's Assistance I Will Someday Be an Artist': John B. Fairbanks's Account of the Paris Art Mission," *Brigham Young University Studies* 50, no. 3 (2011): 133–59. See Heather Belnap Jensen's chapter in this volume for a discussion about Fairbanks's female contemporaries.

5. John B. Fairbanks to Lillie Fairbanks, November 9, 1890, Springville Museum of Art, Springville, Utah.

6. Avard Fairbanks was a sculptor whose work captured many aspects of the Mormon historical experience.

7. Some of John B. Fairbanks and Florence Gifford Fairbanks's manuscript records are included in the James Austin Cope and Florence Fairbanks Cope Family Papers that are located in the L. Tom Perry Special Collections Library, Harold B. Lee Library, Brigham Young University, Provo, UT.

8. For a historical discussion about Mormon views of eternal families, see Jonathan Stapley, "Adoptive Sealing Ritual in Mormonism," *Journal of Mormon History* 37, no. 3 (2011): 53–118.

9. "Aunt Nellie" was very involved in the lives of Florence Cope's children and grandchildren. Many of Nellie's personal papers and photographs were mixed in with Florence's belongings and are a part of the James Austin Cope and Florence Fairbanks Cope Family Papers.

10. Recent scholarship has considered kinship in broader terms, specifically looking at the many different roles and relationships that have shaped family life across time. Lisa Wilson, *A History of Step Families in Early America* (Chapel Hill: University of North Carolina Press, 2014); C. Dallett Hemphill, *Siblings: Brothers and Sisters in American History* (New York: Oxford University Press, 2011).

11. Kathryn Daynes, *More Wives Than One: Transformation of the Mormon Marriage System, 1840–1910* (Urbana: University of Illinois Press, 2001). Sarah Barringer Gordon, *The Mormon Question: Polygamy and Constitutional Conflict in Nineteenth-Century America* (Chapel Hill: University of North Carolina Press, 2002).

12. For further details about Mormon polygamy, see Daynes, *More Wives Than One*; Gordon, *The Mormon Question*; Kathleen Flake, *The Politics of Religious Identity: The Seating of Senator Reed Smoot, Mormon Apostle* (Chapel Hill: University of North Carolina Press, 2004); Laurel Thatcher Ulrich, *A House Full of Females: Plural Marriage and Women's Rights in Early Mormonism, 1835–1870* (New York: Knopf, 2017); and Annie Clark Tanner, *A Mormon Mother: An Autobiography by Annie Clark Tanner* (Salt Lake City: Tanner Trust Fund, University of Utah Library, 1991)

13. *Fictive kinship* is a term used by anthropologists and ethnographers to describe forms of kinship or social ties that are based on neither consanguineous blood ties nor affinal ties.

14. Samuel Brown, *In Heaven as It Is on Earth: Joseph Smith and the Early Mormon Conquest of Death* (New York: Oxford University Press, 2012).

15. A recent monograph discusses the history behind and the impact of the LDS Indian Student Placement Program. See Matthew Garrett, *Making Lamanites: Mormons, Native Americans, and the Indian Student Placement Program, 1947–2000* (Salt Lake City: University of Utah Press, 2016).

16. The expansiveness of relationships and broad definitions of kinship are a fundamental part of understanding women's experiences within the home, the community, and the church. See, for example, Naomi Tadmor, *Friends and Family in Eighteenth-Century England: Household, Kinship, and Patronage* (Cambridge: Cambridge University Press, 2001); Cynthia Yvonne Aalders, "Writing Religious Communities: The Spiritual Lives and Manuscript Cultures of English Women, 1740–90" (PhD thesis, Trinity College, University of Oxford, 2014).

17. Religious community creates fictive ties that scholars refer to as *spiritual kinship*. Discussions about the importance of such relationships can be found in several sources. For example, see Aalders, "Writing Religious Communities"; Phyllis Mack, *Heart Religion in the British Enlightenment: Gender and Emotion in Early Methodism* (Cambridge: Cambridge Uni-

versity Press, 2008); Anna M. Lawrence, *One Family under God: Love, Belonging, and Authority in Early Transatlantic Methodism* (Philadelphia: University of Pennsylvania Press, 2011).

18. Robert Orsi highlights the formation of religious community and the support that religious communities offer to one another by considering the lived experiences of Catholic women. This crossover work is a superb example of ordinary experiences reflecting larger themes and ideas. See Robert Orsi, *The Madonna of 115th Street: Faith and Community in Italian Harlem* (New Haven, CT: Yale University Press, 1985).

19. Doctrine and Covenants 137.

20. Ann Braude, "Women's History *Is* American Religious History," in *Retelling U.S. Religious History*, ed. Thomas A. Tweed (Berkeley: University of California Press, 1997), 87–107.

Chapter One

Charting the Past and Future of Mormon Women's History

Keith A. Erekson

Women shaped Mormonism from its outset. Church founder Joseph Smith re-counted his earliest visions to his mother, Lucy, whose history of those early events is among the faith's most important records. Joseph took his wife, Emma, with him on the night that he received gold plates from an angel, and she served as one of his scribes early in the process of translating what would be published as the Book of Mormon (1830). Women attended the first meet-ing of the Church in 1830 and were among the earliest converts to embrace the Church's doctrines and be baptized into the new faith. Women gathered alone and in families to the settlements of the Latter-day Saints in New York, Ohio, Missouri, and Illinois. In Nauvoo, women received and administered temple rites and were organized into the Female Relief Society of Nauvoo. They remembered and repeated Joseph's statement that "the organization of the Church of Christ was never perfect until women were organized."[1] At the society's first meeting, its first president, Emma Smith, declared, "We are go-ing to do something extraordinary . . . we expect extraordinary occasions and pressing calls."[2] Women migrated to Utah, participated in plural marriages, tamed the western wilderness, stored grain, and publicly defended the faith by speaking, writing, lobbying, voting, and serving as missionaries. Today, in what has been characterized as "a woman's church," Mormon women around the world lead, speak, make decisions, teach, visit, discuss, persuade, encour-age, strengthen, and develop resources.[3]

Despite their early, ongoing, and significant participation in Mormonism's past and present, women have not found their way into histories of Mormon-ism in equal measure. The literature on Mormon women can be divided into two distinct periods. First, during the first century after the Church's orga-nization in 1830, women were either absent from historical accounts or they were presented as victims or symbols. The public announcement of polygamy drew outsized attention to Mormon women through polemicized critiques and ardent defenses of the practice, though individual women were largely left out or passively portrayed. Second, a century later, in the 1970s, the New Mormon History movement expanded output and increased professionalism while seeking to recover women's voices and inspire modern activism. After four decades of work, much has been written about Mormon women, but their stories have gone largely unintegrated into larger narratives; when present, they are found within a limited set of narrative locations about auxiliaries, polygamy, suffrage, and opposition to the Equal Rights Amendment (ERA).

While women may be technically present in modern histories—though they are still sometimes, inexplicably, awkwardly absent—writers and historians writing about the Mormon past have not adequately recounted and integrated women's choices and voices into the larger narratives. Wallace Stegner's observation in telling "the story of the Mormon trail" that "their women were incredible" illustrates the way that Mormon women are often recognized and forgotten in the same breath.[4] Well might we paraphrase historian Ann Braude's critique of American historical writing to assert that "Mormon women's history *is* Mormon history."[5] Viewed in this light, the history of Mormonism has yet to be written. This chapter reviews the literature on Mormon women to identify important concepts in need of further development—agency, integration, and individuality—and makes five specific recommendations for using historical sources to better understand and incorporate Mormon women's experiences within wider historical contexts.

THE LITERATURE ON MORMON WOMEN

In the earliest institutionally produced histories, Mormon women were little mentioned and frequently unnamed. In 1869, when Church historian George A. Smith outlined *The Rise, Progress and Travels of the Church of Jesus Christ of Latter-day Saints*, he wrote of women as defenseless and sick; they sobbed and suffered; they were massacred and violated. Yet only one of them, Church founder Joseph Smith's wife, Emma, was mentioned by name. Later, B. H. Roberts compiled the most cited history of the early Church, Joseph Smith's *History of the Church*, in which only a few women were mentioned by name.[6]

In contrast to their near absence in official histories, Mormon women were very present in anti-polygamy writing. Though still often nameless as individuals, the plight of the collective served as a call to defend Mormon women who were described as victims, slaves, deluded, downtrodden, dull, senseless, sorrowful, degraded, shameless, and miserable. Also in contrast to official histories read by insiders, anti-polygamy pamphlets and novels targeted national audiences ranging from the curious to the outraged. The printed works were evocatively illustrated, as were the broadsides that announced the lantern-slide lectures that further pushed the image of Mormon women into public consciousness in the United States and England.[7]

The widespread popularity—and power—of the image of Mormon woman as victim provoked three responses from turn-of-the-century Mormon writers. The first reaction to the image of an oppressed collective was to counter it by identifying and profiling "notable" individual women who made contributions to the Church and to the settlement of the American West—an approach common in other studies of religious women throughout the United States. Mormon convert Edward Tullidge worked with influential Mormon leader Eliza R. Snow to compile the volume *The Women of Mormondom* (1877). Part biography, part history, and part theology, the book portrayed Mormon women as the hardworking and independent builders of a tangible Zion in the West.[8] Official Church materials followed suit with Sunday school curriculum outlines on the *Heroines of Mormondom* (1884) that told the life stories of a witness to a miraculous healing (Lydia Knight), the widow of a martyr (Mary Fielding Smith), and the survivor of a massacre (Amanda Barnes Smith). Unfortunately, the series ended after only two years.[9]

If one impulse sought to highlight the contributions of Mormon women, a companion response looked to compensate for the absence of women by placing them in a separate, designated, proper place—their "separate sphere" in the parlance of the times. Periodicals written and edited by Mormon women for their sisters, such as the *Woman's Exponent*, began to publish biographical sketches of individual women.[10] The practice found similar expression outside of women's periodicals, as in the notable case of Orson F. Whitney's four-volume history of the territory and state of Utah. Employing gendered language typical of the historical enterprise of the era, the state of Utah is referenced with feminine pronouns. The final volume compiled the biographies of the state's important citizens, with a few women, properly segregated. Among the twenty entries on "Pioneer Leaders and Their Associates" is one on "Three Pioneer Women" that treats Harriet Page Wheeler Young, Clara Decker Young, and Ellen Sanders Kimball. Among twenty-eight "First Immigrants" of note, two brought named wives—Susan Fairbanks and Susann S. Adams. There were no women named among the "Leading Colonizers" or the "Early Militia Men" or the "Men of Affairs" but one among the eighteen educators (Mary Jane Dilworth Hammond). The pattern continues with no women among the "Manufacturers and Mining Men" or the "Lawyers and Legislators." One farmer had a wife (Mary Spiers), and Margaret and Fanny Steele were named among the "Trades and Professions." Finally, on the last page of the table of contents, in their own little section, we find seventeen "Women of Note." Perhaps the only consolation is that the women appear before sections on "Others" and "Utah in Congress."[11] The practice of collecting and publishing stories of the contributions of women continued throughout the twentieth century in the work of the Daughters of Utah Pioneers.[12]

The third response to the portrayal of women in anti-polygamy literature elevated individual women into typological symbols for all Mormon women. In his four-volume *Comprehensive History of the Church* (1930), B. H. Roberts responded directly to the popular stereotype: "Never was greater mistake made than when it has been supposed that the women of the church were weak, and ignorant, and spiritless." He presented obituaries for two women who served as "Women Types of the New Dispensation." Vilate Kimball stood for the "American born" Mormon woman and Leonora Taylor for the "foreign born" (she was born in Canada). Both were "noble-minded, high-spirited, intelligent, courageous, independent, cheerful, but profoundly religious and capable of great self-sacrifice." After commenting on their service at home and in the Church's female auxiliaries, he concluded that "the social and domestic circles are recognized in the church as the natural sphere of woman's chief activities."[13] Such typological language was common for histories of this era and had been employed most influentially by Frederick Jackson Turner, who identified the frontier as a place of symbolic encounter between "civilization" and "savagery" as traders and hunters, cattle raisers, pioneers, and farmers moved westward. He called out Andrew Jackson and Abraham Lincoln as "typical" of Americans of the frontier ideal: they were "elevated to heroic typological status, serving as thumbnails for the entire mass of white, westward-moving immigrants of their respective eras."[14]

Thus, during the first century after the Church's organization, Mormon women were portrayed as absent, victims, profiles, placeholders, and symbols. Though polygamy added a sensationalized twist, the portrayal of Mormon women paralleled the treatment of other women in contemporary American literature. Mormon women, like American women, were largely left out of narratives or passively portrayed. Polygamy provided one reason to pay attention to women, but the result was a caricature, much like a woman in a barroom with an ax or a woman on a bicycle. Writers came to the subject with an agenda—to defend their faith, to express sexual fantasy, to protect virtue, to proclaim one's own purity in contrast with an "other"—that rarely sought to understand Mormon women and their experiences from their own perspectives. It would be left to another generation of writers to ask: Who were these women? "Would we recognize them? Whose are the faces under the big brimmed sunbonnets?"[15]

New Mormon History Seeks to Catch Up

A new generation of interest in Mormon women arose in the 1970s in an entirely different historical context. By the middle of the twentieth century, anti-polygamy had long since passed as a social movement, and the state of Utah had outlawed polygamy and publicly enforced monogamy. The Cold War fear of nuclear annihilation prompted an emphasis on the "nuclear" family, and the Victorian culture of the late nineteenth century had become "traditional" and popularized in a *Father Knows Best* style.[16] As social movements of the 1950s and 1960s mobilized the public square for civil rights, antiwar efforts, and feminist issues, academic historians began to study the nation's social history. Looking back on the first generation of social historians who trained their focus on women, Nancy Cott and Drew Gilpin Faust observed that "the initial impulses and ambitions in the field of women's history were to make women visible, to put women on the historical record, to correct omissions of women and distortions of their past, to enable and to hear women's voices and to illuminate women's points of view."[17] The climate produced two interwoven impulses in the writing of Mormon women's history, one to recover their lost voices and another that found a history of past women's activism as grounds to advocate in the present.

The need to recover women found resonance in Mormon historical writing. Trailing the academy by a decade, historians of Mormonism aspired to infuse the sensitivities of new social history into their burgeoning effort at professionalization, an effort they consciously named New Mormon History.[18] The Church's Historical Department hired women, including Maureen Ursenbach Beecher, Jill Mulvay Derr, Carol Cornwall Madsen, and Edyth Romney, to research and write about Mormon women. Among the field more broadly, the 1970s and 1980s witnessed an outpouring of activities in the study of Mormon women.[19] Caucuses were held at meetings of the Mormon History Association and as part of Brigham Young University's Women's Conferences. Universities and societies invited lecturers to discuss Mormon women. Academic journals devoted special issues to women.[20] Combing through diaries, letters, and legal records, social historians sought to hear women's voices, uncover their intentions, trace their activism, and recover their "self-presentation."[21]

The "rediscovery" of so many women quickly translated into a decades-long surge in publishing on women's lives and writings. Linda King Newell and Valeen Tippetts Avery's 1984 biography of Emma Smith drew the most attention, written unabashedly from Emma's perspective, but over time biographies of both the well known and unfamiliar appeared, including Eliza R. Snow, Emmeline B. Wells, and Amy Brown Lyman.[22] Utah State University Press began a series titled "Life Writings of Frontier Women" that published diaries, correspondence, and memoirs of polygamous wives, exiled polygamists, disillusioned converts, and leading women.[23] Lavina Fielding Anderson edited Lucy Smith's history of Joseph Smith to reveal just how significantly the work frames the history of Lucy's life and family.[24] The role of Utah women in the struggle for suffrage and against the ERA received attention.[25] Oral history programs in the Church History Department, at Claremont

Graduate University, and under the auspices of the Mormon Women Project recorded modern stories and published collections.[26] Continuing this trend, the Church History Department has recently published an edited volume of historical documents related to the Relief Society and a volume of discourses by Mormon women.[27] Thus, the impulse to restore women to the story—whether in the earliest documentary efforts to recover *Women's Voices: An Untold History of the Latter-day Saints, 1830–1900* (1982) or in a more recent oral history collection, *Mormon Women Have Their Say* (2013)—has proven a continuous and motivating theme.

Alongside the impulse to recover lost women's voices, a second impulse emerged over the past forty years that sought to understand and encourage Mormon women's activism. Here the purpose was not simply to add women back to a story line but also to shift the narrative, to rearrange and reinterpret it. Within wider academic scholarship on women's history and women's studies, the push beyond simply noting women's "contributions" or "compensating" for their absence led to an effort to "reconstruct" all of American history.[28] Writers found new meaning in women's historical agency that motivated them to strike an activist stance on modern issues.

This strain of activist writing found literary expression in a special issue of *Dialogue: A Journal of Mormon Thought* that became known as the "Pink Dialogue" (Summer 1971) and in a new literary vehicle, *Exponent II* (1974–), conscientiously named after the nineteenth-century Mormon women's newspaper. In 1976, Claudia Bushman edited a volume of essays, *Mormon Sisters: Women in Early Utah*, in which she, Laurel Thatcher Ulrich, Beecher, Derr, Madsen, and others explored Mormon women in connection with healing, plural marriage, feminism, and politics. Collectively, they presented a picture of socially and politically active women who handled both polygamy and leadership through their own institutions, including publishing and the Relief Society organization.[29]

Beecher and Lavina Fielding Anderson compiled essays in *Sisters in Spirit: Mormon Women in Historical and Cultural Perspective* (1987) that reexamined scriptural stories of Mother Eve and other women—including "Mother in Heaven," the logically requisite wife of the father of all people— together with the more recent history of female participation in the priesthood, temple rites, and marriage. Five years later, another volume of essays, *Women and Authority: Re-emerging Mormon Feminism* (1992), took the analysis of female agency further to argue that Mormon women's history and Mormonism's distinctive theology offered empowering possibilities for modern Mormon women who could and should reassert themselves to reclaim lost opportunities. Looking back from the twenty-first century, Joanna Brooks summarized that *Women and Authority* "crystallized a new surge of feminist energy and educated a generation of feminists that followed."[30]

The Impact of New Mormon History?

Forty years on, it seems like a good time to assess the impact of New Mormon History on Mormon women's history. The recovery impulse certainly increased the volume of scholarship on Mormon women, and the activist impulse certainly cast women's history in a new light. But have all the talks, special issues, primary sources, biographies, and edited volumes changed the larger story lines? How has the scholarship influenced the writing of Mormon history generally? Has it influenced the teaching of Church history at Brigham Young University or in Church classrooms? Has it shaped wider public discourse? Though there is no single, official narrative, a quick survey of several important and recent histories reveals that the impulses of recovery and activism have resulted not so much in a transformed story line but in a more sophisticated compartmentalization of women's experience.

The heart of the New Mormon History movement originated in the work of Church historian Leonard Arrington, widely seen as the "dean" of 1970s-era Mormon historical studies. He hired women to work for the Church on women's history and regularly endorsed the cause. Early fruits of this effort included single-volume histories of the Church's female-led auxiliaries for children (1979) and women (1992), both of which cast the work of women within the spheres of the organizations.[31] Further, when Arrington and Davis Bitton wrote *The Mormon Experience* (1992), a volume designed for college-course adoption, they relegated their discussion of women to chapters on "Mormon Sisterhood" and "Marriage and Family Patterns." Finally, in the sweeping narrative history produced by Arrington's Church History Department, *The Story of the Latter-day Saints* (1992) by James Allen and Glen Leonard, women again find their places in discussions of the auxiliaries, plural marriage, suffrage, the ERA, and gender roles. Two decades later, Matt Bowman wrote a compelling synthesis of the New Mormon History scholarship that added some of the activist topics—healing and feminism—to the story line of the Relief Society and polygamy.[32] In short, the recovery impulse brought women into separate literary spaces, while the activist impulse has been domesticated and, likewise, treated in its own separate space. The result is something of a professional echo of the nineteenth-century women's periodicals and book sections. The "separate spheres" of nineteenth-century social life transmuted onto twentieth-century historical writing as writers seeking recovery, activism, or synthesis located women as polygamous wives, as wives who stayed home while their husbands served missions, as leaders of the Relief Society and other women's auxiliaries, as activists for suffrage and Utah political issues, as the "leading sisters" of the first few generations of the Church's history.

The confinement of women to separate literary spaces is amplified in the work of Brigham Young University religious history writers. In the comprehensive *Encyclopedia of Latter-day Saint History*, published in 2000, the representation among 1,406 entries includes 435 entries about men (30.9 percent) and sixty-four about women (4.6 percent). The selection among the sixty-four reveals intriguing patterns—thirty-five auxiliary presidents; seven wives or mothers (including Mother in Heaven); five authors (including Fawn Brodie and Juanita Brooks); two each of educators, physicians, African converts, the first female missionaries, and Mormon Miss Americas; and another half dozen or so that include a scribe (Martha Coray), an apostate who prompted a revelation (Doctrine and Covenants 43), and a swimsuit designer (Rose Marie Reid). More than three-quarters of the women receive less than a page of coverage—only Emma Smith and Eliza R. Snow merit two pages each, while four of the auxiliary leaders, two physicians, two African converts, the mother of Joseph Smith, an artist (Minerva Teichert), and a swimsuit designer merit a page. The two-page entry titled "Women, Role of" mentions the Relief Society, plural marriage, and suffrage while quoting five men on what women should do, together with a few lines from the "Relief Society Declaration," a document published in 1999.[33] Further, a historical atlas, published by Brigham Young University faculty in 1994, was updated in 2014 by removing the one woman identified as an "Early Church Leader" (Emma Smith) and reducing the four pages of maps of Relief Society activities to two.[34]

The treatment of women in separate, defined female spaces carries over into history-related Church curriculum. Today the Church's adult Sunday school curriculum examines Church history every four years. In 1996, the Church released a one-volume history, *Our Heritage*, that has been assigned in adult Sunday school classes ever since. Extended discussions of women occur in two of the typical, separate places—women made clothes for temple workers and participated in the Relief Society. Emma Smith is mentioned the most times (five)—once each for marrying, getting pregnant, being the recipient of a revelation (Doctrine and Covenants 25), being concerned about tobacco, and participating in the Relief Society. Lucy Mack Smith raised Joseph and is quoted twice, once on the Church's organization and once while traveling to Ohio. Church president David O. McKay's mother is the only woman to be named in the text and pictured in an illustration—she is the quoted subject of a vignette about urging her husband to serve a mission. Half a dozen other women are quoted, about topics such as the Kirtland temple dedication (Eliza R. Snow), rescuing the Book of Commandments (Mary Elizabeth Rollins), or her reaction to Joseph Smith's death (Louisa Barnes Pratt). Approximately a dozen more are named in conjunction with actions, such as giving George A. Smith a coat (Eliza Brown), attending to the injured at Hawn's Mill (Amanda Smith), suffering with handcarts (Nellie Pucell), sailing on a ship with a husband (Elizabeth Wood), or dying (Flora Benson). Six named women were left behind by their missionary husbands, though Mary Richards "cheerfully recorded" life at Winter Quarters while her husband was away. Women are not specifically mentioned in the context of polygamy, though the topic appears on only three pages in which the Manifesto is mentioned in connection with statehood.[35] Recently, the Church expanded its historical curriculum offerings with a new history of the Relief Society, *Daughters in My Kingdom* (2011). While devoted entirely to the history of women, its use has largely been confined to female learning spaces, such as being quoted in women's sessions of the Church's general conference, excerpted in monthly messages for women, and assigned in instruction only during Sunday meetings of the Relief Society.[36]

If the recent outpouring of New Mormon History scholarship on Mormon women has not found its way into academic syntheses or Church curricula, we might well inquire about its impact—if any—beyond the small circles of Church history and Mormon studies. If activist interpretations are domesticated and important social and cultural studies are shunted into a narrow range of narrative spaces by specialists and insiders, has the work had any impact on wider writing about Mormonism and women? For all of the discussion of Mormon women and the ERA, it is surprising that a prominent history exploring *Why We Lost the ERA* (1986) did not even mention Mormon women.[37] Recent best-selling books on Mormon topics reveal not the recovery of past voices or the rewriting of the narrative but a continued fixation on polygamy and violence, such as Jon Krakauer's *Under the Banner of Heaven* (2003) or the recent mini-boom in "escape from polygamy" memoirs.[38] In popular culture, the Broadway musical *The Book of Mormon* has nothing to say about Mormon women. In American school classrooms, textbooks tend to avoid polygamy (and women), flattening the Mormon story into a story of the quest for religious freedom (like the Pilgrims) or of the settlement of the West.[39] Forty years of scholarship appears to have done little to change the field outside of Mormon history circles.

Thus, after two generations of expansive research and publishing on Mormon women, their voices and stories have been included in larger narratives only in a limited way, in primarily separate spaces. Nineteenth-century writing about Mormon women casts them as absent, victims, profiles, placeholders, and symbols. In the twentieth century, the impulse to recover women's voices addressed their absence while the impulse of activism addressed their victimhood. But women's history has not been integrated successfully into larger narrative syntheses of Mormon history. Instead of being held up as profiled notables or symbolic types, Mormon women remain in separate, albeit newly identified, narrative spaces. Historian Jon Butler's observation that religion is like a "jack-in-the-box" that pops out only at certain times in modern American history[40] certainly holds true for Mormon women within larger Mormon history narratives—they appear in the auxiliaries, in polygamy, in the home, and in the fight against the ERA—but only in these female narrative spaces.

MOVING BEYOND THE CURRENT CROSSROADS

The field of Mormon women's history seems to have arrived at something of a crossroads. The absence, victimhood, and symbolism of the first century of writing have been augmented by significant work in the past forty years to recover their voices, choices, and experiences. Yet, for all of the historical work, women remain largely on the margins of wider histories. However, the expansion of writing about Mormon women has occurred in parallel with a growth in available sources on Mormon women, sources that have the potential to provide new insight into questions of Mormon women's agency, their integration into wider narratives, and their individuality within wider historical contexts.

Historian Catherine Brekus called out the crossroads and the question of agency in an address to the Mormon History Association in 2010. After surveying the literature on Mormon women, she observed, "In terms of its treatment of women, the field of Mormon history stands at a crossroads" and sounded the call to examine women's agency: "Mormon women's history has not yet been integrated into the larger fields of either women's history or American religious history." Further, "While previous generations of historians virtually ignored women," she observed, "recent scholars have been so determined to portray women as historical agents that they have sometimes exaggerated their freedom to make choices about their lives." Mormon women had gone, in the hands of a generation of writers, from downtrodden victims to fiercely independent matriarchs. Brekus argued that we need to challenge both portrayals and offered as "one way forward" a new analytical model of agency that takes into account women's social and collective actions. The model would not, as in the activist impulse of the past forty years, look for "crusading female leaders who challenged male authority." Rather, it would be conceptually broad enough to consider women who reproduce or transform social structures, who choose to challenge or accept social roles, who provide thought leadership and social cohesion. In short, Brekus advocated for a view of agency as relational, social, collective, and expressed on a continuum that is "always shaped by cultural norms and structural constraints."[41]

The call was first taken up by a convening of writers held the following year that resulted in a volume of essays, *Women and Mormonism: Historical and Contemporary Perspectives* (2016), edited by Kate Holbrook and Matt Bowman. The effort to contextualize agency reveals that historical actors made choices not only in opposition to but also in acceptance of polygamy, to found the Primary organization in counsel with priesthood leaders, or to find a spiritually fulfilling life while submitting to the Church's prohibition of black participation in temple rites.[42] The focus on agency presents the opportunity to contextualize the full range of contemporary female action, from calling for priesthood ordination, to challenging the misperceptions of Mormon women, to advocating for the perpetuation of current Church structure while striving for better understanding and inclusion of women at church.[43]

Second, the lack of integration surfaces as a new imperative. Yes, women have moved from the back of the volume on Utah history, but they have gone to special issues, dedicated series, and safe spaces within larger narratives. Perhaps one exception that proves the rule can illustrate the work yet to be done. In *More Wives Than One: Transformation of the Mormon Marriage System, 1840–1910* (2001), Kathryn M. Daynes presented Mormon plural marriage not as the imposition of lecherous men nor as the chosen path of independent agents but as a social, economic, and political marriage system, "the sets of rules used in societies to govern the establishment, continuance, and dissolution of marriage." Drawing conscientiously on theoretical, historical, legal, sociological, and comparative literature on marriage and divorce, Daynes focused on "the place where church, law, and the lives of individuals intersected." Unlike the general push for individual "voices" and biographies, Daynes reconstructed the demographics of Mormon society in Manti, Utah, by scouring its laws, court cases on marriage and divorce, and census and civil records. Unlike writing that found polygamy a source for sensationalism or activism, Daynes found a source for data, thorough research, and controlled analysis. Unlike the convenient approach of assembling a collection of essays, Daynes sifted the data into an integrated story that placed women's experience into wider historical context.[44]

Finally, a question of individuality returns to the fore. As new biographies and edited collections pour forth, we might ask if it is enough simply to record women's voices. Has recent work merely democratized the nineteenth-century impulse to profile selected "notables" by settling for adding many more "voices"? Today, no writer proposes, as did B. H. Roberts, to single out two women as "types" of all Mormon women, but is there not an undercurrent in which individual voices are pulled out from among the many and enshrined as de facto symbols? If, for example, a historical narrative can mention only one black female pioneer, or one Asian female auxiliary leader, or one prominent unmarried Mormon woman, then have we really discovered and understood the experiences of black, Asian, and single Mormon women? On the activist end of the spectrum, there is an impulse to reduce women to the question of priesthood ordination, but at the devotional end a similar symbolic reduction reduces women only to "mothers," elevating for emulation only the "mothers of prophets" or the "wives of [non-polygamous] prophets."[45] In so doing, have we merely traded the old Typological Symbol for new Reductionist Symbols of our own time? How can we place their lives and stories in context? What can be learned from thoughtful analysis?

In the twenty-first century, the crossroads of Mormon women's history lies at the juncture of agency, integration, and individuality. If writers have overcompensated for the portrayal of women as victims by presenting them as activist matriarchs, how can we challenge both extremes? If the outpouring of work *about* women has continued to keep them in separate series and sections, how can we integrate their experience into wider historical narratives? If writers moved away from profiling notables and types to collecting voices and elevating new symbols, how can we view the experience of Mormon women within historical, cultural, and theological contexts?

In the midst of the present crossroads around agency, integration, and individuality, one single, significant premise undergirds five specific recommendations for moving the field forward—there are far more sources to be studied than have yet been studied. Or, stated another way, we will move past the present crossroads only as we better engage the vast and under-examined body of historical sources by and about Mormon women. To illustrate the oversight, consider that in 1950, Whitney Cross justified paying scant attention to women in his seminal *The Burned-Over District* on the basis of lack of sources: "Although women had reached the threshold of their modern freedom, they were still so much the forgotten members of society that little satisfactory direct evidence about them has survived."[46] Not only is this assertion untrue, it belies a lack of creativity and motivation. And, it is just plain out of date.

To quantify the situation, consider Davis Bitton's *Guide to Mormon Diaries & Autobiographies*, compiled in 1977 during the early years of the flourish of activity in Mormon women's history. Reviewing fourteen repositories in the United States, Bitton logged 2,894 diaries or autobiographies, of which 489 were by women (17 percent).[47] Twenty-five years later, the end of 2015 found in the Church History Library—the largest repository of Mormon women's sources in the world—holding 9,001 diaries and autobiographies, of which 1,596 were created by Mormon women (18 percent).[48] The 1881 warning of Emmeline B. Wells certainly applies today: "The historians of the past have been neglectful of woman, and it is the exception if she be mentioned at all; yet the future will deal more generously with womankind, and the historian of the present age will find it very embarrassing to ignore woman in the records of the nineteenth century."[49] No historian can blame such embarrassment on lack of sources, only a lack of inquiry. So how to inquire?

1. Use Newly Available Sources in Creative New Ways

First, we must engage these newly available sources in creative ways. The wave of Mormon scholarship that began in the 1970s tracked sources and edited documents. Inspired by the academic milieu that advocated social history, Mormon writers looked to sources but did not fully apply social historical methods to consider social structure, processes, or demography. And the historical profession has developed new tools since that time through cultural, aesthetic, linguistic, and material turns. Speaking in 2014 to a gathering sponsored by the Mormon Women's History Initiative, historian Susan S. Rugh observed, "It is time to move beyond biography. It is time we apply the methods of social and cultural history to examine women in our collective past."[50]

There are already some examples of such approaches in Mormon women's studies. Laurel Thatcher Ulrich has examined the practices of diary writing and the material culture of homespun objects, Jennifer Reeder has combed through hair art, and Kate Holbrook has sampled foodways.[51] But there is so much more to be done. If anything, Mormons have proven very effective at creating culturally specific artifacts and materials. Mormon women kept diaries and wrote autobiographies, but they have also taken photographs, kept books of remembrance, and compiled scrapbooks. Goal-oriented programs leave in their wake finished and unfinished projects, changing patterns (and physical hardware) of awards and recognitions, formative experiences at camps for young women, theatrical performances ("roadshows"), and youth treks that imitate pioneer experiences. The Mormon life course moves Mormon women through culturally scripted, ritual-like experiences of blessings, baptism, missionary service, marriage, childbirth, anniversaries, family reunions, and death with culturally defined expectations for clothing and meals, celebrating and mourning, speaking and recordkeeping. Long before Sugar-Doodle or Pinterest provided a place to share craft and lesson ideas, there existed an underground of Relief Society meetings and kinship networks through which circulated recipe ideas, lesson handouts, sewing patterns, and flannel board activities. While it is common to laugh at stereotypes of green Jell-O salad or Relief Society meeting centerpieces, we must move toward a richer analysis and understanding of unstated norms, social practices, and cultural products.

The sources for such analysis may be hiding in plain sight. Take as one example the papers of Dorothy Stone, matron of the Salt Lake Temple from 1968 to 1972, that are housed in the Church History Library. Among the journals, correspondence, and photographs are also funeral programs, transcripts of talks given, yearbooks and scrapbooks, notes from Relief Society lessons and visiting teaching visits, calendars, poems, music, newsletters, and items related to a fiftieth wedding anniversary celebration.[52] Certainly many other examples may be found by researchers who will look for new materials on which to conduct creative cultural analyses.

2. Pay Attention to Function (as Well as to Form)

A second avenue of inquiry into Mormon women's experience requires a reconsideration of formal participation. Over the years, it has proven both tempting and easy to view Mormon women as part of a formal church institution. The approach is not inaccurate as Mormon women did (and do), in fact, join the Church and participate in its formal meetings and activities. However, such formal analysis invariably finds (and limits) women into specific social spaces—leaders and teachers in auxiliaries, mothers and wives in homes. Looking only for the forms of participation creates an immediate bias against discovering the active influence of women.

For example, consider a study of Book of Mormon witnesses that assumes the importance of formal roles. Accordingly, the researcher will open the volume, find the names of the eleven men listed as formal witnesses, and then set out to describe their experience and testimony. If, however, we were to ask not "Who was listed formally as a Book of Mormon witness?" but, rather, "Who witnessed the golden plates?" we will find those eleven men as well as four more people, all of whom were women. Joseph Smith's mother, Lucy Mack Smith, saw the outline of the plates, handled them, and helped to hide them. His wife, Emma, accompanied him when the plates were acquired, served as a scribe during translation, moved the plates, and rustled their pages. Mary Whitmer was shown the plates by a mysterious stranger. Lucy Harris saw the plates in a dream that prompted tangible action.[53] Here, attention to the function of witnessing uncovers women who did not occupy the formal role of official published witness.

Another example emerges from a manuscript collection in the Church History Library. Mary Moyle "Reba" Booth worked as a schoolteacher in Provo and Alpine, Utah. On her income, she supported her husband, Joseph Wilford Booth, while serving a mission to Syria in 1898. She served with him as a missionary in Armenia from 1903 to 1909 and then served with him when he was a mission president. To look at the form of her experience, Reba was a stay-at-home missionary wife, an in-field missionary, and a mission president's wife. But to look at the functions she performed reveals that she spent time with members and missionaries preaching and ministering. She spoke in tongues and founded the first Primary in Turkey. Her husband died in office, so she assumed direction of day-to-day mission affairs and oversaw the closure of the mission before World War I.[54] We cannot simply ask what position women held in the Church; we must ask what they were doing and how they did it.

3. Uncover Participation in Institutions

A third approach to understanding Mormon women's experience necessitates re-visioning participation in social and institutional structures. Modern life is characterized by the existence of institutions. Institutions and bureaucracies are designed to hide the contributions of individuals. Leaders of governments, schools, and corporations want the public to pay attention to services, successes, and stock prices rather than to individual incidents, failures, or employees. The writer of a company's promotional materials (whether male or female) will be invisible—by design—when the CEO (whether female or male) delivers the public speech. Institutional planning activities intentionally erase the role of contributors. Thus, whenever a man announces a Church program at a general conference or dedicates a historic site, one must ask how many women and men were involved—and one cannot assume that the director of the work that led to the announcement was a man.

One important example from Mormon history involves the Relief Society grain storage work that became the precursor to the Church's modern welfare, family, and humanitarian services programs. After consultation with Brigham Young in the early 1870s, Emmeline Wells mobilized Mormon women to the task of saving grain. She began by penning an editorial in the newspaper she edited, and women responded by saving grain immediately. By the first decade of the twentieth century, the grain had been used to fight hunger in Mormon communities and to provide relief after earthquakes in San Francisco and China. During World War I, Emmeline served as president of the Relief Society and sold grain to the US government. The cash generated from the transaction was invested, and its interest revenues provided health care and insurance for pregnant women and their children. During the Great Depression, Church leaders put men to work building a large grain silo at what is now known as "Welfare Square," but the silo was filled with grain donated from the Relief Society's stores. In the 1970s, the auxiliary officially transferred its assets to the Church's Welfare Department. Today, one of the most common public images of the Church is the picture of Church members dressed in yellow delivering food and supplies after natural disasters—work that has its root and foundation in the work of Mormon women.

A few tactical hints will help when researching in archival and manuscript collections. Remember that modern institutions erase individuals, both in the final outcomes and (importantly) in the internal records and processes. Don't assume that the minutes will tell you that individuals are being erased! Creativity is needed to look for different kinds of sources than simply minutes, to consider the timing and settings in which to uncover women. These strategies are especially important in more recent history, marked by a rising number of female missionaries, female missionaries filling leadership positions, women serving on internal church committees, and women participating in public affairs at stake and regional levels.[55] Women most certainly contribute to bureaucratic institutions (that erase all individuals, female and male), and the best researchers must uncover them.

4. See the Significance of Conversion

A fourth strategy by which to integrate women involves reassessing the measures of significance. A common way that historians measure significance is by causation—a missionary preached. Another way to measure significance is to look at impact and change—a person converted and a life story transformed. More than anything, the story of Mormonism is a story of converts and conversion. Historian Amy Harris perceptively asked, "What would Mormon history look like if we began with the converts instead of the converters?"[56]

If we begin with converts, we will find women and men in every time and place. Beginning with conversion will allow historians to look outside of Utah, beyond polygamy, to global experiences beginning in the nineteenth century. Beginning with conversion allows for the exploration of relationships between individuals and institutions. Beginning with conversion transforms the Mormon Pioneer Overland Travel database, with its 57,000 individuals identified (49 percent of whom were women), into a database of converts.

Here's another example, unpacked by analyzing a rare, early Mormon pamphlet. Published in Philadelphia in 1849, the pamphlet begins with a caustic letter by Reverend Abraham De Witt, chastising a young girl for even considering Mormonism, declaring that she has an "excitable and unstable mind" and warning her to "escape as for [her] life from this vortex of fanaticism." This is clearly an anti-Mormon letter, and for this reason the pamphlet was not included in the Mormon bibliographies produced by Crawley or Flake and Draper.[57] But, upon closer examination, it becomes apparent that the pamphlet was not assembled by De Witt. Rather, his letter is presented first so that the young girl could rhetorically dismantle it. That girl, Sarah Stageman, had been born in England in 1826 and immigrated to Maryland in 1840 at age fourteen with her parents and four younger siblings. At age twenty-three, she encountered the Mormon Church and shared the good news with her pastor's wife who, in turn, told her husband, and he wrote the letter and circulated the message to his flock in print and in whispers. Sarah began her defense by pointing out that he cited no scripture; she then writes an eight-and-a-half-page tour de force of biblical exposition, testifying of themes common in Mormon preaching—truth, the last days, visions and revelations, Joseph Smith as a prophet, apostasy, the gathering of Israel, dispensations, priesthood restoration, and the workings of God in His own way. Asked by what inspiration she knows that the minister and his parishioners have no religion, Sarah responds that it certainly was not in his church, because he did not give the gift of the Holy Ghost by laying on of hands as did the apostles of old. When asked why Joseph Smith's temple was never finished, she charges De Witt with being like the mockers at the cross who called Jesus to come down and said he wouldn't believe Joseph if the temple had been completed. Besides, the Bible itself cites prophecies of temples that were never built, and Joseph's was only the first of many temples to be built across the earth. This is not an anti-Mormon pamphlet. It is a record of the significance of conversion in the life of a young woman who would convert to Mormonism and then lead her parents and siblings west. It likewise demonstrates a significant place for women in interpreting scripture and making public commentary.[58] All this from a pamphlet initially ignored for being presumed to be anti-Mormon.

5. Historicize the Mormon Family

A final method for understanding Mormon women's agency, integration, and individuality is to see how Mormon families have functioned over time and in historical context. In Latter-day Saint doctrine, the "family" is traced back timelessly to Adam and Eve and projected forward through marriage that endures beyond death. But while "family" may be eternal as a Mormon doctrinal concept, Mormon "families" are historical, both as lived experience and as a reflection of their times.

Demography offers a starting point for such inquiry. For examples, the family structure characterized by a breadwinning husband, homemaking wife, and schooling children did not become a majority in the United States until the 1920s. How did Mormon families operate before (and after)? The most rapid increase in unwed pregnancies occurred in the United States between 1940 and 1958 (not during the 1960s). Teenage childbearing was higher in the 1950s than today.[59] How do Mormon families compare? How did the demographic surge of the baby boom generation impact Mormon missionary work in the 1950s and 1960s, marital practices in the 1960s and 1970s, and post-retirement missionary service in the twenty-first century? Katherine Daynes offered a case study in nineteenth-century polygamy, but far more could be done on the transformations over time in family roles, functions, and dynamics.[60] We need to better understand Mormon single parents, working mothers, unmarried and childless women, infant mortality, orphanhood, loss of parents, relationships, and kinship beyond nuclear relations.

Beyond demographics, we must explore how the cultural construct of "Mormon families" interacts over time with wider cultural stereotypes and assumptions. How did Mormon family life in the nineteenth century participate in (not just differentiate from) norms, assumptions, and values of home industry, the family as an economic unit, notions of patrimony, and contemporary advice

literature? How did the cultural construct of a non-nuclear, non-Victorian polygamous family transform into a construct idealizing a monogamous, nuclear,
"American" family during the Cold War? How do Mormon conceptions of
true love, the romantic ideal, and companionate marriage change over time and
reflect and resist wider cultures? How do cultural constructs that resonate with
white, western, conservative American political values find expression and
resistance in other political contexts? Future inquiries need to explore change
over time, comparative family experiences, life-cycle family development,
Mormon family intersection and interaction with major events and public policy, and family rituals. We need to explore the impact of socioeconomic class
on family expectations and experiences. And Mormon genealogists clearly
need to historicize their research and storytelling.[61]

CONCLUSION

In conclusion, Mormon women have been the subject of study and writing for
nearly two centuries. In the present crossroads of Mormon women's history
that wrestles with agency, integration, and individuality, we can move forward by a studied return to the thousands of sources that have been collected
and made available in libraries and archives. We need scholars and writers
who will use sources creatively, pay attention to function (as well as to form),
uncover the participation of women in institutions, see the significance of
conversion, and historicize the Mormon family. Mormon women's history
truly *is* Mormon history and American history—it must be integrated into the
work of every writer on every topic. It can no longer be acceptable to discuss
women in separate places—either the experts on Mormon women's history
must write integrated syntheses or the writers of syntheses must integrate the
scholarship on Mormon women.

Because women continue to be omitted or underrepresented in academic
literature as well as Church curriculum materials, it may run the risk of
openly stating the obvious to name several practices to avoid. These should
be obvious, but writers still do them. Historical inquiry and analysis needs to
be complex and nuanced, and there are many more ways than one to do good
history, but avoiding these few problems is a good way to begin:

- Don't *omit* women, ever.
- Don't *add* women simply as a vignette, sidebar, chapter, or section.
- Don't view women *only* as wives, daughters, or Church auxiliary members.
- Don't suppose women's history is only for *women* or *historians*.
- Don't assume you have seen *all* of the sources.

More and richer sources on Mormon women's history exist than ever before, and they are more comprehensive than for many other women in American and world history. Engagement with Mormon women and their sources can reshape the stories told about the Church and its people, as well as about American and international social, cultural, and intellectual histories.

NOTES

1. Joseph Smith, in *The First Fifty Years of Relief Society: Key Documents in Latter-day Saint Women's History*, ed. Jill Mulvay Derr, Carol Cornwall Madsen, Kate Holbrook, and Matthew J. Grow (Salt Lake City, UT: Church Historian's Press, 2016), 6n13.

2. Emma Smith, Nauvoo Relief Society Minute Book, March 17, 1842, 11, in Derr et al., eds., *First Fifty Years of Relief Society*, 35.

3. Sharon Eubank, "This Is a Woman's Church" (presented at the FairMormon Conference, Provo, UT, August 8, 2014), https://www.fairmormon.org/fair-conferences/2014-fairmormon-conference/womans-church.

4. Wallace Stegner, *The Gathering of Zion: The Story of the Mormon Trail* (New York: McGraw-Hill, 1964), 13.

5. Ann Braude, "Women's History *Is* American Religious History," in *Retelling U.S. Religious History*, ed. Thomas A. Tweed (Berkeley: University of California Press, 1997), 87–107.

6. George A. Smith, *The Rise, Progress and Travels of the Church of Jesus Christ of Latter-day Saints* (Salt Lake City, UT: Deseret News Office, 1869); B. H. Roberts, *History of the Church* (Salt Lake City, UT: Deseret News, 1902).

7. For examples, see Metta Victoria Fuller, *Mormon Wives: A Narrative of Facts Stranger Than Fiction* (New York: Derby & Jackson, 1856); Ring Jepson, *Among the Mormons: How an American and an Englishman Went to Salt Lake City, and Married Seven Wives Apiece; Their Lively Experience, a Peep into the Mysteries of Mormonism* (San Francisco, CA: San Francisco News Company, 1879); Jennie Anderson Froiseth, ed., *The Women of Mormonism; or, The Story of Polygamy as Told by the Victims* (Detroit: C. G. G. Paine, 1882), 20, 23, 26, 144, 191, 259; Mrs. A. G. Paddock, *Saved at Last from among the Mormons* (Springfield, OH: Mast, Crowell, and Kirkpatrick, 1894); Charles Felton Pidgin, *The House of Shame: A Novel* (New York: Cosmopolitan Press, 1912). For analysis, see Sarah Barringer Gordon, "'Our National Hearthstone': Anti-polygamy Fiction and the Sentimental Campaign against Moral Diversity in Antebellum America," *Yale Journal of Law & the Humanities* 8 (Summer 1996): 295–350; Terryl L. Givens, *The Viper on the Hearth: Mormons, Myths, and the Construction of Heresy* (New York: Oxford University Press, 1997), 97–167.

8. Edward W. Tullidge, *The Women of Mormondom* (New York: Tullidge and Crandall, 1877). On Tullidge see Claudia L. Bushman, "Edward W. Tullidge and *The Women of Mormondom*," *Dialogue* 33, no. 4 (Winter 2000): 15–26. An interesting inversion of this practice—inverted by being written by a non-Mormon and by featuring homes rather than women—is Elizabeth Wood Kane's *Twelve Mormon Homes Visited in Succession on a Journey through Utah to Arizona* (Philadelphia: William Wood, 1874).

9. [Susa Young Gates], *Lydia Knight's History* (Salt Lake City, UT: Juvenile Instructor Office, 1883); *Heroines of Mormondom* (Salt Lake City, UT: Juvenile Instructor Office, 1884). See also Melvin L. Bashore, "Index to Books in the Noble Women's Lives Series" (Salt Lake City, UT: Historical Department, Church of Jesus Christ of Latter-day Saints Church History Library, 1979).

10. *Woman's Exponent* 15, no. 21 (April 1, 1887), 163.

11. Orson F. Whitney, *History of Utah* (1892–1904), vol. 4 (1904); the entries are for Eliza Roxcy Snow Smith, Zina Huntington Young, Bathsheba Bigler Smith, Jane Snyder Richards, Mary Isabella Horne, Emmeline B. Woodward Wells, Ellen Brooke Ferguson, Emily S. Richards, Elizabeth Ann Claridge McCune, Ruth Mosher Pack, Charilla Abbott Browning, Emily Hill Woodmansee, Hannah Cornaby, Luisa Lula Green Richards, Romania Bunnell Pratt, Inez Knight Allen, and Lucy Jane Brimhall Knight. On gendered language in nineteenth-century historical writing, see Bonnie G. Smith, "Gender and the Practices of Scientific History: The Seminar and Archival Research in the Nineteenth Century," *American Historical Review* 100 (1995): 1150–76.

12. See Kate B. Carter, comp., *Heart Throbs of the West* (Salt Lake City: Daughters of Utah Pioneers, 1939–1951); Kate B. Carter, comp., *Treasures of Pioneer History* (Salt Lake City: Daughters of Utah Pioneers, 1952–1957); Kate B. Carter, comp., *Our Pioneer Heritage* (Salt Lake City: Daughters of Utah Pioneers, 1958–1977).

13. B. H. Roberts, *A Comprehensive History of the Church of Jesus Christ of Latter-day Saints*, 6 vols. (Salt Lake City, UT: Deseret News Press, 1930), 5:253–56.

14. On Turner's typological language and its appropriation in history, see Keith A. Erekson, *Everybody's History* (Amherst: University of Massachusetts Press, 2012), 90–92, 102–4.

15. Maureen Ursenbach Beecher, "Under the Sunbonnets: Mormon Women with Faces," *BYU Studies* 16, no. 4 (October 1, 1976): 471.

16. See H. W. Brands, *The Devil We Knew: Americans and the Cold War* (New York: Oxford University Press, 1993); Stephen J. Whitfield, *The Culture of the Cold War*, 2nd ed. (Baltimore: Johns Hopkins University Press, [1991] 1996); John Lewis Gaddis, *We Now Know: Rethinking Cold War History* (New York: Oxford University Press, 1997); Lizabeth Cohen, *A Consumer's Republic: The Politics of Mass Consumption in Postwar America* (New York: Alfred A. Knopf, 2003).

17. Nancy F. Cott and Drew Gilpin Faust, "Recent Directions in Gender and Women's History," *OAH Magazine of History* 19, no. 2 (March 2005): 4.

18. See D. Michael Quinn, "Editor's Introduction," in *The New Mormon History: Revisionist Essays on the Past* (Salt Lake City, UT: Signature Books, 1992), vii–xx; Thomas G. Alexander, "Historiography and the New Mormon History: A Historian's Perspective," *Dialogue: A Journal of Mormon Thought* 19 (Fall 1986): 25–49; Roger Launius, "The 'New Social History' and the 'New Mormon History': Reflections on Recent Trends," *Dialogue: A Journal of Mormon Thought* 27, no. 1 (Spring 1994): 109–27.

19. See Christy Best, *Guide to Sources for Studies of Mormon Women in the Church Archives* (Salt Lake City, UT: Historical Department of the Church of Jesus Christ of Latter-day Saints, 1976); Carol Cornwall Madsen and David J. Whittaker, "History's Sequel: A Source Essay on Women in Mormon History," *Journal of Mormon History* 6 (1979): 123–45; Patricia Lyn Scott and Maureen Ursenbach Beecher, "Mormon Women: A Bibliography in Process, 1977–1985," *Journal of Mormon History* 12 (1985): 113–27; Linda Thatcher, comp., *Guide to Women's History Holdings at the Utah State Historical Society Library* (Salt Lake City: Utah State Historical Society Library, 1985).

20. *Utah Historical Quarterly* 38, no. 1 (Winter 1970); *Utah Historical Quarterly* 46, no. 2 (Spring 1978).

21. Carol Cornwall Madsen, "'Feme Covert': Journey of a Metaphor," *Journal of Mormon History* 17 (1991): 58.

22. Linda King Newell and Valeen Tippetts Avery, *Mormon Enigma: Emma Hale Smith, Prophet's Wife, "Elect Lady," Polygamy's Foe, 1804–1879* (Garden City, NY: Doubleday, 1984); Keith Terry and Ann Terry, *Eliza: A Biography of Eliza R. Snow* (Santa Barbara, CA:

Butterfly Publishing, 1981); Karen Lynn Davidson and Jill Mulvay Derr, *Eliza: The Life and Faith of Eliza R. Snow* (Salt Lake City, UT: Deseret Book, 2014); Martha Sonntag Bradley and Mary Brown Firmage Woodward, *4 Zinas: A Story of Mothers and Daughters on the Mormon Frontier* (Salt Lake City, UT: Signature Books, 2000); Carol Cornwall Madsen, *An Advocate for Women: The Public Life of Emmeline B. Wells, 1870–1920* (Provo, UT: Brigham Young University Press, 2005); Carol Cornwall Madsen, *Emmeline B. Wells: An Intimate History* (Salt Lake City: University of Utah Press, 2017); Dave Hall, *A Faded Legacy: Amy Brown Lyman and Mormon Women's Activism, 1872–1959* (Salt Lake City: University of Utah Press, 2015). For collections of biographical sketches, see Vicky Burgess-Olson, *Sister Saints* (Provo, UT: Brigham Young University Press, 1978); Kenneth W. Godfrey, Audrey M Godfrey, and Jill Mulvay Derr, *Women's Voices: An Untold History of the Latter-day Saints, 1830–1900* (Salt Lake City, UT: Deseret Book, 1982); Janet Peterson and LaRene Gaunt, *Elect Ladies: Presidents of the Relief Society*, rev. ed. (Salt Lake City, UT: Deseret Book, 1990); Janet Peterson and LaRene Gaunt, *Keepers of the Flame: Presidents of the Young Women* (Salt Lake City, UT: Deseret Book, 1993); Carol Holindrake Nielson, *The Salt Lake City 14th Ward Album Quilt, 1857: Stories of the Relief Society Women and Their Quilt* (Salt Lake City: University of Utah Press, 2004); Richard E. Turley Jr. and Brittany A. Chapman, eds., *Women of Faith in the Latter Days*, 3 vols. (Salt Lake City, UT: Deseret Book, 2011–2014); Brittany Chapman Nash and Richard E. Turley, eds., *Fearless in the Cause: Remarkable Stories from Women in Church History* (Salt Lake City, UT: Deseret Book, 2016).

23. Juanita Brooks, *Quicksand and Cactus: A Memoir of the Southern Mormon Frontier* (Logan: Utah State University Press, 1992); Maurine Carr Ward, ed., *Winter Quarters: The 1846–1848 Life Writings of Mary Haskin Parker Richards* (Logan: Utah State University Press, 1996); Donna T. Smart, ed., *Mormon Midwife: The 1846–1888 Diaries of Patty Bartlett Sessions* (Logan: Utah State University Press, 1997); S. George Ellsworth, *The History of Louisa Barnes Pratt: Mormon Missionary Widow and Pioneer* (Logan: Utah State University Press, 1998); Noel A. Carmack and Karen Lynn Davidson, eds., *Out of the Black Patch: The Autobiography of Effie Marquess Carmack, Folk Musician, Artist, and Writer* (Logan: Utah State University Press, 1999); Maureen Beecher, *The Personal Writings of Eliza Roxy Snow* (Logan: Utah State University Press, 2000); Charles M. Hatch and Todd M. Compton, eds., *A Widow's Tale: The 1884–1896 Diary of Helen Mar Kimball Whitney* (Logan: Utah State University Press, 2003); Edward Lyman, Susan Ward Payne, and S. George Ellsworth, eds., *No Place to Call Home: The 1807–1857 Life Writings of Caroline Barnes Crosby, Chronicler of Outlying Mormon Communities* (Logan: Utah State University Press, 2005); Sandra Ailey Petree, ed., *Recollections of Past Days: The Autobiography of Patience Loader Rozsa Archer* (Logan: Utah State University Press, 2006); Melissa Lambert Milewski, ed., *Before the Manifesto: The Life Writings of Mary Lois Walker Morris* (Logan: Utah State University Press, 2007); Linda DeSimone, ed., *Exposé of Polygamy: A Lady's Life among the Mormons, Fanny Stenhouse* (Logan: Utah State University Press, 2008); LuAnn Faylor Snyder and Phillip A. Snyder, eds., *Post-Manifesto Polygamy: The 1899–1904 Correspondence of Helen, Owen and Avery Woodruff* (Logan: Utah State University Press, 2009); Margaret E. P. Gordon and Claudia L. Bushman, *Pansy's History: The Autobiography of Margaret E. P. Gordon, 1866–1966* (Logan: Utah State University Press, 2011); Martha Sonntag Bradley, ed., *Plural Wife: The Life Story of Mabel Finlayson Allred* (Logan: Utah State University Press, 2012). Several volumes are available for free download at http://digitalcommons.usu.edu/usupress_lifewritings/.

24. Lavina Fielding Anderson, ed., *Lucy's Book: A Critical Edition of Lucy Mack Smith's Family Memoir* (Salt Lake City, UT: Signature Books, 2001).

25. Carol Cornwall Madsen, ed., *Battle for the Ballot: Essays on Woman Suffrage in Utah, 1870–1896* (Logan: Utah State University Press, 1997); Martha Sonntag Bradley, *Pedestals and*

Podiums: Utah Women, Religious Authority and Equal Rights (Salt Lake City, UT: Signature Books, 2005).

26. James N. Kimball and Kent Miles, *Mormon Women: Portraits and Conversations* (Salt Lake City, UT: Handcart Books, 2009); Claudia Bushman and Caroline Kine, eds., *Mormon Women Have Their Say: Essays from the Claremont Oral History Collection* (Salt Lake City, UT: Greg Kofford Books, 2013); Neylan McBaine, ed., *Sisters Abroad: Interview from the Mormon Women Project* (Englewood, CO: Patheos Press, 2013).

27. Derr, Madsen, Holbrook, and Grow, *First Fifty Years of Relief Society*; Jennifer Reeder and Kate Holbrook, eds., *At the Pulpit: 185 Years of Discourses by Latter-day Saint Women* (Salt Lake City, UT: Church Historian's Press, 2017). For excerpts from women's speeches organized by topics that attempt to align with Church curriculum, see Janiece L. Johnson and Jennifer Reeder, eds., *The Witness of Women: Firsthand Experiences and Testimonies from the Restoration* (Salt Lake City, UT: Deseret Book, 2016).

28. Madsen, "'Feme Covert,'" 43–61.

29. Claudia L. Bushman, ed., *Mormon Sisters: Women in Early Utah*, 2nd ed. (Logan: Utah State University Press, 1997).

30. Maureen Ursenbach Beecher and Lavina Fielding Anderson, eds., *Sisters in Spirit: Mormon Women in Historical and Cultural Perspective* (Urbana: University of Illinois Press, 1987); Maxine Hanks, ed., *Women and Authority: Re-emerging Mormon Feminism* (Salt Lake City, UT: Signature Books, 1992); Joanna Brooks, in *Mormon Feminism: Essential Writings*, ed. Joanna Brooks, Rachel Hunt Steenblik, and Hannah Wheelwright (New York: Oxford University Press, 2016), 9.

31. Carol Cornwall Madsen and Susan Staker Oman, *Sisters and Little Saints: One Hundred Years of Primary* (Salt Lake City, UT: Deseret Book, 1979); Jill Mulvay Derr, Janath Russell Cannon, and Maureen Ursenbach Beecher, *Women of Covenant: The Story of Relief Society* (Salt Lake City, UT: Deseret Book, 1992). The history of the young women's auxiliary has not been told since Susa Young Gates, *History of the Young Ladies' Mutual Improvement Association of the Church of Jesus Christ of Latter-day Saints, from November 1869 to June 1910* (Salt Lake City, UT: Deseret News, 1911).

32. Leonard J. Arrington and Davis Bitton, *The Mormon Experience: A History of the Latter-day Saints* (Urbana: University of Illinois Press, 1992), 185–205, 220–42; James B. Allen and Glen M. Leonard, *The Story of the Latter-day Saints*, 2nd ed. (Salt Lake City, UT: Deseret Book, 1992), 175–76, 401–4, 659–62; Matthew Bowman, *The Mormon People: The Making of an American Faith* (New York: Random House, 2012), 72–78, 126–36, 136–37, 174–76, 234–38, 258–59.

33. Arnold K. Garr, Donald Q. Cannon, and Richard O. Cowan, eds., *Encyclopedia of Latter-day Saint History* (Salt Lake City, UT: Deseret Book, 2000), 1357–59; I thank Lis Allen for conducting the content analysis. Entries include Amanda Inez Knight Allen, May Anderson, Janette Hales Beckham, Fawn Brodie, Juanita Brooks, Elaine Cannon, Lucy Cannon, Martha Hughes Cannon, Camilla Cobb, Martha Coray, Ruth May Fox, Ruth Hardy Funk, Susa Young Gates, Michaelene P. Grassli, May G. Hinckley, Mary Isabella Hales Horne, Adele C. Howells, Ms. Hubble, Colleen Hutchins, Elaine L. Jack, Florence S. Jacobsen, Ardeth Kapp, Sarah Granger Kimball, Lucy Jane Brimhall Knight, Polly Knight, Ann Lee, Amy Brown Lyman, Julia N. Mavimbela, Coleen K. Menlove, Mother in Heaven, Margaret D. Nadauld, Lavern W. Parmley, Patricia P. Pinegar, Bertha S. Reeder, Rose Marie Reid, Alice Louise Reynolds, Louise Y. Robison, Aurelia Spencer Rogers, Mary Elizabeth Rollins, Priscilla Sampson-Davis, Ellis Reynolds Shipp, Naomi M. Shumway, Barbara B. Smith, Bathsheba Wilson Smith, Emma Hale Smith, Lucy Mack Smith, Mary Duty Smith, Mary Fielding Smith, Mary Ellen Smoot, Eliza R. Snow, Belle S. Spafford, Annie Clark Tanner, Elmina Shephard Taylor, Minerva Teichert, Martha Horne Tingey, Emmeline

B. Wells, Sharlene Wells, Mary Whitmer, Helen Mar Whitney, Clarissa Smith Williams, Barbara W. Winder, Ann Eliza Young, Dwan J. Young, and Zina D. Young.

34. S. Kent Brown, Donald Q. Cannon, and Richard H. Jackson, eds., *Historical Atlas of Mormonism* (New York: Simon & Schuster, 1994), 2–3, 104–7; Brandon S. Plewe, ed., *Mapping Mormonism: An Atlas of Mormon History* (Provo, UT: Brigham Young University Press, 2014), 12–13, 102–3.

35. The Church of Jesus Christ of Latter-day Saints, *Our Heritage* (Salt Lake City, UT: Church of Jesus Christ of Latter-day Saints, 1996), Emma Smith, 7, 21, 25, 61–62; Lucy Mack Smith, 1–2, 15, 19; McKay's mother, 115 (only five of the book's twenty-six illustrations have women in them); Eliza R. Snow, 35; Mary Elizabeth Rollins, 41; Louisa Barnes Pratt, 62; Mary Richards, 72; polygamy, 97–98, and the Manifesto, 100–101.

36. The Church of Jesus Christ of Latter-day Saints, *Daughters in My Kingdom: The History and Work of Relief Society* (Salt Lake City, UT: Church of Jesus Christ of Latter-day Saints, 2011). On the book's creation and uses, see "Frequently Asked Questions, History—Daughters in My Kingdom," https://www.lds.org/callings/relief-society/messages-from-leaders/news-and-announcements/frequently-asked-questions; Julie B. Beck, "Preserving the Heritage of Latter-day Saint Women" (presented at the Church History Symposium, June 3, 2016), https://history.lds.org/article/preserving-the-heritage-of-latter-day-saint-women.

37. Jane J. Mansbridge, *Why We Lost the ERA* (Chicago: University of Chicago Press, 1986); Utah is acknowledged on page 34.

38. Jon Krakauer, *Under the Banner of Heaven: A Story of Violent Faith* (New York: Doubleday, 2003); Carolyn Jessop with Laura Palmer, *Escape* (New York: Broadway Books, 2007); Elissa Wall and Lisa Pulitzer, *Stolen Innocence: My Story of Growing Up in a Polygamous Sect, Becoming a Teenage Bride, and Breaking Free of Warren Jeffs* (New York: Harper, 2009); Ruth Wariner, *The Sound of Gravel: A Memoir* (New York: Flatiron Books, 2016); Anna LeBaron and Leslie Wilson, *The Polygamist's Daughter: A Memoir* (Carol Stream, IL: Tyndale House Publishers, 2017).

39. Peter Cannon, "The Mormons: Saints or Sinners?" *Social Studies Review*, no. 3 (Winter 1990): 9–10; Kyle Ward, *Not Written in Stone: Learning and Unlearning American History through 200 Years of Textbooks* (New York: New Press, 2010), 186–91.

40. Jon Butler, "Jack-in-the-Box Faith: The Religion Problem in Modern American History," *Journal of American History* 90 (March 2004): 1357–478.

41. Catherine A. Brekus, "Mormon Women and the Problem of Historical Agency," *Journal of Mormon History* (Spring 2011): 67–68, 71, 77, 83, see 59–87.

42. Kate Holbrook and Matthew Burton Bowman, eds., *Women and Mormonism: Historical and Contemporary Perspectives* (Salt Lake City: University of Utah Press, 2016); see especially Rachel Cope, "Reexploring Mormon Women and Agency in the Context of Polygamy" (56–67); Kate Holbrook and Rebekah Ryan Clark, "'A Wider Sphere of Action': Women's Agency in 1870s Utah" (165–82); Quincy D. Newell, "Jane James' Agency" (136–48).

43. Sheri L Dew, *Women and the Priesthood: What One Mormon Woman Believes* (Salt Lake City, UT: Deseret Book, 2013); Neylan McBaine, *Women at Church: Magnifying LDS Women's Local Impact* (Salt Lake City, UT: Greg Kofford Books, 2014).

44. Kathryn M. Daynes, *More Wives Than One: Transformation of the Mormon Marriage System, 1840–1910* (Urbana: University of Illinois Press, 2001), 2, 14.

45. Leonard J. Arrington, Susan Arrington Madsen, and Emily Madsen Jones, *Mothers of the Prophets* (Salt Lake City, UT: Deseret Book, 1992); Mary Jane Woodger and Paulette Preston Yates, *Courtships of the Prophets: From Childhood Sweethearts to Love at First Sight* (American Fork, UT: Covenant Communications, 2015). The slim 138-page courtship volume omits most of the polygamist prophets—Taylor, Woodruff, Snow, Joseph F. Smith, and Grant. The chapter on Joseph Smith tells of his marriage to Emma with not a word on polygamy

(40–45); the chapter on Brigham Young tells of his marriage as a widower to his second (non-plural) wife, Mary Ann Angell, and closes only with this cryptic comment: "The marriage not only survived but flourished . . . even under the uniquely traumatic shock of being called to live polygamy" (74–80). Eight years after their marriage, Brigham took on his first plural wife; Mary Ann outlived Brigham by five years, dying in 1882.

46. Whitney Cross, as cited in Rachel Cope, "The Unexplored Drama within the Drama," *Journal of Mormon History* 35, no. 3 (Summer 2009): 198.

47. Davis Bitton, *Guide to Mormon Diaries & Autobiographies* (Provo, UT: Brigham Young University Press, 1977). The repositories searched were LDS Historical Department, University of Utah, Utah Historical Society, Brigham Young University, Utah State University, Genealogical Society of Utah, Bancroft Library, Huntington Library, Yale, Princeton, Library of Congress, Idaho State University, Denver Public Library, Daughters of Utah Pioneers (v–vi, xi). I thank Anya Bybee for performing this analysis.

48. I thank Ed Riding for providing the analysis; for a starting point on the holdings, see "Women in Church History: A Research Guide," March 3, 2016, https://history.lds.org/article/women_in_church_history_research_guide.

49. Emmeline B. Wells, "Self-Made Women," *Woman's Exponent* 9 (March 1, 1881): 148.

50. Susan S. Rugh, e-mail to Keith A. Erekson, February 17, 2016, relating remarks at http://www.mormonwomenshistoryinitiative.org/mwhit-symposium-program.html.

51. Laurel Thatcher Ulrich, *A House Full of Females: Family and Faith in 19th-Century Mormon Diaries* (New York: Alfred A. Knopf, 2017); and from Holbrook and Bowman, eds., *Women and Mormonism*, see Laurel Thatcher Ulrich, "Remember Me: Inscriptions of Self in Nineteenth-Century Mormonism" (42–55); Jennifer Reeder, "Turning the Key: Understanding Mormon Women's Material Culture" (68–81); and Kristine Wright, "'We Baked a Lot of Bread': Reconceptionalizing Mormon Women and Ritual Objects" (82–100).

52. O. Leslie and Dorothy C. Stone Family Papers, 1916–1985 (MS 28910), Church of Jesus Christ of Latter-day Saints Church History Library, Salt Lake City, UT (hereafter cited as LDS Church History Library).

53. Amy Easton-Flake and Rachel Cope, "A Multiplicity of Witnesses: Women and the Translation Process," in Dennis L. Largey, Andrew H. Hedges, John Hilton III, and Kerry Hull, eds., *The Coming Forth of the Book of Mormon: A Marvelous Work and a Wonder* (Provo, UT: Brigham Young University Religious Studies Center, 2015), 133–53.

54. "Sketch of Mary Rebecca Moyle Booth" (MS 15817), LDS Church History Library, Salt Lake City, UT; Mary R. Moyle Booth Papers, 1904–1906, 1923–1933 (MS 15414), LDS Church History Library, Salt Lake City, UT.

55. Tad Walch, "Women Hired by LDS Church History Department Making Huge Strides in Mormon Women's History," DeseretNews.com, February 7, 2016, http://www.deseretnews.com/article/865647165/Women-hired-by-LDS-Church-History-Department-making-huge-strides-in-Mormon-womens-history.html?pg=all. For a proactive approach to working within institutions, see McBaine, *Women at Church*.

56. Amy Harris, "Converting Mormon History," *Journal of Mormon History* 35, no. 3 (Summer 2009): 226.

57. Peter Crawley, *A Descriptive Bibliography of the Mormon Church*, 3 vols. (Provo, UT: Brigham Young University Religious Studies Center, 2005), 2:68–112; Chad J. Flake and Larry W. Draper, eds., *A Mormon Bibliography, 1830–1930: Books, Pamphlets, Periodicals, and Broadsides Relating to the First Century of Mormonism*, 2nd ed., 2 vols. (Provo, UT: Brigham Young University Religious Studies Center, 2004), 1:331, 1:343, 2:324–25.

58. *Correspondence between Rev. Abraham De Witt, Pastor of Rock Church, Cecil Co., Md. and Miss Sarah Stageman, One of His Flock, regarding the Principles and Faith of the Church*

of Jesus Christ of Latter-day Saints (Philadelphia: Bicking & Guilbert Printers, 1849). See also Kathryn Webb Wikert, "Home to Iowa: Letters from the Western Trails," *Iowa Heritage Illustrated* 84, no. 1 (Spring 2003): 30–46.

59. Steven Mintz, "Does the American Family Have a History? Family Images and Realities," *OAH Magazine of History* 15, no. 4 (Summer 2001); see also Stephanie Coontz, "The Challenge of Family History" in the same issue.

60. Daynes, *More Wives Than One.*

61. Steven Mintz, "Teaching Family History: An Annotated Bibliography," *OAH Magazine of History* 15, no. 4 (Summer 2001).

Chapter Two

Sifting Truth from Legend

Evaluating Sources for American Indian Biography through the Life of Sally Exervier Ward

Jenny Hale Pulsipher

If you were to combine all the family stories of the life of my fourth great-grandmother, Sally Exervier Ward, into one story, it would go something like this: Sally, the daughter of Komootze, a Shoshone chief, was born near the headwaters of the Green River around 1808. While she was still a baby, a battle took place in Wyoming between the Shoshone Indians and American soldiers (or Crow Indians) in which almost all the Shoshones were killed. After the battle, some soldiers (or fur traders) saw a movement on the battlefield. Going to inspect, they discovered an Indian baby suckling at the breast of her dead mother. They took the baby to St. Louis, where a merchant adopted her. (Or she was taken to St. Louis when she was around twelve years old, after being shot in the neck by a Sioux Indian, and placed in the care of a relative for several years.) Sally lived with the merchant for several years; then, unhappy with her situation, she ran away, swimming across the Missouri (or Mississippi) River. She traveled upriver and took shelter at the home of a trapper, and it was there that she met and fell in love with Baptiste Exervier, a French mountaineer. (Or she may have met Exervier in the mountains of the West, after being reunited with her Shoshone kin.) After they married, they settled with the Shoshones at Fort Laramie (or Fort Bridger). They had two children, a girl named Adelaide (or Adeliette) and a boy named Ish-a-mana (or John or Lewis). When Adelaide was four years old, her father died of Rocky Mountain spotted fever (or from being shot in the back by a fellow mountaineer during a drunken "frolic"). Sally later married Barney Ward, a handsome Irishman (from Virginia), who promised Baptiste Exervier on his deathbed to care for his wife and children. Sally had two daughters with Ward, Polly and Louisa. After the Mormons arrived in the West, the family moved to Salt Lake City, where Adelaide was taken into the home of Brigham Young and "learned the ways of the refined white people." Barney Ward joined the Latter-day Saints (LDS) Church and

served in the Fort Supply, Wyoming, mission to the Shoshone Indians, taking along Sally and her daughters. While there, Adelaide met and married
Ward's fellow missionary James Morehead Brown. When Johnston's Army
arrived, Sally felt that she would be safer among the Indians and left Ward to
live with them. Soon thereafter, she fell sick and died. Ward and his daughters
later moved to Sanpete County, and he was killed by Indians at the start of the
Blackhawk War in 1863 or 1865. (Or Sally died shortly after being widowed
in the Blackhawk War. Or Sally and her son John continued to live with the
Shoshones but traveled to Ogden regularly to stay with her daughter Adelaide.
After one such visit, she left with her son but never returned, probably dying
among her people.)[1]

As this combined account demonstrates, family histories of Sally are riddled
with contradiction and anachronism. Clearly, all these details cannot be right,
but how do you sift the factual from the fanciful? In this chapter, I will discuss
the challenges of determining the truth about poorly documented individuals,
including Sally and most other American Indians before 1900. But I will also
argue that there is truth to be found even in fanciful accounts, particularly
when they are placed in historical context. They help us uncover how people
in previous eras understood their history and how that informed their identity.
Additionally, I will use the events of Sally's family history to illustrate how a
Native perspective not only illuminates family history but provides vital insight
into the causes of conflict and the role of race in Mormon-Indian relations.

The compiled account above drew entirely from oral history sources—
family stories passed by word of mouth and later written down. The contradictions demonstrate why many historians and genealogists have taken
a dim view of oral history. These historians claim that oral sources *cannot*
be trusted, that they have been corrupted by the biases of the tellers as they
passed down through the generations. However, some American Indian historians argue that *only* oral history can be trusted, that the written sources
are too tainted by white cultural imperialism to give a true account. This is a
false dichotomy; thoughtful scholars acknowledge that *all* sources, private or
public, written or oral, require careful attention to the circumstances of their
production, their purpose, and their audience to account for inevitable biases.[2]
In fact, oral sources can be used profitably in concert with documentary
sources, each serving to validate, discredit, or shed light on the other.[3]

Family stories of Sally Exervier Ward, based on oral accounts, are clearly
problematic. They show evidence of faulty memory—Barney Ward dying in
1863 rather than 1865, for example—and of guessing about facts even contemporaries did not know—when and where Sally died, for instance. They
are also contradictory. Take the example of Exervier's death. The earliest
family account—Adelaide's 1896 obituary—says he was shot in the back by
a fellow mountaineer. The next account (chronologically), given in 1919 by

Sally and Barney Ward's daughter Polly, reports Exervier's death, but not how he died. The next account, from which most of the succeeding accounts were drawn at least in part, was written in 1937 by a granddaughter of both Adelaide and Louisa, Naomi Brown. She claimed that Exervier died of "the dreaded scourge of the pioneer days," Rocky Mountain spotted fever. When such mistakes or contradictions appear, primary written documents can assist in selecting which detail is true. Barney Ward's death and the start of the Black Hawk War are documented in multiple contemporary accounts, as is the death of Baptiste Exervier. (He actually was shot in the back in a drunken "frolic.")[4] Thus, contemporary written reports allow us to corroborate or correct oral histories passed down through families. But the oral history accounts, even when they directly contradict the facts, are not worthless. Examining contradictions can give us insight into how families reconciled their sense of what kind of people they were or aspired to be with the details of their family history and the events and attitudes of their historical milieu.

One of the biggest discrepancies among family accounts is the explanation of how Sally ended up in St. Louis—something that all the accounts agree occurred. Adelaide's obituary describes Sally being wounded at age six or seven, cared for by a relative until age twelve, and later being taken to St. Louis by a "wealthy merchant." Naomi Brown's 1937 account tells a very different tale: She says,

When she was only a baby, in the early part of 1800 a terrific battle took place at Battle Creek, Wyoming between the Indians and a party of white soldiers who had been sent to this locality to investigate some Indian thefts.

As was so often the case, instead of trying to make peace with the Red Men, these self-righteous defenders of the law, took it upon themselves to settle the trouble by killing every one of this little band. But some kind fate had decreed a different ending for one soul, for as the victors were preparing to leave the field of battle, some one noticed a slight movement on the ground. On closer scrutiny, a wee infant was discovered suckling at its dead mother's breast.

Some brave full grown man exclaimed, "Nits make lice, hit it in the head." But another spoke up and said, "No, let me have it, I will take it home with me, it will be quite a curiosity." And so the life of little Sally of the Shoshones was spared.

She was taken to St. Louis and adopted by some merchant with whom she lived for several years.

Naomi Brown's story draws from Polly Ward Williams's 1919 account, which was published in the widely available *LDS Biographical Dictionary*. But it does not take into account details that appear in Adelaide's obituary. If Naomi did not have access to the obituary, the details in her account that are consistent with it—Sally's adoption by a St. Louis merchant, running away, swimming a river (although not the same one), meeting and marrying the

French trader Exervier, his death (though not the manner of it), and marrying Barney Ward—are probably key elements of the family story, details that survived four generations after Sally.

Naomi Brown's account of Sally's time in St. Louis suggests both that she was unaware of the obituary and that she filled in the missing gaps by drawing on the mythology of the American frontier. Hundreds of firsthand accounts of traveling in the American West exist, as well as "blood and thunder" novels that peddled Western stereotypes to a broad audience, some of whom would travel west with those hackneyed expectations firmly in place.[5] Two of the governing tropes of Western mythology were the "savage Indian" and the "vanishing Indian." According to the first of these tropes, Indians were the antithesis of civilization, lacking the Euro-American traits of Christianity, education, cleanliness, and a work ethic. Instead of these civilized traits, Indians were frequently associated with theft, laziness, filth, and drunkenness.[6] The nineteenth-century ideology of manifest destiny envisioned "the sons of the Pilgrims" carrying "the progress of industry and enterprise" to regions that were previously "known only as remote and unexplored wildernesses."[7] Indians were depicted as antagonists to that march of progress in countless lurid tales of violence against white settlers, particularly women and children.[8] By emphasizing the incompatibility of Indians with modern society, these depictions of Indians undergirded another dominant trope—the vanishing Indian. Indians were presumed to be incapable of or unwilling to adapt to modern life. One nineteenth-century immigrant declared of them, "These little savages . . . come nearer supplying Darwin's missing link than any other human beings on the face of the globe."[9] Thus they were doomed to disappear—or be exterminated—before the advance of dominant white civilization.

Naomi Brown's story fits neatly into this Western mythology. Her description of "a party of white soldiers who had been sent to this locality to investigate some Indian thefts" implies that Indian theft was an understood and common occurrence. The derogatory attitudes many whites held toward Indians are also apparent in her account. White soldiers proposed killing the orphaned Sally because "Nits make lice."[10] The vanishing Indian trope appears in Naomi Brown's description of the Indians slaughtered by US soldiers, who afterwards discovered on the battlefield "a wee infant . . . suckling at its dead mother's breast." The suckling infant evokes a picture of the diminished survivors of Native peoples trying in vain to derive nourishment from their dying culture. This striking image, with its symbolic echoes, appears repeatedly in narratives of early Indian-Euroamerican contact.[11]

Family accounts were influenced by more positive myths about American Indians as well. Savagery and civility were concepts constantly in tension in depictions of Indians. The counterpart to the barbarous savage was the noble chief or, more often, the virtuous princess.[12] The earliest family account,

Adelaide's 1896 obituary, claims that Sally's father was a "chief" of the Shoshone Indians. The likeliest source for the information was Adelaide's husband of forty years, James Morehead Brown, or one of their children. Outside of the obituary, there is no evidence for the claim. Of course, that does not disprove it, but it is worth considering the high frequency of claims of descent from "chiefs" or "princesses" by people claiming American Indian ancestry. Genealogist Sharon DeBartolo Carmack explains that "for those who frowned upon a white male ancestor marrying an Indian woman, elevating the woman's status to princess made the truth easier to swallow."[13] Sally's father may have been a chief of the Shoshone Indians, or he may have had aristocracy conferred on him by his descendants.[14] Claiming the equivalent of "royal" ancestry was one way to make Indian ancestry more respectable during a time long before Native descent attained its modern cachet. Like chiefs, Indian "princesses" were more acceptable relatives. These figures offered assistance to white explorers or settlers, as Pocahontas did to John Smith and Sacagawea to Lewis and Clark; they embraced white civilization, sometimes abandoning their own people in the process; and they were often depicted as falling in love with white men.[15] This romantic trope is evident in Adelaide Exervier Brown's obituary, which asserts that her Shoshone mother Sally's relationship with Baptiste Exervier was a love match: "Their acquaintance ripened into love and after a few weeks courtship they were married." Adelaide's granddaughter Ella Brown Hale added, "They were very happy."

Another romantic trope of the era—loyal male friendship—also appears in Naomi Brown's account as an explanation for Sally's second marriage to Elijah Barney Ward.[16] While Adelaide's obituary scarcely mentions Ward (Adelaide was Exervier's daughter), Polly Williams (Barney's daughter) recounted this of him:

> A very dear friend of his, a Mr. Exervid, a Frenchman, died. Just before his death he called Mr. Ward to his bedside and confided to his care his young wife, a handsome Indian girl, and also his little daughter, Adelaide. Mr. Ward accepted the trust and was true to his charge, in time marrying the woman by whom he subsequently had two daughters.

The story of Exervier entrusting his family to Ward on his deathbed cannot be corroborated in any sources, including the three contemporary journals that mention Exervier's death.[17] Indeed, Ward is not even present in any of these accounts, but after the incident appeared in Polly's story, it made its way into the Brown family tales as well.

Historian Daniel Richter argues that, for most people, history is "a serious, essentially mythic business of defining group identity."[18] When Richter said history was a "mythic business," he did not mean that the stories told in history were necessarily false. *Myth*, in the sense he used, was associated with stories about origins and identity. In other words, the stories we tell about ourselves, our families, our cultures, and nations line up with who we think we are. We remember the stories that reinforce our identity. Stories that contradict our identity are forgotten or, in some cases, consciously altered. The selection of remembered and forgotten pieces of Sally's family stories demonstrates this process. It is clear that the Browns and Wards were proud of their American Indian heritage but also somewhat defensive. A number of family stories recount experiencing prejudice based on appearance or self-identification as Indian, including teasing at school, disapproval within the extended family, and exclusion from dating relationships because of "Negro blood."[19] Responding defensively to such prejudice may explain Naomi Brown's sarcastic description of the "brave full grown man" (a white US soldier who proposed killing the infant Sally) as well as her presentation of her Indian ancestors as refined and well educated—thus reversing the stereotypical assignment of civility to whites and savagery to Indians. Aspects of family history that smacked of incivility—such as dying in a drunken frolic—undermined that genteel identity. Thus, the death of Exervier was handed down as spotted fever rather than murder. Uncomfortable details extant in Sally's family history could also undermine presentation of a civilized, respectable identity. Those, which included the birth of an illegitimate daughter to Louisa Ward and the abandonment of Polly Ward by her first husband, remain absent from all family stories.[20] Family stories also demonstrate that the tellers were influenced by contemporary ways of thinking and writing about Indians and by themes in American storytelling. Thus, to create a complete narrative out of the surviving fragments of Sally's life, family members plugged in familiar tropes and romantic themes, connecting the family story to larger stories about the American West, progress, persecution, friendship, and romance.

* * *

The tellers of these stories about Sally were passing on their family history, but for the most part, they were not historians. Even if they had been, they would have found it rough going adding to Sally's story because of an issue endemic to American Indian history—a dearth of sources, compounded by the fact that the sources that do exist are largely from a Euro-American, rather than a Native, perspective. Historians interested in telling Native histories often have to draw them from primary documents produced by people who had no interest in Indians, were actively fighting Indians, or held attitudes toward Indians that modern people find offensive. Contemporary Native voices occasionally appear, but they are usually reported by Euro-Americans and thus filtered through their biases.[21] Oral histories preserved among American Indians offer one promising source of historical material. Like written sources, they reflect the biases of their creators and transmitters, but their biases are at least different ones. While it is impossible to entirely escape bias in historical research and writing, obtaining multiple perspectives whenever possible—those of Native people as well as white settlers—provides needed balance.

Given the scarcity of Native sources and perspectives, it is no wonder that the Indians who appear in pre-twentieth-century records often lack names and come across as undifferentiated figures, easily conflated with each other. That conflation is clearly evident in the early twentieth-century historian Grace Hebard's scholarship on Sacagawea. According to Hebard's account, Sacagawea was a powerful figure long after the end of the Lewis and Clark expedition. Hebard asserts that Sacagawea was an important participant in the 1868 Fort Bridger treaty that led to the establishment of the Wind River Indian reservation, was influential in Shoshone adoption of agriculture, acted as a frequent interpreter and counselor to both Indians and white settlers, was honored and trusted by the Mormon community in Utah, and traveled all over the West, welcomed by Indians and whites wherever she went.[22] Hebard has been sharply criticized by scholars for jumping to conclusions with no evidence, pressuring oral history informants, and "fabricating" sources. These historians point to contemporary documents describing Sacagawea's early death and argue that the things Hebard describes must have been done by other Shoshone women, a large number of whom were wives to white trappers.[23] In fact, Hebard conflates Sacagawea with Sally Exervier Ward more than once: she references the accounts of Exervier's death, which mention his (unnamed) wife and children, and claims that this Shoshone wife of a French trapper must have been Sacagawea. Hebard's claims that Sacagawea had close ties with the Mormon Church, that she helped establish agricultural practices among the Shoshone, and that she was a valued interpreter were largely based on information she received from the LDS Church historian's office, which she does not seem to have visited in person.[24] These records were summaries from the Church's "Journal History," a chronological scrapbook with condensed accounts of events. The more detailed accounts reveal that many of the events Hebard claims for Sacagawea actually involved Sally, Adelaide, and several other Shoshone women living with LDS missionaries at Fort Supply, a Mormon agricultural settlement in the Green River area, near Fort Bridger. This settlement was intended to help "supply" Mormon emigrants and, at the same time, provide instruction in agricultural techniques and Mormon doctrine to nearby Shoshones.[25]

It is likely that Hebard's assumption that Sacagawea was responsible for actions carried out by other Indian women was connected to her ideological stance. Hebard was a committed promoter of women's rights. Like her contemporary and friend Eva Emery Dye, whose novel *The Conquest* spawned monuments to Sacagawea nationwide, Hebard saw Sacagawea as a perfect subject for promotion as an American feminist icon.[26] Hebard's conflation also may have arisen from a too-narrow focus on Sacagawea's life at the expense of the broader historical context of the nineteenth-century American West.

That broader context reveals a multitude of issues and events that impacted Sacagawea's life, including the Indian slave trade. If she had lived to an advanced age, as Hebard argues, she and her Shoshone people would also have been affected by Mormon and other Euro-Americans' settlement of the Rocky Mountain region, Mormon missions to the Shoshone, the tensions between Mormons and Indians that resulted in the Black Hawk War, Walker's War, and other local conflicts, and the Utah War between federal troops and Mormon settlers. All these events, as well as the adoption of Indian children by Mormon families, Mormon interference in the Indian slave trade, and Mormon attitudes toward Indian and mixed-race people, also affected the Shoshone woman Sally Exervier Ward. A careful reading of the life of Sally Exervier Ward brings American Indian and Mormon history together to illuminate the causes and consequences of these significant events and issues, deepening and complicating both Mormon and American Indian history.

* * *

Sally and her family lived in Utah during a time of significant change and conflict, encompassing the arrival of the Mormon pioneers, their settlement across the region, and several wars involving Mormon settlers, American Indians, and "gentile" travelers and officials.[27] This was a time of transition from an American Indian to a Euro-American world. Seeing this transition through an American Indian lens provides a vital perspective on the causes of conflict and the role of race in Mormon-Indian relations.

When the Mormon pioneers arrived in the Salt Lake Valley on July 24, 1847, Sally Exervier Ward and her daughter Adelaide, her second husband Elijah Barney Ward, and their newborn daughter Polly were already living in the region. Barney Ward, an American trapper from Virginia, had worked in the fur trade throughout the West, including stints at Fort Hall and Fort Bridger. His decades in the trade had given him a facility with Native dialects, including Ute, Shoshone, and Flathead. This skill made Ward an attractive ally to the newly arrived Mormons. Indeed, he may have encountered them at Fort Bridger before they reached the Valley.[28] Polly Ward was born at Fort Bridger on July 15, 1847. Barney Ward soon began working as an interpreter for Brigham Young, moving his family into the Old Fort in Salt Lake by the spring of 1848. Louisa Jane, Sally and Barney's second daughter, would be born there on May 26, 1848.[29]

Having an American Indian family—a Shoshone mother, American father, and three mixed-race children—living in the Old Fort must have raised considerable interest among the exiled Saints. Indian-European marriages were common in the fur trade, but fur trade society was far removed from mainstream American life, as alien to nineteenth-century white families as

American Indian society itself. Americans in general were intrigued and un-nerved by Indians, but Mormons had additional doctrinal reasons for their interest. They believed that their sacred scripture, the Book of Mormon, was an account of Lehi and his family, Jewish emigrants to the New World whose descendants were among the American Indians. These descendants, called "Lamanites," were children of Israel whom God had promised to restore to a knowledge of the Christian gospel in the latter days.[30] Mormon missionaries had already carried their message to tribes living in Indian territory near the city of Nauvoo. Once the Mormons settled in the West, they were surrounded by new Indian peoples and felt an obligation to teach them the gospel and introduce them to the benefits of white civilization, thus fulfilling the modern prophecy that before the second coming of Jesus Christ "the Lamanites shall blossom as the rose."[31]

Sally's daughter Adelaide Exervier participated in one of the first efforts to meet this obligation. At the age of ten, she attended Zina D. H. Young's school in Salt Lake City, probably beginning in the latter months of 1848. Zina re-corded in her journal in January 1849: "A lamanite girl by the name of Adalade is coming to school thus fulfilling Old Father Smiths words on my head when but 14 years old."[32] Zina Young's blessing from Father Smith and her claim that it was fulfilled by teaching Adelaide highlight early Latter-day Saints' special relationship to American Indians. Like the Puritans three hundred years before, Mormons believed their role was to restore the Indians to a knowledge of the truth they had once had. (Interestingly, some Puritans also believed Indians descended from the lost tribes of Israel.) While Mormons and Puritans believed that Native peoples were their spiritual equals, they also believed themselves to be culturally superior to Indians and, therefore, able to raise them to a higher level of civilization through precept and example. This paternalistic approach created resentment and conflict between the two peoples.[33] Nevertheless, Zina and Adelaide developed what seems to have been a mutually affectionate rela-tionship. Adelaide would later name one of her daughters Martha Zina in her teacher's honor and cherished a signed photograph of her.[34]

There was some delay in evangelizing the surrounding Indians as the Mor-mons settled into their new home in the American West, but in 1853, Brigham Young called a group of missionaries to preach to the Shoshone people of southwestern Wyoming. Barney Ward, who by then had been baptized into the LDS Church, was one of those sent on the new mission to Fort Supply, and he took along his wife Sally and their two younger daughters.[35] Later, Adelaide, who had been continuing her schooling in Salt Lake City, joined them, and she and Sally served as language instructors to the LDS missionar-ies, thus facilitating the missionaries' teaching of the Shoshones and probably influencing their attitudes about Native Mormons as well. Ward's fellow mis-sionary Henry W. Sanderson notes that he "took lessons in the Shoshonean language from a young half-breed woman that had been raised among the

Indians, a step-daughter of Barney Ward."[36] Fort Supply was located near the Green River, a traditional gathering place for the Shoshone Indians, and the presence of Sally Ward at the mission undoubtedly helped make it a magnet for other Shoshones of the area. It is possible that Sally's marriage to Barney Ward prompted apostle Orson Hyde's suggestion that the other missionaries intermarry with local Shoshone women, something they thought would pave the way to widespread conversion.[37] Following this counsel, James S. Brown visited the Shoshone chief Washakie and indicated the missionaries' interest in taking Indian wives. Washakie replied, "white men might look around, and if any one of us found a girl that would go with him, it would be all right, but the Indians must have the same privilege among the white men."[38]

Washakie's response was a clear indication of American Indian expectations of reciprocity in their interactions with white settlers. Reciprocity—an assumption that relationships entailed mutual obligations—was a foundational principle in many American Indian societies, both within their own tribes and between themselves and other Native people. As Europeans settled North America, Indians tried to establish reciprocal relations with them, too. One form of reciprocal relations was alliance, which usually accompanied trade. But Native trade and alliance almost always intertwined with kinship. Trade gatherings were opportunities for alliance-building intermarriages, and alliances always included expressions of kinship, fictive and actual. Thus, ties between two distinct peoples occurred on multiple levels, and reciprocity was expected in all these exchanges.[39]

The fur trade, which drew in both European and Native peoples, modeled these multi-level interconnections. Intermarriage between whites and Indians had long been practiced in the fur trade, although the arrangement, known as "the custom of the country," often lacked the imprimatur of church or civil authority. The marriage of Barney Ward and Sally Exervier was probably of this variety. White traders married into Indian families for strategic reasons: to learn Native languages or gain a live-in interpreter, to secure favorable trade relations with a tribe, or to have the comfort of a hardworking wife. Indian women's reasons for intermarrying with whites were equally strategic. Once a trader married an Indian woman, her family was guaranteed access to his trade goods, the marriage smoothed relations between Indians and the home community of the trapper, and Indian women may have believed that their bicultural children would enjoy special advantages.[40] Thus, intermarriage was a form of cultural reciprocity that built strong cross-cultural relationships.

Like many other nineteenth-century Americans, most Mormons were not open to intermarriage with Indians, and that lack of full reciprocity introduced distrust into Mormon-Indian relations.[41] An example of this occurred after the Walker War of 1853. Soon after Mormons settled Manti in Sanpete Valley, the Ute chief Wakara visited Brigham Young to ask for permission to marry a Mormon woman. Wakara had, by this time, been baptized a member of the Mormon Church and received the priesthood, so there was no religious barrier to intermarriage. Young said certainly, if Wakara could find one who would have him. Wakara returned to Sanpete and asked Mary Artemesia Lowry, the 21-year-old daughter of Manti's bishop, to marry him—a choice likely connected to her status as the daughter of the local Mormon "chief." Her status would enhance his own and strengthen ties between the Utes and Mormons. A contemporary account of Wakara's proposal fairly drips with the contempt Mormons felt for their Indian neighbors: "He poured into her ears the tale of a splendidly elegant and imposing wickiup he would build for her, told her how rich he was, what numberless droves of horses he owned, and how he would furnish her future home in such barbaric splendor as should astonish all beholders."[42] Mary was horrified. She feared snubbing the chief might endanger her family and even her town, so she cast about for the only solution she could think of: she claimed she was already polygamously married to her sister's husband. As the story goes, Wakara plunged his knife into the kitchen table, stalked out, and later complained loudly of the insult.

The Mormons had rejected Wakara's request for reciprocal kin relations and made it clear that they did not consider the Indian chief a suitable partner for the Mormon bishop's daughter. They had demonstrated that Mormons shared nineteenth-century Anglo-Americans' cultural distaste for what they increasingly viewed as "inferior races," despite the religious imperatives that pushed them to believe—and behave—otherwise.[43] Even among LDS missionaries to the Indians, who had been specifically directed to take Native wives, there were very few white-Indian marriages, and most of those that did occur did not last long. Historian Richard Kitchen suggests that the reluctance of the missionaries to intermarry with the Indians was a significant factor in the failure of the first phase of the Fort Supply mission that Sally and Barney Ward participated in.[44]

Repugnance for intermarriage seems to have extended to the Indians being raised within Mormon families, very few of whom married white Mormons.[45] Around four hundred Indians lived in Mormon households in the nineteenth century, mostly in the first decade of Mormon settlement.[46] They were there as a result of the Mormon encounter with the New Mexican trade in guns, horses, and Indian slaves. The slave trade was practiced in Utah long before the Mormons arrived. By the early nineteenth century, it had become a violent and destructive system in which the women and children of nonequestrian tribes like the Paiutes were taken captive by Ute Indians, who exchanged them for guns and horses.[47] When the Mormons arrived in 1847, they found this system firmly in place. Looking for closer sources of trade, the Utes immediately offered Indian slaves to the Mormon newcomers, who were appalled and refused to buy them. The consequences of their refusal were immediate and game changing. In one incident, the Ute chief Arapeen offered to sell a child to a Mormon. When he refused, Arapeen dashed the child's brains out against a rock, threw the body at the Mormon's feet, and declared, "You have no heart or you would have bought [him] and saved [his] life."[48] Given the horrifying alternative, Mormons began purchasing Indian captives and placing them in their own households. Eventually, the territorial legislature legalized the practice as an indenture system, including the stipulation that children from seven to sixteen years of age attend school at least three months a year.[49] Indians in the indenture system were released upon reaching adulthood or after repaying their purchase price. Mormons viewed this system in two ways. At the basic economic level, the Indian children in Mormon homes provided needed household or agricultural labor. At the religious level, the system allowed Mormons to teach Indians their religion and "civilize" them, thus fulfilling their religious obligations.

Indians experienced a range of conditions within the LDS indenture system, but full acceptance within the larger community was exceedingly rare. Like the Indian indenture system in place in Catholic New Mexico, the LDS system rested on the need for labor as well as a desire to teach Indians Christianity. In some Mormon households, as in Catholic households, Indians were overworked, beaten, or abused. In others, they were treated as members of the family; some were even provided with legacies in wills. But almost none of them were accepted as marriage partners within Mormon society.[50] Richard Kitchen's study of Mormon-Indian relations in the intermountain West found only seven examples of Indians marrying white Mormon partners before 1870, and most of these marriages occurred in the context of missions to the Indians.[51] Racial and cultural prejudice prevented widespread intermarriage, leaving fostered Indians in a cultural no-man's-land. One Native woman living with the Mormons responded to the limbo by choosing to have children outside of wedlock. She declared, "I have a right to children. No white man will marry me. I cannot live with the Indians. But I can have children, and I will support the children that I have . . . God meant that a woman have children."[52] The woman's declaration that she could not live with the Indians is a poignant comment on being caught between two cultures. A Native woman raised in white society would likely imbibe all the prejudices of that society, making it difficult for her to imagine returning to her own people, even though "no white man" would marry her. Such examples from the lives of American Indian women highlight the failure of nineteenth-century Mormons to bring their cultural and religious beliefs into harmony. Their religion may have taught them that Indians were heirs of Israel, God's chosen people, but their culture taught them that Indians were uncivilized and inferior, not fit to marry their daughters.

Sally's family provides another illustration of Mormons disappointing Native expectations of reciprocity. On April 10, 1865, Barney Ward and James Hansen were ambushed by Ute Indians who killed both men and then mutilated Ward's corpse. As a trader and interpreter, Ward was well known to the Ute Indians, and his murder and mutilation seem to have been payback for previous incidents, including Ward's participation in the 1850 Fort Utah fight between Mormon settlers and Ute Indians. Following the murders, the Ute chief Sanpitch claimed that Ward had previously promised him his two young daughters, Polly and Louisa, as wives and demanded that they be delivered to him. Because Ward was dead when Sanpitch made his claim, it is impossible to know whether he had really promised the girls to Sanpitch. Ward had a history of telling people what they wanted to hear, so it is certainly possible.[53] Local Mormons claimed that Sanpitch had mistreated his other wives, so they refused to comply with his demand, alerted Church leaders to the crisis, and hustled Louisa Ward off to Salt Lake City under heavy guard. (Polly Ward was away from home at the time, visiting her sister Adelaide in Ogden.)[54] It is probable that Sanpitch's demand was, like Wakara's earlier request, an attempt to secure the truly reciprocal relations intermarriage represented. The public repudiation of a Ute chief's demand was undoubtedly humiliating to Sanpitch and certainly could have contributed to the outbreak of the Black Hawk War, as some contemporaries claimed.[55] Native legend offers insight into the potentially violent consequences of such humiliation: A Comanche chief was promised the hand of a beautiful maiden once she was old enough to marry, but when he came to claim her, she was betrothed to someone else. In retaliation, the chief and his fellow tribesmen "sack[ed] the village . . . to seize what in honor had been promised him."[56]

The Native men who sought marriage with Mormon women were all of high status—chiefs or subchiefs. Among Natives of the Southwest, elite polygyny had become increasingly common with the dramatic growth in the horse and slave trade. Prominent men needed multiple wives to process hides and to be living illustrations of their wealth and status. Additional marriages also allowed them to form beneficial ties with other high-status families.[57] Polygamy among Mormons was also connected to status. Those men who had enough wealth to support more than one wife were generally the ones asked to take additional wives, and high-ranking Church leaders were more likely than other Mormons to practice polygamy.[58] Despite these similarities, and despite the fact that Mormon theology equated Indians with the children of Israel, Mormons were aghast at the idea of their women intermarrying with Indians. Mormons shared with other Anglo-Americans the "squaw drudge" stereotype, the perception that Indian women were overworked and mistreated by Indian men, an idea evident in Mormon settlers' justification for rejecting Sanpitch's demand for the daughters of Barney Ward.[59]

As the incident involving Sanpitch and Ward's daughters indicates, failures of reciprocity could lead to conflict. Mormons not only refused to intermarry with Indians to any significant extent but also refused to engage in the trade that had previously enriched the Ute Indians. At the same time Mormons began purchasing Indian captives, they prohibited New Mexican traders from entering the territory. This action cut Utes off from the stream of horses, guns, and goods of the New Mexican trade, creating tension between the Mormons and local Indians.[60] Mormon settlement itself also created tremendous—and rapidly increasing—tensions, cutting off Indians from normal food sources. Had Mormons and Indians become "one people," as the Natives seemed to desire, their kin networks could have balanced some of the losses brought on by Mormon settlement.[61] Kin shared their resources with each other. In the absence of that reciprocal relationship, Indians responded to their losses with violence. They raided livestock and engaged in a series of wars with local residents. As astute observers of Mormon-Federal relations, the Indians attacked at times of particular tension, trusting that the Mormons would get little help from Washington.[62]

* * *

Sally's family offers the opportunity to examine a range of outcomes of Indian-white intermarriage. She herself married within fur trade society to two white men in succession—a French Canadian trapper and an American trapper. Interracial marriage was widely accepted within fur trade society, but even there, racial prejudice kept many white trappers from retaining ties to their Indian wives and children after returning to live permanently in white society. The children of mixed marriages found themselves in between white and Native society. Some exploited that position, becoming cultural intermediaries. Most, as children of Native mothers, remained in Native society, particularly if their fathers eventually broke ties with their mothers; some grew up in white society. Mixed-race children suffered prejudice in both Indian and white environments.[63] Nevertheless, intermarriage between whites and mixed-race individuals seems to have been more acceptable to whites than white-Indian intermarriage. Of the eighty Indian-white marriages Richard Kitchen found in the intermountain West, seventy of them occurred after 1870.[64] Based on the evidence of Sally's daughters, it is likely that the higher number of Indian-white marriages after 1870 included mixed-race partners.

Like Sally, all three of her daughters married white men. Her oldest child, Adelaide, joined her mother at Fort Supply in 1854 after several years of education in Salt Lake City. Apparently, she also remembered enough of her previous education among her mother's Shoshone people to serve as a language instructor to the missionaries at Fort Supply. One of these missionaries was the twenty-year-old James Morehead Brown, son of Mormon Battalion captain James Brown, the founder of Ogden. Young James Brown recalled that when he saw Adelaide sitting on a fence with curly black hair falling down her back, he announced that she was the girl he was going to marry. They were wed a month later and went on to have eleven children. Newspaper stories and local histories of Ogden, Utah, indicate the family of James and Adelaide Brown was prominent and beloved.[65] The three censuses in which Adelaide appears all indicate her race differently. In 1860, she was listed as "Ind," or Indian. In 1870, a *w* for white was written in under race, with an *I* superimposed over it. In the census of 1880, Adelaide was identified as white, as were all of her children. Unlike the vast majority of Mormon men who married Indian women, James took Adelaide as his first and only wife. He did not remarry until after her death in 1895 and never had children by another woman.

Polly was living with her sister Adelaide in Ogden at the time her father was killed. By 1870, she was living in the household of Brigham Young. The census identified her with an *I* for Indian and "domestic servant" for her status.[66] In 1872, she married a white man named Upton Donely, who may have entered the territory as part of the construction of the Union Pacific Railroad. They had two children, and then Donely abandoned her. She and her children moved in with Adelaide and James. Some years later she entered a polygamous marriage with a Mormon man, moved to Idaho, had five sons, and died in 1947, just short of her hundredth birthday.[67] Louisa was living with her father at the time of his murder. She was taken to live in Brigham Young's household for a time, then moved to Ogden. Louisa was still living in Ogden in 1870, working as a domestic servant in the household of Thomas and Emma Browning. The census taken that year listed her as white. In 1870, she had an illegitimate daughter, Nelly Ward. In 1877, Louisa married a Mormon man named James Daley. Louisa had one son with Daley and died around 1880.[68]

While all three of Sally's daughters eventually married Mormon men, Polly and Louisa's status seems to have been significantly lower than Adelaide's. Both worked as domestic servants before their marriages; one bore a child out of wedlock, and the other was abandoned by her non-Mormon first husband. Both of these events would have been considered shameful in nineteenth-century America. While both later married Mormon men, neither enjoyed the status of a first wife. Even Adelaide, whose family history suggests a love match with James M. Brown and who was the matron of a prominent and wealthy family in Ogden, was sometimes referred to within the extended Brown family as "that Indian woman."[69]

It is clear that despite a theology that suggested a noble spiritual heritage for the American Indians, Mormons found it difficult to transcend the cultural prejudice against Indians and mixed-race people prevalent in nineteenth-century America. That prejudice belied Mormon professions of spiritual kinship with the Lamanites and undermined relations between the two peoples, triggering violence that led to many deaths among Indians and Mormons. American Indian family history—including legends, oral history, and critical reading of documentary sources—helps us better understand the causes and consequences of this violence by providing perspectives and information not available in traditional sources alone. Together, these approaches offer us a more complete and nuanced view of the past.

NOTES

1. This combined account is drawn from Adelaide Exervier Brown's obituary (*Deseret News* [Salt Lake City, UT], January 6, 1896); a short biography of Elijah Barney Ward based on an interview with Polly Ward Williams, appearing in Andrew Jenson's *Latter-day Saint Biographical Encyclopedia*, vol. 4 (Salt Lake City, UT: Andrew Jenson History Co., 1901); Mrs. Albert F. Brown (Naomi Brown Brown)'s account; Mrs. William W. Hale (Ella Brown Hale)'s account; and Ruth Hudson Hale (daughter-in-law of Ella Hale)'s account. Other family accounts, which draw primarily on the first three accounts, include those of Elizabeth Jo Daley and Wayne K. Brown. Another account, by Amy Mirafxal, granddaughter of Joan and Albert Clark, draws on Adelaide's obituary and on primary accounts such as the Sage, Talbot, and Fremont discussions of Exervier's death. All of the family accounts are in my personal collection.

2. Elizabeth Tonkin, *Narrating Our Pasts: The Social Construction of Oral History* (Cambridge: Cambridge University Press, 1992). On debates over the reliability of American Indian oral history, see Daniel K. Richter, "Whose Indian History?" *William and Mary Quarterly*, 3rd ser., 50, no. 2 (April 1992): 384–87. On the problems of authentically representing American Indian speech and perspectives, see Jacqueline M. Henkel, "Represented Authenticity: Native Voices in Seventeenth-Century Conversion Narratives," *New England Quarterly* (March 2014): 10; Hilary E. Wyss, *Writing Indians: Literacy, Christianity, and Native Community in Early America* (Amherst: University of Massachusetts Press, 2000); Joshua David Bellin, "'A Little I Shall Say': Translation and Interculturalism in the John Eliot Tracts," in *Reinterpreting New England Indians and the Colonial Experience*, ed. Colin G. Calloway and Neal Salisbury (Boston: Colonial Society of Massachusetts, 2003); Kristina Bross and Hilary E. Wyss, *Early Native Literacies in New England: A Documentary and Critical Anthology* (Amherst: University of Massachusetts Press, 2008). For a range of views on the writing of American Indian history, see Devon A. Mihesuah, ed., *Natives and Academics: Researching and Writing about American Indians* (Lincoln: University of Nebraska Press, 1998).

3. This is an approach used by Andrew Wiget, who examined oral histories of events surrounding the Pueblo Revolt, compared them to Spanish written accounts, and found fascinating corroborations as well as new perspectives. See, for example, his "Father Juan Greyrobe: Reconstructing Tradition Histories, and the Reliability and Validity of Uncorroborated Oral Tradition," *Ethnohistory* 43, no. 3 (Summer 1976): 459–82, and "Truth and the Hopi: An Historiographic Study of Documented Oral Tradition concerning the Coming of the Spanish," *Ethnohistory* 29, no. 3 (Summer 1982): 181–99.

4. Accounts of Exervier's 1843 death appear in Rufus B. Sage, *Rufus B. Sage: His Letters and Papers, 1836–1847*, Far West and the Rockies Historical Series, 1820–1875, ed. Leroy R. Hafen and Ann W. Hafen (Glendale, CA: Arthur H. Clark Company, 1956), 2:268–69; John Charles Fremont, *Report of the Exploring Expedition to the Rocky Mountains in the year 1842, and to Oregon and North California in the Years 1843–'44* (n.p.: Readex Microprint, 1966 [1845]), 120–30; Theodore Talbot, *The Journals of Theodore Talbot, 1843 and 1849–52: With the Fremont Expedition of 1843 and with the First Military Company in Oregon Territory, 1849–52*, ed. Charles H. Carey (Portland, OR: Metropolitan Press, 1931), 24, 28; and Charles Preuss, *Exploring with Fremont: The Private Diaries of Charles Preuss, Cartographer for John C. Fremont on His First, Second, and Fourth Expeditions to the Far West*, trans. and ed. Erwin G. and Elisabeth K. Gudde (Norman: University of Oklahoma Press, 1958), 83–84.

5. Hampton Sides, *Blood and Thunder: The Epic Story of Kit Carson and the Conquest of the American West* (New York: Anchor Books, 2006), 310–13.

6. There is a vast literature on white American attitudes toward the "savagery" of American Indians, including Roy Harvey Pearce, *Savagism and Civilization: A Study of the Indian and the American Mind* (Baltimore: Johns Hopkins University Press, 1953 [1965]); Richard

Slotkin, *Regeneration through Violence: The Mythology of the American Frontier, 1600–1860* (Middletown, CT: Wesleyan University Press, 1973); Robert F. Berkhofer Jr., *The White Man's Indian: Images of the American Indian from Columbus to the Present* (New York: Knopf, 1978); and Philip J. Deloria, *Playing Indian* (New Haven, CT: Yale University Press, 1998). Recent scholarship places the savagery of American Indians within the context of the violence of colonialism. See, for example, Ned Blackhawk, *Violence over the Land: Indians and Empires in the Early American West* (Cambridge, MA: Harvard University Press, 2006); and Brian DeLay, *War of a Thousand Deserts: Indian Raids and the U.S.-Mexican War, 1846–1848* (New Haven, CT: Yale University Press, 2009). On American Indians and alcohol, see Peter C. Mancall, *Deadly Medicine: Indians and Alcohol in Early America* (Ithaca, NY: Cornell University Press, 1995); and Stephen F. Evans, "'Open Containers': Sherman Alexie's Drunken Indians," *American Indian Quarterly* 25, no. 1 (Winter 2001): 46–72.

7. Daniel Webster, quoted in Daniel K. Richter, *Facing East from Indian Country: A Native History of Early America* (Cambridge, MA: Harvard University Press, 2001), 243–44.

8. Colin Ramsey, "Cannibalism and Infant Killing: A System of 'Demonizing' Motifs in Indian Captivity Narratives," *Clio* 24, no. 1 (Fall 1994): 55–68.

9. James B. Marsh, *Four Years in the Rockies; or, The Adventures of Isaac P. Rose of Shenango Township, Lawrence County, Pennsylvania* (New Castle, PA: W. B. Thomas, 1884), 88.

10. This trope appears in Northwestern Shoshone Mae Timbimboo Parry's account of the Bear River Massacre of 1863. She attributes the phrase to Colonel Patrick O'Connor, "meaning that it was his intention to kill all Indian children and babies before they had a chance to grow to adulthood." Mae Parry, "The Northwestern Shoshone: Utah's Native Americans," accessed July 22, 2016, http://historytogo.utah.gov/people/ethnic_cultures/the_history_of_utahs_american_indians/chapter2.html. Paul Reeve discusses the history of the phrase "nits make lice" in his *Religion of a Different Color: Race and the Mormon Struggle for Whiteness* (New York: Oxford University Press, 2015), 52–55.

11. Ann Marie Plane, *Colonial Intimacies: Indian Marriage in Early New England* (Ithaca, NY: Cornell University Press, 2000), 26; Duane Schultz, *Over the Earth I Come: The Great Sioux Uprising of 1862* (New York: St. Martin's Press, 1992), 134; John G. Neihardt, *Black Elk Speaks* (Albany: State University of New York Press, 2008 [1932]), 210. The image also appears in folktales and histories of many cultures. See, for example, Stith Thompson, *The Folktale* (Berkeley: University of California Press, 1977 [1946]), 256; Rev. John Graham, *Annals of Ireland* (London, 1817), 65; Sir Joshua Reynolds, *The Discourses of Sir Joshua Reynolds* (London, 1842), 21.

12. For examples of the popularity of claiming American Indian "princesses" or "chiefs" as ancestors, see Alexia Kosmider, "Strike a Euroamerican Pose: Ora Eddleman Reed's 'Types of Indian Girls,'" *American Transcendental Quarterly* 12, no. 2 (June 1998): 4–5; Courtney Miller, "Cherokee Misconceptions, Part 7: The Cherokee Princess," December 26, 2013, accessed June 8, 2016, http://nativeamericanantiquity.blogspot.com/2013/12/cherokee-misconceptions-part-7-cherokee.html; Jamie K. Oxendine, "My Grandmother Was a Cherokee Indian Princess," accessed June 8, 2016, http://www.powwows.com/2011/11/18/my-grandmother-was-a-cherokee-indian-princess/#ixzz49i7wjIzg; "Why Your Great-grandmother Wasn't a Cherokee Princess," accessed June 8, 2016, http://www.native-languages.org/princess.htm.

13. Sharon DeBartolo Carmack, "Family Legends and Myths: Watching Out for Red Flags," accessed June 8, 2016, http://www.genealogy.com/articles/research/90_carmack.html.

14. Thomas P. Slaughter argues that the status of princess accorded to the two most famous American Indian women, Pocahontas and Sacagawea, supports American "myths of discovery and conquest": Sacagawea "becomes a princess of equal standing with Pocahontas when Lewis and Clark declare her brother a 'great chief.' The two princesses thereafter serve as complementary symbols of racial fusion by 'saving' white men and bearing biracial sons." Thomas P. Slaughter, *Exploring Lewis and Clark: Reflections on Men and Wilderness* (New York: Alfred A. Knopf, 2003), 86.

15. Rayna Green, "The Pocahontas Perplex: The Image of Indian Women in American Culture," *Massachusetts Review* 16, no. 4 (1975): 698–714.

16. April Selley, "I Have Been, and Ever Shall Be, Your Friend': *Star Trek, The Deerslayer* and the American Romance," *Journal of Popular Culture* 20, no. 1 (Summer 1986): 89–104.

17. See footnote 4.

18. Richter, "Whose Indian History?," 389.

19. Personal correspondence with Joan and Albert Clark, April 29, 2002 and September 8, 2003. A number of Sally's descendants intermarried with each other, including Naomi Brown Brown, who was a granddaughter of both Adelaide and Louisa and married a grandson of Adelaide. It is possible that this pattern of intermarriage was a result of ostracism because of Native ancestry or self-segregation, or both.

20. Ogden City Cemetery burial plot map for Nellie Ward Brown, location K-0-4-1E. The burial record lists her birth date as April 27, 1870 in Ogden, Utah, and her death date as October 5, 1924. Her mother is listed as Louisa Ward and her father as James Daley. While it is possible that Daley was the father, there is no evidence that he knew Louisa at the time of her pregnancy. He married her as a plural wife in 1877 (Daughters of Utah Pioneers Obituary Scrapbook for James L. Daley, accessed May 29, 2017, http://search.ancestry.com/cgi-bin/sse.dll?_phsrc=SIM5&_phstart=successSource&usePUBJs=true&indiv=1&db=obit&gss=angs-d&new=1&rank=1&msT=1&gskw=James%20L.%20Daley&MSAV=1&MSV=0&uidh=u1c&pcat=34&fh=0&h=3835&recoff=&ml_rpos=1). Upton Donley abandoned Polly Ward Donley August 4, 1876 (date of abandonment stated in divorce decree for Polly Ward Donley and Upton Donley, June 24 and June 27, 1879, Utah State Archives).

21. Berkhofer, *White Man's Indian.*

22. Hebard's argument appears in Grace Hebard, *Sacajawea: Guide and Interpreter of Lewis and Clark* (Glendale, CA: A. H. Clark, 1933). Some of the depositions Hebard collected from Shoshone, Comanche, and white settlers appear in the appendices of her book. A more recent book making the same argument for Sacagawea's later death is Esther Burnett Horne with Sally MacBeth, *Essie's Story: The Life and Legacy of a Shoshone Teacher* (Lincoln: University of Nebraska Press, 1998).

23. Historians critical of Grace Hebard and her claims about Sacagawea include W. Dale Nelson, *Interpreters with Lewis and Clark: The Story of Sacagawea and Toussaint Charbonneau* (Denton: University of North Texas Press, 2003), 125; Ella E. Clark and Margot Edmunds, *Sacagawea of the Lewis & Clark Expedition* (Berkeley: University of California Press, 1979), 93; Pennie L. Magee, "What Ever Happened to Sacagawea? The Debate between Grace Hebard (1861–1936) and Blanche Schroer (1907–1998)," *Heritage of the Great Plains* 37, no. 1 (2004): 27–39; Thomas H. Johnson with Helen S. Johnson, *Also Called Sacajawea: Chief Woman's Stolen Identity* (Long Grove, IL: Waveland Press, 2008), 40–42; and Donna J. Kessler, *The Making of Sacagawea: A Euro-American Legend* (Tuscaloosa: University of Alabama Press, 1996), 101.

Evidence for Sacagawea's early death appears in the note "Se car ja we au - Dead" penned next to a list of expedition members on the front cover of Clark's cash book and journal for 1825–1828 (transcribed and reprinted in Donald Jackson, ed., *Letters of the Lewis and Clark Expedition with Related Documents, 1783–1854* [Urbana: University of Illinois Press, 1978], 2:638–39). For a discussion of how race and status may have influenced the debate over when Sacagawea died, see Slaughter, *Exploring Lewis and Clark,* 90.

On the possibility that other Shoshone or Native women did what Hebard claimed Sacagawea did, see Virginia Scharff, *Twenty Thousand Roads: Women, Movement, and the West* (Berkeley: University of California Press, 2002), chapter 1. William R. Swagerty counted at least sixteen Shoshone women who were wives to Euro-American trappers (William R. Swagerty, "Marriage and Settlement Patterns of Rocky Mountain Trappers and Traders," *Western Historical Quarterly* 11, no. 2 [April 1980]: 165).

24. Grace Hebard to Mrs. Mary F. Kelly Pye, secretary of the Historian's Office, March 24, 1926, in "Papers Pertaining to Chief Baziel," Church of Jesus Christ of Latter-day Saints Church History Library, Salt Lake City, UT (hereafter cited as LDS Church History Library).

25. Hebard identifies the Shoshone wife of Baptiste Exervier, mentioned in several 1843 explorers' journals (see footnote 4), as Sacajawea (Hebard, *Sacajawea*, 156–57). Hebard's attribution of the action of other Shoshone women to Sacagawea is rooted in her assumption that the woman identified as "Basil's mother" on an 1877 census and in a number of other accounts was Sacagawea. Basil frequently visited the missionaries and their families, including Sally Exervier Ward, at Fort Supply. Primary accounts of the Fort Supply mission that mention Basil's visits and describe Sally and Adelaide teaching the Shoshone language include James S. Brown, *Giant of the Lord: Life of a Pioneer* (Salt Lake City, UT: Bookcraft, 1960 [1902]), 320–85; Henry Weeks Sanderson, "History of Henry Weeks Sanderson," typescript copy of original, 1916 (Provo, UT: L. Tom Perry Special Collections, Harold B. Lee Library, Brigham Young University); Isaac Bullock diary, LDS Church History Library, Salt Lake City, UT; John Pulsipher, "A Short Sketch of the History of John Pulsipher," L. Tom Perry Special Collections, Harold B. Lee Library; "A Sketch of the History of a Company of Elders . . . on the Shoshone Mission," LDS Church History Library, Salt Lake City, UT. See also Fred Gowans and Eugene Campbell, *Fort Supply: Brigham Young's Green River Experiment* (Provo, UT: Brigham Young University Press, 1976).

26. Kessler, *The Making of Sacagawea*, 87.

27. Mormons considered themselves to be modern Children of Israel, if not by descent, then by adoption into the covenant family of Abraham. Thus, they considered non-Mormons (with the exception of the Jews and Indians) "gentiles." "Gentiles," in *The Encyclopedia of Mormonism*, accessed September 22, 2016, http://eom.byu.edu/index.php/Gentiles.

28. George D. Smith, ed., *An Intimate Chronicle: The Journals of William Clayton* (Salt Lake City, UT: Signature Books, 1995), July 7, 1847.

29. Transcription of Columbia River Fishing and Trading Company Accounts at Fort Hall from 1834 to 1837, when it was sold to the Hudson Bay Company, listed under Ward, Elijah, on pages 165 and 166, 295, 452, www.xmission.com/~drudy/mtman/html/fthall/index.html, originals held at Oregon Historical Society, Portland, Oregon; Leroy R. Hafen, "Elijah Barney Ward," in *The Mountain Men and the Fur Trade of the Far West*, ed. Leroy R. Hafen and Ann W. Hafen (Spokane, WA: A. H. Clark, 2002), 7:343–51; Smith, ed., *Journals of William Clayton*, 399, 404, 406, 410.

30. *The Book of Mormon* (Salt Lake City, UT: Church of Jesus Christ of Latter-day Saints), Enos 1:9–18; Alma 37:19; 3 Nephi 5:13–15; Ether 12:22; Mormon 5:12.

31. John S. Price, "Mormon Missions to the Indians," in *Handbook of North American Indians, Northeast*, ed. Bruce G. Trigger, vol. 4, *History of Indian-White Relations*, ed. Wilcomb A. Washburn (Washington, DC: Smithsonian Institution, 1978), 459–63; *Doctrine & Covenants of the Church of Jesus Christ of Latter-day Saints* (Salt Lake City, UT: Church of Jesus Christ of Latter-day Saints), section 49:24.

32. Zina D. H. Young, *"A Weary Traveler": The 1848–50 Diary of Zina D. H. Young*, ed. Marilyn Higbee (Honors thesis, Brigham Young University, 1992), 18.

33. Blackhawk, *Violence over the Land*, 231; Christina Skousen, "Toiling among the Seed of Israel: A Comparison of Puritan and Mormon Missions to the Indians" (master's thesis, Brigham Young University, 2005); Richard W. Cogley, "John Eliot and the Origins of the American Indians," *Early American Literature* 21 (1986–1987): 210–25.

34. Private correspondence with Joan Clark, September 30, 2003, October 8, 2003, and July 13, 2006. The photo of Zina D. H. Young is in the possession of descendants of Adelaide and James M. Brown's son Moroni Franklin Brown. This inscription appears on the back: "Zina D Young, To Mrs Adalad Brown."

35. Charles E. Dibble, "The Mormon Mission to the Shoshoni Indians," *Utah Humanities Review* 1 (January/April/July 1947): 53–73, 166–77, 279–93.

36. Sanderson, "History of Henry Weeks Sanderson," 49.

37. Juanita Brooks, ed., *On the Mormon Frontier: The Diary of Hosea Stout, 1844–1861* (Salt Lake City: University of Utah Press, 1964), 2:515–17.

38. Brown, *Giant of the Lord*, 334.

39. Kathleen J. Bragdon, *Native People of Southern New England, 1500–1650* (Tulsa: University of Oklahoma Press, 1996), 43–45; Jean M. O'Brien, *Dispossession by Degrees: Indian Land and Identity in Natick, Massachusetts, 1650–1790* (Cambridge: Cambridge University Press, 1997), chapter 1; Daniel K. Richter, *Ordeal of the Longhouse: The Peoples of the Iroquois League in the Era of European Colonization* (Chapel Hill: University of North Carolina Press, 1992), chapter 2.

40. John Mack Faragher, "The Custom of the Country: Cross-Cultural Marriage in the Far Western Fur Trade," in *Western Women, Their Land, Their Lives*, ed. Lillian Schlissel, Vicki Ruiz, et al. (Albuquerque: University of New Mexico Press, 1988), 199–216; Swagerty, "Marriage and Settlement Patterns"; Sylvia Van Kirk, *Many Tender Ties: Women in Fur-Trade Society, 1670–1870* (Norman: University of Oklahoma Press, 1980); Susan Sleeper-Smith, *Indian Women and French Men: Rethinking Cultural Encounter in the Western Great Lakes* (Amherst: University of Massachusetts Press, 2001).

41. Richard Darrell Kitchen, *Mormon-Indian Relations in Deseret: Intermarriage and Indenture, 1847 to 1877* (PhD diss., Arizona State University, 2002), 23–24, 38, 51, 56.

42. Kathryn M. Daynes, *More Wives Than One: Transformation of the Mormon Marriage System, 1840–1910* (Champaign: University of Illinois Press, 2001), 43.

43. Sondra Jones, *The Trial of Don Pedro Leon Lujan: The Attack Against Indian Slavery and Mexican Traders in Utah* (Salt Lake City: University of Utah Press, 2000), 108.

44. Kitchen, *Mormon-Indian Relations*, 150–51, 171.

45. Jones, *Trial of Don Pedro*, 104.

46. Kitchen, *Mormon-Indian Relations*, 34; Sondra Jones says the slave trade in Utah was mostly over by the end of the 1860s (Jones, *Trial of Don Pedro*, 97–103).

47. Pekka Hämäläinen, *The Comanche Empire* (New Haven, CT: Yale University Press, 2008); James F. Brooks, *Captives and Cousins: Slavery, Kinship, and Community in the Southwest Borderlands* (Chapel Hill: University of North Carolina Press, 2002); Blackhawk, *Violence over the Land*; Jared Farmer, *On Zion's Mount: Mormons, Indians, and the American Landscape* (Cambridge, MA: Harvard University Press, 2008); Jones, *Trial of Don Pedro*.

48. Daynes, *More Wives Than One*, 42.

49. Kitchen, *Mormon-Indian Relations*, 126.

50. Jones, *Trial of Don Pedro*, 31, 35–38, 41–42, 94; Brooks, *Captives and Cousins*, 234–57; Kitchen, *Mormon-Indian Relations*, chapter 4, 208–9.

51. Kitchen, *Mormon-Indian Relations*, appendix C, 233–37.

52. Jones, *Trial of Don Pedro*, 103.

53. For an example, see Joseph Alonzo Stuart, *My Roving Life: A Diary of Travels and Adventures by Sea and Land, during Peace and War* (Auburn, CA, 1895), 52.

54. John Alton Peterson, *Utah's Black Hawk War* (Salt Lake City: University of Utah Press, 1998), 19–21, 57, 135–45, 266; Andrew Jenson biographical file, Elijah Barney Ward, MS 17956, box 24, folder 53, LDS Church History Library, Salt Lake City, UT; Brigham Young Office Files, LDS Church History Library, Salt Lake City, UT, box 25, folder 13, to Brigham Young (BY), December 31, 1857; box 30, folder 12, David Holladay to BY, August 18, 1865; box 40, folder 4, Orson Hyde to BY, April 14, 1865, April 23, 1865; box 40, folder 14, Andrew Moffitt to BY, April 23, 1865.

55. John Codman, *The Round Trip by Way of Panama* (New York: G. P. Putnam's Sons, 1879), 219–20.

56. Brooks, *Captives and Cousins*, 6.

57. Hämäläinen, *Comanche Empire*, 247–49.

58. Daynes, *More Wives Than One*, 128–29.

59. Kitchen, *Mormon-Indian Relations*, 56.

60. Jones, *Trial of Don Pedro*, 52, 93, 105.

61. In 1848, Parley P. Pratt recorded that the Indians were "much pleased and excited with every thing they saw, and finally expressed a wish to become one people with us, and to live among us and we among them, and to learn to cultivate the earth and live as we do" (quoted in Farmer, *On Zion's Mount*, 50–51).

62. Peterson, *Utah's Black Hawk War*, 3.

63. Van Kirk, *Many Tender Ties*, 49–50; Jones, *Trial of Don Pedro*, 103.

64. Kitchen, *Mormon-Indian Relations*, appendix C, 233–37.

65. Evidence of the affection Ogden residents felt for James M. and Adelaide Brown appears in a specially printed card titled "Loved Ones Gone" and bearing the names and dates of five of their children who had died, presented to console the couple on the death of their twenty-year-old son Hubert in May 1888 (copy in my possession). James M. Brown served as a policeman for Ogden City and on the High Council of the Weber Stake, and Adelaide was a member of the Ogden 1st Ward Relief Society (James M. Brown obituary, *Deseret News*, December 27, 1924; Ogden 1st Ward RS Minutes, Microfilm LR 6391 15, LDS Church History Library, Salt Lake City, UT). Their son Moroni Franklin Brown served as bishop of the Ogden 1st Ward from 1890 until his death in 1897 (Ogden 1st Ward Manuscript History and Historical Reports, Microfilm LR 6391 2, LDS Church History Library, Salt Lake City, UT).

66. Andrew Jenson biographical file, Elijah Barney Ward, MS 17956, box 24, folder 53, LDS Church History Library, Salt Lake City, UT.

67. Polly Ward Donley and Upton Donley, filing for divorce, April 29, 1879, Weber County, Utah Probate Court Civil and Criminal Case Registers of Actions, 1868–1887, book 1, p. 85, series 83901; Polly Ward Donley and Upton Donley, divorce decree, June 27, 1879, Utah State Archives; Polly Ward Williams, Idaho Death Index, 1890–1964, certificate number 152092, accessed May 29, 2017, http://search.ancestry.com/cgi-bin/sse.dll?_phsrc=SIM16&_phstart=successSource&usePUBJs=true&indiv=1&db=IdahoDeathIndex&gss=angs-d&new=1&rank=1&msT=1&gsfn=Polly&gsfn_x=1&gsln=Williams&gsln_x=1&msddy=1947&msdpn__ftp=Idaho,%20USA&msdpn=15&msdpn_PInfo=5-%7C0%7C1652393%7C0%7C2%7C0%7C15%7C0%7C0%7C0%7C0%7C0%7C&MSAV=1&MSV=0&uidh=u1c&pcat=34&fh=0&h=169276&recoff=8%2010&ml_rpos=1.

68. US Census, 1870, Weber County, Utah Territory, p. 483; Nelley, age 9, was living in the household of James M. and Adelaide Brown in the 1880 US Census, Weber County, Utah Territory; Daughters of Utah Pioneers Obituary Scrapbook for James L. Daley. While this obituary lists Louisa's death in 1880, her sister Adelaide's obituary lists Louisa's death as "about twelve years" before January 1896 (*Deseret Weekly*, January 25, 1896, 31).

69. Personal correspondence with Albert and Joan Clark, September 8, 2003.

Chapter Three

Silent Memories of Missouri

Mormon Women and Men and Sexual Assault in Group Memory and Religious Identity

Andrea G. Radke-Moss

A young bride and new convert to Mormonism, Mary Isabella Horne experienced the terror of the Mormon-Missouri War (1838–1839) from her small house in Far West, Missouri, at the tender age of twenty. Years later, in her 1884 autobiography, she remembered the horrific occasions when "the mob entered Far West [and] entered houses, taking what they pleased, jeering and intimidating the women." Mary Isabella recalled her own defiant reaction to the mob violence: "She would not humble herself to let them see she was afraid."[1] Mary Isabella's autobiography endures as one of a few important memory accounts by survivors of the conflict that resulted in the persecution and expulsion of thousands of members of the Church of Jesus Christ of Latter-day Saints (LDS) from the state of Missouri. Both women and men left important memories of the war, often in autobiographical form and written years after the event. In an 1859 autobiography, John Loveless, another survivor of the war, remembered that "in the fall of 1838, the mob arose and we were expelled from the State of Missouri and compelled to sign over all our property by force of arms."[2] John continued, "In this I was an eye witness to scenes that until this day, when called to mind, make my blood run cold and would almost make me fight a legion." His list included the range of crimes committed against the Mormons: "Women were ravished, men murdered, houses burned, property destroyed, the Prophet and Patriarch, with many others, taken and cast into prison."[3]

These two autobiographical memory accounts of the Mormon-Missouri War, taken together, represent the general terror experienced by members of the Mormon faith before their expulsion to the state of Illinois in 1838 and 1839. Both accounts mention threats or assaults against women, but Mary Isabella's memory is ambiguous and personal, while John's is specific and oriented to the whole community. These memory accounts in part capture the ways that Mormon women and men have constructed and memorialized their persecution in Missouri in different ways and for different purposes, and particularly how they have remembered the sexual violence committed against Mormon women in that conflict.[4] While Mormon men remembered the Mormon-Missouri War with explicit references to the rape of Mormon women, especially through public testimonies and published memory accounts, women themselves have kept their experiences with sexual violence as "silent memories," mostly unspoken but lingering in the group consciousness through intimate conversations and private confidences. For Mormon men, rape memories are typically oriented toward the religious group as a whole, recounted along with other crimes to unify their community as victims of outside political-religious persecution, and for reasserting a construction of their masculine identity against the violation of the group. For Mormon women, rape memories are situated in silent, individual suffering and oriented toward self, either for the need to endure the shame of their victimization or for more intimate purposes of finding spiritual and personal meaning in those experiences.

This is a history of rape and memory in the Mormon-Missouri War and how individuals and communities construct their recollections of wartime trauma. It is not a history of the war itself, nor is it a history of the specific sexual assaults against Mormon women within that conflict, a topic that I have examined elsewhere.[5] I am more concerned with investigating Mormons' collective memories of the conflict as "sites of *traumatic memory preservation*,"[6] and how that preservation has taken different gendered forms. Certainly historians are interested in verifying memories, but for this study, as David Thelen has emphasized, "the social dimensions of memory are more important than the need to verify accuracy."[7] Specifically, I am interested in how Mormon men and women have recalled, preserved, and transmitted their memories of sexual violence and constructed them in different ways for the purposes of community building.

The study of Mormon memories of Missouri provides an important insight into the relevance of gender in the collection, recovery, and uses of memory. Historians have generally lacked engagement with gender and memory, and especially with how subjects engage or disengage with their sexual assault experiences in wartime. In her work on the Holocaust and memory, Anna Reading has noted that "there is a gender gap in most of the key studies on collective memory" and that we need to know more about "the ways in which gender is a factor in the collective construction, mediation and articulation of memories of historical events."[8] More specifically, Nicola Henry has lamented that memory studies have neglected "the relationship between collective memory and wartime rape."[9] Most studies of gendered memories of rape and war focus solely on the divergence between the female victims' accounts of their own rapes and the denials of those rapes by authoritative male voices on the opposing side.

"Although gender may be neglected or overlooked in memory studies," Henry observes, "it is paradoxically and vividly apparent in official, nationalistic recollections of the past."[10] This chapter breaks new ground by examining the differences between male and female accounts of rape memories that come from *within* the victimized Mormon community. Indeed, even when accounts of sexual violence are produced from the same group, male- and female-generated memories take significantly different forms and are remembered and used in different ways for community building and group cohesion.

HISTORICAL BACKGROUND

For Mormonism's first generation of followers, the Mormon-Missouri War of 1838–1839 was a defining moment in cementing a communal character that centered on shared loss, flight from persecution and violence, physical survival in the face of imminent danger, and the spiritual endurance of the group. According to accounts of the war by survivors themselves, Mormon women partook of that loss in more sinister ways, in that some women were possibly victims of rape during the conflict. Mormons first arrived in Jackson County, Missouri, in 1831, with the hope of establishing a Utopian society called Zion, near Independence. Arriving mostly from Ohio, these immigrants were also joined by new converts from British Canada and New England. The Mormon presence in western Missouri immediately met with tensions over economics, politics, land and property, slavery, and of course, Mormons' revolutionary religious ideas.[11] Mormons were evacuated from Jackson County to the neighboring Clay County in 1833, and then eventually settled farther north in Caldwell, Ray, and Daviess counties, which had been carved out of Clay County by the Missouri Legislature exclusively for them. Relations between Mormons and Missourians did not improve, but deteriorated so badly that mob violence escalated to all-out war between Missouri state militias, who sought to dampen Mormon political and economic power in the state, and various ad hoc Mormon militias, who believed Missouri was their sacred Zion.[12] The violence centered on the Mormon community of Far West in Caldwell County between August 6 and November 1, 1838, and Gallatin and Adam-Ondi-Ahman in Daviess County, during the same months. Tensions led to an official "Exterminating Order" by Governor Lilburn W. Boggs and the forced expulsion of an estimated ten thousand Latter-day Saints out of Missouri into neighboring Illinois in 1838 and 1839. The violence has been well documented: arson, destruction of property, the killing of livestock, confiscation of weapons, physical assaults, imprisonment, and murder. Less well documented, but still present in the collective memory of the war, is the rape of Mormon women and teenage girls.

The sexual assault of Mormon women during the Mormon-Missouri War has been a long-debated topic. When it comes to the retrieval of memories associated with rape, historians' work is limited by many factors, including the lack of victims' accounts, the absence of eyewitness testimonies, the small amount of identifying information about the rape survivors, and finally, counterevidence and testimonials that bring doubt upon the occurrence of rapes during the war. The complications of documenting that history have even led some historians to downplay or dismiss their occurrence. Leland Homer Gentry's 1965 dissertation was the first to acknowledge with some hesitation that "several Mormon women and girls" had been sexually assaulted.[13] Other historians have given more credence over time to the accusations of rape, but they have still raised questions about the difficulty of verifying these crimes.[14] For memory studies, the verification of rapes in war is not as important as how the memories of those rapes are constructed and transmitted for meaningful purposes within the group. The same is true for Mormon women's experiences in Missouri in 1838 and 1839.

The possibility of rapes committed in the Mormon-Missouri War is set against a backdrop of nineteenth-century society that either denied that rapes could be possible in gentlemen's warfare or accepted some sexual violence as the inevitable collateral damage of war. Sharon Block notes that "wartime rapes have occurred throughout history as victors claimed their success in a sexual right to their defeated enemy."[15] And as a particular type of trauma inflicted on a community during a military conflict, wartime rapes are what historian Susan Brownmiller has called "part of a recognizable pattern of national terror and subjugation" in which "the effect is indubitably one of intimidation and demoralization for the victims' side."[16] Brownmiller's seminal 1975 work, *Men, Women, and Rape*, was the first to document a comprehensive history of rape in warfare and how military conflicts specifically affect women. Surprisingly, she even included a brief discussion of Mormon women as victims of sexual assault in Missouri.[17] And since, as Brownmiller has noted, "rape is considered by the people of a defeated nation to be part of the enemy's conscious effort to destroy them," I submit that members of that community tend to formulate lasting group memories around the crimes of sexual violence.[18]

GENDER, RAPE, AND MEMORY

The impact of the Missouri violence has been significant to the larger historical narrative of Mormons as a people and the memories of sexual assault have persisted as part of that story, working toward the reinforcement of a collective group identity rooted in shared historical consciousness.[19] Groups reclaim their traumatic memories through both the silence of loss and public testimony of victimization, allowing them to build a community around that suffering. As Nicola Henry has observed:

> The unspeakability and contestation of traumatic histories reveals the complexity of memory and the nature of competing truths in the aftermath of conflict. And yet at the same time, the memorialization of the past also provides and sustains social cohesion and solidarity, serving as an antidote to amnesia and silence; a potent marker of trauma, justice and injustice. Memory validates the experiences and identities of victims and may bolster conceptions of national, religious, community and personal identity.[20]

The process of "gendering of memory" can allow historians to see both similarities and dissimilarities in how men and women mark the past because "people construct memories in response to changing circumstances."[21]

For Mormon men, how they memorialized rape in the Mormon-Missouri War exposed their larger concerns about the need to preserve the cohesiveness of the group and about how the war had threatened their masculine ability to protect women from outsiders. Susan Brownmiller has summarized this anxiety best:

> Men of a conquered nation traditionally view the rape of "their women" as the ultimate humiliation, a sexual *coup de grace*. Rape is considered by the people of a defeated nation to be part of the enemy's conscious effort to destroy them. In fact, by tradition, men appropriate the rape of "their women" as part of their own male anguish of defeat. Rape by a conqueror is compelling evidence of the conquered's status of masculine impotence. Defense of women has long been a hallmark of masculine pride, as possession of women has been a hallmark of masculine success. The body of a raped woman becomes a ceremonial battle-field, a parade ground for the victor's trooping of the colors. The act that is played out upon her is a message passed between men—vivid proof of victory for one and loss and defeat for the other.[22]

When communities interpret the rape of their women as a symbolic assault on the cohesiveness of group security, Elizabeth Son has labeled this "woman-as-nation," which suggests "gendered narratives of lost sexual and moral innocence represented in the imagery of young women."[23] Thus, male voices have tended to dominate the war narrative, leaving behind a group memory heavily centered on the preservation and defense of the Mormon community. Transmission of memory has usually taken the form of these public and institutionally significant male voices, while women's memories have been transmitted primarily in private, intimate settings.

Female memorialists have been remarkably silent in conveying their own sexual trauma in war, mostly because of the cultural shame associated with that trauma. Henry calls wartime rape an "unspeakable" crime for women but also suggests that silence itself becomes a form of memory.[24] Silence as a conveyer of memory is a concept born out of explorations of how women experience the violence of war differently from men. Indeed, "a staggering silence has come to define wartime rape, nonetheless that has not precluded the subject of rape from forming part of collective memory or memories in a variety of complex ways."[25] Taken together, male- and female-generated memories of rape in the Mormon-Missouri War have kept alive the threat and reality of sexual violence against women as a vivid part of their collective consciousness, while also revealing significant gendered differences and purposes in the relaying of those memories.

RAPE IN MORMON MALE MEMORY

Most rape memories in the Mormon historical identity are male generated, and of those sources, most are hearsay sources, with some claiming to be eyewitnesses. Beginning in the 1840s and 1850s, a few male veterans of the war committed their reminiscences to autobiographies, memorials, testimonies, and contributions to family and Church histories, mostly in order to achieve redress for the loss of property. By examining and unpacking this diversity of memory sources, I hope to find relevant themes throughout male memories of the Mormon-Missouri War. Some of these include, for example, reinforcement of Mormon persecution narratives, the rhetorical use of the gang rape of one woman as a symbolism for Mormon nationhood, the idolizing of the Mormon prophet Joseph Smith as a "defender of female virtue," and in more sinister constructions, the justification of revenge motives for the Mountain Meadows Massacre.

Mormon men recalled and reported rape, often in the form of listing sexual assault as part of the litany of abuses committed against the Mormons as a group. Apostle Parley P. Pratt was the first to employ this formula: "Much property has been plundered, provision destroyed, *Chastity of women* violated, houses burned."[26] John Loveless also used the listing pattern: "Women were ravished, men murdered, houses burned, property destroyed, the Prophet and Patriarch, with many others, taken and cast into prison."[27] And Church apostle Heber C. Kimball's Missouri memoir took a decidedly stronger tone of outrage, sarcasm, and hyperbole: "Oh lavish generosity! Two thousand dollars for a city sacked and pillaged, fields and farms laid waste, and homes given to the flames; not to mention murders, *rapes*, expulsions and other outrages nameless for their enormity, committed upon a helpless people by a ruthless mob in the sovereign name of the state of Missouri!"[28] Note also Church historian Andrew Jenson's 1893 history of the Mormons, compiled for the *World's Fair Ecclesiastical History of Utah*, which dramatically called up the Missouri violence in similar fashion: "the Saints were indiscriminately massacred, *women ravished*, houses plundered, horses stolen, cattle and hogs shot in their pens for sport, corn fields robbed, thousands of acres of grain destroyed by turning horses into the fields, and fences burnt up."[29] By listing the physical abuses committed against the Saints—including rape—Mormon men's retelling of the Missouri persecutions took a decidedly political tone, in that "rape has been used to construct a narrative of nationalistic victimization."[30] Male testimonials lamented the lack of financial, legal, and political redress for the expelled Saints and reminded observers that the rape of Mormon women had been a crime committed against the community as a whole, not just against individual women.

Building upon this general approach of listing the crimes against the Mormon body, male accounts of transmitted war memories also emphasized three main narratives referencing rapes in Missouri. One repeated a common telling of the gang rape of one or two women on a meetinghouse bench located in the center of Far West. The second retold the story of Joseph Smith's and other Church leaders' imprisonment in the Richmond Jail in November 1838, in which Joseph famously stood against the guards who were boasting about raping Mormon women. The third narrative showed how a second and third generation of Mormon men used the history of the Missouri violence to explain their fears of external assault against the Mormon political body, leading to retributive violence at the Mountain Meadows Massacre in September 1857. All of these types of retellings spoke to the gendered concerns of male leadership of the Church, in highlighting the attacks on the community's cohesive identity, even its sense of nationhood.

Tied to a Bench: Female Victimhood as Religious Victimhood

The first way that Mormon men memorialized the rape of Mormon women was in a common retelling of the gang rape of one or two women that occurred in either Far West or Haun's Mill, and usually on a meetinghouse bench. The account has minor variations depending upon the teller but was traumatic enough to the observers that it was incorporated into multiple memory accounts of the Mormon-Missouri War. The incident exposes the ways in which male members of a community memorialize rape in war in terms of female victimhood as religious victimhood.

Hyrum Smith's 1843 testimony before the Nauvoo Municipal Court introduced this narrative, in that he had heard the guards at Liberty Jail brag "that they lashed one woman upon one of the damned 'Mormon' meeting benches, tying her hands and her feet fast, and sixteen of them abused her as much as they had a mind to, and then left her bound and exposed in that condition."[31] Smith's early memory of rape in Missouri introduced a scene so graphic and horrifying into the Mormon consciousness that it was repeated in numerous other male accounts of the war over the next century.

Mosiah Hancock's 1864 memory is one of the most quoted and known of Missouri rape descriptions, because he claimed he had personally witnessed the assault. "I saw the fiends tie a young person to a bench—she was scarcely sixteen years of age, . . . and fourteen things in human form performed 'that' upon their victim which would cause a hyena to revolt at their fiendish orgies! It continued long after their fainting victim had become unconscious."[32] Hancock's supposed eyewitness account is informative but also suspect, since his age at the time of the attack would have been just over four and a half years old. It is possible that he witnessed the attack exactly as he described and that the violence of it burned into the memory of a young, impressionable child. If not, a contested memory account because of age or other problems invites us to think about the fragility of memory and how communities might still build their identity around those contested memories. Using the work of Marita Sturken, Nicola Henry has argued that the "instability of memory means that the past is constantly being 'verified, understood and given meaning' but that our focus should not be on reliability, rather we need to think about the way in which the past affects the present. This can happen once personal memory is shared in a social context."[33]

The contested group memories of the Mormon-Missouri War present a challenge to the goal of uncovering the verifiable truth of the conflict. In the case of Mosiah Hancock, the reliability of his account comes under the most suspicion exactly because he is one of the few who claimed to have personally witnessed the attack. And yet, in the context of how Mormons already remembered the war, Hancock's account is valuable, especially in relation to the other accounts of the sexual assault taking place on a "meetinghouse bench."[34] There is little variation in the story; the details vary, but the elements are sticky and persistent. A memory may be a fragment, a trace, or a hybrid of other memories, partially borrowed from someone else in the group. If he was inventing a new memory or adapting one of his own, it is possible that he conflated his recollection with accounts he had overheard from others. Hancock's autobiography repeated elements of the bench narrative from earlier leader testimonies and then reconfigured them for his own audience, because "collective memory does not necessarily imply a shared and solidifying consensus of the past because memory is not fixed or static, but rather it is in a state of constant transformation."[35]

Mosiah Hancock's memory, whether exact, modified, or invented, has left an inestimable effect on Mormon group memory, as his autobiography has been used and reused by historians for telling the story of the war. High-ranking Church elder and historian B. H. Roberts wrote a 1900 history of the conflict that included this description, remarkable in that it followed two of the patterns of Mormon men's telling of rape memory. It provided a "listing" of the crimes committed against the Saints and also retold the account of the gang rape on a bench, with a description very similar to Hancock's in language and content:

> The mob was now let loose upon the unarmed citizens of Far West, and under the pretext of searching for arms they ransacked every house, tore up the floors, upset haystacks, wantonly destroyed much property, and shot down a number of cattle, just for the sport it afforded them. The people were robbed of their most valuable property, insulted and whipped; but this was not the worst. The chastity of a number of women was defiled by force; some of them were strapped to benches and repeatedly ravished by brutes in human form until they died from the effects of this treatment.[36]

Memory studies scholars would agree that "because of the inherent power and fragility of memory, it functions in the present as something deeply contested and fundamentally omnipresent. As a consequence, memory is also manifestly political."[37] For Hancock, that meant that he sought to claim his place as an eyewitness to a grand tragedy by documenting the war as he knew it, and to garner sympathy for the Church's plight during those years from a larger public audience. By dramatizing the events of war in epic fashion—including the use of a shocking rape narrative—Hancock placed himself at the center of the most known and tragic actions of early Church history and succeeded in keeping alive the rape of Mormon women as a vivid part of their past.[38]

Hancock's was not the only late memoir to incorporate the gang rape of a woman "tied to a bench." For example, in June 1860, Brigham Young also claimed that "at Haun's Mill 100 men ravished a young woman after tying her to a bench."[39] Young's account is clearly an exaggeration, and the location (Haun's Mill) differs from other late memory accounts of the rape on a bench. Still, Young's telling worked toward the perpetuation of a larger Mormon group consciousness of persecution that centered on sexual violence in Missouri, particularly an account of a gang rape so shocking in its horror that it bore repeating in several Missouri narratives, even if the narrator, like Young, had not witnessed the act in person. His hyperbole follows a pattern of other dramatic accounts of early persecutions, especially in working toward the promotion of a tragic Mormon narrative that was useful in nineteenth-century America. Such late-memory retellings remind us that "in each construction of a memory, people reshape, omit, distort, combine, and reorganize details from the past in an active and substantive way.[40]

The repeated accounts of the gang rape of one or two Mormon women on a meetinghouse bench works as an allegory for religious persecution against the whole Mormon community. Again, as with Mosiah Hancock's account, certain elements of the story are persistent in every version. That it is always a gang rape evokes a feeling of overwhelming attack by numberless outsiders against one or two helpless innocents, potently incorporated here to represent blameless Latter-day Saint members against an onslaught of anti-Mormon persecutors in the nineteenth century. Once again, Nicola Henry's employment of the "metaphor of the 'raped nation'" is useful for understanding how memorialists portrayed the violation of women as a symbolic violation of the religion's own nationhood.[41] Susan Brownmiller has described how "rape has been used to construct a narrative of nationalistic victimization. The invocation of rape as memory . . . is essentially premised on the ulterior motive of expounding a nation's virtue in opposition to another nation's barbarity."[42] That the rape persistently occurs on a church or meetinghouse bench is a necessary reminder of the stakes of religious persecution in America. It is a double violation of the woman herself (and by extension, the religious community) and of the religious freedom supposedly guaranteed by the Constitution but clearly not applied to the Latter-day Saints. As Mormon men consistently returned to the memory of one or two women violated on a bench by Missouri mobbers, they simultaneously reaffirmed their claims to religious purity and their own rightness of cause against widespread anti-Mormon hatred.

Remembering the Prophet Joseph Smith as the Honorable Defender of Female Virtue

The "gang rape on a bench" formula for remembering Missouri rapes served as an important trope for reviving male indignation on behalf of Mormon nationhood. But a more well-known construction of the rape of Mormon women came in a now celebrated, impromptu discourse delivered by the Church's prophet leader, Joseph Smith, while he was incarcerated in the Richmond Jail in November 1838. Now referred to as the "Majesty in Chains" speech, perhaps his most famous discourse, it has employed a significant idolization of the Prophet that has persisted in Mormon narratives to reaffirm Smith's prophetic role and noble calling. This account came from the pseudo-official voice of early Church apostle Parley P. Pratt, regarding an event that occurred while he, Joseph Smith, and others were incarcerated together in the Richmond Jail in November 1838. Pratt told the story in 1853—fifteen years after the event—in a letter to Church historian Willard Richards, which was later reprinted in the Mormon-owned *Deseret News* in Salt Lake City and then published posthumously in 1874, "becoming the main source for the narrative."[43] According to Pratt, while lying on the floor, the men had to listen to the guards' "dreadful blasphemies, and filthy language," especially as they "recounted to each other their deeds of rapine, murder, robbery, etc., which they had committed among the 'Mormons,' while at Far West, and vicinity. They even boasted of defiling by force, wives, daughters, and virgins." As the men lay quietly listening to these verbal persecutions, Joseph suddenly arose to his feet, and spoke in a voice of thunder, or as the roaring lion, uttering, as near as I can recollect, the following words: "SILENCE—Ye fiends of the infernal pit. In the name of Jesus Christ I rebuke you, and command you to be still; I will not live another minute, and hear such language. Cease such talk, or you or I die THIS MINUTE."[44]

Pratt described Smith's presence as "[c]hained, and without a weapon; calm, unruffled and dignified as an angel." The Prophet's commanding indignation had its effect: "the quailing guards whose weapons were lowered or dropped to the ground; whose knees smote together, and who, shrinking into a corner or crouching at his feet, begged his pardon, and remained quiet until a change of guards."[45]

This episode, as recounted by Pratt, gained traction in the wider community narrative, and has since been told and retold as part of Mormon memorializing of the Prophet Joseph as an honorable and noble leader who stood defiantly against a verbal assault on Mormon women. Pratt summarizes the significance of this event to his memory of Joseph Smith:

> I have seen a Congress in solemn session to give laws to nations; I have tried to conceive of kings, of royal courts, of thrones and crowns; and of emperors assembled to decide the fate of kingdoms; but dignity and majesty have I seen but once, as it stood in chains, at midnight, in a dungeon in an obscure village of Missouri.[46]

This characterization of Joseph as dignified and magisterial in his defense of female virtue was an interesting and ironic reversal considering the accusations against Smith as a philanderer and for his later introduction of polygamy and polyandry. The "Majesty in Chains" speech even made it into the family and personal histories of other veterans of the Richmond Jail incarceration. Morris Phelps quoted Pratt's version of the speech, down to the exact word, "uttering as near as Morris could remember latter [*sic*] the following words."[47] He then added: "The guards quailed and begged his pardon, and remained quiet the rest of the night."[48] Indeed, the "Majesty in Chains" speech powerfully captured the culmination of all the Mormon suffering during the Missouri conflict, which included the incarceration of the Church's beloved leaders.

The long-term memorializing of the "Majesty in Chains" speech, while honoring Joseph's reputation, has negatively resulted in the omission of any specific mention of individual Mormon women and their experiences from the story. Thus, the elevation of Joseph comes with the simultaneous erasure of Mormon women, or their need to receive any individual justice for the rape crimes that guards bragged to Mormon leadership in the Richmond Jail. This pars with Nicola Henry's statement that "rape throughout history has been drawn upon not simply to raise the status of victim nations during armed conflict, but to construct a narrative of victorious masculinity, as opposed to any concern or understanding for women's human rights."[49] This was also one more step in the process of silencing female memories of rape, since

> the experiences of women in warfare, particularly of sexual violence, have been co-opted by a nationalist historiography that excluded the authentic voices of the victims and ultimately consolidated them and culminated in an extraordinary silence. This happened to such an extent . . . that silence has in and of itself become part of the collective memory of wartime rape."[50]

By placing Joseph Smith at the center of this narrative, the crimes committed against Mormon women have been overshadowed by the need to construct Smith's image in terms of noble, courageous, and virtuous manhood that defended Mormon femininity and honor. In fact, "Majesty in Chains" is what historians Matthew Grow and Terryl Givens have described as "the most famous in Pratt's autobiography, [and] has become the prime ingredient in the hagiographic tradition surrounding Joseph Smith."[51]

Joseph Smith's speech to the Richmond Jail guards has become so iconized in Mormon lore that it is the subject of numerous forms of commemoration—literature, painting, and dramatic film portrayals of early Church history, all working toward the formalizing of Joseph Smith's honored status in Mormon group memory. This is all part of creating what Eviatar Zerubavel has described as "ritualized remembrance," in that "[c]ollective memory is substantiated through multiple forms of commemoration . . . [which] reproduce(s) a commemorative narrative, a story about a particular past that . . . provides a moral message for the group members."[52] "Majesty in Chains" has been artistically rendered no fewer than six times for Mormon audiences, all focusing on the male participants and all highlighting a holy, even sublime aura surrounding the Prophet. The earliest depiction of the event, by Danquart Anthon Weggeland (1827–1928), stands out for being the only one to depict a woman in the scene—Athalia R. Robinson, Sidney Rigdon's seventeen-year-old daughter and the wife of fellow prisoner George Robinson.[53] Her presence in this narrative has gone unnoticed because no other artists' renditions include her, but she is vital as a symbolic reminder of the effects of the Mormon-Missouri War on women, a feminine specter in the jail of the masculine.[54] In this image, a heavenly light from a lone prison lantern shines upon Joseph's magisterial form as he addresses the prison guards. The light then passes through Joseph and casts upon the serene face of the seated Athalia holding her sleeping baby, as she represents *all* Mormon women, an embodied allegory of divine motherhood and virtuous womanhood juxtaposed against the terror of sexual violence.

"Majesty in Chains" reached a point of formal inclusion in the LDS community narrative when it was incorporated into various official film offerings in the early 2000s. In fact, these film portrayals of the Missouri violence and, more particularly, Joseph Smith's Richmond Jail experience have recovered a context of rape in Missouri that had been lost to lay Mormons. In each, the litany of abuses builds from bragging about general acts of violence to more specific criminal acts against children and women. Only when the jailers brag about the rape of Mormon women is Joseph pushed over the edge; it is rape that finally merits his standing up to the jailers.

But the films also provide telling differences. In the earlier, lengthier version of *Joseph Smith: Prophet of the Restoration* (Theatrical Release, 2005), the plot includes a husband and wife as the central characters with allusions to her being a victim of rape, whereas the second, shortened version of *Joseph Smith: Prophet of the Restoration* (DVD Release, 2005) omits the couple's identities entirely to focus solely on Joseph's "Majesty in Chains" speech.[55] These variations in the official narratives demonstrate that the filmmakers made conscious choices for the inclusion of women's experiences into the story of rape. But then the removal of that plot for a later film version, along with the un-naming of the female character, likewise symbolizes the erasure of female rape victims that has followed all Mormon-Missouri War memorialization in Mormon group identity. Still, the persistent inclusion of Joseph Smith's speech in official Church narratives has kept it a part of the collective memory for new generations of members, working toward a story of persecution and hardship for early Saints but still mostly reaffirming the prophetic image of the Joseph that is noble, divine, and virtuous.

Gerald Lund, in his bestselling novelization of Mormon history, *The Work and the Glory*, also returned to "Majesty in Chains" as a significant pivotal point in his own retelling of the Missouri events:

"Then we found this woman hiding under the bed. She had a young 'un, but we drove him out of the house screamin' and hollerin'. We took her outside and called a bunch of our comrades. She was screamin' and cryin' and beggin' for mercy."

"And I'll bet you were real merciful!" someone hollered.

"We were," he retorted seriously. "We tied her hands down to a bench so she wouldn't hurt herself thrashing around and all that. Then we—"

There was a sudden and sharp rattle of the chain, and Benjamin saw movement out of the corner of his eye. His head came up just in time to see Joseph leaping to his feet.

"*Silence, ye fiends of the infernal pit!*"[56]

Lund's portrayal is striking for how it incorporates both predominant Mormon male narratives of the Missouri rapes. In this case, the guards aren't just bragging about general rapes, but about a woman whose hands have been "tied . . . down to a bench." It is this vile boast that makes Joseph finally stand to rebuke his oppressors. By unifying both male accounts into one narrative, Lund offered a new construction that highlighted Mormon persecution and revived a noble and virtuous image of the Prophet Joseph. In some ways, the security of the Mormon community has often been bound up in portraying Joseph as a righteous leader who spoke against vulgarity, violence, and the defiling of women, and so the in-group use of "Majesty in Chains" to idolize the Prophet Joseph remains the predominant narrative for memorializing rape in Missouri.

Defending against Outsider Threat; or, The Mountain Meadows Massacre as Revenge for Rape

In the short-term aftermath of the Mormon-Missouri War, the memories were held and invoked by men who had experienced the violence firsthand (and/ or knew the women who did). Their memories were used for more immediate purposes for the community, in seeking justice and compensation for losses in Missouri, and as a pivot point on which to center their persecution narrative. In the later decades of the century, that narrative gradually gave way to reinforcing Mormons' self-identity as an outcast group who required constant vigilance against outsider threats. Eventually, the uses of defensiveness in memory made space for Mormon militancy and retribution for the Missouri persecutions. More specifically, memory sources began to embrace a new and more sinister construction of the Missouri rape narrative—one that explained, understood, and even justified revenge that a group of Mormon leaders took against an emigrant wagon train at the Mountain Meadows Massacre on September 11, 1857, wherein 120 men, women, and children were brutally murdered by Mormon men, and seventeen children under the age of seven were spared.[57] The 1850s was a transformative decade for Mormons, as they officially and publicly sanctioned polygamous practice, as they began the Reformation efforts to recommit members to the faith and their loyalty to the Restoration and Joseph Smith's prophetic role, and as the challenges of overland migration frayed at the edges of Mormon cohesiveness and economic and political growth. It was also during this decade that survivors and veterans of the Missouri violence put to paper their memories from fifteen and twenty years earlier, like Pratt's account of Joseph Smith rebuking the guards and Hancock's 1864 autobiography.

Historians have yet to make a strong link among all these forces across lines of creating and transmitting memories of trauma in Missouri, but the 1857 Massacre presents a compelling case for how the memory of rape was inserted into the Mormon past to make sense of later traumatic events. As the president of the United States sent troops to put down a so-called Mormon rebellion in 1857, rumors circulated that a few emigrants from Missouri had merged with the Baker and Fancher parties from Arkansas and that the Missouri "Wild-cats" were blamed for, or at least associated with, numerous acts of aggression in the weeks leading up to the massacre.[58] Some emigrants boasted that they had helped drive the Saints out of Missouri and that they were "among the mob at Carthage when Joseph and Hyrum were murdered."[59] Tensions heightened even further when in Utah County, "Provo stake president James C. Snow called Haun's Mill massacre survivor Charles Jameson to the pulpit during that town's Sunday services. 'I feel like fighting,' Jameson said, '& if any Mob comes here I feel like giving them the best I have got in the locker.'"[60] Reports like these of vague threats and boastings by emigrants against Mormons regarding either Missouri or Nauvoo were conflated in memory because the similarities of persecution narrative and expulsion still did not point to specific accusations about past rapes of Mormon women.

But for many southern Utahans, memories of the Mountain Meadows Massacre of 1857 had trickled into and woven through group consciousness, even to the second and third generations, leaving behind shadow traces of eyewitness accounts as remembered through reconstructed stories. In the 1920s, one southern Utah resident, Joseph Fish, reported in his autobiographical materials a compelling account of how tensions at the Klingensmith Mill in 1857 had escalated. While not an eyewitness to either the massacre or the specific event at the mill, he remembered that "the subject of the Mountain Meadow Massacre has been written up very many times, and some of these have been colored more than the facts would justify."[61] But as a resident of southern Utah, who had grown up surrounded by tales of the massacre, Fish felt he could only "give the outlines or main items as I understood them at the time." Regarding the members of the Baker and Fancher parties, popular memory suggested that as the wagon train members "got a little more of this [whisky] than they should" and became intoxicated, "they talked very freely, and boasted of what they had done to the Mormons, and what they would do." Fish then recalled a "story told of this affair, but I cannot say how much truth there is in it. It is about as follows:"

> During the persecutions of the saints in Missouri, about forty of the mob came to a Mormon's house and after destroying everything in it, they took two girls that were there and lashed them to some benches and ravished them. One of the girls died from the effects of this treatment, but the other finally recovered and was at this time a resident of Southern Utah.[62]

Fish's account is striking for its similarities to other memory accounts of the Missouri rapes from Mosiah Hancock, Hyrum Smith, and Brigham Young, particularly in referencing the female victims being "lashed . . . to some benches." Fish also provides details about the victim's identity that are not found in other accounts. The tensions between group memory transmission still allow for specifics to persist and thrive, even as consolidated memories merge. Fish also perpetuates the associations of the Mountain Meadows Massacre as a revenge for the Missouri crimes.

From the talk and boasts that these emigrants made at the mill, it was understood that one or perhaps two or more of these men were in that company of the mob that had so inhumanly treated these girls. These statements and threats aroused those at the mill and a general fight was about started, but the emigrants withdrew before there was any blood shed. The Mormons in this district were thoroughly aroused, and under the circumstances thought that this company should be killed. It was an easy matter for John D. Lee and others to set the Indians to attack the company which they did a short time after."[63]

In casting a direct line between the emigrants' supposed boasting about Missouri rapes to the agitation of the Mormons leading to mass murder in 1857, Fish accepted a framework of outrage that gave post-facto meaning to the massacre. Even as a sympathetic observer, Fish repeats a risky pattern, in which a late-memory account of the massacre has adopted a rape narrative and then linked that memory to explaining, understanding, and even justifying the motivations behind the massacre.

Another late-memory account added to the suspicion that Lee's anger was set off due to the boasting about rape, but in this account, the rape had occurred in Nauvoo, not Missouri, making it difficult to pin down the origins of specific Mormon outrage in the context of the massacre. In 1996, ninety-three-year-old Alva Matheson remembered in an oral interview some of the stories he had heard as a little boy. Matheson had grown up in Cedar City, close to a mill built by Louis Chaffin, who owned it with his son, Henry, and Joseph Walker and John D. Lee. Matheson remembered eavesdropping on a conversation between John M. Higbee and Matheson's own father, where "Higbee recounted a confrontation between Lee and members of the Fancher party at the Chaffin Mill" that involved "Charles Fancher taking 'what mill stuff he wanted, spit in Lee's face,' said that he had helped to kill Joseph Smith, and participated in a gang rape of one of Lee's daughters in Nauvoo." That boast "turned the very devil loose inside of brother John D." and ultimately "[led] to the Mountain Meadows."[64]

The narrative of revenge-for-rape became so important to Mormon memory constructions of the Mountain Meadows Massacre that it got a helpful boost from various non-Mormon depictions of the massacre, written four or five decades after the massacre. In these examples, non-Mormon narratives successfully merged into Mormon out-group memory. For example, Lily Dougall's *The Mormon Prophet* (1899) traces the history of the Church through fictional characters who grapple with the persecutions against the Mormons during the Restoration period. One young man, after experiencing the actions of the Mormon-Missouri War, declares his justifications for affiliating with the Danites to defend the Saints: "Look here! I'm a Danite. Do you mean to say that the Lord's not going to accept of me because I can't stand by and see weak men and women and children killed, *or worse than killed*, without punishing the murderers?"[65] In this scenario, Mormon indignation toward revenge could be pushed to the edge with the murder and rape of innocents. And when pressed on that possibility, the Danite responded, "The Scripture also says 'There's a time for wrath,' and 'he that sheddeth man's blood, by man shall his blood be shed.'"[66]

Most of the literary depictions of Mormon vengeance showed how some outside observers had been able to construct a post-facto link between the murder of women and children at Mountain Meadows and the attacks against Mormon women in Missouri. In one widely read fictionalized Mormon history, *The Lions of the Lord* (1903), Harry Leon Wilson follows the life of a young man, Joel Rae, who experienced the trials of Missouri, including witnessing his sister being raped at Haun's Mill, and then finds himself at the Mountain Meadows, being goaded into murdering women and children by Church leaders. Although many of the book's characters were actual historical individuals, Wilson imagines a fictional family's conversations and motivations for this account.

In the narrative, Brother Rae hears reports that the Fancher Party that is traveling through southern Utah "was composed chiefly of Missourians, many of whom were said to be boasting that they had helped to expel the Saints from Jackson County in that State."[67] As he reached Paraowan he was told

> that the wagon-train coming south—their ancient enemies who had plundered and butchered them in Jackson County—was to be cut off before it left the basin, it seemed but right to him, the just vengeance of Heaven upon their one-time despoilers, and a fitting first act in the war-drama that was now to be played.[68]

Naturally conflating the Missouri persecutors with the emigrants of the California-bound train, he claimed that "once more the mob was marching upon them to despoil and murder and put them into the wilderness." And then interpreting the arrival of these "Missourians" as an opportunity for the retribution he had long sought for the crimes against Mormons in Missouri, he declared it a "a token of [God's] favour and His wish, [that] here was a company of their bitterest foes delivered into their hands."[69]

As Brother Rae steeled himself for the arrival of these enemies, he continued to revisit his memories of Missouri, particularly the trauma of watching his sister raped and murdered at Haun's Mill: "When he closed his eyes, there, like an echo, was the vision of a woman's face with shining eyes and lip,—a vision that after a few seconds was washed away by a great wave of blood."[70] With the emigrant trains' arrival imminent and his terror and anxiety mounting, he "saw his sister, the slight, fair girl, in the grasp of the fiends at Haun's Mill." Turning to his leaders for validation of the next cause of action, he engaged them over the morality of how to proceed against the settlers.

"And there are women?" he asked, feeling a great sickness come upon him. "Plenty of them," answered Klingensmith, "some mighty fine women, too; I could see one yesterday, a monstrous fine figure and hair shiny like a crow's wing, and a little one, powerful pretty, and one kind of between the two—it's a shame we can't keep some of them, but orders is orders!" "These women must be killed, too?" "That's the orders from headquarters, Brother Rae." . . . "But women and children—" . . . He repeated the words as if he sought to comprehend them.[71]

Feeling his own doubts and hesitancy about committing murder of innocent women and children, Rae then turned again to John M. Higbee for reassurance of their decision. Higbee answered, "There ain't a drop of innocent blood in the whole damned train. And what are you, to be questioning this way about orders from on high? . . . seems to me you get limber like a tallowed rag when an order comes along." Whereas most outside critics in the aftermath of the massacre and the later trial blamed Mormons as violating standards of chivalrous manhood for being willing to murder women and children, in this account, Higbee questions Rae's manhood for being reluctant to follow those orders. But still, Rae hesitated, "'Defenseless women and little children—' he was still trying to regain his lost equilibrium." And then John D. Lee "interposed," "Yes, Brother Rae, as defenseless as that pretty sister of yours was in the woods there, that afternoon at Haun's Mill."[72]

Leon's book served to formalize into popular literature the long-circulating rumors that had connected the Mountain Meadows Massacre as an act of revenge for the violence in Missouri. That he centralized the massacre as a specific response to memories of sexual assault shows how significantly the constructions of the massacre had become rooted in notions of gendered retribution. Wilson added another layer of sexual predation to the act of revenge against women and children; as Klingensmith is describing some of their soon-to-be female victims, he laments the lost opportunity to kidnap potential plural wives: "it's a shame we can't keep some of them, but orders is orders!"[73] In remembering the Utah War and the Mountain Meadows Massacre as a response to the rape of Mormon women, the history and telling of the massacre has evolved to show how "the venue of struggle had changed from the battlefield to the landscape of memory."[74]

By the late nineteenth century, Mormon narratives about the Mormon-Missouri War had filled volumes of official and pseudo-official histories, working toward keeping alive the memories of early Mormon events for new generations of Saints. By the second half of the nineteenth century, memories of the war had passed from first-generation eyewitnesses to the second and third generations, who had heard or read of these events as they circulated through the community. The Mormon community identity continued to be forged amid the early stories of persecution that reinforced the insider/outsider or us/them dynamic (which, in the case of the Mountain Meadows Massacre, had turned toxic). Mormon men contributed to that historical memory of the war in uniquely gendered ways, by referencing the rape of women through one of three main formulas: in the use of a common narrative of a "gang rape on a bench," in recrafting versions of the "Majesty in Chains" speech, and in linking the Mountain Meadows Massacre to feelings of indignation and revenge for the rape of women in Missouri. By retelling these hardships of the Restoration period, men sought to correct anti-Mormon perceptions of their religion and people, to reaffirm their allegiance to their founding prophet, and to earn the sympathies of outsiders against anti-polygamy persecution and federal prosecution. As the century came to a close, the needs of the community were changing, and the earlier persecution-centered memories lent themselves to reorientation toward Mormons' broader effort to integrate into American society and to claim sympathy as a formerly persecuted minority and pioneering group that played a part in the settlement of the West.

RAPE IN MORMON FEMALE MEMORY

Whereas Mormon men took the lead in forming group remembrances regarding the Mormon-Missouri War, women's voices and memories have also found their way into the collective memory of wartime rape. Male accounts have focused on the political and larger group persecution, while Mormon women's remembrances tended toward the personal, intimate, and spiritual. Mormon men often spoke with indignant outrage; Mormon women spoke with sadness, resignation, and mostly with silence. Memory studies have had limitations in the incorporation of female voices and in understanding how women transmit their stories outside of conventional forms. This is especially true when it comes to sexual assault, where any mention might be considered delicate, sensitive, and private or would have invited shame for a woman in a nineteenth-century context. For historians, the challenge of understanding women's unique forms of memory transmission is crucial. Sources surrounding war and memory are complicated, and for women's early memory sources, even more troubling.[75]

Any study of women, war, and memory requires more careful consideration of women's unconventional sources as part of the documentary record of the nineteenth century, particularly as the transmission of female memories often comes through oral traditions, private confession to diaries and letters, intimate conversations in their close social circles, and poetry with its veiled expressions and revealing subtexts. Although private and limited, these types of sources allow for women to contribute to the larger public memory of their communities. In describing her experiences in Missouri, early Mormon convert Bathsheba W. Smith referred to a few details of the specific crimes committed against the Mormons: "I saw much, very much, of the suffering that were brought upon our people by those lawless men. The Saints were forced to sign away their property and to agree to leave the state before it was time to put in spring crops."[76] Her format followed the "listing" patterns of male remembrances, but like other Mormon women's memories, Bathsheba's remembrance ended with how the trials helped refine her personal faith and sense of community:

> In these distressing times, the spirit of the Lord was with us to comfort and sustain us, and we had a sure testimony that we were being persecuted for the Gospel's sake, and that the Lord was not angry with none save those who acknowledged not his hand in all things.

Smith's remembrance is also emblematic of how Mormon women typically addressed the instances of sexual violence in the war: by not mentioning them at all. The absence of *female* memories of Missouri rapes stands in stark contrast to how often they are memorialized in *male* late-memory sources and autobiographies. Silence, then, is its own form of memory transmission, in that through the absence of significant events in the stored record, women are actually pointing to their importance. These whispered memories need to be drawn out through evaluation of other sources: public statements without comment, private family lore, oral traditions, and the privacy of female social circles.

Memory (of Hannah Kinney Johnstun) in Oral Tradition and Family History

The transmission of female memories of trauma in the nineteenth century often flowed through the unconventional channels of oral tradition and family lore. Historian Joseph Johnstun has suggested a strong circumstantial case for the rape in Missouri of one of his ancestors, Hannah Kinney Johnstun, whose story comes down, not through the traditional documentary record of the Mormon-Missouri War, but through Johnstun's own family history. Hannah was a young woman and convert to the Church with her family when they arrived in Far West and experienced the raw violence and expulsion of the rest of the Saints. Her brother, Jesse, recalled that "I had an aged mother and four sisters that were young women to protect, and I knew too well the disposition of the enemy that we were to be surrendered to."[77] Jesse left no direct evidence or statement about how or which of his sisters was raped. But after fleeing to Quincy in April 1839, his sister Hannah, twenty-three years old and unmarried, gave birth to a baby girl sometime in summer 1839, after which the baby was given to another couple to raise as their own. The story had a tragic conclusion: the baby died, and Hannah soon followed, "after a lingering illness of three months."[78] A reading of the historic circumstances of this tragedy point to the probability that Hannah has been raped in Missouri and the child was the result of the rape. And yet, Hannah's anonymity and death kept this evidence unknown except through private family transmission.

In the case of Hannah Johnstun, the silent female memories of wartime rape in Missouri manage to surface in more traditional ways, allowing her story to blend into Mormon collective memory. Sometime during her pregnancy, Hannah received a patriarchal blessing, in which Joseph Smith Sr. told her "thy character stands fair; no sin is chargeable against thee." What other "sin" might Patriarch Smith have been referring to, for a woman who was unmarried and pregnant in 1839? Johnstun considers this a veiled reference to Hannah's status as victim of sexual assault, as it appeared "that Father Smith was not among those who saw victims of rape as anything other than a victim. He told her, 'thy virtue is unsullied; thy name stands pure, and Heaven acknowledges thy work.'"[79] In this case, one woman's experience, shrouded in silence, was passed through family oral tradition and then read against another source—the patriarchal blessing—to create a new institutional memory of sexual violence in Missouri. In recovering the memory and identity of Hannah, Joseph Johnstun has added a secondhand female account of the war that had previously been kept outside of the male-centered public and institutional Mormon history of the war.

Memory (of Eliza R. Snow) in Female Social Circles

Mormon women who passed along their traumatic memories of the Mormon-Missouri War benefited from their intimate circles of feminine sociality, providing countless opportunities for confidential transmissions of memory. This context set the stage for another late-memory account of a possible rape victim, which comes from Alice Merrill Horne, a famous Mormon art critic and patroness of Minerva Teichert, as well as the granddaughter of Apostle George A. Smith and General Relief Society president Bathsheba W. Smith. Alice Merrill Horne came from the most elite heritage within Mormonism, as her grandparents had experienced the events of the Restoration in person. In her later years—probably in the 1930s—Horne wrote a personal autobiography, in which she remembered visiting her grandmother as a young girl and "hearing the most important Mormon women of the nineteenth century often gathered at the Smith home abutting the Church Historian's Office" remembering the early days of the Church. Writing of her childhood in the third person, she remembered how "Alice would sit on her grandmother's lap and listen, catching 'the whispered word unraveling, spelling, and signs made by those ladies.'"[80] It was there, at one of these rendezvous of feminine confidences in the late 1870s, that young Alice overheard the account of the brutal gang rape of Eliza R. Snow. "There was a saint—a Prophetess, a Poet, an intellectual, seized by brutal mobbers—used by those eight demons and left not dead, but worse. The horror, the anguish, despair, hopelessness of the innocent victim was dwelt upon. What [*sic*] future was here for such a one?"[81] Horne's language reveals the tensions and fears embedded in a culture that was hyper-focused on the sexual purity of unmarried women. "All the aspirations of a saintly virgin—that maiden of purity—had met martyrdom!" In this case, according to Horne, the rape left its victim not only emotionally scarred but also permanently affected physically:

> The Prophet heard and had compassion. This Saint, whose lofty ideals, whose person had been crucified, was yet to become the corner of female work. To her, no child could be born and yet she would be a Mother in Israel. One to whom all eyes should turn, to whom all ears would listen to her sing (in tongues) the praises of Zion. She was promised honor above all women, save only Emma, but her marriage to the Prophet would be only for heaven.[82]

It is clear that Alice Merrill Horne inferred that Eliza R. Snow would never be able to bear children because of a rape committed against her. Snow's infertility, in this particular memory construction, became a visible, tangible reminder of the violence against women in Missouri, but it also gave her the status of martyr.

The case of Eliza R. Snow invites us to think about the gendered ways that traumatic memories are transmitted for women. Barring more public and outward forms of remembering, women turned to private and subtle means of communicating their loss. Poetry, as an appropriate nineteenth-century venue for female expression, also provided an unconventional format for memory transmission and allowed women subtle and cloaked revelations of private emotions and experiences. Already a published poet by 1838, Eliza R. Snow, like most Mormon writers and diarists, went through the Missouri trials with a silent pen, and she provided no direct written testimony of any act of sexual violence committed against her in Missouri. Snow's poetry allowed her to direct her deep and unrelenting rage at the "peace-destroying mob," with ambiguous accusations, while still capturing the general tenor of violence against women. In October 1838, she declared with indignation,

'Twas Autumn: Summer's melting breath was gone,
And winter's gelid blast was stealing on.
To meet its dread approach, with anxious care
The houseless Saints were struggling to prepare.
When round about a desp'rate mob arose,

Like tigers waking from a night's repose—
They come like hordes from nether shades let loose—
Men without hearts—just made for Satan's use!
With wild demoniac rage they sally forth,
Resolv'd to drive the Saints of God from earth.[83]

Examining Eliza's poetry allows us to look at how she remembered the Missouri experience: "But see, the threat'ning foe in terror hide, Dark guilt and cowardice go side by side."[84]

In January 1841, Snow gave further poetic expression to her built-up frustrations after three years of violence, expulsion, and dispossession, but with a tone of hope. Snow encouraged her readers, "Though deepening trials throng your way, press on, press on, ye Saints of God!" Her positive stance was by no means a way to dismiss the wrongs committed against her and her people. In fact, her language is a haunting reminder of the sinister actions of Missouri mobs: "What though our rights have been assailed? What though by foes we've been despoiled? Jehovah's promise has not failed; Jehovah's purpose is not foiled."[85] Now memorialized in Mormon hymnody, Eliza's poetry allowed Mormons to find "solace" and to draw courage from the text.[86]

If Eliza's poetry was referencing a more specific threat against women, she veiled it in ambiguity and what Henry has called the "unspeakability" of rape.[87] Silence then becomes a language of memory, in that while she is not talking about it, she *is* talking about it. Nicola Henry has noted that some female victims of rape take as long as fifty years to come forward with their testimonies, demonstrating the "resilience of the culture of silence surrounding wartime sexual violence."[88] Eliza evoked similar reminders about the silent forms of memorial and suffering for women. At the deaths of Hyrum and Joseph Smith in 1844, she noted, "What it was for loving wives and children, the loyal heart may *feel*, but let *language keep silence!*"[89] The hymn "Though Deepening Trials" is also an honor to Eliza's silent and individual path through unnamed trials because "no one knew better than she the hardships and indignities suffered by the early saints."[90]

The case of Eliza R. Snow reminds us of the limitations of unexpressed and undocumented memories, but also that traumatic memory can be partially unwrapped out of the silence of the past. Henry describes this process: "the silence—or at least the collective memory of silence—has helped create a powerful political counter-memory, particularly . . . when women began to speak out publicly about their horrific experiences."[91] Ultimately, Alice Merrill Horne's hearsay account confided to her autobiography is a counter-memory, a multigenerational witness to another's experience. On the one hand, the account of Snow's rape becomes a tool for reinforcing the Missouri narrative that had been controlled by male voices and male lists, as well as the institutional framing of the Mormon-Missouri War—that *men knew* that some women had, in fact, been victims of rape. But it is also a transgressive memory, a counter-witness to the dominant group narrative of Eliza R. Snow's path to infertility and childlessness, which had traditionally been linked to either age or trauma. For in this account, Horne effectively assigned a new meaning of traumatic infertility to Eliza R. Snow's rape.

Snow's childlessness was commonly known to most early Mormons. And it mattered greatly, especially to a community for whom motherhood held the ultimate importance for female purpose and identity. Another story had tried to lay the blame for Snow's childlessness on Emma Smith, because of a supposed altercation, in which Emma pushed Eliza down the stairs of the Mansion House in a fit of jealousy and caused her to miscarry a baby. The Emma-Eliza-Stairs story is likely an invented memory, constructed for very specific purposes of undermining the reputation and status of the Prophet Joseph's widow and for characterizing the introduction of polygamy with all of the sordid taint of a henhouse. The story's origins and evolution are problematic, and probably even false, making it the "stuff of legend, a folk tradition, perpetuated orally, and likely to continue."[92]

But in examining the story and its genesis, historians have asked similar questions regarding the problems of group memory transmission: "Why was [the story] told and why is it still told? What does the telling say about the tellers? What 'truths of the humans heart,' their own human hearts, do people reinforce through the telling?"[93] Ironically, at the same time that Alice Merrill Horne was privately constructing her autobiographical materials in the 1930s, Church history researcher and Eliza's own nephew LeRoi C. Snow (youngest son of Eliza's brother, the Prophet Lorenzo Snow) was grappling with the Stairs account, which "loomed large in his mind." Snow examined numerous sources of the story and tried to decide whether to formally include it in some biographies he had planned to publish for the Church History Department; he even relayed one of the historical versions to the famous Joseph Smith biographer Fawn Brodie.[94] That these two clashing memory narratives were developing side by side in the group discourse is informative. As Nicola Henry has reminded us, memory is almost always "multiple and contested rather than unifying and consensual."[95] And in those "conflicting narratives" we might discover ways that "marginalized memories have been excluded from dominant understandings of past events."[96]

As communities work through their contested memories, they find multiple uses and meanings for their past traumatic events, which historians must examine very carefully, because "understanding the political decisions regarding which memories are retained and which memories are discarded or ignored is thus important for understanding the politics of memory."[97] In the case of Eliza R. Snow, the group memory of her supposed infertility was ascribed to one of two possible traumatic events. One memory allows the group to feel collective anger toward Emma Smith as a traitor whose actions caused personal injury to the Mormons' beloved Eliza and denied her the possibilities of motherhood. The other memory redirects Mormon anger outward toward Missouri militias, reminding members of the need for vigilant unity against external political persecutions. One memory exposes Emma Smith's hatred of polygamy as a tool for internally fracturing the Church and upsetting the in-group dynamic of loyalty to the Prophet Joseph Smith (although conversely it also *undermines* a narrative of a romanticized polygamy for later members of the Church, by revealing all of the imperfections, secrecy, and jealousies of its practice). The other memory *reinforces* a concept of divine and virtuous polygamy, by portraying it as an eternal and loving solution to one spinster's unmarried and motherless status that had resulted from a violent rape. It reifies Joseph's Smith position as a noble leader and defender of feminine and motherly virtue. It is in the vivid tensions between these two competing memory constructions that Mormon women will effectively search for a meaning relevant to their lived experience. Horne's memory transmission of Snow's trauma never functioned for the Mormon community in the way that other, more publicized male sources had succeeded in doing; it was, after all, only confided to a private autobiography. Still, in discovering and now publishing this memory, Eliza's story might serve to recenter women's voices and experiences into the Missouri narrative, creating a new group memory that allows women to see themselves in the violence of the past. This scenario exposes two overlapping problems of memory: how sexual violence was remembered by those who experienced, witnessed, or knew about it, and how historians now "remember" it, by recovering a memory that was largely lost, for our own purposes.

If Eliza's memory, as transmitted through Alice Merrill Horne, had remained in total isolation—buried in obscurity and lost to history—the question of its usefulness would not be relevant. But perhaps surprisingly, others found meaning in it, too. On February 18, 1942, a polygamous wife named Olive Kunz, of the fundamentalist Jessop clan, was recovering from a recent hysterectomy and other health problems that had placed her near death. Feeling physical exhaustion for the trauma to her body and reproductive system, plus the emotional devastation that she could not have more children, she still felt the need to attend her Tuesday Relief Society meeting: "I dressed myself and with help got outside and into the car. The sisters gave me a loving welcome which touched me greatly and for which I thanked God. I was called to speak a few minutes, and remaining seated, I did so." [98] Olive's address to her Relief Society sisters turned quickly to finding spiritual meaning in her medical trial and infertility: "I longed to tell the sisters that it was not of their faith or mine that I was not completely healed, but for a glorious purpose of

God, of which He and I knew and I would try to be patient and return thanks-giving to Him that He had found me useable in any way." Olive also turned to a well-known historical subject for emulation:

> How near I felt to Sister Eliza R. Snow that nite! How I longed to tell them of her and her blessings. She, whose every righteous desire was granted save one . . . that of child bearing; and that she knew why she suffered and that it was for a noble cause in God's sight and she would yet stand before the bar of God, a witness against the wicked mobocrats of Missouri who had caused her affliction, with oth-ers whose bodies were attacked by "sons of the devil." [99]

Olive Kunz's astonishing retelling of the Eliza R. Snow rape account invites us to give urgency to the question of the transmission of memory and history within a group. How might one hearsay memory, confided to a private autobi-ography by an elite Mormon woman in Salt Lake City, have found its way into the personal thoughts of an obscure polygamist wife in a fundamentalist group in 1941? Perhaps the reminiscences were passed down through separate arter-ies of transmission, unrelated but originating in the murky past of Mormon women's private meetings and conversations. Of course, it is impossible to trace the direct line of memory diffusion. It lies somewhere in the dark matter of how members of groups share their stories, in the whispered conversations, in the passing of oral tradition through families, and in following the informal lines of communication as they flow across a group in motion.

Both Alice Merrill Horne and Olive Kunz accepted and communicated a meaning in the Eliza R. Snow account, especially as it related to female in-fertility. Kunz even drew a direct line between Eliza's trial, the sufferings of the prophets and apostles, Christ's suffering, and herself:

> Was it lack of faith that God suffered? Or that the Apostle Paul suffered from afflictions until death or that Pres. John Taylor lived and died a martyr, receiv-ing wounds at the time of the Prophet Joseph's martyrdom? No! But each for a different purpose, which purpose was shown to them and they knew they but lacked here, to received greater blessings hereafter." [100]

Indeed, the Eliza R. Snow rape account shows how the memory of sexual assault of Mormon women has been constructed by different individuals and groups for varying and sometimes competing purposes. The work of American studies scholar Elizabeth W. Son is informative here. Son has examined the attempts by various Korean groups to memorialize the sexual victimization of Korean "comfort women" by the Japanese military during World War II. Son asks, "How do subjects memorialize loss that is in turn generative of subjection formation and diasporic belonging?" [101] Even more, how do sub-jects find and transmit memory out of silence and loss? As the Japanese state has strongly contested the history of military-based sexual slavery of Korean "comfort women," this has worked to deny the survivors any reparative measures. The Mormon rape victims of the Mormon-Missouri War have likewise been silenced, through lack of effective engagement with forms of justice and the absence of publicized female transmissions of memory. Still, even in that group silencing, Mormon women employed nontraditional methods of sharing their memories within a group. For memory scholars, the lack of female memories in the aftermath of war does not preclude the possibility that women kept the confidence of their own assaults. Indeed, "it is worth noting that silence can also be constructive and sometimes very powerful," even working toward the "formation of a collective memory of wartime rape." Silence even "forms a central part" of that memory.[102] The dismissal of rape claims further abuses the female victims for whom memories are often contested, disallowing them their voice, their experience, and historical justice for those crimes.

The process of memory consolidation is both challenging and empowering, as when counter memories conflict with the common narrative, since "creating, remembering, and agreeing on certain historical narratives (and ignoring, forgetting, and contesting others) are the primary methods by which group identities are created and maintained."[103] Mormons' collective memory remains a space of contested memories, where some will choose to accept a sexual crime committed against Zion's prophetess and some will choose to reject that memory. As the possibility of Eliza R. Snow's rape in Missouri enters into the Mormon collective narrative about the war, Mormon women will find new meaning and significance in her memories for their own lived experiences.

CONCLUSION

There are no physical monuments to Mormon victims of the Mormon-Missouri War. But the rapes against Mormon women have lingered in historical and cultural memory in other ways, in verbal monuments, silent monuments, textual monuments, and media monuments, all of which speak out through years of storytelling about the war. Elizabeth Son has described these abstract forms as symbolic memorials, which "reflect and constitute individual, collective and national desires over . . . war memory."[104] They remind us not only of the stark importance of recovering women's individual memories but also how those memories might be used for group purposes. As Nicola Henry observed:

> Rape is a profoundly private, individualized experience of bodily violation, and yet it is also highly politicized and collectivized at certain points in time. In some contexts, rape has been used as a way to build a shared or communal tragedy that binds a nation or group of people.[105]

As Mormons independently retrieved, collected, and formulated their memories of the Mormon-Missouri War of 1838, the gendered memories of sexual violence were inserted and adapted for these various intentions. But within these purposes, the voices and memories of women have too often been absent. Or, as Henry has articulated, "Wartime rape enters the realm of the political when it becomes utilized for the explicit political purposes of nation building."[106] Mormon autobiographers rarely named specific female victims for the purposes of gaining justice for the individual; instead, they have memorialized sexual assaults as part of marking the crimes committed against the religious community as a whole. Mormon narrators, novelists, and filmmakers have since used rape memories as a method to garner sympathy: "to mobilize national support . . . they tapped into this narrative of sexual victimhood as national victimhood."[107] The innocent, pure rape victim becomes an allegory for the Mormon group body, and the "notion of innocence finds expression in a language of chastity and images of youth."[108]

The persistent male accounts of Mormon-Missouri War rapes point to a representation of victimized nationhood: the virtuous and anonymous young woman violated by Missourians represents the young religion, symbolically brutalized by anti-Mormon persecution. While there is an implied honoring of Mormon womanhood in these memories, the purposes of their telling lie not in achieving justice for individual victims but in reinforcing the larger persecution narrative of Mormonism's troubled beginnings. Female accounts, on the other hand, have lurked in silent and unexpressed tension until hints of memories have emerged from that darkness. Taken together, male and female memories of the Mormon-Missouri war have kept alive the threat and reality of sexual violence against Mormon women as a vivid part of the religion's consciousness of the Mormon community. Only in recovering individual women's experiences can the project of memorializing a war seek to find justice for the losses felt by female victims. For Mormon memorialists, that honoring begins with the shadowy and terrible image of a virgin strapped to a church bench on a cold November day in Missouri in 1838.

NOTES

1. Mrs. Joseph [Mary Isabella] Horne, "Migration and Settlement of the Latter-day Saints," 7; Bancroft Library, California. Far West, in Caldwell County, Missouri, was the main settlement for Mormons and headquarters of the Church. Founded in 1836, its population reached somewhere between 3,000 and 5,000 before the Saints were forced to evacuate in November 1838.

2. John Loveless, Autobiography 1859, Church of Jesus Christ of Latter-day Saints Church History Library, Salt Lake City, UT (hereafter cited as LDS Church History Library).

3. Loveless, Autobiography.

4. See Ann Taves, *Religious Experience Reconsidered: A Building Block Approach to the Study of Religion and Other Special Things* (Princeton, NJ: Princeton University Press, 2009).

5. For the purposes of clarifying and confirming rape in the historical record of the Mormon-Missouri War, I have documented all known historical accounts of sexual assaults against Mormon women, found in contemporary testimonials, hearsay accounts, eyewitness reports, and later reminiscences and autobiographies in Andrea G. Radke-Moss, forthcoming. Also, I choose to use the terms *rape* and *sexual assault* interchangeably.

6. Nicola Henry, *War and Rape: Law, Memory, and Justice* (New York: Routledge, 2011), 14.

7. David Thelen, "Memory and American History," *Journal of American History* 75 (March 1989): 1122.

8. Anna Reading, *The Social Inheritance of the Holocaust: Gender, Culture and Memory* (New York: Palgrave Macmillan, 2002), 5; see also Henry, *War and Rape*, 20.

9. Henry, *War and Rape*, 20. She recalls that, as late as 2010, one conference specifically called for papers on gender and memory, but "aside from my own presentation, I did not come across any that specifically dealt with the connection between gender and memory." Henry, *War and Rape*, 134n12.

10. Henry, *War and Rape*, 20.

11. At this point, Mormons had not yet begun practicing polygamy (polygyny), which would be introduced in Nauvoo a decade later.

12. For more on the history of the Mormon-Missouri War of 1838–1839, see Leland Homer Gentry, "A History of the Latter-day Saints in Northern Missouri from 1836 to 1839" (PhD diss., Brigham Young University, 1965); Stephen C. LeSueur, *The 1838 Mormon War in Missouri* (Columbia: University of Missouri Press, 1987); Alexander L. Baugh, *A Call to Arms: The 1838 Mormon Defense of Northern Missouri* (Provo, UT: Joseph Fielding Smith Institute for Latter-day Saint History and BYU Studies, 2000); and Leland H. Gentry and Todd M. Compton, *Fire and Sword: A History of the Latter-day Saints in Northern Missouri, 1836–39* (Salt Lake City, UT: Greg Kofford Books, 2011).

13. Gentry, "A History of the Latter-day Saints in Northern Missouri from 1836 to 1839," 338.

14. LeSueur, *The 1838 Mormon War in Missouri*, 180–81; see also Baugh, *A Call to Arms*; and Gentry and Compton, *Fire and Sword*, 370.

15. Sharon Block, *Rape & Sexual Power in Early America* (Chapel Hill: University of North Carolina Press, 2006), 81.

16. Susan Brownmiller, *Against Our Will: Men, Women, and Rape* (New York: Simon & Schuster, 1975), 37.

17. Brownmiller, *Against Our Will*, 124. Henry has also shown that "rape has nonetheless occupied a central part of wartime collective memory [and] wars are well remembered not only for pillage and murder, but also for the rape of women." Henry, *War and Rape*, 117.

18. Brownmiller, *Against Our Will*, 38.

19. David W. Grua, *Surviving Wounded Knee: The Lakotas and the Politics of Memory* (Oxford: Oxford University Press, 2016), 3; see also Maurice Halbwachs, *On Collective Memory*, ed. and trans. Lewis A. Coser (Chicago: University of Chicago Press, 1992); Maurice Halbwachs, *The Collective Memory*, trans. Francis J. Ditter Jr. and Vida Yazdi Ditter (New York: Harper Colophon Books, 1980). According to Halbwachs, "Memories are constructed within social frameworks, meaning that people filter and organize their memories according to the values and concerns espoused by whatever group or groups to which they belong," quoted in Grua, *Surviving Wounded Knee*, 3.

20. Henry, *War and Rape*, 10.

21. Thelen, "Memory and American History," 1118. See also Michael Kammen, *Mystic Chords of Memory: The Transformation of Tradition in American Culture* (New York: Knopf,

1991); Michael Kammen, "Commemoration and Contestation in American Culture: Historical Perspectives," *Amerikastudien/American Studies* 48, no. 2 (2003): 185–205.

22. Brownmiller, *Against Our Will*, 37–38.

23. Elizabeth W. Son, "Memorializing Loss" (paper presented at the Histories of Violence Symposium, Northwestern University, Evanston, IL, April 27, 2013), 1; see also Elizabeth W. Son, *Embodied Reckonings: Comfort Women, Performance, and Transpacific Redress* (Ann Arbor: University of Michigan Press, forthcoming).

24. Henry, *War and Rape*, 59.

25. Henry, *War and Rape*, 52.

26. Parley P. Pratt to "Sister" [Manuscript 2], December 9, 1838, in Dean C. Jessee and David J. Whittaker, "The Last Months of Mormonism in Missouri: The Albert Perry Rockwood Journal," *BYU Studies* 28, no. 1 (Winter 1988): 32.

27. Loveless, Autobiography.

28. Orson F. Whitney, *Life of Heber C. Kimball: An Apostle, the Father and Founder of the British Mission*, 3rd ed. (Salt Lake City, UT: Bookcraft, 1940), 234. Emphasis mine.

29. Andrew Jenson, comp., under the direction of Franklin D. Richards, "An Epitome of the History of the Church of Jesus Christ of Latter-day Saints," in *World's Fair Ecclesiastical History of Utah*, ed. Sarah Granger Kimball (Salt Lake City, UT, 1893), 40.

30. Henry, *War and Rape*, 20. Historians have even noted similar patterns of documenting war crimes in other settings. This occurred, for example, in Belgium during and after the First World War when "the German Army cut a swath of horror. Houses were burned, villages were plundered, civilians were bayoneted, and women were raped." Brownmiller, *Against Our Will*, 41.

31. Hyrum Smith, "Testimony of Hyrum Smith," July 1, 1843, Nauvoo Municipal Court, reprinted in *Mormon Redress Petitions: Documents of the 1833–1838 Missouri Conflict*, ed. Clark V. Johnson (Provo, UT: Religious Studies Center, Brigham Young University, 1992), 629.

32. Mosiah Lyman Hancock, Autobiography (1834–1865), comp. Amy E. Baird, Victoria H. Jackson, and Laura L. Wassell, http://www.boap.org/LDS/Early-Saints/MHancock.html; quoted in Baugh, *A Call to Arms*, 158n108.

33. Henry, *War and Rape*, 14. See also Marita Sturken, *Tangled Memories: The Vietnam War, the AIDS Epidemic, and the Politics of Remembering* (Berkeley: University of California Press, 1997).

34. For a more thorough discussion of the various accounts of a gang rape committed on a "meetinghouse" bench, please see my forthcoming article documenting the Mormon-Missouri War rape accounts.

35. Henry, *War and Rape*, 27. See also Katharine Hodgkin and Susannah Radstone, eds., *Contested Pasts: The Politics of Memory*, Routledge Studies in Memory and Narrative (London: Routledge, 2003).

36. B. H. Roberts, *The Missouri Persecutions* (Salt Lake City, UT: George Q. Cannon & Sons, 1900), 243–44.

37. Henry, *War and Rape*, 14.

38. Steven C. Harper, comment on Mormon History Association panel, "Contested Memories of the Mormon-Missouri War of 1838," June 11, 2016, Snowbird, UT; C. R. Barclay, "Schematization of Autobiographical Memory," in *Autobiographical Memory*, ed. D. C. Rubin (Cambridge: Cambridge University Press, 1986), 97; Edmund Blair Bolles, *Remembering and Forgetting: An Inquiry into the Nature of Memory* (New York: Walker, 1988), 58, 64–65.

39. "The Latest Brutal Outrage," *Deseret News*, June 6, 1860, 108–9; "Important from Utah: the Indian Troubles at the West-Conduct of the Mormons, a Case of Personal Revenue-Assassinations, &c," *New York Times*, July 3, 1860; and Fred C. Collier, ed., *The Office Journal of President Brigham Young: 1858–1863, Book D* (Hanna, UT: Collier's Publishing, 2006),

101, June 15, 1860, and 104, June 23, 1860; see also Steve C. Taysom, *Shakers, Mormons, and Religious Worlds: Conflicting Visions, Contested Boundaries* (Bloomington: Indiana University Press, 2011), 236n4.

40. From Frederick C. Bartlett, *Remembering* (1932), quoted in Thelen, "Memory and American History," 1120.

41. Henry, *War and Rape*, 41.

42. Brownmiller, *Against Our Will*, 37–38. See also Henry, *War and Rape*, 20.

43. Alexander L. Baugh, "'Silence, Ye Fiends of the Infernal Pit!': Joseph Smith's Incarceration in Richmond, Missouri, November 1838," *Mormon Historical Studies* 13, no. 1–2 (Spring/Fall 2012): 143.

44. Parley P. Pratt to Willard Richards, November 7, 1853, Journal History of the Church of Jesus Christ of Latter-day Saints, 1; also *Deseret News*, November 12, 1853. See also Parley P. Pratt, *The Autobiography of Parley Parker Pratt* (Chicago: published for Pratt Bros., 1888).

45. Pratt to Richards, Journal History, 1, and Pratt, *Autobiography*, 229.

46. Pratt to Richards, Journal History, 1, and Pratt, *Autobiography*, 229–30.

47. Morris Calvin Phelps, "Biography of Laura Clark," 2, LDS Church History Library, Salt Lake City, UT; see also Morris Calvin Phelps, undated reminiscence, LDS Church History Library, Salt Lake City, UT.

48. Phelps, "Biography of Laura Clark," 2–3.

49. Henry, *War and Rape*, 43.

50. Henry, *War and Rape*, 63.

51. Terryl L. Givens and Matthew J. Grow, *Parley P. Pratt: The Apostle Paul of Mormonism* (New York: Oxford University Press, 2011), 144. For an excellent examination of the history of narrative and visual depictions of the "Majesty in Chains" event, see Baugh, "'Silence, Ye Fiends,'" 134–59.

52. Eviatar Zerubavel, *Time Maps: Collective Memory and the Shape of the Past* (Chicago: Chicago University Press, 2004), 5–6; see also Henry, *War and Rape*, 17.

53. Baugh, "'Silence, Ye Fiends,'" 141.

54. Baugh, "'Silence, Ye Fiends,'" 141.

55. *Praise to the Man*, directed by T. C. Christensen and Gary Cook (Salt Lake City, UT: Excel Entertainment, 2005. DVD), 39:18–43:00, https://www.lds.org/media-library/video/2006-05-01-joseph-smith-prophet-of-the-restoration-2002-version; *Joseph Smith: Prophet of the Restoration*, directed by T. C. Christensen and Gary Cook (Salt Lake City, UT: Church of Jesus Christ of Latter-day Saints, 2005. DVD), 39:35–41:13, https://www.lds.org/media-library/video/2011-03-01-joseph-smith-the-prophet-of-the-restoration?category=feature-films&lang=eng.

56. Gerald Lund, *The Work and the Glory*, vol. 4, *Thy Gold to Refine* (Salt Lake City, UT: Deseret Book, 2006), 443.

57. For histories of the 1857 Mountain Meadows Massacre, please see Ronald W. Walker, Richard E. Turley Jr., and Glen M. Leonard, *Massacre at Mountain Meadows* (Oxford: Oxford University Press, 2008); see also Janiece Johnson, "In Search of Punishment: Mormon Transgressions and the Mountain Meadows Massacre" (PhD diss., School of History, University of Leicester, 2014); and Richard E. Turley and Janiece Johnson, eds., *Mountain Meadows Massacre: Complete Legal Papers*, 2 vols. (Norman: University of Oklahoma Press, 2017).

58. Walker, Turley, and Leonard, *Massacre at Mountain Meadows*, 82, 87.

59. Walker, Turley, and Leonard, *Massacre at Mountain Meadows*, 93.

60. Walker, Turley, and Leonard, *Massacre at Mountain Meadows*, 107.

61. Joseph Fish, *The Life and Times of Joseph Fish, Mormon Pioneer*, edited by John H. Krenkel (Danville, IL: Interstate Printers & Publishers, 1970), 81.

62. Fish, *Life and Times of Joseph Fish*, 81.

63. Fish, *Life and Times of Joseph Fish*, 81.

64. Alva Matheson, "John D. Lee and the Chaffin Mill," 1996 July 15. Oral history received by John Eldredge Matheson; CR 100 385 inventory, folder 35, 1, LDS Church History Library, Salt Lake City, UT.

65. Lily Dougall, *The Mormon Prophet* (New York: D. Appleton and Company, 1899), 237. Emphasis mine.

66. Dougall, *Mormon Prophet*, 238.

67. Harry Leon Wilson, *The Lions of the Lord: A Tale of the Old West*, illustrated by Rose Cecil O'Neill (Boston: Lothrop Publishing, 1903), 201.

68. Wilson, *Lions of the Lord*, 202.

69. Wilson, *Lions of the Lord*, 203–4.

70. Wilson, *Lions of the Lord*, 201.

71. Wilson, *Lions of the Lord*, 202–3.

72. Wilson, *Lions of the Lord*, 210–11.

73. Wilson, *Lions of the Lord*, 210–22.

74. Grua, *Surviving Wounded Knee*, 182.

75. See Henry, *War and Rape*, for a thorough discussion of the difficulties recovering memories of war.

76. Bathsheba W. Smith Autobiography, typescript, L. Tom Perry Special Collections, Harold B. Lee Library, Brigham Young University.

77. Joseph Johnstun, "A Victim of the 1838 Mormon-Missouri War: The Life and Tragedy of Hannah Kinney Johnstun" (paper presented at Mormon History Association Conference, Independence, MO, May 2010; copy in possession of the author and used with permission), 9.

78. Johnstun, "A Victim," 11.

79. Johnstun, "A Victim," 9–10.

80. Alice Merrill Horne, Autobiography, 7, transcript courtesy of Lavina Fielding Anderson and in possession of the author.

81. Horne, Autobiography, 7.

82. Horne, Autobiography, 8.

83. Eliza R. Snow, *Poems, Religious, Historical, and Political, also Two Articles in Prose* (Liverpool, England: Franklin D. Richards, 1856; Salt Lake City, UT: Latter-day Saints' Printing and Publishing Establishment, 1877), 1:11, http://archive.org/stream/PoemsReligiousHistoricalAndPolitical/poemsreligioushi01snow_djvu.txt. See also "Eliza Roxie Snow Smith: A Tribute of Affection," *Woman's Exponent* 16 (December 15, 1887): 109.

84. Snow, *Poems, Religious, Historical, and Political*, 1:11–12; see also "Eliza Roxie Snow Smith," 109.

85. Eliza R. Snow, "Though Deepening Trials" (January 1841).

86. Snow, "Though Deepening Trials."

87. Henry, *War and Rape*, 49.

88. Henry, *War and Rape*, 52.

89. Eliza R. Snow, "Sketch," in *Personal Writings of Eliza R. Snow*, ed. Maureen Ursenbach Beecher (Logan: Utah State University Press, 2000), 17.

90. Karen Lynn Davidson, *Our Latter-day Hymns: The Stories and the Messages*, rev. ed. (Salt Lake City, UT: Deseret Book, 2009), 163.

91. Henry, *War and Rape*, 59.

92. Maureen Ursenbach Beecher, Linda King Newell, and Valeen Tippetts Avery, "Emma and Eliza and the Stairs," *Brigham Young University Studies* 22, no. 1 (Winter 1982): 87. For more on the sources and critique of the Stairs narratives, see Brian C. Hales, "Emma Smith,

Eliza R. Snow, and the Reported Incident on the Stairs," *Mormon Historical Studies* 10, no. 2 (Fall 2009): 63–76.

93. Beecher, Newell, and Avery, "Emma and Eliza and the Stairs," 87.

94. Beecher, Newell, and Avery, "Emma and Eliza and the Stairs," 89.

95. Henry, *War and Rape*, 17.

96. Henry, *War and Rape*, 19.

97. Henry, *War and Rape*, 19.

98. Diary of Olive Kunz, reprinted in Rhea Allred Kunz, *Voices of Women Approbating Celestial or Plural Marriage*, vol. 2, *Treasured Memories* (Draper, UT: Review and Preview Publishers, 1985), 335.

99. Diary of Olive Kunz, 335.

100. Diary of Olive Kunz, 335.

101. Son, "Memorializing Loss," 1, and Son, *Embodied Reckonings* (forthcoming).

102. Henry, *War and Rape*, 59.

103. Matthew Kester, *Remembering Iosepa: History, Place, and Religion in the American West* (Oxford: Oxford University Press, 2013), 140.

104. Son, "Memorializing Loss," 3.

105. Henry, *War and Rape*, 52.

106. Henry, *War and Rape*, 52–53.

107. Son, "Memorializing Loss," 4.

108. Son, "Memorializing Loss," 4.

Chapter Four

Early Mormonism's Expansive Family and the Browett Women

Amy Harris

Between 1878 and 1889, the widowed and childless Elizabeth Browett acted as proxy for four women's posthumous marriages to the same deceased man: her husband, Daniel Browett.[1] Daniel had died in 1848, leaving behind Elizabeth, his wife of fourteen years, and Harriet, his plural wife of five years. The intervening years had brought not only Daniel's death but also Harriet's only two years later. They also brought two additional marriages and a divorce for Elizabeth. So why did Elizabeth seal other women to Daniel thirty years after his death, women who were never married to him during his lifetime? The answer to that question lies in her and the other Browett women's pre-Mormon ideas about marriage and family, in the radically reconsidered notions of family and community embodied in nineteenth-century Mormonism, and in their own unique marital and maternal experiences. The function of what Elizabeth did in the 1870s and 1880s—adoptive sealings to a deceased or living, priesthood-holding Latter-day Saint (LDS) man—was not unusual, but her participation in it, along with the combined action of the other Browett women, illuminates how early LDS women made sense of Mormon teachings about kinship, both mortal and eternal. Together, their stories illuminate how women combined their preexisting beliefs and practices with LDS teachings about the possibilities of divine, eternal kinship.

The Browett women included Elizabeth, Harriet, Martha, and Martha Rebecca. The oldest of the women, Elizabeth's mother-in-law, Martha Pulham Browett (later Winchester), was born in 1782 in Gloucestershire in western England. Her two daughters-in-law, Elizabeth Harris Browett Johnstun and Harriet Barnes Clifford Browett, were also born in Gloucestershire, in 1813 and 1808, respectively. The youngest of the women, Martha's daughter, Martha Rebecca Browett Hyde McKenzie, was born in 1817.[2] Harriet was the first to die, in 1850 in Iowa, followed by Martha in 1865 in Salt Lake City.

Elizabeth and Martha Rebecca lived the longest, dying in 1899 and 1904, respectively, in Utah. From bits of information about the Browett women scattered in church and government documents as well as passing references to them found in the diaries and letters of others, it is possible to piece together a story of their lives—a story that reveals just what it was like for women to grapple with Mormonism's largest claims about a priesthood designed to conquer the dissolution of kinship ties and reify them across eternity. Ultimately, this type of approach is often the only way to gather and understand the stories of numerous women who left so little record of their lives.

The Browett women's family and religious background coupled with nineteenth-century Mormonism's wide-ranging view of family and its connections to theology and faith provide a rich set of tools for situating and interpreting the Browett women's experiences. Recent work by Jonathan Stapley, Samuel Brown, and Kathleen Flake has illuminated how Mormon teachings about salvation, family, and priesthood became intertwined over the course of the nineteenth century. In Jonathan Stapley's words, "Mormon sealing, whether for marriage, for children, or for the fullness of the priesthood, sealed in the traditional sense (i.e., guaranteed salvation) inasmuch as it formalized eternal bonds in the interconnected network of the cosmological priesthood."[3] Stapley and Brown refer to a cosmological priesthood that, while not always clearly defined, was different from an administrative priesthood used to perform rituals necessary for salvation. Cosmological priesthood, instead, remapped priesthood as a power granted to men and women via a heavenly structure based on kinship connections and leading to exaltation: in other words, to a progression that ended in a life like God's. It grew from Joseph Smith's revelations and innovations about temple ordinances that bound, or "sealed," women and men into a heavenly kinship. The priesthood Joseph Smith imagined was not confined to pastoral or preaching roles. Instead, it comprised "the eternal structure of heaven" and made it possible for men and women to reign "through eternity as kings and queens, priests and priestesses."[4] Strikingly, the conflation of priesthood and family did not exclude women. Instead, it explicitly included a "matriarchal dimension of patriarchal priesthood" that rendered kinship "a source of divine blessing and . . . priesthood blessings."[5] Heavenly kinship, therefore, consisted of men and women sealed in marriage and all people sealed as children to parents who had been sealed in marriage as well. In this way, "salvation transformed to encompass the heavenly kinship network."[6]

The effort to bring all believers into this heavenly kinship had an enormous impact on early Mormonism's rituals and practices. Sealing rituals that bound spouses to each other, and children to sealed, priesthood-bearing parents, raised questions about those who died without the opportunity to participate in such rituals and about how to account for the many converts who could not be connected to their parents because the parents were not sealed or even a part of the Mormon faith. Joseph Smith creatively solved this conundrum by the introduction of proxy participation in sacred ordinances on the behalf of deceased ancestors (particularly baptism, which for many early LDS leaders signaled inclusion in the heavenly family as much as it signaled personal redemption).[7] A further elaboration by Smith and his successors was to allow for "adoption" sealings—rituals that spiritually bound Church members to priesthood-bearing parents who were already sealed. In particular, rank-and-file members could be sealed as children to Church leaders (and their wives). In this framework, polygamy, both in practice and in name only, similarly offered eternal, priestly marriages for all women. Blessings by priesthood leaders, called patriarchal blessings, also offered sacred kinship connections. Pronounced by the patriarch of the Church, the blessings were recorded and kept with official Church records. Patriarchal blessings also included personalized blessings on individuals and simultaneously discussed their lineage as descendants of Israel and their future possibilities in establishing Zion and having a righteous posterity. Taken together, these rituals offered an eternity populated by a sacred kinship and a mortality that blurred the lines between spiritual connections to fellow believers and connections to biological families.[8]

Most early accounts of sealing rituals, proxy ordinances for the dead, and adoptions come from accounts written by male leaders, but the Browett women's experience shows that such teachings and practices had deep and meaningful resonance in women's lives as well. The evidence of the Browett women's views of Mormon teachings about kinship and salvation is not as explicit as that left by LDS leadership; it is revealed more by their actions than by written evidence. Discovering their actions required using the tools more often associated with genealogy to piece together a story based on minimal evidence. Other than two letters Elizabeth wrote in 1856, there are no surviving writings by any of the women. Elizabeth also left short accounts of her migration and marriage history, but these were recorded by others in a fiftieth-anniversary celebration of the 1847 pioneers and in a widow's army pension application. With so little firsthand evidence from the women themselves, their stories are only revealed by painstakingly patching together the fragments of information they left in newspapers; temple and church records (LDS, Anglican, Quaker, and Methodist); immigration, probate, military, cemetery, census, and vital records; and the mention of them found in others' diaries and letters. Therefore, the conclusions about their beliefs or attitudes are an interpretation based on their actions and the trail those actions left in a variety of historical records. The advantage of this approach is that it allows women's actions to come to the forefront, even when they did not leave voluminous written records. Combined, these records reveal rank-and-file women negotiating Mormonism's heady mixture of kinship, priesthood, salvation, and exaltation (an extension of salvation that sanctified a person until she or he became godlike).

Before they encountered that heady mixture, however, the Browett women were shaped by a preexisting English kinship and religious milieu. The women, particularly the oldest three, who were all born before 1815, came of age in a culture shaped by England's broad, flexible notions of kinship. While relatively late marriage (British women were often five to ten years older than their Continental counterparts and two years older than their American counterparts) and nuclear household structures were typical in England since the middle ages, the kinship ties beyond and between households were essential to familial, social, and financial survival well into the nineteenth century.[9] For the laboring or trades classes (as the Browetts and connected families were), connections with siblings, in-laws, cousins, aunts, and uncles were essential to the raising of children, supporting marriages, and providing financial and social support. Family relationships had yet to fully undergo the rhetorical compression and collapse of all affectionate and intimate relationships into a romantic couplehood.[10] Instead, early nineteenth-century English families blurred the lines among blood relatives, in-laws, step relations, and even friends—emphasizing the instrumental and functional aspects of relationships over a narrower, romanticized definition of those relationships.[11]

The interconnected and functional nature of kinship was assumed, as anyone who has made the briefest of forays into Jane Austen novels can attest. Numerous characters, much like Austen's own brother, were sent to live with an aunt and uncle when parental health or fortunes failed, distant cousins offered housing to destitute relations, uncles gave ecclesiastical appointments to nephews, and siblings offered lifelong emotional and social support. Even if they did not read Austen, the Browett women inhabited a very similar world to the one Austen described. They cared for their nieces and nephews; married friends of their siblings; witnessed their siblings' marriages; executed estates in conjunction with siblings, siblings-in-law, and cousins; and joined the same nonconformist religious groups as their cousins and in-laws. In addition, they layered spiritual kinship onto this expansive family structure. Like Protestants on both sides of the Atlantic, particularly Methodists, the Browett women saw themselves as belonging to a vast spiritual kinship built by all those who "adopted" themselves, via baptism, as children of God.[12]

How the Browett women came to combine their experiences within the English kinship system and Protestant notions of spiritual kinship into their Mormon beliefs and practices begins in late eighteenth-century Gloucestershire with the birth of Martha Pulham in 1782.[13] She was baptized in the Church of England and presumably raised in that tradition, though there is no evidence of her parents' religious beliefs. Though no account of her early years survives, it is possible to piece together a picture of her life from surviving evidence in church records and from the context provided by historical scholarship. If her childhood and youth were typical of rural England at the turn of the nineteenth century, she would have received a basic education in Church of England catechetical teachings and rudimentary literacy. She would have also begun paid labor in her mid-teens, probably as a servant—the most common occupation for young women from laboring or trades families.[14] Employment, or perhaps participation in a market, is probably how she met Thomas Browett, a Quaker man five years her junior from Tewkesbury, a nearby market town.

Brief entries in Society of Friends (Quaker) and Anglican Church records reveal how kinship and religion intertwined in Martha's life. The relationship between her and Thomas seems to have displeased Thomas's family, especially when Martha gave birth to a son in December 1809. An unwed pregnancy for an Anglican of Martha's class was not uncommon, especially when the couple intended to marry, as Thomas and Martha did.[15] For a Quaker, however, it was far more serious. While English Quakers emphasized replacing "genetic kin with spiritual kin," they kept strict boundaries of who belonged to that spiritual kin by "erecting severe marriage disciplines to prevent Quaker children from marrying outsiders."[16] Reading between the lines of the local Society of Friends Monthly Meeting minutes highlights the impact this notion of kinship had on Martha's life. The minutes record that members of the congregation questioned Thomas about his relationship with Martha, and when he did not deny paternity, the meeting removed him from full membership.[17] It would have been possible for Thomas and Martha to mend this rift, had they complied with Quaker standards, but Martha's apparent continued connection to Anglicanism made that impossible. She had their son, Daniel, christened in the Church of England under her maiden name in 1810.[18] Despite seeming religious differences, the couple continued their relationship, but they did not marry until nearly three years later. They married in the Church of England in November 1812, eight months after Thomas's father's death—the timing suggesting that his father's disapproval might have been the central obstacle in making their relationship official.[19] The location of their marriage, however, does not reveal much about their religious beliefs. Between 1754 and 1837, all marriages in England and Wales (except those between Quakers or between Jews) had to be performed in the established church and by a regularly ordained Anglican minister. An Anglican ceremony was the only legal marriage available to Martha and Thomas since they were not in good standing with the Quakers.

The Tewkesbury Quaker records reveal that whatever Martha's religious beliefs, her marriage to Thomas brought a continued association with Quakerism, and thereby with Thomas's family who were also attending Quaker meetings. Those kinship connections, and those maintained with her family of origin, were important to the young Browetts over the coming years. Over the next nine years, they had five additional children, one of whom died as an infant. All of those births were registered with the local Friends' meeting despite neither parent being in full membership.[20] Though the family remained in Tewkesbury where Thomas had a large extended family, Martha's proximity to the Browetts did not prevent her from maintaining ties with her parents and siblings who lived a few miles away, if later involvement with LDS proxy baptisms for her family members is any indication. Maintaining connections with both families would have been typical and essential to the survival of Martha and Thomas's household. Because English couples typically established their own households upon marriage, those households could be particularly fragile if one of the couple was incapable of working. Buttressing such households required strong relationships across households: people who could loan money, apprentice children, and provide resources in time of need.[21] Though no record of it survives, it was probably through such connections that Martha and Thomas apprenticed their teenage sons to a local carpenter, tailor, gardener, and dairyman, respectively, and their daughter to a seamstress.

Even with the support of other households, the death of a spouse could drastically alter a family's outlook, as Martha discovered with Thomas's unexpected death in 1824 when he was only thirty-seven years old.[22] This left Martha with five children between the ages of three and fourteen. Thomas's will left Martha with some resources, mostly their household goods, or the money those goods could produce if she had to sell them. The will also suggests Martha continued to enjoy the support of his siblings and Quaker associates who lived in Tewkesbury; a brother, along with one of Thomas's Quaker friends, acted as trustees of Thomas's will.[23] However, with so many children and years of care and training to provide, Martha would have been concerned about providing for them for the duration. Parish registers from her hometown, a few miles from Tewkesbury, show that, within a few months of Thomas's death, Martha had the children baptized Anglican. Since she was not in full membership with the Friends, who provided support for their poor, she perhaps had the children baptized in the established church as a contingency if she ever needed poor relief, which was administered via the state church.[24] Again, with so little documentary evidence, it is difficult to untangle whether Martha's actions can be attributed to purely religious convictions or to the need to have instrumental as well as spiritual kinship.

Martha's religious convictions between 1825 and 1840 cannot be determined from surviving evidence, but her extended kin were making large changes to their religious practices and affiliations. According to a list of local preachers, in the late 1830s Martha's son Daniel and his wife, Elizabeth Harris, along with some of Elizabeth's extended family, were circuit preachers with the United Brethren, a sect of Primitive Methodists centered at the borders of Herefordshire, Worcestershire, and Gloucestershire.[25] Similar to many Protestant sects of the time, Methodists emphasized spiritual kinship and the bonds of friendship between fellow believers.[26] It is not known whether Martha was involved with the group, but if she was involved, perhaps its sense of spiritual kin and combination of doctrines appealed to her in a way Quakerism had not. In any event, it would have been hard for her to avoid interaction with the United Brethren because there were hundreds of members based in the small villages along the Severn River, south of Tewkesbury.

Whatever Martha's connection to the United Brethren, the group itself experienced enormous changes in 1840. The LDS apostle Wilford Woodruff had begun his missionary work in England in January 1840 and had already spent time in Staffordshire when he felt called to travel to Herefordshire to preach. Recent converts recommended him to their relations who lived in that county—kinship connections thereby laying the foundation for religious connections. There he encountered the United Brethren and met an enthusiastic reception—the vast majority converted to Mormonism in short order.[27] This rapid inclusion of the majority of United Brethren adherents is partially explained by their shared notions of spiritual kinship. Like other contemporary Protestants, both missionaries and converts viewed themselves as joining a godly family, being "adopted" into the proselytizer's spiritual family.[28] Woodruff was particularly enthusiastic about this concept, describing those he converted in familial terms: "The first fruits of my ministry . . . are bound to me closer than the ties of consanguinity."[29] By late spring 1840, three of the Browett women (Martha, Elizabeth, and Martha Rebecca), along with some of their in-laws, cousins, and siblings, had joined the Mormons.[30] References to the Browetts in Woodruff's journal kept at the time, as well as a journal entry from 1881 that states he baptized Elizabeth's brother in 1840, indicate that the lasting friendship between the Browetts and Woodruff augmented their spiritual kinship. Daniel and Elizabeth were particularly close to him, regularly having him stay with them for long visits and writing him letters once he left Gloucestershire.[31] The Browett women were literally among the "first fruits" Woodruff spoke of, and, at least for Elizabeth, spiritual kinship with Woodruff bore fruit for decades to come.

Elizabeth Harris was born and christened Anglican in 1813 and grew up some five miles from where the Browetts were living.[32] From letters written later in life, we learn that as a young woman she helped care for her nieces and nephews, particularly Charles Robert Bloxham, her sister's oldest child.[33] She probably met Daniel Browett via his close friendship with her older brother. After five years of "keeping company," she married Daniel in 1834, when they were already involved with Methodism.[34] The overlap between her sibling relationships, religious convictions, and marital choices was not unusual. Siblings were important across the lifespan, and during adolescence and young adulthood, they heavily influenced one another's social, political, and religious views.[35] Similarly, they consistently sought each other's advice about marital choices. Marrying her brother's friend and both of them participating in the United Brethren with cousins and siblings strengthened the bonds between family members and between coreligionists.

While three of the Browett women were connected to each other as soon as the 1820s, the last woman, Harriet Barnes (who eventually became Daniel's plural wife), was living at a distance of some twenty miles from where the Browetts and Harrises lived. She was born in 1808 and was also raised in a nonconformist family—though of a Congregational bent instead of Methodist.[36] She married Elijah Clifford in 1835, and they encountered Mormonism shortly after the Browetts did; from a missionary's diary it appears they converted to Mormonism in the first half of 1840.[37] By so doing, they acquired a large network of spiritual kin. Missionary journals show the Browetts and the Cliffords regularly hosting and conversing with Mormon missionaries, and associating with hundreds of other recent converts, throughout that year and into early 1841.

Conversion to Mormonism dramatically altered the daily rhythms of Browett family life because it almost immediately brought geographic separation. Estate agent papers show that the Browetts, and connected families, were already preparing to depart for America by the end of 1840, when they began to auction off their household goods.[38] Martha, Elizabeth, Martha Rebecca, Daniel, and their relations (including two of Elizabeth's siblings and their spouses) started for America in early 1841, traveling up the Mississippi River and arriving in Nauvoo, Illinois, in April 1841, leaving behind Martha's other three sons, aged between twenty and twenty-six, who remained at least nominally Anglican.[39] Later census and birth records hint that despite the religious differences and geographic distance, the family maintained amicable contact for years to come. One of Martha's sons who remained in England named children after Daniel and Martha Rebecca in the 1840s and 1850s.[40]

It is not clear when Harriet traveled to Nauvoo, but she was there by March 1845, when she received her patriarchal blessing. What happened to her husband, Elijah Clifford, is also unknown. While the details of Harriet's life between her conversion in early 1840 and her receipt of her patriarchal blessing in 1845 cannot be traced, it is possible to piece together a likely scenario. She appears in the England 1841 census with Elijah, but while there is a man in Nauvoo who matches the scant details known about Elijah, there is no immigration record for either him or Harriet. Whether Elijah died or he and Harriet parted ways, it is likely that she was in Nauvoo by 1843—the probable date for her marriage, as a plural wife, to Daniel Browett.[41] Even if Elijah survived, Harriet's lack of further contact with him suggests that the marriage may have dissolved before her marriage to Daniel in the way many marriages, particularly on the frontier, informally ended.

At the time of their arrival in the United States, the three younger women were all childless, and at least two of them were unmarried, but Nauvoo was about to offer them all a host of spiritual kin connections and a sacralized understanding of their existing relationships with their in-laws and siblings. The America the Browetts encountered was a decidedly Mormon one. The Mormons, fleeing conflict and persecution in Missouri, had settled Nauvoo in late 1839. The Browetts and connected families arrived just as Joseph Smith's revelations about proxy ordinance work for the deceased were solidifying; a January 1841 revelation read at the April general conference just prior to the Browetts' arrival described the necessity to build a temple, including a font where baptisms on behalf of the dead could be performed. And in rhetoric that would continue in the Browett women's lives long after they left Nauvoo, the revelation blurred the lines among spiritual, eternal, and earthly kinship and associations; discussions about building the Nauvoo House—Joseph Smith's family residence and a boarding house for visitors—were colored with the same revelatory language used to describe the temple.[42]

The Browetts' first encounter with Mormonism's elaboration of sacralized kinship occurred when they obtained patriarchal blessings in Nauvoo. Martha and Elizabeth were the first of the Browett women to participate in this revealed practice within their new faith. They received patriarchal blessings in October 1841, the same day as Daniel; Elizabeth's sister-in-law and sister followed suit within three months, with Martha Rebecca following an additional three months later and Harriet some four years later.[43] For the younger three women—childless Elizabeth and Harriet and unmarried and childless Martha Rebecca—promises about their posterity (a common feature of the blessings) could have rung hollow. However, patriarchal blessings combined with the timeless kinship promised via proxy ordinances meant those promises did not need to be confined by time or death. Elizabeth was promised that her and her husband's "Names shall be honored for Ever" and that she would "be blessed with posterity" in the first of three patriarchal blessings she received.[44] That posterity was not necessarily confined by biology; patriarchal blessings were the first Mormon ritual to explicitly tie members to a priestly kinship, pronouncing the person's spiritual lineage as a descendant of a tribe of Israel under the hands of a spiritual father (patriarch).[45] At the same time, however, they did not completely jettison biological kinship—recipients' parents (often including mothers' maiden names) were listed at the beginning of the blessing.

The Browetts arrived in Nauvoo just as another aspect of Mormonism's sacred kinship system was falling into place: baptisms for the dead. Joseph Smith had been preaching the idea since 1840, but he had been working for years before to resolve the Christian necessity for baptism and the apparent injustice of denying salvation to those who were not baptized while alive.

Smith's own losses and grief for deceased family members undergirded the desire for revelation and answers.[46] And he was not alone in this desire—once the doctrine was preached, the Saints rushed to perform baptisms for their deceased friends and family in the Mississippi River.[47] Elizabeth immediately acted as proxy for her brother who had died the day before Wilford Woodruff began baptizing members of the United Brethren and four days before Elizabeth herself was baptized into the LDS Church. Similarly, Martha was baptized for her parents and deceased siblings.[48]

Martha and Elizabeth's early enthusiasm for baptism for the dead, which also functioned as a way of adopting deceased ancestors into Mormonism's priestly family, suggests that the idea of eternal families resonated with them because they saw a spiritual way to perpetuate the broad and useful kinship network they had enjoyed in England. Their new faith now offered a similarly rich, supportive kinship network across time and distance, and now even across death. Death did not dissolve the bonds and shared connections of siblings and parents. Instead proxy work thickened these bonds with a spiritual, priestly, exalting capacity.

In addition to patriarchal blessings and baptisms for the dead, the Browett women engaged in temple rituals that began to be elaborated upon in the early 1840s. They participated in both endowment ceremonies and husband-wife sealing ceremonies (both monogamous and polygamous). Temple endowment rituals "amplifi[ed] . . . concepts behind baptisms for the dead" by initiating men and women with priestly powers and linking them to all other priesthood-bearing men and women, past, present, and future.[49] At the end of 1845 and beginning of 1846, the Browett women, and their kin, were endowed in the temple, as were hundreds of Saints just as they fled Nauvoo, again due to conflict with and persecution by their neighbors.[50] Beyond establishing connections with their immediate family, endowment and sealing rituals brought them into the spiritual kinship of God's family, a sibling-based spiritual kinship as Quakerism and Methodism had done but now coupled with an understanding that such kinship connections were eternal and were *essential* for exaltation. In Samuel Brown's words, Mormonism not only "plac[ed] humans beside God" but also "position[ed] humans durably with other humans."[51]

Similarly, sealing of husbands to wives was linked to creating heavenly, eternal families endowed with and bound by priestly power. Sealing linked spouses, but it was not simply a marriage ceremony. Sealing brought holiness and sanctification to individuals via their sacred priesthood bond with one another.[52] And sealing brought all similarly sealed people into one grand family—one large, divine kinship. The complex practice—and teachings surrounding the practice—of plural marriage is further illuminated by this context. For while teachings about polygamy did not grapple with the possibilities of unattached men, plural marriages did create a path for all women to participate in saving and exalting rituals, no matter their original marital status. As Samuel

Brown has elucidated, "polygamy is the marital amplification and application of adoption theology. 'Plural' not only indicated that there would be multiple wives . . . but that such ritual marriages would unite worshippers as part of the celestial plurality of . . . heaven."[53] In this context, polygamy was as much about expanding the reach of God's family as it was about marriage.

Though documentation for Daniel and Elizabeth's sealing does not survive, it is likely that it occurred around the same time Martha Rebecca was married and sealed to an apostle, Orson Hyde, early in 1843. It is also likely that Daniel was sealed to Harriet at the same time.[54] Many of the early sealings done in Joseph Smith's red brick store in 1842 and 1843 were reconfirmed in the Nauvoo Temple in 1846 (as Martha Rebecca's was). However, Elizabeth's and Harriet's sealings to Daniel do not appear there or in other known accounts of the early 1843 sealings. Elizabeth's later behavior—referring to Harriet as Daniel's plural wife and never sealing herself for eternity to another man—suggests she was already sealed to Daniel. Similarly, Harriet used the Browett surname when she was endowed in January 1846, suggesting she had already been sealed. While Harriet used the Clifford surname for her patriarchal blessing in 1845, using both married and previous names was not uncommon for plural wives at the time.[55] Taken together, these bits of evidence suggest that the Browett women were among the first to participate in eternal and plural sealings. That early participation was, at least in part, facilitated by their previous experiences with patriarchal blessings and proxy baptisms, as well as by lasting social ties with Wilford Woodruff. It was further assisted by their lifelong association with broad and instrumental kinship—where family ties were essential to survival.

The instrumental aspect of kinship was of even greater importance as the Browetts joined their fellow saints in fleeing Nauvoo for temporary refuge along the Missouri River between Iowa and Nebraska in 1846.[56] After the murder of Joseph Smith and his brother Hyrum in the summer of 1844, tensions had run high between Mormons and their neighbors, culminating in the Latter-day Saints' mass exodus from Nauvoo. Such a large group migration required cooperation—cooperation that leaders explicitly tied to the sacred rituals that symbolically bound all of the Saints together.[57] And the Saints, including the Browett women, seemed to have taken those connections seriously. According to letters written to Orson Hyde's wives, Martha Rebecca and her mother, despite the secrecy surrounding the practice of polygamy, were not isolated from the other Hyde households in Nauvoo and Iowa. The other wives incorporated the elder Martha into their family and referred to her as "Mother Browett."[58] Additionally, Harriet's use of the Browett surname when she was endowed in January 1846 and her presence in Martha's household in Winter Quarters at the end of that year (listed as Harriet Clifford) suggest that all the women maintained close ties with one another—residential ties that reified relationships with other women they had acquired when they entered plural marriage.

In addition to the general disruption of fleeing Nauvoo, trudging across Iowa in the winter of 1846, and suffering in Winter Quarters (near present-day Omaha, Nebraska), the latter half of the 1840s was a personally trying time for all the Browett women, but for Elizabeth in particular. Her kinship network was about to undergo dramatic alterations. In what must have felt like a miraculous turn of events, she had a son in September 1845, her first child in eleven years of marriage. In addition to her own son, Elizabeth maintained close ties with her Harris nieces and nephews (children of her siblings who had converted to Mormonism when Elizabeth did) and continued to act as a surrogate mother for her sister Dianah's children, particularly the teenaged Charles Robert, whom she had helped raise since his infancy. Disruptions in family life started when both Daniel and Elizabeth's brother Robert joined the Mormon Battalion in the summer of 1846.[59] But that was just the beginning of her difficulties; Elizabeth's connection to her brother was one of the few things to survive the next three years. First, along with so many others that fall and winter, her sister Dianah died in September or early October 1846 after a prolonged illness.[60] Then Elizabeth's son died in November 1846, leaving her childless once again. While in Winter Quarters, other relationships persisted; Elizabeth, Harriet, and Elizabeth's sister-in-law, Maria (who was expecting her seventh child), assisted one another and were also helped by a neighbor in their husbands' absence.[61] The spiritual and biological continued to collide in practical and supportive ways.

In letters to their wives sent in September and October 1846, Daniel and Robert emphasized their kinship connections and their desires to be reunited. The letters also hint at ways blessings and temple ordinances bound them across space and even across death. Daniel assured Elizabeth that her sister Dianah's death, after years of suffering, was a relief because of a "pronunciation upon her" of an unspecified blessing. Robert reminded his wife to "be faithful and not forget the things which you and I heard and seen [sic] in the Temple of the Lord."[62] Their fellow Saints emphasized their spiritual kinship connections to one another during the exodus to Iowa and the overland trail experiences of the late 1840s. The ubiquitous presence of familial language on the trail was encouraged by Church leaders who emphasized adoption sealings—the binding of Church members to leaders, and thereby their priestly families.[63] The Browett women did not participate in those early adoptions, but in all other ways they continued to believe and hold on to spiritually reified kinship ties.

From Winter Quarters, Elizabeth and Harriet traveled to Salt Lake City in the fall of 1847, in anticipation of meeting Daniel returning from the Mormon Battalion.[64] But he never returned; he was murdered in June 1848 in the Sierra Mountains while scouting a trail for other Battalion veterans returning from Sutter's Fort to Salt Lake.[65] Elizabeth and Harriet probably learned of his death directly from other returning Mormon Battalion veterans; Martha and

Martha Rebecca probably learned of it via letters (those letters do not survive, but another woman's letters indicate that the sisters-in-law corresponded while Martha Rebecca was in Iowa and Elizabeth in Utah).[66] That loss was compounded in the coming years. The following year, 1849, Harriet returned to Iowa, intending to come back to Utah, but she died during the return journey in 1850.[67] She probably encountered Martha and Martha Rebecca while she was there, as they remained in the Kanesville (later Council Bluffs) area until they migrated to Salt Lake City late in the summer of 1852.

Despite being part of an apostle's family at the center of Mormon leadership and despite continued connection with Elizabeth, Martha Rebecca's encounter with Mormonism was more complicated than the other Browett women's, and she seems to have been less enthusiastic for elements of Mormonism's reimagined kinship than the others were. She, too, had received a patriarchal blessing but, tellingly, six months later than her mother, brother, and sister-in-law. A few months later, she also learned of plural marriage and became Orson Hyde's third wife in early 1843, bringing her into an aspect of the Church not yet widely practiced or acknowledged.[68] According to an 1859 letter from Hyde to Martha Rebecca, the lack of recognition as a wife was particularly galling to her, but the tension between polygamy and the surrounding culture's celebration of monogamous marriages was not unique to Martha Rebecca.[69] As in many of the early, secret polygamous marriages, Martha Rebecca and Orson's union was not smooth—a situation that caused "considerable anguish."[70] This is understandable, as marriage was central to women's social identities in the nineteenth century and had been for centuries. And Martha Rebecca was not alone; polygamy put strain on even the strongest and most resilient of relationships.[71]

It is not known if the birth of her daughter in April 1850 made the situation better or worse, but the child's death three months later put more strain on the marriage than Martha Rebecca could withstand. Despite living near other members of Hyde's family, she did not officially use the Hyde surname, and she and her mother were listed as a separate household in the 1850 census.[72] If the outsider perspective found in letters written to Martha Rebecca and her sister-wives is accurate, Martha Rebecca's relationship with the other wives offered a version of inclusion and belonging, an essential element for any polygamous marriage that hoped to function.[73] In Martha Rebecca's case, however, the secrecy added a pressure to her marriage that does not seem to have been present in Elizabeth's and Harriet's plural marriage. Unlike Martha Rebecca, her sisters-in-law had had over a decade of monogamous marriage behind them before they entered polygamy. Martha Rebecca's first introduction to marriage, however, was to join a marriage that already had established routines and rhythms. She was also marrying for the first time in a period of intense valorization of monogamous marriage as the epitome of womanhood.[74]

According to the 1859 letter, the tension surrounding Martha Rebecca's desire to be publicly recognized as a wife and the continued pressures associated with plural marriage eventually became untenable; Orson Hyde recommended a divorce, even suggesting an alternative spouse for Martha Rebecca: the recently widowed Thomas McKenzie.[75] Hyde and Martha Rebecca divorced informally (and without altering their temple sealing), and she married McKenzie, in a ceremony officiated by Hyde, on December 9, 1850, in Kanesville.[76] There is no record that explains this unusual circumstance, but since the marriage was civil only, perhaps the combination of an eternal sealing to Orson, a formal separation from him, and a civil marriage to Thomas gave Martha Rebecca both priestly/spiritual connections and a publicly recognized marriage. The recognized marriage also brought with it the chance for children who lived in a household with their father (Thomas had a young daughter from his previous marriage). Combined, these factors seem to have been her motivation in marrying McKenzie. Martha Rebecca used the McKenzie surname, lived, along with her mother, in Thomas's household in Iowa, and migrated together with him and her mother in 1852. But the marriage did not last. In Church divorce files, there are two brief entries confirming her official divorces from both Hyde and McKenzie within weeks of her arrival in the Salt Lake Valley.[77] It is not clear why she divorced McKenzie. It should be noted, however, that divorce was relatively common and available in early Utah, due to the recognition of the pressures of polygamy and a desire to have incompatible couples remarry and have children with a more suitable spouse.[78]

While Martha Rebecca was struggling with her marital and maternal status in the late 1840s and early 1850s, Elizabeth was undergoing her own transition. In July 1849, she married a Mormon Battalion veteran, William Johnstun, a man more than ten years her junior, and they, along with her nephew Charles Robert, decamped for California as part of the "gold mission" not long afterward.[79] It is not clear whether William Johnstun had been officially asked to join the few other missionaries called to this "mission" to mine gold and return it to LDS Church leaders in Utah in order to support settlement there, but he and Elizabeth seemed to have been there with the Church's acknowledgment.[80] While most gold missionaries left for the more traditional proselytizing mission fields of Hawaii in 1850, the Johnstuns, including William's brother, remained. Elizabeth, who was also bereft of her sister-wife, Harriet, who died in 1850, had been anxious to get to California in the hopes of finding Daniel's remains, which had been buried by other returning Battalion members who found Daniel and his two slain companions at a place they named Tragedy Spring.[81] She spoke of the desire openly in 1849 to one of Brigham Young's plural wives and continued to dwell on it when she wrote Young and Woodruff in 1856.[82]

For a woman who was not literate enough to sign her own 1834 marriage record, Elizabeth left two remarkable letters behind. Sometime before she wrote the letters in May 1856, she had learned basic writing skills, and in so doing, she provided the only firsthand account from any of the Browett women. The letters show how unhappy she was in the gold fields, mostly because she was isolated from family—both biological and spiritual. The letters, in combination with diary entries of a missionary returning from Polynesia in 1857, show she had been ill most of the years she had been in California, she had not heard the gospel preached in years, and William's religious devotion did not seem to match the depth of her own. Those general disappointments were compounded in the spring of 1856 when Charles Robert died at only twenty-four years old. His death was the impetus behind the two letters, one to Brigham Young and his wife and the other to Wilford Woodruff and his wife (she did not stipulate which wives she was addressing). In addition to her grief over Charles Robert's death, she felt abandoned by her brother, who had not responded to her many letters, and neglected by her spiritual "father," Woodruff. She longed to return to Salt Lake City and the communion of the Saints. The communion she most longed for centered on the temple and the spiritual kinship offered via its associated rituals.

Many Church members had been sealed, by adoption, to Church leaders in the late 1840s, and many of those relationships functioned temporally as well as spiritually.[83] But Elizabeth seemed to be operating beyond those confines—she was not merely seeking a link to priesthood-holding leaders. Analyzing the language she used reveals how important the possibility of eternal kinship, whether marital, biological, or adopted, had become for Elizabeth. She begged Young for news of the temple under construction in Salt Lake and pleaded to return. "I wants to com [*sic*] back," she wrote, "to do my work for my ded [*sic*]."[84] She also wrote Woodruff about her desire to complete temple work for Daniel. At the time, the only work available for the dead was baptism (performed in the recently erected Endowment House in Salt Lake), something Daniel did not require.[85] Despite the practice waning after 1847, she might have been referring to an adoption sealing, however, because in the same letter she told Sister Woodruff about the loss of Charles Robert and asserted "that Browett wanted him," suggesting she wanted to seal Charles Robert to herself and Daniel. She also seemed to consider herself permanently connected to Woodruff; beyond referring to him as her father, she recounted to Young that while in England she had washed the elders' feet, probably a reference to a ritual she performed for Woodruff in echo of the spiritual kinship between Christ and his apostles. She also told Woodruff that she had followed the advice he had given her when they met on the trail to Utah, that she "was not to promis to go into nother [*sic*] family."[86]

Despite these connections and her desire to further participate in temple rituals, Elizabeth remained with William, but, as an account from a visiting missionary reveals, she "felt overjoyed" the following year when Mormon missionaries returning from Polynesia stopped to preach and visit with local members. She reveled in having more of her spiritual kin around her. She had "quite a comfortable chat" with them one night and had them administer a blessing to her when she was ill. While there they also rebaptized William, who "expressed a desire to live his religion."[87] Shortly after this visit, Elizabeth, William, and six other Saints left northern California for San Bernardino, but they did not linger long there, returning to Utah due to the threat of the Utah War and Brigham Young's request for outlying settlements to gather to central and southern Utah.

Meanwhile, Martha Rebecca, twice divorced and childless, and her mother settled in Salt Lake City and, according to census records, often boarded with other families. But Martha Rebecca had not quite given up on marriage. Sometime in 1858 or 1859 she wrote Orson Hyde about the possibility of remarrying him and rejoining the family. Polygamy was now openly practiced; perhaps she assumed the marriage would work better without the pressure of secrecy. She may have also been seeking stability for herself and her aging mother (who was seventy-seven at the time). Or perhaps she was partially motivated by the lingering effects of the Mormon Reformation, particularly the call for expanded polygamy.[88] Her letter to Hyde does not survive, but Hyde's response does, and its tone and content suggest reasons why the remarriage never occurred. He admonished her for her insistence during those early days on being publicly acknowledged as his wife. He proposed allowing her to remarry him, as long as she agreed to his "conditions": that she not complain about "former troubles and difficulties" and that she acknowledge his "will must be the law of [his] family." He ended the letter in a more sympathetic tone, stating he could not look "with indifference, upon any woman who, through my agency, has endured the afflictions of a mother."[89] In the end, Martha Rebecca apparently spurned his conditions and they never remarried; she and her mother continued to board in others' homes in Salt Lake City. After her mother's death, Martha Rebecca continued boarding in homes until her own death in 1904.[90] For Martha Rebecca, the eternal possibilities embodied in Mormonism's intertwining of family, priesthood, and salvation did not fully compensate for difficult marital relations.

Martha died on August 15, 1865, and was buried in the Winchester family plot in the city cemetery.[91] Her inclusion in the Winchester family was due to her marriage on August 13 to Stephen Winchester, a seventy-year-old polygamist member of the First Quorum of the Seventy, who already had three living wives.[92] She spent two days, at the age of eighty-three, as a plural wife; the last act she accomplished before her death was to connect herself to a priestly, spiritual marriage and kinship.[93] From the sparse bits of information recorded in the Endowment House register and the cemetery records, Martha's belief in Mormon teachings that conflated marital sealings, posterity, and salvation is revealed.[94] Participating in a sealing as her last mortal act underscores an acceptance of a purported teaching of Joseph Smith: that unless men and women were married eternally during mortality, they would "cease to have increase when they die."[95] For a woman who lost one child as an infant and lived to see most of her other children live beyond the capacity to have children, or die without children of their own, the possibility of eternal increase must have had special resonance.

On the other hand, Martha Rebecca's lack of participation in proxy or adoption sealings for herself or others, other than her marriage to Orson Hyde, reveals a different response to expansive aspects of Mormon familial cosmology. Among the Browett women, she seems to have been the one who struggled the most with Mormonism's practical and spiritual kinship, though she maintained her membership and participation in the Church. As the youngest of the group and the one most likely influenced by early Victorian attitudes about romantic couplehood and a narrow definition of family that focused on the nuclear family and motherhood at the expense of broader kinship networks, her struggle is not surprising. Scholars have emphasized that one of the pressures of polygamy was the disconnect between its contours and the Victorian ideals of monogamous marriage.[96] That disconnect helps explain Martha Rebecca's difficulties.

How much of those difficulties can be attributed to Martha Rebecca's personality and how much was a function of her circumstances is difficult to know. But shifts in LDS teachings about families and their eternal structure changed the context of Martha Rebecca's final years. First, the practice of polygamy officially ended in 1890, and the practice of adoption sealings officially ended in 1894. In the place of adoption sealings, Wilford Woodruff revealed a new approach to Mormon eternal kinship. Instead of being sealed to priesthood-holding men, Latter-day Saints would now search out their own ancestors and perform proxy ordinances for them. Early baptisms for the dead had already emphasized individuals' intimate relationships with family and friends, but Woodruff's elaboration of this principle ushered in a new era in Mormon understandings of their place within their families and the eternities. If baptism, priesthood, and temple endowments and sealings could be bestowed on the dead, then everyone could be stitched together into one large heavenly family; finding and connecting to those deceased ancestors became imperative.

Martha Rebecca died in 1904, a decade after Woodruff's revelation. Four years after that, another woman performed proxy temple ordinances on Martha Rebecca's behalf, sealing her to her biological parents. The woman who acted as proxy, Persis Louisa Young Richards, was herself a plural wife who had had only one child, a child who died in infancy, and she seems to have known Martha Rebecca well enough to know her birthplace and date and details about her marriage and death.[97] She knew Martha Rebecca's brother's and mother's details as well. She did not know Martha Rebecca's father's information, or correct name, but she knew he had died in the 1820s. It is possible Persis researched Martha Rebecca, but this seems unlikely given that Martha Rebecca had died poor and without kin and was not prominent enough to appear in many public or church records. It is more likely that Persis knew Martha Rebecca personally and acted on her wishes. The details she provided about the Browett family suggest Martha Rebecca gave Persis the information and that maybe, in the end, Martha Rebecca was more drawn to the newer practice of sealing to one's biological family than she ever was to the adoptive sealings of the previous century.[98]

Unlike her sister-in-law, Elizabeth Harris was consistently involved with Mormon practices centered on kinship. She and William Johnstun settled in Kaysville in northern Utah near her brother and sister-in-law and remained there for several years. A personal history and William's application for a military pension produced decades later illuminate Elizabeth's complicated marital story. In 1863, she agreed to William's decision to marry an additional woman, Ellen Jane Perks. However, Ellen was not comfortable being a second wife, so Elizabeth agreed to divorce William. They divorced on January 9, 1864, just over two weeks before he married Ellen.[99] As Elizabeth continued to refer to her deceased husband as "my dear Browett" eight years after his death, and seven years into her marriage with William, it appears that their marriage did not conform to Victorian ideals of a romantic match. It must have functioned well enough for them to stay married, but William was probably concerned he would not have children if he did not marry an additional wife. Elizabeth was fifty and beyond whatever limited fertility she had; William was thirty-nine, and Ellen was not quite twenty—they had every likelihood of becoming parents. As posterity was doctrinally entangled with discussions of priesthood and exaltation, the desire for children was shared by Elizabeth and goes a long way to explain the seemingly amicable, though unusual, shift in her marital status. The new Mr. and Mrs. Johnstun moved to southern Utah/Nevada as part of a settlement mission known as the Muddy Mission, and Elizabeth retained ownership of the Kaysville house.[100] But her connections to the Johnstuns did not end there.

In the mid-1860s, Elizabeth's marital and maternal statuses underwent unusual changes that reflect her beliefs about the flexibility of eternal kinship and its echoes in mortal family relationships. In 1867, William, Ellen, and their young daughter returned to Salt Lake; the couple was sealed in the Endowment House in March of that year. They then traveled on to Kaysville and stayed with Elizabeth for an extended visit. According to a personal history written by Ellen, Elizabeth, who had remained childless since the death of her son in 1846, "was devoted" to Ellen and William's children and asked if she could become William's plural wife and join the family, to which Ellen "gave [her] consent."[101] Sealings, both for spouses and for children to parents, allowed Elizabeth to think of marriage in flexible terms as well as hope the eternities would bring the children she could not have in mortality.

Similar to her mother-in-law, Martha, Elizabeth's actions demonstrate a belief in the possibilities of "eternal increase" that would compensate for mortal childlessness. Plural marriage to William offered a version of mortal motherhood she had tasted only briefly in Nauvoo and only vicariously with Charles Robert. While she did not see William as a substitute for Daniel (her "eternal" spouse), a plural sealing to William for mortality allowed her to participate in motherhood, a motherhood not defined by biology or confined by Daniel's death.[102] Even biological children born before their parents were sealed had to be "adopted" to the family just as nonbiological relations did; spiritual kinship was more meaningful and longer lasting than biological relationships alone.[103] This context is behind Elizabeth and William's sealing in July 1867.[104] In August, while still in Kaysville, Ellen gave birth to a son. Elizabeth, weeping while walking the floor with the baby, was overheard to say, "I'm so happy for we have a boy."[105] By being sealed to the Johnstuns, Elizabeth was sealed to their children and joined in a shared motherhood. This echoed the childrearing she had shared with her sister and sister-in-law in England, Nauvoo, Winter Quarters, and Utah. This familiar practice meant that for Elizabeth plural marriage became a mechanism that bound her to children and brought with it the potential for motherhood in the eternities, a motherhood that was intertwined with divinity.[106]

Now connected to the Johnstuns by a sealing and in the practical ties of a shared household, Elizabeth's next few years were punctuated by movement and by efforts to maintain ties with spiritual kin in her local congregations. They, along with Elizabeth's brother and one of his sons, spent the next few years at the Muddy Mission, north of present-day Las Vegas.[107] Always fraught with difficulties, not the least of which was discovering that they had settled on the Nevada side of the border and the state wanted five years' back taxes, the mission was abandoned in 1870. Before they left the Muddy Mission, Elizabeth was rebaptized in 1870—a common occurrence in the middle decades of the nineteenth century when Mormons reaffirmed their faith by undergoing an additional baptism.[108] Reemphasizing her spiritual kinship underscores the deep meaning Elizabeth found in her connections to spiritual kin as well as biological and marital ties, a system of connections Samuel Brown has described as the "Mormon Chain of Belonging."[109]

As she aged, Elizabeth's place within that chain of belonging increasingly revolved around her Harris family—her brother's widow and children. For the next two decades, she shuttled between the Johnstun family as they moved to southern Utah and Arizona and her Harris family in northern Utah.

She was rebaptized again in 1877 in Kaysville, along with her widowed sister-in-law, Maria.[110] After Maria's death in 1888, Elizabeth moved between her nieces' and nephews' homes in Kaysville and Portage on the Utah-Idaho border. By the time of her death in 1899, her ties with the Johnstuns had waned. Ellen claimed Elizabeth left them once polygamy ended in 1890, but Elizabeth seems to have been more connected to her Utah kin before then. It is possible that William and Ellen's move to New Mexico in 1883 was too great a distance for Elizabeth, either due to age (she turned seventy that year) or distance from her nieces and nephews in Utah, or perhaps distance from a temple. In any event, by the mid-1880s she lived exclusively among her Utah relations, who cared for her in her declining years.[111] As her eyesight failed her and her health declined, they housed her, wrote her account for the jubilee celebration of the pioneers of 1847, and eventually wrote her obituary.

Elizabeth's desire to perform temple work for her dead began in Nauvoo, remained important to her even when isolated in California, and was finally possible with the completion of the St. George Temple in 1877.[112] Temple records describe not only that proxy work was performed but highlight how Elizabeth saw her place within Latter-day Saint cosmological, and familial, priesthood. In the 1870s and 1880s, she engaged in multiple proxy sealings. She started sealing her deceased sisters and others to Daniel as eternal sister-wives in 1878—just after the completion of the St. George Temple and under Wilford Woodruff's direction. Woodruff, who was president of the St. George Temple and who became church president in 1887, was much more enthused about adoption sealings than Young had been, and the newly completed temple allowed, for the first time, access to the full spate of temple ordinances for the dead.[113] In this way, Elizabeth participated in the shift toward "temple consciousness"—an increased awareness of, and participation in, proxy temple work as a marker of unique Mormon identity and purpose—that occurred during Woodruff's presidency.[114]

Elizabeth eagerly participated in this early phase of widespread adoption sealings. In the late 1880s, when she lived in northern Utah and southern Idaho, she took advantage of the newly finished Logan Temple to continue to perform proxy work. Three of the four women Elizabeth sealed as wives to Daniel were her close relations: her sister, her mother (whom she also sealed by proxy to her father), and a woman who was most likely her niece. In addition, she acted as proxy for the posthumous sealing of her brother, who had never joined the LDS Church, to his wife.[115] She also had herself, her sister Dianah (listed as Browett, not Harris or her married name, Bloxham), Daniel, and his plural wife Harriet all sealed as children to Wilford Woodruff in 1879, the person she had considered her spiritual father for the better part of three decades.[116] In addition, after more than a twenty-year wait, she had baptism and confirmation ordinances performed for Charles Robert at the same time.[117]

Unlike her male leaders who were concerned with the spiritual social climbing and jealousy expressed in some attitudes about adoption sealings, Elizabeth used adoption to deepen connections with people she was already connected with, whether that connection was biological, marital, sealed, adopted, or spiritual.[118] She cared about kinship, not connections to powerful leaders. She was anticipating the post-1894 practice of emphasizing connecting biological families via temple rituals but without its exclusion of nonbiological relationships.

In her final years, Elizabeth simultaneously sustained ties of social and spiritual kinship with the living. She maintained strong ties with the local Saints, who called her "Aunt Browett," and local newspapers recounted her speaking in tongues on more than one occasion in large Church meetings.[119] Though no official documentation survives, a personal account of a student suggests she began the first school in west Layton.[120] She also wrote a poetic tribute to Wilford Woodruff upon his death.[121] When she died in 1899, one obituary lauded that she was "universally respected."[122] And in the end, her original kinship echoed one last time for Elizabeth—she was buried beside her brother and sister-in-law in the Kaysville cemetery.[123]

Elizabeth's example shows the most complex understanding of spiritual kinship and cosmological priesthood among the Browett women. Her persistent attachment to Daniel has all the elements of nineteenth-century romantic matches, but her broad understanding of family and kinship shows elements of both preexisting, expansive ideas of kinship and the remapped version found in Mormonism's cosmological, priestly family. Long before she converted to Mormonism, Elizabeth shared the responsibility of raising her nephew Charles Robert; additionally, her participation in Methodism's version of spiritual kinship and her shared religious conversions with her existing kin are some of the ways that she already worked in an inclusive kinship system. That practicality and inclusion were in turn channeled by early Mormonism's approach to family. Patriarchal blessings, proxy baptisms, sealings, plural marriages, and adoptions echoed and elaborated Elizabeth's lived experience. She emphasized kin connected to her by biology and by sealing/priesthood bonds: her nieces and nephews, the Johnstuns, Harriet, and Wilford Woodruff. Elizabeth neatly stitched together early modern ideas of friends and family as a large, flexible group to proxy baptisms, plural marriage, and adoption sealings. She fully embraced the astounding implications of Mormonism's claims about the "remarkable role other humans could play in the salvation drama."[124]

CONCLUSION

The details of the Browett women's lives reveal what it was like, at ground level, to make sense of Mormonism's radical reimagining of family ties. These four British converts to Mormonism brought their cultural traditions of broadly defined family ties with them when they joined the Saints in the United States. Their acceptance of patriarchal blessings, proxy baptisms, and sealings—polygamous, proxy, adoptive, eternal, and temporal—shows what cosmological priesthood looked like on the ground in women's lives. Sealings provided a way for the Browett women, childless and unmarried for long stretches of time, to build kinship for mortality and for eternity. In a time that reified marriage and childbearing for women and in a time when fewer than 3 percent of Utah women remained childless throughout their lives, these women's experiences with singleness and childlessness should have marginalized them.[125] However, their English kinship background combined with Mormon practices offered additional paths to socially and religiously supported kinship. If "childbearing" was listed as one of "the pleasures and duties of Mormon women," proxy temple work, adoptive sealings, and even polygamous sealings offered an alternative path not just to childbearing but to kinship more broadly.[126] Polygamy's potential attractiveness to women otherwise socially or emotionally marginalized has recently been recognized, but it was not just plural marriage that offered the Browett women access to Mormonism's capacious spiritual kinship.[127]

Polygamy was just one constellation within a cosmological priesthood, but it did not encompass that new cosmos. Mormon leaders had asserted since the 1830s and 1840s that baptism for the dead brought salvation to all and that sealing ordinances brought exaltation via family connections.[128] Through temple rituals "all of humanity could be interconnected in indissoluble connections." Such a "sacerdotal genealogy" encompassed all those bound by temple sealing rituals, no matter their earthly kinship relationships.[129] Mormon priesthood, intertwined as it was with notions of a functional and spiritual kinship that bound even the unmarried and the childless into the family of God for the eternities, "offered a metaphysical substitute" kinship for women as well as men.[130]

Martha and Elizabeth's efforts at proxy baptisms, Martha's marriage sealing two days before her death, Elizabeth's remarriage in order to have a shared motherhood and her proxy sealing to Wilford Woodruff, and even Martha Rebecca's consideration of remarrying Orson Hyde suggest that the Browett women found resonance in a cosmological priesthood. Mormonism did not create an expansive family for the Browett women—they already had that—but it sacralized familial and social bonds in day-to-day life and extended those ties across time and eternity.

NOTES

1. For Latter-day Saints, "sealing refers to the marriage of a husband and wife and to the joining together of children and parents in relationships that are to endure forever. This special

type of sealing of husband and wife in marriage is referred to as 'eternal marriage' or 'celestial marriage.' It contrasts with civil and church marriages, which are ceremonies . . . only for the duration of mortal life. The sealing together of husband, wife, and children in eternal family units is the culminating ordinance of the priesthood." See Paul Hyer, "Sealing: Temple Sealings," in *Encyclopedia of Mormonism*, ed. Daniel H. Ludlow (New York: Macmillan, 1992), http://eom.byu.edu/index.php/Sealing#Sealing:_Temple_Sealings.

2. I have included all the women's marital names to indicate just how complex their marital histories were. For simplicity, however, for the remainder of the chapter I will refer to them primarily by their first names—as tracking just which surname applied at any given point would needlessly complicate the narrative.

3. Jonathan A. Stapley, "Adoptive Sealing Ritual in Mormonism," *Journal of Mormon History* 37, no. 3 (Summer 2011): 60–61.

4. Stapley, "Adoptive Sealing Ritual," 56.

5. Kathleen Flake, "The Development of Early Latter-day Saint Marriage Rites, 1831–53," *Journal of Mormon History* 41, no. 1 (January 2015): 89–90.

6. Stapley, "Adoptive Sealing Ritual," 60.

7. Stapley, "Adoptive Sealing Ritual," 61.

8. Stapley, "Adoptive Sealing Ritual," 62.

9. Craig Muldrew, *The Economy of Obligation: The Culture of Credit and Social Relations in Early Modern England* (Houndmills, England: Palgrave, 1998), 121–72; Mary S. Hartman, *The Household and the Making of History: A Subversive View of the Western Past* (Cambridge: Cambridge University Press, 2004); Adam Kuper, *Incest and Influence: The Private Life of Bourgeois England* (Cambridge, MA: Harvard University Press, 2009).

10. Ruth Perry, *Novel Relations: The Transformation of Kinship in English Literature and Culture 1748–1818* (Cambridge: Cambridge University Press, 2004).

11. Naomi Tadmor, *Family and Friends in Eighteenth-Century England: Household, Kinship, and Patronage* (Cambridge: Cambridge University Press, 2001).

12. Samuel M. Brown, "Early Mormon Adoption Theology and the Mechanics of Salvation," *Journal of Mormon History* 37, no. 3 (Summer 2011): 11, 13, 15. This sense of adoption was more figurative than the literal sense Mormons come to preach in the second half of the century.

13. Martha Pulham, christening June 23, 1782 (birth June 4, 1782), Church of England, Bishop's Cleeve, Gloucestershire, England, Bishop's Transcripts, Family History Library (hereafter FHL) film 417123, Salt Lake City, UT.

14. Raefaella Sarti, "Forum: Domestic Service since 1750," *Gender and History* 18, no. 2 (August 2006): 187–98; Hartman, *Household*, 1–69; Bridget Hill, *Servants: English Domestics in the Eighteenth Century* (Oxford: Clarendon Press, 1996).

15. Richard Brown, *Society and Economy in Modern Britain 1700–1850* (New York: Routledge, 1991), 24; Richard Adair, *Courtship, Illegitimacy, and Marriage in Early Modern England* (Manchester: Manchester University Press, 1996), 92–109.

16. Barry Levy, *Quakers and the American Family: British Settlement in the Delaware Valley* (Oxford: Oxford University Press, 1988), 51.

17. Society of Friends, Gloucester Monthly Meeting Minutes, October 24, 1809, November 21, 1809, and January 23, 1810, GA D1340 B2/M4/7/19/2.

18. Daniel Pulham, christening, April 22, 1810, Church of England, Bishop's Cleeve, Gloucestershire, Bishop's Transcripts, FHL film 417123.

19. Thomas Browett and Martha Pulham, marriage, November 30, 1812, Church of England, Bishop's Cleeve, Gloucestershire, parish registers, GA P46.

20. Society of Friends, Quarterly Meeting Birth Register, Gloucestershire, 1642–1857, Gloucestershire Archives, Gloucester, England, (GA) D1340/A1/R1.

21. Rosemary O'Day, *The Family and Family Relationships, 1500–1900: England, France, and the United States of America* (New York: St. Martin's, 1994).

22. Joanne Bailey, *Unquiet Lives: Marriage and Marriage Breakdown in England, 1660–1800* (Cambridge: Cambridge University Press, 2003).

23. Thomas Browett, will, written March 10, 1824, proved May 7, 1825, GA GDR Wills 1825/90.

24. Thomas Browett, burial, March 14, 1824, Friends' Burial Ground, Tewkesbury, Gloucestershire, England, Society of Friends Gloucestershire Quarterly Meeting Burial Registers, FHL film 812211; Christenings of Martha and Thomas Browett children, October 1, 1825, Church of England, Tewkesbury, Gloucestershire Parish Registers, 1595–1873, Baptisms and Burials, 1779–1847, FHL film 856927; Patricia Crawford, *Parents of Poor Children in England, 1580–1800* (Oxford: Oxford University Press, 2010).

25. "United Brethren Preachers' Plan of the Frooms Hill Circuit, 1840," 284.6 U58p 1840, Church of Jesus Christ of Latter-day Saints Church History Library, Salt Lake City, UT (hereafter LDS Church History Library); V. Ben Bloxham, James R. Moss, and Larry C. Porter, *Truth Will Prevail: The Rise of the Church of Jesus Christ of Latter-day Saints in the British Isles, 1837–1987* (Salt Lake City, UT: Church of Jesus Christ of Latter-day Saints, 1987), 136–40; Carol Wilkinson, "The Restoration of the Gadfield Elm Chapel," in *Regional Studies in Latter-day Saint Church History: The British Isles*, ed. Cynthia Doxey, Robert C. Freeman, Richard Neitzel Holzapfel, and Dennis A. Wright (Provo, UT: Religious Studies Center, Brigham Young University, 2007), 41–59.

26. Cynthia Aalders, "'Your Journal, My Love': Constructing Personal and Religious Bonds in Eighteenth-Century Women's Diaries," *Journal of Religious History* 39, no. 3 (September 2015): 386–98; Brown, "Early Mormon Adoption Theology," 10–11, 13.

27. The United Brethren converts were just one part of a large LDS missionary effort in mid-nineteenth-century Britain. Thousands joined the Church and immigrated to Utah between 1837 and the end of the century. See Stephen J. Fleming, "The Religious Heritage of the British Northwest and the Rise of Mormonism," *Church History* 77, no. 1 (March 2008): 73–104; Malcolm Thorp, "Religious Backgrounds of Mormon Converts in Britain, 1837–1852," *Journal of Mormon History* 4 (1977): 51–66; Richard L. Jensen and Malcolm Thorp, *Mormons in Early Victorian Britain* (Salt Lake City: University of Utah Press, 1989).

28. Brown, "Early Modern Adoption Theology," 19.

29. Wilford Woodruff, "President O. Cowdery, Dear Brother," *Messenger and Advocate* 3, no. 3 (December 1836): 432, quoted in Brown, "Early Mormon Adoption Theology," 19.

30. Wilford Woodruff, Baptismal Record, 1840, FHL film 889347, item 6; Joseph Smith, *History of the Church of Jesus Christ of Latter-day Saints* (Salt Lake City, UT: Deseret Book, 1978), 4:134–35, 147, 297, 300; Scott G. Kenney, ed., *Wilford Woodruff's Journal 1833–1898* (Midvale, UT: Signature Books, 1983–1985), 1:450, 456, 458–60, 479, 488, 492, 549–50; 2:30. It is difficult to identify the exact baptism dates for the other women due to inconsistent record keeping in early LDS missionary and membership records.

31. Wilford Woodruff, journal, ed. Scott G. Kenney, vol. 1, typescript, March–August 1840, BX 8670.1.W868jo 1983, LDS Church History Library, Salt Lake City, UT; Wilford Woodruff, London, November 13, 1840, to Daniel Browett, George A. Smith papers, box 4, folder 5, LDS Church History Library, Salt Lake City, UT.

32. Elizabeth Harris, christening, June 16, 1813, Church of England, Sandhurst, Gloucestershire Parish Registers, 1537–1921, FHL film 991298, item 3.

33. Elizabeth Johnstun, Salmon Falls, California, to Brigham Young, Salt Lake City, May 1, 1856, CR 12341, Brigham Young Incoming Correspondence, 1839–1877, box 25, folder 1, images 46–48, LDS Church History Library, Salt Lake City, UT.

34. Mormon Battalion (Mexican-American War) Pension File, Elizabeth Browett application (widow of Daniel Browett), original no. 12509, can no. 278, bundle no. 27, Deposition June 13, 1895, in Ogden, UT, FHL film 480132; Ernest A. Lister and Rev. Arthur S. Lister, transcribers and collators, *The Leigh Parish Register Transcripts* (England, 1925), FHL film 91309.

35. Leonore Davidoff, *Thicker Than Water: Siblings and Their Relations, 1780–1920* (Oxford: Oxford University Press, 2011); Amy Harris, *Siblinghood and Social Relations in Georgian England: Share and Share Alike* (Manchester: Manchester University Press, 2012).

36. According to the patriarchal blessing index, Harriet was the daughter of Thomas and Esther Barnes. While she reported her birth year as 1810 or 1811, the best match for her is an Anglican christening in 1808. However, her parents had their other children (born 1811–1821) baptized in an Independent Chapel. See Church of England, Blaisdon, Gloucestershire Parish Registers, Gloucestershire Archives, P49 IN 1/2, digital image at "Gloucestershire, England, Church of England Baptisms, Marriages and Burials, 1538-1813," www.ancestry.co.uk; Mitcheldean Independent Chapel (Mitcheldean, Gloucestershire), Births, Baptisms, and Burials, RG-4 series no. 764, 13, 14, 16, and 19, FHL film 595449, item 10.

37. Elijah Clifford and Harriet Barnes marriage, December 25, 1835, Church of England, Hempsted, Gloucestershire, Bishop's Transcripts, GA GDR/V1/370, digital image accessed August 13, 2015, https://www.ancestry.co.uk, accessed August 13, 2015; James Barnes, missionary diary, 1840–1841, MS 1870, LDS Church History Library, Salt Lake City, UT.

38. Moore and Sons of Tewkesbury [Gloucestershire], estate agents, sales and valuation books, 1840–1841, GA D2080, vol. 555.

39. Ship *Echo*, United States, Immigration and Naturalization Service, passenger lists of vessels arriving at New Orleans, 1820–1945, NARA Series M259, Roll 20, FHL film 200148.

40. Thomas David Browett (1815–1865) married Harriet Simpson in 1846 and had four children. Among those children were Harriet Rebecca (1848–1852), Thomas Daniel (1850–1859), and Isabella Rebecca (1855–1908).

41. The Church of Jesus Christ of Latter-day Saints, *Early Church Information File* (card index), Harriet Barnes Clifford entry, FHL film 1750668. Twentieth-century accounts of Harriet claim that she was a widow when she was sealed to Daniel, but a man somewhat matching Elijah Clifford's description lived in Nauvoo and later settled in Salt Lake City. If this is the same Elijah Clifford, it is possible that Harriet was one of several early plural wives who were also simultaneously married to two men. There is an Elijah Clifford of approximately the right age who was in the Quorum of the Seventy in Nauvoo, in Winter Quarters with the Saints, and in the first big company of migrants to Utah in the fall of 1847 (the same company as Elizabeth and Harriet). However, it is not clear whether this man was born in England and therefore a match for Harriet's husband. Darryl Harris, *Life History of Robert Harris, Jr., and Hannah Maria Eagles Harris, Daniel Browett, Elizabeth Harris Browett* (Idaho Falls, ID: self-published, 2002), 10.

42. Alex D. Smith, "Organizing the Church in Nauvoo: D&C 124, 125," *Revelations in Context*, June 10, 2013, https://history.lds.org/article/doctrine-and-covenants-organizing-nauvoo?lang=eng.

43. The Church of Jesus Christ of Latter-day Saints, *Early Church Information File* (card index), Browett entries, FHL film 1750663; The Church of Jesus Christ of Latter-day Saints, *Index to Patriarchal Blessings 1833–1963*, FHL film 392639.

44. Elizabeth Harris Browett, patriarchal blessing, September 13, 1841, Nauvoo, IL, vol. 4, p. 16, LDS Church History Library, Salt Lake City, UT.

45. Brown, "Early Mormon Adoption Theology," 20–28.

46. Richard E. Turley, "The Latter-day Saint Doctrine of Baptism for the Dead," BYU Family History Fireside, 2001, https://cfhg.byu.edu/pdf/firesides/2001-11-09.pdf; Brown, "Early Mormon Adoption Theology," 33, 35–36.

47. Ryan Tobler, "'Saviors on Mount Zion': Mormon Sacramentalism, Mortality, and the Baptism for the Dead," *Journal of Mormon History* 39, no. 4 (Fall 2013): 182–238.

48. William Harris, burial, March 23, 1840, Deerhurst with Apperley, Gloucestershire, England, parish registers, *Gloucestershire, England, Church of England Burials, 1813–1988*, accessed December 12, 2015, https://www.ancestry.co.uk; *The* Church of Jesus Christ of Latter-day Saints, Nauvoo Temple, Baptisms for the Dead, 1840–1845, FHL film 820152. In these early days of proxy baptisms, it was not uncommon for people to be baptized for deceased family members of either sex; the requirement that the living proxy be the same sex as the deceased person was a later development.

49. Brown, "Early Mormon Adoption Theology," 46.

50. The Church of Jesus Christ of Latter-day Saints, Temple Index Bureau, compiler, *Nauvoo Temple Endowment Register 10 December 1845–8 February 1846* (Salt Lake City, UT, 1974). FHL US/CAN 977.343/N1 K29c.

51. Brown, "Early Mormon Adoption Theology," 49.

52. Flake, "Development," 92.

53. Brown, "Early Mormon Adoption Theology," 38.

54. The Church of Jesus Christ of Latter-day Saints, Nauvoo Temple Sealing Records, 1846–1857, sealing of Orson Hyde and Martha Rebecca Browett, January 11, 1846, FHL Special Collections film 183374, p. 309; *Nauvoo Temple Endowment Register*, FHL US/CAN 977.3431 N1 K29c; Myrtle Stevens Hyde, *Orson Hyde: The Olive Branch of Israel* (Salt Lake City, UT: Agreka Books, 2000), 158, 497–98.

55. Kathryn Daynes, *More Wives Than One: Transformation of the Mormon Marriage System, 1840–1910* (Urbana: University of Illinois Press, 2001), 31.

56. William G. Hartley, "Council Bluffs/Kanesville, Iowa: A Hub for Mormon Settlements, Operations, and Emigration, 1846–1852," *John Whitmer Historical Association Journal* 26 (2006): 17–47.

57. Stapley, "Adoptive Sealing Ritual," 75–76.

58. Louisa Beaman, April 8, 1849, Salt Lake Valley, to Marinda, Martha, and Mary Ann Hyde, Iowa, in Todd Compton, "'Remember Me in My Affliction': Louisa Beaman and Eliza R. Snow Letters, 1849," *Journal of Mormon History* 25, no. 2 (1999): 51–53.

59. Norma Baldwin Ricketts, *The Mormon Battalion: U.S. Army of the West, 1846–1848* (Logan: Utah State University Press, 1996).

60. Daniel Browett, Santa Fe, October 17, 1846, to Elizabeth Browett, Winter Quarters, Mormon Battalion Correspondence Collection, MS2070, LDS Church History Library, Salt Lake City, UT.

61. Job Smith had worked for the Browetts in Nauvoo in 1844, and then he and his uncle assisted the Harris and Browett families during the summer of 1846 when Daniel and Robert joined the Mormon Battalion. See Job Smith, Diary and Autobiography, 1849–1877, pp. 50, 60, MSS 881, BYU L. Tom Perry Special Collections.

62. Daniel Browett, Santa Fe, October 17, 1846, to Elizabeth Browett, Winter Quarters, and Robert Harris, near Ft. Leavenworth, September 19, 1846, to Maria Harris, Winter Quarters, Mormon Battalion Correspondence Collection, MS 2070, LDS Church History Library, Salt Lake City, UT. All four women are referenced in the letters, along with a suggestion that some of them had written letters. Sadly, any letters from them do not survive.

63. Stapley, "Adoptive Sealing Ritual," 75–76.

64. Utah Pioneer Jubilee, *Semi-Centennial Book of Pioneers* (Utah, 1897), 110, FHL film 497713.

65. Ricketts, *Mormon Battalion*; B. H. Roberts, *Comprehensive History of the Church* (Salt Lake City, UT: Church of Jesus Christ of Latter-day Saints, Deseret New Press, 1930), 3:368–69.

66. Louisa Beaman, April 8, 1849, Salt Lake Valley, to Marinda, Martha, and Mary Ann Hyde, Iowa, in Compton, "'Remember Me in My Affliction,'" 49–54.

67. The Church of Jesus Christ of Latter-day Saints, "Mormon Pioneer Overland Travel, 1847–1868," database, LDS Church History Library (www.history.lds.org/overlandtravels), entry for Harriet Browett, June 8, 1850, Aaron Johnson Company; Harriet Browett's death, "From the Plains," *Frontier Guardian*, September 4, 1850, Kanesville, Iowa, Harold B. Lee Library, Special Collections, SCM 140, item 1, 2. Harriet appears in the 1850 census in Pottawattamie County, Iowa, despite it being recorded months after her death. This was due to the census taker enumerating several people who had left for Utah in the summer of 1850 (when the census taking was supposed to be completed). I wish to thank my research assistant, Rebecca Johnson, who puzzled out just what the census taker was doing. See Martha Browett household, 1850 US Federal Census, Pottawattamie County, Iowa, District 21, dwelling 816, digital image at www.ancestry.com.

68. Daynes, *More Wives Than One*, 20–28, 31; Hyde, *Orson Hyde*, 158, 497–98.

69. Brown, "Early Mormon Adoption Theology," 50.

70. Daynes, *More Wives Than One*, 26.

71. Paula Kelly Harline, *The Polygamous Wives Writing Club: From the Diaries of Mormon Pioneer Women* (Oxford: Oxford University Press, 2014).

72. Martha Browett household, 1850 US Federal Census, Pottawattamie County, Iowa.

73. Harline, *Polygamous Wives Writing Club*.

74. Jodi Vandenberg-Daves, *Modern Motherhood: An American History* (New Brunswick, NJ: Rutgers University Press, 2014), 11–31; Stephanie Coontz, *The Social Origins of Private Life: A History of American Families, 1600–1900* (New York: Verso, 1988).

75. Given the transient nature of frontier life, this "divorce" seems to have been similar to the ways many marriages officially, but informally, ended. Hendrik Hartog, *Man and Wife in America: A History* (Cambridge, MA: Harvard University Press, 2000), 29–30.

76. Pottawattamie County, Iowa, Early Marriage Records, 1848–1869, Marriage Licenses, December 9, 1850, FHL film 1476888, item 1, p. 80.

77. Brigham Young Papers, divorce files, Martha Rebecca Browett, November 16, 1852 (from Orson Hyde) and October 26, 1852 (from Thomas McKenzie), LDS Church History Library, Salt Lake City, UT; information provided by Randall Dixon (Church archivist), e-mail to author, September 15, 2008.

78. Daynes, *More Wives Than One*, 142–43, 163.

79. Compton, "Remember Me in My Affliction," 53; Eugene Edward Campbell, "The Mormon Gold Mining Mission of 1849," *BYU Studies* 1, no. 2 (1959–1960): 19–31.

80. William James Johnstun file, no. XC2664739, *Selected Pension Application Files for Members of the Morman [sic] Battalion, Mexican War, 1846–48* (Washington, DC: National Archives and Records Service, 1934), FHL US/CAN Film 490139.

81. Ferol Egan, "Incident at Tragedy Springs: An Unsolved Mystery of the California Trail," *American West* 8, no. 1 (1971): 36–39; Elizabeth Johnstun, Salmon Falls, California, to Brigham Young, Salt Lake City, May 1, 1856.

82. Louisa Beaman, April 8, 1849, Salt Lake Valley, to Marinda, Martha, and Mary Ann Hyde, Iowa, in Compton, "Remember Me in My Affliction," 53.

83. Stapley, "Adoptive Sealing Ritual," 75–76.

84. Elizabeth Johnstun, Salmon Falls, California, to Brigham and Sister Young, Salt Lake City, May 1, 1856, CR 12341, Brigham Young Incoming Correspondence, 1839–1877, box 25, folder 1, images 46–48, LDS Church History Library, Salt Lake City, UT.

85. After the Saints fled Nauvoo, they did not have a building wherein they could perform temple rituals. Along the trail and once in Utah, various rituals were performed in a variety of places, and a more lasting solution was found by constructing the Endowment House in Salt

Lake City in 1855. See Lisel G. Brown, "'Temple pro Tempore': The Salt Lake City Endowment House," *Journal of Mormon History* 34, no. 4 (Fall 2008): 1–68.

86. Elizabeth Johnstun, Salmon Falls, California, to Wilford and Sister Woodruff, Salt Lake City, May 1, 1856, CR 12341, Brigham Young Incoming Correspondence, 1839–1877, box 25, folder 1, images 46–48, LDS Church History Library, Salt Lake City, UT; Stapley, "Adoptive Sealing Ritual," 80.

87. Frederick William Hurst, diary, May 8–12, 1857, compiled by Samuel H. and Ida Hurst (1961), transcribed by Joyce Holt (2001), joyceholt.4t.com/FWHurst/FWHhome.html.

88. Paul H. Peterson, "The Mormon Reformation of 1856–1857: The Rhetoric and Reality," *Journal of Mormon History* 15 (January 1989): 549–87; Thomas G. Alexander, "Wilford Woodruff and the Mormon Reformation of 1855–57," *Dialogue: A Journal of Mormon Thought* 25, no. 2 (Summer 1992): 25–38.

89. Orson Hyde, Salt Lake City, to Martha Rebecca Browett, Salt Lake City, February 28, 1859, Romania Jeanette Hyde Woolley Collection, MS 9681, folder 2, LDS Church History Library, Salt Lake City, UT.

90. Sarah Pearson household, 1900 US Federal Census, Salt Lake City, Salt Lake, Utah, ED 10, sheet 2A, 775 East 4th Street; Martha Browitt [*sic*], death certificate, Utah Office of Vital Records and Statistics, Utah State Archives—Utah History Research Center, Series 81448, Reel 2, certificate 630; Salt Lake City, Utah Cemetery Records, 1848–1992, accessed June 4, 2008, https://www.ancestry.com.

91. It is not known how Martha knew the Winchesters. Stephen and his wife, Nancy, had lived in the Nauvoo Third Ward in the 1842 census, as had Martha, and they both lived in Salt Lake City (though their proximity to one another is not known).

92. David J. Whittaker, "East of Nauvoo: Benjamin Winchester and the Early Mormon Church," *Journal of Mormon History* 21, no. 2 (1995): 31–83.

93. The Church of Jesus Christ of Latter-day Saints, Endowment House, sealing records, vol. C & D, FHL Special Collections film 183395; The Church of Jesus Christ of Latter-day Saints, *Millennial Star* (1865), 27:768, FHL film 1402732; Salt Lake County Death Registers, pre-1898, Utah State Archives—Utah History Research Center, Series 21866, reel 1, entry 188; Salt Lake City, Utah Cemetery Records, 1848–1992, accessed June 4, 2008, https://www ancestry.com.

94. Flake, "Development," 77–103.

95. Quoted by William Clayton in Gary Bergera, "The Earliest Eternal Sealings for Civilly Married Couples Living and Dead," *Dialogue: A Journal of Mormon Thought* 35 (Fall 2002): 48.

96. Harline, *Polygamous Wives Writing Club*, 11–60.

97. Maureen Ursenbach Beecher and Lavina Fielding Anderson, eds., *Sisters in Spirit: Mormon Women in Historical and Cultural Perspective* (Urbana: University of Illinois Press, 1992), 167; Martha Rebecca Browett Hyde sealing to parents, September 11, 1908, The Church of Jesus Christ of Latter-day Saints, Salt Lake Temple Sealings of Children to Parents, 1893–1942, FHL Special Collections film 1239612, Book H, p. 275.

98. If the shift to sealing children to their ancestors instead of to Church leaders was the more appealing factor for Martha Rebecca, she shared it with many of her fellow Saints. According to Jonathan Stapley, the year after the policy change, proxy parent-child sealings increased 675 percent compared to the previous year. See Stapley, "Adoptive Sealing Ritual," 96, 112.

99. Ellen Jane Perks Johnstun, "Personal History," submitted by Agnes J. Rose, Salt Lake City, Daughters of Utah Pioneers Museum (DUPM); William James Johnstun file, no. XC2664739, *Selected Pension Application Files*, FHL film 480139.

100. Audrey M. Godfrey, "Colonizing the Muddy River Valley: A New Perspective," *Journal of Mormon History* 22, no. 2 (Fall 1996): 120–42.

101. Ellen Johnstun, "Personal History."

102. Bergera, "Earliest Eternal Sealings," 63–64.

103. Stapley, "Adoptive Sealing Ritual," 64.

104. The Church of Jesus Christ of Latter-day Saints, Endowment House Sealing Records, vol. E, p. 47, FHL Special Collections film 1149515.

105. Ellen Ashcroft Kleinman, comp., "History of Ellen Jane Perks Johnstun, Handcart Pioneer of 1856," DUPM.

106. Flake, "Development," 93–94.

107. Ellen Johnstun, "Personal History."

108. The Church of Jesus Christ of Latter-day Saints, St. Thomas, Nevada, Record of Members, 1865–1933, FHL film 14924. Rebaptism as a sign of rededication was common for those called on colonizing missions. H. Dean Garrett, "Rebaptism," in *Encyclopedia of Mormonism*, ed. Daniel H. Ludlow (New York: Macmillan, 1992), 1194.

109. Samuel M. Brown, "Early Mormon Chain of Belonging," *Dialogue: A Journal of Mormon Thought* 44, no. 1 (Spring 2011): 1–52.

110. The Church of Jesus Christ of Latter-day Saints, Kays Ward Membership Records, 1851–1939, FHL film 26050.

111. Mary Ann Parkinson Harris, life story, ca. 1930s, Utah, transcript in possession of the author.

112. She was not the only one with such a long-lasting desire. See Brown, "Early Mormon Adoption Theology," 4.

113. It should be noted that access to living or proxy work was forbidden to those of African descent until 1978. Elizabeth's interaction and appreciation of Mormonism's expansive ideas about family was a decidedly white experience in the 1870s and 1880s.

114. Richard Bennett, "Wilford Woodruff and the Rise of Temple Consciousness among the Latter-day Saints, 1877–84," in *Banner of the Gospel: Wilford Woodruff*, ed. Alexander C. Baugh and Susan Easton Black (Provo, UT: Religious Studies Center, Brigham Young University; Salt Lake City, UT: Deseret Book, 2010), 233–50.

115. Proxy sealing of Hannah Harris and Daniel Browett, December 5, 1878, St. George Temple, FHL Special Collections film 170596; Proxy sealing of Eleanor Davis and Daniel Browett, March 1, 1879, St. George Temple, FHL Special Collections film 170597; Proxy Sealing of Susannah Harris and Daniel Browett, March 6, 1889, Logan Temple, FHL Special Collections film 178062; Proxy sealing of Sarah Harris and Daniel Browett, and proxy sealing of John Harris and Elizabeth Gillett, December 4, 1890, Logan Temple, FHL Special Collections film 178062.

116. Proxy sealings of Daniel Browett, Elizabeth Harris Browett, Harriet Browett, and Diana Browett as children to Wilford Woodruff and family and Maria Marks Harman as representing the female line, March 1, 1879, St. George Temple, FHL Special Collections film 170583.

117. Proxy baptism of Charles Robert Bloxham, December 3, 1878, St. George Temple, FHL film 170847 and March 4, 1879, St. George Temple, FHL film 170848.

118. Stapley, "Adoptive Sealing Ritual," 77, 85, 87–88, 91.

119. "Kaysville Ward Relief Society minutes and records," Kaysville Ward, North Davis Stake, Church of Jesus Christ of Latter-day Saints, LR 4531 14, May 28, 1878, LDS Church History Library, Salt Lake City, UT; "Layton Lines," *Davis County Clipper*, June 5, 1896, and March 10, 1898, Utah Digital Newspapers, https://newspapers.lib.utah.edu.

120. Dan and Eve Carlsruh, eds., *Layton, Utah: Historic Viewpoints, Kaysville-Layton Historical Society* (Salt Lake City, UT: Moench Printing, 1985), 125, 128.

121. Elizabeth Browett Woodruff, poetical tribute to Wilford Woodruff, Wilford Woodruff Papers, reel 2, box 2, folder 16, LDS Church History Library, Salt Lake City, UT. Note that while the item is cataloged, it is closed to research.

122. "Woman Pioneer Dead," *Salt Lake Herald*, March 8, 1899, Utah Digital Newspapers, https://newspapers.lib.utah.edu.

123. Davis County Death Registers, 1898–1904, Utah State Archives—Utah History Research Center, Series 84244, reel 1; *Cemetery Records and Index of Utah* (Salt Lake City, UT: Genealogical Society of Utah, 1943–1955), FHL US/CAN 979.2 V3c.

124. Brown, "Early Mormon Adoption Theology," 40, 47, 49.

125. M. Skolnick et al., "Mormon Demographic History I: Nuptiality and Fertility of Once-Married Couples," *Population Studies* 32, no. 1 (March 1978): 5–19; S. Philip Morgan, "Late Nineteenth- and Early Twentieth-Century Childlessness," *American Journal of Sociology* 97, no. 3 (November 1991): 784–85.

126. Rolander Guy McClellan, *The Golden State: A History of the Region West of the Rocky Mountains: Embracing California, Oregon, Nevada, Utah, Arizona, Idaho, Washington Territory, British Columbia, and Alaska, from the Earliest Period to the Present Time . . . with a History of Mormonism and Mormons* (n.p.: W. Flint, 1876), 677. Harvard University, Google-Books, accessed May 10, 2009.

127. Laurel Thatcher Ulrich, "Runaway Wives, 1830–1860," *Journal of Mormon History* 42, no. 2 (April 2016): 1–26; Laurel Thatcher Ulrich, *A House Full of Females: Plural Marriage and Women's Rights in Early Mormonism, 1835-1870* (New York: Knopf, 2017).

128. Gordon Irving, "The Law of Adoption: One Phase of the Development of the Mormon Concept of Salvation, 1830–1900," *BYU Studies* 14, no. 3 (Spring 1974): 293.

129. Brown, "Early Mormon Adoption Theology," 5–6.

130. Brown, "Early Mormon Adoption Theology," 29; Flake, "Development," 89–90.

Chapter Five

Poetry in the *Woman's Exponent*

Constructing Self and Society

Amy Easton-Flake

In the pages of the *Woman's Exponent*, we find a back-and-forth conversation between Mary J. Tanner and Emily Scott that showcases how women came to one another's aid and drew strength and comfort through one another's words. What contemporary readers may find surprising about this conversation is that it is written entirely in verse. In "I'll Lay by the Harp," Tanner expresses an oft-found theme in Mormon women's poetry of the difficulty of being able to write because of the many time demands and life difficulties these women face:

> But my hands have grown weary with many a task,
>   And my heart has grown heavy with waiting.[1]

Tanner fears her poems have not captured the visions she wishes to impart and consequently resolves to relinquish her poetic ambitions:

> Then I'll lay by the harp, for its strings are undone,
>   And the sound of its music is dying;
> The hopes I have cherished have passed one by one,
>   And their fragments around me are lying.

Seeing this poem in the *Exponent*, Scott writes a poem to assure Tanner that her poetry is

> Lighting a path for others to tread,
>   Aye, the light of a guiding star.
> A morning star for youth's glad spring,
>   To pilot a voyage of life;
> A beacon light to the wayfaring,
>   Seen above sin and strife.[2]

Scott also assures her that her poetry is powerful not in spite of her trials and experiences as a woman but precisely because of them. In an ensuing poem, Tanner then expresses the strength she gains from Scott's poem.

> And how often a friend true assistance may lend,
>   The weary and faint to uphold;
> For a word of true love, comes like balm from above,
>   And light to our vision unfolds.[3]

Tanner subsequently commits to renew what she sees as her poetic mandate:

> I will hold to the task that is given;
> And point to the star that is shining afar,
>   Guiding to God—and to heaven.

From this poetic conversation, we gain access to these women's thoughts and feelings as well as insight into the social role poetry played in America at this time. During the past ten years, literary scholars have begun to offer compelling studies demonstrating poetry's expansive and central place in nineteenth-century America, while historians have largely continued to overlook the insights poetry offers into people, culture, and events.[4] This dismissal of poetry is likely a legacy of the "new critical" approach to poetry, which constructed the literary critic as an "expert" who could unlock the meaning of poetry in ways not accessible to those untrained in the method. The modernist view of poetry as an ambiguous, "apolitical and asocial aesthetic object" has also obscured its usefulness to historians.[5] Reading contemporary notions of poetry onto nineteenth-century poems is unfortunate and limiting, particularly for historians of nineteenth-century women, as poems were a primary medium of expression and communication for women in that period. Consequently, the focus of this chapter is to exhibit what historians will gain by recognizing poems as legitimate and valuable primary sources, using the case study of Mormon women's poetry found in the *Woman's Exponent* from 1872 to 1914. Analyzing poetry from the *Exponent*, I illustrate how poems construct and promote the ideologies and collective identity Mormon women worked within; how poems provide unique access into women's interiority; and how poems reveal questions and experiences left obscure in other sources because the subject material was often deemed too personal, sacred, or transgressive for other mediums. When we view poems as our nineteenth-century subjects did, we will readily embrace the insights they offer into collective groups and individual points of view; to aid in this process, I begin with an overview of nineteenth-century poetic conceptions.

NINETEENTH-CENTURY CONCEPTIONS OF POETRY

As historians, we will be most interested in approaching poetry from an understanding of nineteenth-century conceptions of poetry and of how poems functioned in the lives of women. These perspectives often elude twenty-first-century scholars and readers because our understanding of poetics differs so markedly from our nineteenth-century predecessors. In the distinctly modern poetics of today, poetry is no longer part of everyday discourse; it is not taught in school except occasionally as an artifact, and its association with modernist aesthetics privileging irony, paradox, and ambiguity have caused it to be seen as "an autonomous discipline" inaccessible to most people.[6] In direct contrast, nineteenth-century poetry held a predominantly social function and was intended to impart moral, theoretical, or even practical knowledge. It was expected, as it always was until the advent of the twentieth century, to delight and to teach.[7] So while some nineteenth-century readers turned to poems for the literary and aesthetic pleasure they offered, Michael C. Cohen convincingly explains in his work *The Social Lives of Poems in Nineteenth-Century America* that many more individuals looked to "poems for spiritual and psychic well-being; adopted popular song tunes to spread rumor, scandal, satire, and news; or used poems as a medium for personal and family memories, as well as local and national affiliations."[8]

Sentimental poetry—characterized by its presentation of domestic, pious, and morally uplifting topics through smooth-flowing, regular meter and rhyme—was the dominant rhetorical mode in nineteenth-century America. And while both men and women wrote genteel, sentimental poetry, women writers and readers clearly dominated the American literary marketplace for most of the nineteenth century.[9] As Patricia Okker explains in her seminal work, "By establishing a market for periodicals by and for women, nineteenth-century women rejected the gendered public-private dichotomy and created the idea of a public sphere for women."[10] Poetry was a place where women created and validated their lived experience. As Janet Gray writes, "Forging the stories and icons of national identity, women writers and editors gave primacy to everyday life and human connection, building networks of community—centered on women and children."[11] In direct contrast to the modern poetics of today, where art is often regarded as "a separate realm with its own, sometimes antisocial, values and resonance," nineteenth-century women poets believed art was to provide memorable expression of familiar aspects of life. As Cheryl Walker further explains, "For the most part, these women saw their task as providing memorable expression for the prevailing sentiments of liberal Christianity, domestic piety, American nature romanticism, and nationalistic fervor."[12] Consequently, these poems are valuable historical sources as "they encode and transmit ideas pervading the . . . culture of their time."[13]

Readers most often understood women's poetry to be an extension of the writer herself. They believed the poet's life and works to be identical, even when they were not. Hence, poetry was often seen as a place to reveal rather than to mask an individual. Correspondingly, because of the elasticity of the medium and the elevated feelings it evokes, poetry was believed to capture events that may otherwise be difficult to express, such as love, death, mourning, and spiritual awakenings and identification. Knowing this, historians may turn to poetry to access an intimate picture of women's internal reality that allows us to see the many real questions with which individuals struggled and more accurately understand how women dealt with different life events.[14]

Important also to understand is that nineteenth-century poetry could at once be both a venue for personal disclosure and reflection as well as a social instrument and entrée into public discourse. Regarded as the province of women and occupying a position on the boundary between public and private worlds (because it was written in the private realm but published for public consumption), poetry became an acceptable place for women to express their views on society, politics, and theology.[15] Nineteenth-century women also recognized poetry's capacity to reach large audiences and appeal to their emotions, to personalize complex political and social situations, and to promote views without alarming readers.[16] Consequently, women used poetry because it was not only an acceptable but also a highly influential platform from which they could engage with pressing contemporary issues. Unfortunately, today the literary texts that furthered the proliferation of many ideas and the success of many movements are largely neglected or lost in our historical understanding of the period.

Because poetry held a primarily communicative function, poems also played an important role in building real and imagined communities.[17] Poetry of mourning, for instance, promoted a sense of cohesion within nineteenth-century reading communities, as they publicly offered words of consolation and sympathy.[18] Poems focused on everyday life also shaped and bound communities as they implicitly—and explicitly, at times—taught what it meant to be a part of a certain community. As Cohen cogently explains, "poetry [was] constitutive of public culture" because poems were able to reach a popular audience, carry ideas into people, popularize them, and unite people behind the ideals they professed. The succinct, rhythmic, memorable aspect of many nineteenth-century poems gave them "pride of place as carriers of group identity, collective history, and social meaning."[19]

When we view poetry from a nineteenth-century perspective—where poems are seen as a medium for personal and collective memories; an appropriate space for sharing one's political, social, and religious views; and an extension of women themselves—we may more readily see what nineteenth-century poems offer as legitimate sources of historical inquiry. While poetry's foregrounding of formal artifice and individual emotion presents layers of complexity in accepting poems as accurate portrayals of history or individuals,[20] the same could be said of most historical documents since a gap "always exists between what actually happened and our perceptions, memories, and narratives of what happened. Indeed, a large part of being human involves negotiating and evaluating the competing narratives that make up our experience of the world and its past."[21] For historians, this acknowledgment of the indeterminate gap becomes even more significant as we take seriously our task to gather information from diverse individuals and sources in hopes that, in sorting through all the different narratives, we can arrive at a better grasp of lived reality and what it meant and looked like to the people at the time.

POEMS IN THE *WOMAN'S EXPONENT*

The Mormon *Woman's Exponent* provides a rich case study in poetry as a historical source. The *Exponent* was the first journal "owned by, controlled by and edited by Utah ladies," and its stated impetus was to build one another through the "diffusion of knowledge and information" and to correct the "gross misrepresent[ations]" of Latter-day Saint (LDS) women found within the popular press by providing them with a means of representing themselves.[22] Latter-day Saint women had a complex and unique understanding of what it meant to be a woman in nineteenth-century America, but as recognized by the first editor of the *Woman's Exponent*, Louisa Lula Greene, they were often misunderstood and misrepresented by others. Consequently, she proclaimed, "Who are so well able to speak for the women of Utah as the women of Utah themselves? It is better to represent ourselves than to be misrepresented by others!"[23] As we look at how Mormon women have been represented (and most often misrepresented) in the century and a half since she penned these lines, we see how well placed her concern was. What is more intriguing, though, is how the journal through which she hoped to correct these "gross misrepresentations" in her day now provides historians with a powerful tool for correcting historical misrepresentations of Latter-day Saint women in late nineteenth-century and early twentieth-century America.

The *Exponent* was an eight-page, three-column, quarto newspaper issued bi-monthly for most of its forty-two-year run from 1872 to 1914. Never owned or officially sponsored by the LDS Church—although official Church leadership did approve of it—the *Exponent* was considered the organ of the Relief Society, the women's organization of the Church. It provided a space for women to express their viewpoints and interests. The first edition stated that "the aim of the journal will be to discuss every subject interesting and valuable to women,"[24] and a detailed index of its content over its forty-two years in print reveals that it lived up to its aim.[25] Topics of particular interest were women's rights and roles in the home, church, and community; suffrage; education for women; Church and Relief Society news; and defending polygamy and other aspects of Mormonism. Along with editorials and articles, it regularly published original poems, short stories, essays, biographical sketches, and obituaries, as well as reports from the other women's organizations in the Church and from local units of the Relief Society. The surprisingly dialogic views expressed in the *Exponent*'s pages provide scholars today with insight into the diverse opinions that existed in the Mormon community. While scholars such as Sherilyn Cox Bennion and Carol Cornwall Madsen have provided invaluable overviews of the rich material contained within the *Exponent*, much of its rich content remains unknown and undigested.[26] Not surprisingly, the poetry within the *Exponent* has been almost entirely forgotten.[27]

This is unfortunate, as poetry held a prominent place in both the Latter-day Saint community and the *Exponent*. Brigham Young, for instance, often requested Eliza R. Snow, one of his plural wives and the general president of the Relief Society, to write and read poems at important occasions and then at times had them printed and distributed. He also sent Snow's volume of poetry along with the Book of Mormon, the Doctrine and Covenants, and works of Parley P. Pratt and Orson Pratt in response to requests for Church literature on several occasions.[28] Jill Mulvay Derr and Karen Lynn Davidson note in their work on Eliza R. Snow's poetry that "occasionally, Snow's polemical political poems were picked up by eastern papers that featured them as 'a fair index of the view of the more orthodox Mormons.'"[29] This fact offers a quick illustration of the status accorded to poems in nineteenth-century America. Poetry was also an integral part of the *Exponent*. Similar to other women's journals in nineteenth-century America, the *Exponent* had a poet's corner in each issue. Located on the upper-left corner of the second page, the poet's corner featured over eighteen hundred poems, usually written by local women, during its forty-two-year run. Consequently, this poet's corner not only helped cultivate female literary ambition among Mormon women but also contributed to the journal's explicit goal of image correction of Mormon women "by offering abundant evidence of the sensibility, literary taste, and education of [these] women."[30] Even a cursory glance at the poems indicates that these women were aware of and influenced by a variety of poetic influences as they imitated neoclassical and romantic poets in using a variety of verse forms, including ballad stanzas, heroic couplets, blank verse, psalm-like prose poems, and short lyric patterns. Often the poetry appears to be more didactic and pragmatic than aesthetic, which was in keeping with the other public or journalistic poems of nineteenth-century America.[31] With this brief background in place, the question then becomes, what do these poems reveal about these women? How do poems supplement, augment, challenge, or re-inforce information learned within other sources? Nineteenth-century poems played a significant role in creating and promoting ideals and expectations for women, so that is where we begin.

POETRY'S CREATION OF AND
ACCESS TO IDEALS OF WOMANHOOD

Poem after poem in the *Exponent* gives us access to how Mormon women viewed themselves and each other—and by extension, how they viewed all women and their potential. Since Barbara Welter's seminal article in 1966 on true womanhood, numerous scholars have complicated Welter's findings and documented well nineteenth-century conceptions of American womanhood. While a few scholars have used poems as a small part of their source material, the vast majority have relied on advice literature and popular fiction to con-struct what they believe to be nineteenth-century America's conception of ideal womanhood. The ideals that have gained the most traction are Welter's "true woman," who is pious, pure, submissive, and domestic, and Frances Cogan's "real woman," who is intelligent, competent, self-sufficient, and physically fit.[32] While we may find poems in the *Exponent* that simply support each of these competing composites, we may also find a more complex and nuanced image of ideal womanhood—one clearly influenced by Mormon women's reli-gious beliefs—when we analyze poems in the *Exponent* collectively.

One of the most striking themes running throughout the poems is the deep respect these women have for one another. Female friendship was clearly central to these women's lives and identities just as it was to most women living in nineteenth-century America.[33] In hundreds of poems, they praise one another for their virtues and accomplishments. At times, the rhetoric raises these women to near epic status as authors insist that the righteousness of their poetic subjects exceeds that of biblical women:

> They are as noble women
>   As heaven ere smiled upon.
>
> There are none in ancient story
>   Excelling them in deeds;[34]

In other instances, poets would associate their poetic subjects with Christ: "Here are thy children, and grand children round thee / T' call thee their savior, and say thou art blest."[35] As illustrated here, religious overtones are often central to women's valorization of one another. Poets also often bemoan that the world does not recognize, let alone herald, these women and their labors, and call on one another to "acknowledge woman's worth."[36] As such, they participate in what Susanna Morrill sees as "a self-conscious and oft-expressed program by LDS women writers to acknowledge and praise the lives and roles of women within the community."[37]

While Morrill, Madsen, Derr, and others have already established this discourse of deep female bonds among nineteenth-century Mormon women,[38] poems written for public consumption are important additions to this conversation because, for nineteenth-century women, poems were often "the medium of their fellowship," and their poems helped shape and form collective identity and expectations.[39] Consequently, by discovering the expectations women established for themselves and others within their poems, we may access ideals as they were codified and recognize the central role women played in creating shared ideals for their community.

When we note the virtues and accomplishments consistently promoted in these poems, the expectation that women are to be doing good and helping those in need is the unmistakable dominant ideal. The words of one memorial poem—

How tender she was at the couch of pain,
    How willing her sisters to bless;
The poor felt her liberal hand in theirs;
    Her works were of righteousness.[40]

—may stand in for all, as woman's unselfish service is found at the center of every single memorial, tribute, and birthday poem. As such, these poems participate in the ideology of female benevolence readily found in the American press throughout the nineteenth century. The unrelenting pervasiveness of this ideal in Mormon women's poetry, however, indicates that this ideal remained absolutely essential to living up to late nineteenth-century Mormon women's self-created expectations, while in nineteenth-century America it was early in the century an expectation but later in the century more of a recommendation.[41] So integral to Mormon women's identity is helping others that the climax of many poems is a woman's ability to continue this service in the next life: "Then may her usefulness extend / Throughout all time. Life has no close!"[42]

The essential nature of unselfish, unrelenting service to Mormon women's ideal becomes clearer when we recognize that authors most often present service as the vehicle to developing the desired qualities of a saint and qualifying for eternal life with God:

Experience [serving others] has left behind
Its rare and radiant traces,
Enriching heart, and soul, and mind,
Thus adding loveliest graces,

Of sweetest sympathy and love,
Of wisdom, and humility,
Reliance on our God above
In faith, with hope and charity.[43]

This and countless other poems show the necessary qualities of a saint—kindness, obedience, humility, wisdom, and love—to be direct outgrowths of women's untiring service. In turn, poems present these saintly attributes as giving women the strength to overcome trials in this life and to stand as the vanguard in a battle against vice. As one woman wrote of another,

We have lost a standard bearer,
   Who was foremost in the fight;
True and tender, brave and loving,
   With a heart that loved the right;[44]

As these poems make clear, "womanly" qualities were essential to building the kingdom of God.

While most poems in the *Exponent* implicitly taught women how to think and behave, there were some poems that explicitly created and promoted a shared community ideal. A poem that encapsulates this particularly well is Marian Adams Gudmensen's "Past and Future." Gudmensen begins the poem by setting forth quintessential ideal attributes of Mormon womanhood, but in her eloquent phrasing, they appear not just as an ideal but as a reality—a picture of what these women have already accomplished:

Relief Society, ah well art thou named!
Thy mission has ever been one of succor;
Comfort and cheer have been thy watchwords;
To minister unto the afflicted to bind up the broken hearted,
To aid the needy and distressed in all the land.
Skillful have been the hands of thy workers,
To fashion fabrics unto useful forms.
Industry and thrift have characterized thy members;[45]

By stating these actions and attributes as past and ongoing achievements of Relief Society women, Gudmensen presents a collective identity that they have already achieved. Significantly, any Mormon woman may become a part of this community by simply identifying with the poem.[46]

Gudmensen continues to establish and promote a single collective ideal for Mormon women as she meshes singular and collective pronouns and images.

Not pleasure, but "pleasure in duty" has been thy motto,
And when the work of thy hands was completed,

Thou hast not given thyself to idle recreation,
But ever has thou turned thy mind to study,
For wisdom and knowledge hast thou sought,
In good books and in counsel together.
To what, then, shall we liken thee?
To a colony of ants, toiling indefatigably;
To a hive of bees gathering the golden honey
Of wisdom, and from thy precious store
Sweetening the daily life of all around thee.
This has been thy history—one long labor of love.

Gudmensen's merging of the singular and collective helps her create a cohesive community as every individual is acknowledged and yet consumed in the organization. Notice in particular the prevalent themes of duty, labor, love, knowledge, and learning from one another—while ideals of Mormon womanhood draw from prevalent American ideals, they are not confined to them. According to the poem, Relief Society women are consistently seeking to improve themselves through learning so that they in turn can bless and teach others.

Both the content and form contribute to the significance of these pieces because, by presenting these attributes of Relief Society women as a given in a memorable, pleasing form, Gudmensen powerfully helps create the collective identity of this community and inspires them to live up to it, as it is simply who they already are and what they already do. Gudmensen's poem exemplifies well Cohen's contention that nineteenth-century poems were "constitutive of sociality," written "to change hearts and minds, to recruit new members, and to build solidarity within local organizations."[47] In Cohen's words, the poem's literary value, which allows it to better "reach larger numbers of people and ignite their passions" than does prose, is subsidiary to its "broader social value, its ability to be carried in people and to carry people away."[48]

While many poems help create this collective identity, Gudmensen's poem is particularly good at giving these women an expansive destiny to rally behind:

Thou shalt in time to come assist in freeing woman
From all restraining shackles which yet encircle her about;
Conventions, prejudices, senseless fashions,
And all that seems to raise her up but holds her down.
Preventing her from gaining and adorning,
The loftier summits of a nobler womanhood.
Thou shalt encourage, strengthen, lead her
Along the steep and thorny path which she must climb
To grander realms of thought, a broader vision,
A wider scope of action, clearer light.

As Gudmensen presents it, Mormon women are to free and then lead all of "Earth's mighty sisterhood" to "a wider scope of action, clearer light." God has an expansive vision for all women of the world, and it is the responsibility of Mormon women to help them obtain "grander realms of thought, a broader vision." Furthermore, it is up to them to relieve the "moral suffering, social wrong . . . [and humanity's] crushing burden / Of dire oppression and injustice which doth weigh it down." Succeeding at this grand task is critical if they are to accomplish their greatest goal of helping "To usher in the great millennial day." While similar sentiments may be found in the writings of other nineteenth-century women activists,[49] Gudmensen places Mormon women and their particular religious knowledge at the center of women's reform efforts. Part of what their religious theology offered these women was an expansive vision of women's potential and field of action, and this theology infuses the womanhood ideals found throughout their poems. And while many historians have previously noted that nineteenth-century Mormon women saw their religion as being particularly empowering,[50] a look at their poetry gives us insight into how Mormon women defined themselves and their collective identity by these ideas and how they went about establishing and promoting their beliefs.

Both the poetry and the prose of the *Exponent* capture and promote many aspects of this expansive vision; one aspect in which poetry seems particularly adroit is in providing insight into the great regard women had for one another's teachings. While the respect women held for the teachings of Eliza R. Snow, second president of the Relief Society, has been well documented,[51] poems in the *Exponent* make it clear that this was a much wider phenomenon—with Mormon women greatly respecting the teachings and inspiration of countless other women. As one author writes:

God bless Sister Horne;
   I love to hear her voice;
   I love to hear her warn
     The people of God's choice.
. . .
Oft have I sat and listened,
   Yea, many years ago,
And wondered how such wisdom
   From woman's lips could flow.

Her words unlike "weak woman,"
   But like God's servant brave;
Called forth to preach the Gospel,
   Such words of life she gave.[52]

This poem captures well how Mormon women saw one another as teachers and God's messengers. Women warn and teach; they impart wisdom and preach the Gospel. Their connection with the Spirit and/or the gospel empowers them, so that their words are not like "'weak woman,' / But like God's servant brave."

Mormon women clearly looked to each other for direction and leadership and viewed one another as inspired of God and capable of revealing truth—an important corrective to the image of the Mormon Church as being directed and led solely by men. A tribute poem to Eliza R. Snow written by Emmeline B. Wells more than twenty years after Snow's death encapsulates this well:

> Here she taught us life's great lessons,
>   From the fount above obtaining;
> . . .
> Precious truths, the choicest gems,
>   Fairer than earth's diadems.
>
> Rarest, sweetest songs of Zion
>   That are sung with sacred feeling—
> Given her thro' inspiration,
>   Holy principles revealing
> . . .
> Poet! Priestess, Prophet too—[53]

The emphasis throughout the poem is Snow's prophetic capabilities. Wells looks upon her as a prophet because she obtains knowledge through revelation that she imparts to others. Significant for this chapter is the specific mention of Snow's poetry as revealing inspired truth. The most well-known example of this is her poem "My Father in Heaven," now known as "O My Father," where she writes of a Heavenly Mother; however, Snow, Hannah Tapfield King, Emily H. Woodmansee, Lu Dalton, Lydia D. Alder, and many other women consistently grapple with theological issues through their poetry. Perhaps most useful to note when considering women's respect for one another's teachings and words is simply the pervasiveness of this theme throughout the poems. One of the most powerful examples of this is a poem where Lula Greene Richards, first editor of the *Exponent*, captures in poetic form her remembrance of a speech by King in which King called for women to speak out—to "write, or sing, or speak." "Hold up your heads! My Sisters! Speak! / And sing! That you may be heard!"[54] As this and many other poems illustrate, women are still reverencing and drawing strength from one another's teachings many years after the spoken utterance.

Poems in the *Woman's Exponent* also indicate that Mormon women saw themselves as central rather than peripheral to history and current events, as they consistently present women as integral actors. This is particularly true of poems recounting Latter-day Saint history, with many authors emphasizing how women, too, were

> Raised up, inspired as it were, to help ushering forth
> Those principles, which in their embryo and birth,
> Struggled against tradition, and the creeds of men,
> At fearful odds; to bring the priesthood back again.[55]

One of the most noteworthy examples of this is Ellen Jakeman's "The Lady Pioneers," in which Jakeman presents women and men as equals through paralleling their labors and showing their reliance on one another.

> But man came not alone—a conquering hero
>   To pioneer this land, our Deseret,
> But true and brave, and his own strength completeness
>   Woman shared the toil and each privation met,
> "Dwell not alone Oh man" for Heaven decreed it
>   Earth has not changed much though it's older grown,
> And it is true—reluctant sound to own it
>   Man never did accomplish much alone.
>   . . .
> Beside his plane and chisel stood her scissors
>   His ax, her broom; his scythe, her buzzing reel;
> She matched against his harrow, plow and saddle,
>   The labors of her loom and spinning-wheel.[56]

Referencing a divine decree, Jakeman strengthens her argument that men and women must work together as partners because "Man never did accomplish much alone." Her pointed quips indicate her displeasure that men often receive more credit than women do, and the ensuing parallel upon parallel of a man's task with a woman's task creates a particularly memorable and efficacious call for a recognition of men and women's equality.

Later in the poem, Jakeman displays an acute awareness of the role her poems and other acknowledgments of women's contributions will have on the status of women when she explains that it is the "fame" or the recognition of women's contributions that will "lift her up . . . to his side." Many authors recognized this as well, and that is in part why Emily H. Woodmansee insists "That the Mothers of Zion, should share the applause" when we talk about the settlement of Utah,[57] why Hannah T. King writes an entire narrative poem extolling Queen Isabella's role in the discovery of America,[58] and why Lydia D. Alder writes of war from the mother's perspective and sacrifice,[59] to name just a few examples. Mormon women understood that for women to hold an equal place in society their works and deeds must be known and extolled. They saw poetry as an ideal medium for accomplishing this agenda, and consequently we, as historians, will greatly benefit by looking at poems to see how authors built women and their place in society.

POETRY'S ACCESS TO INTERIORITY

Thus far, we have looked at how poems were integral in the creation and promotion of a shared ideal and how we can access a more nuanced view of ideal Mormon womanhood through incorporating poetry into our source material. Perhaps of even greater use to historians, though, are poems that grant unique access into one individual's interiority. While historians are often more concerned with what individuals did than what they said, understanding women's mental world is an important background and supplement to what we know about their actions. Deeply personal poems where women are processing and working through difficult experiences or questions offer more intimate pictures of women's internal reality and draw readers into the experience and feelings of each poet. A particularly poignant example of this from the *Exponent* is the poem "Number Nine" in which the speaker discusses having her ninth child after more than one of her previous children have passed away.[60] The opening stanzas immediately draw the reader in by granting her access to the author's feelings at the birth of her child and the questions it evokes.

> I've passed again the ordeal of pain,
> Been close to the shore of "The River" again,
>   But this innocent babe of mine,
> Makes it seem but as a troubled dream,
> And life again takes a luminous gleam,
>   Although it is number nine.
>
> As I gaze in the depths of its innocent eyes
> Gazing around in such mute surprise
>   Wondering what life can be;
> I too am filled with wondering,
> Why it is that fate should bring,
>   Another wee babe to me?

With striking brevity, the author captures both the pain and wonder of childbirth and allows the reader to feel the emotional tug-of-war evoked by the birth of a ninth child. In turn, this may allow us to better speak for our subjects as we understand them more fully and can present them from an empathetic point of view, or as Stuart Parker describes it, from "the hermeneutics of generosity."[61]

The next stanza gives us insight into the type of theological questions these women grappled with as it moves beyond the emotional to capture questions about agency and individual's placement on this earth that arise for this woman with the birth of her child:

> And I wonder if spirits in spirit-land
> Ere they come to us an earthly band
>   Can choose where they will to come,
> If so it seems that this babe of mine
> Would surely not have been number nine,
>   But have chosen a better home.

These lines capture a woman questioning an oft-found theological supposition within the pages of the *Exponent* that individuals chose, or helped to choose, their earthly home and illustrate how one's personal circumstances certainly influenced one's belief of different theological concepts. They also provide unique access into the feelings of inadequacy this woman feels as she recognizes the limitations and disadvantages that exist when parental and other resources are divided among so many children. These ideas are in tension with the collective Mormon ideal of fulfilling motherhood and confidence in women's capacity to raise their children well;[62] consequently, this poem provides insight into the chasm that at times existed between the ideal and the reality.[63] For poems to be more useful as sources, we often must differentiate poems that speak to an ideal versus a lived reality—fortunately, the distinction is readily apparent in most nineteenth-century poems.

Quite likely, the most affecting turn (and insight in the poem) occurs in the last two stanzas as the speaker openly rejects what one is supposed to say and feel and instead expresses what she actually feels. The author's poignant question of whether she should weep more for the just-born child or her children that have already passed on is precisely the type of courageous honesty one hopes to encounter in point-of-view sources:

> As I lovingly clasp my babe so pure,
> And think of what she must endure,
>   My heart is filled with misgiving.
> And I hardly know for which I should weep,
> The innocent babe in my arms asleep,
>   Or those that are not with the living.

This question highlights both the speaker's deep awareness of the pain and struggles of mortality and her faith in the afterlife. In turn, the painful honesty of this question helps break down walls between the author and the reader, forcing the reader to recognize and grapple with the author's intense sorrows and hardships as well as her faith in God and the next life. In this case, a poem provides insight into the emotions, questions, and theology of an individual in a way that makes them tangible and personal to the reader. The poetics and language of the poem together create a transference from author to audience that prose struggles to duplicate.[64]

The value for historians of the emotional transference that poems may enable is that it helps accomplish what religious historians John Coffey, Alister Chapman, and Brad S. Gregory argue is historians' principal obligation: "to do everything possible to see things their way—to understand past agents on their own terms in their own contexts."[65] As Donald A. Yerxa writes, "Historians have become increasingly interested in looking at past human experience from the inside, the way people experienced various things in their lives."[66] In Mormon history, a prominent example of this is Richard Bushman, who in *Rough Stone Rolling* "attempts to think as Smith thought and to reconstruct the beliefs of his followers as they understood them" in order "to recover the world of a prophet."[67] As increasing numbers of historians follow the lead of such notable scholars as Gregory, Bushman, Karen Armstrong, and Mark Noll to first and foremost understand subjects in their own terms, then sources such as women's poems will become increasingly valuable because they contain the sought-after point of view and emotional state of these women.

POETRY REVEALING WHAT PROSE CANNOT

Poems take on even greater importance for historians in those moments when authors express sentiments that they simply could not or would not in prose. Most often for Mormon women this seems to be due to the private, sacred, or theological nature of what they wrote. As Susanna Morrill writes, "poetry was viewed as a particularly suitable vehicle for female communication and expression, especially the expression of revelatory messages from the divine realm . . . repeatedly, in practice, we see that LDS women writers actually attempted to use poetry as a means of religious, even revelatory communication."[68] Consequently, when we take these poems seriously, we at times glean sacred, private information that we will not find in other sources. For instance, Lydia Alder writes a poem about a vision she had of Christ. Proclaiming unequivocally at the end,

> And now I know! But never more while on the sea of time,
> Will my heart forget the vision; but sing of its adored,
> For I have seen the Lord! mine eyes have seen the Lord![69]

Likely, because of the sacredness of this experience, poetry is the place Alder chooses to record her experience.

Poetry is an ideal forum to share such sacred moments because it not only enables an expression of heightened emotion and vision but also allows for a multiplicity of meanings. The potential for possible meanings and layers of interpretation leaves authors less exposed than if they recorded the experience in prose. Of course, this potential for multiplicity is also part of what keeps historians from embracing poetry, as we at times struggle to know if a poem is describing an actual event or exploring emotions based on hypothetical events. While this is a very real tension within poetry, as it is essential to the poetic cover that enables greater freedom within poetry, I would argue that this tension need not discourage historians for two reasons. First, in many instances, whether an event is real or hypothetical does not matter as what we are seeking to gain through these poems is greater insight into how these women felt and thought or into the ideologies of the time, and both of these aspects are often unaffected by the real versus hypothetical question. Second, I would argue that, in most instances, if we have a working knowledge of the author's life combined with adequate exposure to nineteenth-century poems and poetic conventions, it becomes clear what the author is speaking about and whether it is a real or hypothetical event. I offer one example of this latter assertion.

In August 1883, Hannah T. King, frequent contributor to the *Woman's Exponent*, published "Lord Thou Knowest!"—a highly significant poem because it is the only place where King provides insight into how she felt about Brigham Young and her sealing to him (a sealing is an ordinance performed in the temple to make possible the existence of marriage and family relationships through eternity).[70] As background, King (age sixty-five) was still married to her husband Thomas King when she was sealed to Young for eternity only. The marriage sealing to Young was to come into force only in the next life and seems to have come as a result of King's worry about not being sealed to anyone because her husband was insufficiently motivated to receive his endowment and be sealed to her. King's sealing to Young seems to have been kept secret, and nowhere in her voluminous writings both published and unpublished (at least that have survived) does King write of her sealing to Young.[71] How we know this sealing occurred is from temple records.[72] That King would have chosen poetry as the one place to express her thoughts on Young and their sealing is not surprising, as she most often turned to poetry to convey her deepest emotions and interesting ideas. At the time, poetry also provided her a unique space where she could publicly express her feelings for Young while maintaining the secrecy of their attachment. Since people did not know of their sealing, her opening stanza—

> There is a love that God may see,
>   But must be hid from mortal eyes,

> Because it human law defies;
> Because of earth it cannot be"[73]

—would most likely have been read as speaking to polygamy in general.

However, knowing of King's sealing to Young and the contents of a short letter she wrote to him seven-and-a-half months after Thomas's death—"I have to ask one favour of you vis. That you will give me your picture to put in my room, that I may have you ever present with me; . . . I remain Ever thine Hannah T: K: Young,"—the poem becomes a clear expression of her relationship to Young and the sorrow she feels at his passing.[74]

> The sorrow that must not be seen,
>   When death that hidden treasure steals,
>   And all that loneliness reveals,
> And all that's left is what has been!
> . . .
> Wisdom, prudence, veneration too,
>   All mingled in that humble friend,
>   Whose sole appointment was to tend
> His queen!—for such devotion love was due.
>
> He served her husband, by reflection, he
>   Shone into her heart—until
>   He earned a niche that he himself should fill,
> That by her gratitude unveiled should be.
> . . .
> For queenship, who would sigh! to be
>   Watched and judged, the inner life to scan,
>   And all within the court of erring man!
> Thou knowest Lord! we wait for thy decree.

Knowing of Young's relationship with the King family, the poem's biographical references to this relationship become striking.[75] Further placing the poem in connection to her letter indicating her desire to have Young, through his picture, "ever present before me" and her salutation, "I remain Ever thine," allows us to recognize that in this poem King expresses her affection for Young, the sorrow she feels at his passing, and the joy with which she looks forward to being "His queen" in the next life. While King's sealing to Young has been seen as a pragmatic rather than romantic decision, this poem reveals that at least on King's side deep feelings originally (or at least eventually) accompanied this sealing. If we disregard poetry, we miss an important aspect of the story. This example illustrates well the type of information that may be found only in poems as well as the clarity that often comes to poems when one has contextual knowledge of authors' lives.

Accepting poetry as a valid primary source also allows us to see how women contributed to conversations and influenced ideas that generally were understood to be under male stewardship, such as theology. The most well-known example of a woman influencing Mormon theology is Eliza R. Snow's poem "My Father in Heaven," now known as "O My Father," in which Snow declares the reality of a Mother in Heaven. Although debate exists over how Snow came to believe in the existence of a Mother in Heaven, most of the evidence points to her being taught the doctrine by Joseph Smith. No debate, however, exists over the role her poem played in popularizing the idea. The doctrine and Eliza R. Snow's hymn have been irrevocably linked from the time she penned the lines in 1845 until today.[76] Past prophet Wilford Woodruff further raised the status of this poem when he declared it a revelation: "That hymn is a revelation, though it was given unto us by a woman—Sister Snow. There are a great many sisters who have the spirit of revelation. There is no reason why they should not be inspired as well as men."[77] Woodruff's statement reiterates how nineteenth-century Mormons often saw poetry as a language or means of revelations—and significantly, a method of revelation particularly suited to women. Consequently, if we want to access or acknowledge women's revelatory experiences we must often look to their poems. The influence of this poem on the Mormon Church is also an excellent example of how poetry may at times popularize ideas more effectively than prose because of the succinct, rhythmic, memorable aspect of many poems.

While this is the most well-known example of Mormon women shaping and influencing Mormon theology through their writing, many others exist as well. For instance, Boyd Jay Petersen in his work on Mormon conceptions of Eve shows that the "version of Eve as hero . . . most common in today's [LDS] discourse" is virtually absent in male LDS thought in the nineteenth century but dominant in the *Woman's Exponent*, thus indicating the significant role women played in shaping our current understanding of Eve.[78] And Susanna Morrill in her groundbreaking work on Mormon women's popular theology illustrates how women employed nature-centered theological imagery in their popular literary discourse to argue "for the importance of the abstract concept of femaleness, as well as the centrality of women's roles within the family, everyday life of the community, and even within the overarching LDS plan of salvation."[79] As Morrill's work convincingly illustrates, acknowledging the theology found in popular literary discourse (including poems) is important because it "shifts our horizons and our views of the LDS community as a whole. Instead of seeing simply a patriarchal theology and institution, we discover women and femaleness emerging as powerful forces and symbols within the practical reality of the Mormon community."[80] Morrill is among the many historians of religion who are now looking to alternative sources to bring women's voices into the conversation and thereby providing a much richer understanding of faith traditions and communities.

These scholars' work validates the germaneness of my own; in turn, what I hope to add to the conversation are specific explanations and illustrations of how poems are an essential part of a historical project committed to incorporating women's ideas and experiences. In particular, I argue for the relevancy of poetry in understanding women's theological contributions because poetry was a nonthreatening, socially acceptable genre that allowed women to share their theological ideas. Again, a poem and incident from the life of Eliza R. Snow illustrates this well. In December 1873, Snow published an article in the *Exponent* sharing her views on the resurrection. Seeking to answer objections to the idea of resurrection offered by those who observed the decomposition of the body and the recycling of its elements, Snow divided matter into "two distinct classes or grades." One grade of matter was subject to decay and would not be part of a resurrected body, while the other grade of matter was "capable of resisting every law of infraction of dissolubility" and would compose the resurrected body. When Snow's article began to gain traction, Brigham Young wrote a letter rejecting her theory (published in the *Exponent*) and then offered an address in general conference to explain his position on resurrection. Snow subsequently wrote an open letter retracting her ideas, which was published in the *Exponent* and reprinted in the *Deseret News.*[81]

For my argument, what is significant about this story is not simply that it demonstrates women constructing and sharing their own theological views—though this point should be emphasized—but that it shows a woman being censored for theological views that she had already expounded on in her poetry. A year and a half earlier, Snow expressed these precise sentiments in a poem written to commemorate the death of her sister Leonora and published in the *Exponent.*[82] In great detail and many lines, Snow explains her thoughts on resurrection and two distinct grades of elements, yet no one censored her theological discussion because, at least in part, it appears in verse rather than prose.[83] As women found greater freedom of expression in poems than in other written mediums, individuals seeking women's theological perspectives will need to consider these sources. Morrill's work provides a compelling example of how we may profitably use these sources, but it will be unfortunate if her work is seen as summative of rather than an introduction to these fruitful sources.

To give an idea of the type of insights that are still dormant within theological poetry, I turn to poems in the *Exponent* that reflect on humanity's pre-existent state with God. Looking at these poems collectively, we find definite themes as women fleshed out vague doctrine surrounding premortal existence with God. One of the most prevalent images in the poetry is of individuals being taught by Heavenly Parents in an atmosphere of love and joy.

Dost remember the palace where primeval you strayed,
The gardens of grandeur where soft breezes played?

Or Father or Mother in whose courts you were reared,
With love past revealing—and nothing was feared?[84]

The poems become more interesting when we note the prominent place they
accord women and friendship. A Mother in Heaven is present in the majority
of these poems:

And our Mother, Queen in Heaven,
    Smiled on us every one,
Smiled on each Eve, each Sarah,
    Rachel, Rebecca and Ruth,
Elizabeth, Mary and Martha,
    Each daughter that stood for truth.[85]

As this stanza demonstrates, not just Heavenly Mother but also women as her
daughters are at the center of these authors' images of premortal existence,
once again illustrating how these women often used poetry to place women
at the center rather than the periphery.

Interestingly, though, while the parent-child relationship between humanity and heavenly parents is key to the poems, the bond most commonly mentioned among humanity is not familial but friendship—underlying once again
how important female camaraderie was to these women. Many poems speak
of the friendships established in premortality as the basis for friendships here:

So, when we met in earth-life,
The same old kinship true
Brought each unto the other—
A mystic tie drew me to you.[86]

Some also suggest that we were able to choose those with whom we would
come to earth:

We were *all* ALL there, my sisters;
    And we loved each other well;
And doubtless selected classmates,
    With whom upon earth to dwell.[87]

Collectively these poems reveal these women's understanding that individuals had a part in choosing where they came to earth and that God then selects
for each individual the place where they will find "The greatest satisfaction
in the sphere / For which His wisdom hath this life designed!"[88] Recognizing
the theology women created and advocated in their poems is important because, as Morrill successfully illustrates, this literature "became a loose, but

coherent theological force within the church."[89] The theological richness and complexity within any faith tradition may best be realized when all relevant sources are given due consideration.

CONCLUSION

Returning to the initial poetic conversation between Tanner and Scott, it is striking to recognize how their conversation encompasses many of the established definitions of female identity revealed through a collective analysis of the poems as a whole. For instance, most prominent in their poems is their appreciation for one another's teachings and words. They find comfort and assistance in one another's friendship and writings, and they see each other and their poetic works not as peripheral but as central to their lived realities. Not surprisingly, given the centrality of duty and service to female identity, while both women note the importance of poetic expression to their own sense of self, they ultimately state that they write because they see it as their God-given task and their way of uplifting humanity:

> If the voice could go forth to the weak ones of earth,
>   To raise the down-trod and oppressed,
> To comfort the sad, or to make the heart glad,
>   We should feel that our labors were blessed.
>   . . .
> Though feeble the light that is shining to-night,
>   I will hold to the task that is given;
> And point to the star that is shining afar,
>   Guiding to God—and to heaven.[90]

This one poem may represent all in illustrating how poetry helps shift our understanding of the Mormon community by placing women at the center of their lived religion, as Mormon women value their female identity and community and turn to one another for support and religious guidance.

More important, the poetic conversation also serves as a microcosm displaying why historians of nineteenth-century women should embrace nineteenth-century poems as valuable primary sources. First, the poems illustrate how poetry aids the historical task by drawing us into the experience, point of view, and feelings of the author. Readers gain an intimate understanding of how Mormon women felt about themselves and each other as they use poetry as the medium of choice to ask questions and explore life's difficulties. Second, the poems encode and transmit both the implicit and explicit ideologies that Mormon women worked within, such as duty, service, and appreciation for women's work and words, as they provide memorable expression of prevailing sentiments. Third, the poems reveal how poetry provides a space for women to ask questions and share experiences that are too personal, sacred, or transgressive for other mediums. Fourth, the poems demonstrate the expansive social role poetry played in nineteenth-century America. When we view poetry from a nineteenth-century perspective—where poems are recognized as a medium for personal and collective memories; an appropriate space for sharing one's political, social, and religious views; and an extension of women themselves—we will come to embrace nineteenth-century poems as valuable sources for historical inquiry. And in the process of embracing women's poems, we will allow these women to define their own lives and society and receive recognition for affecting social change through their writings.

NOTES

1. Mary J. Tanner, "I'll Lay by the Harp," *Woman's Exponent* 12, no. 12 (November 15, 1883): 91.

2. Emily Scott, "To Mary J. Tanner," *Woman's Exponent* 12, no. 15 (January 1, 1884): 11.

3. Mary J. Tanner, "To Mrs. Emily Scott," *Woman's Exponent* 12, no. 18 (February 15, 1884): 139.

4. Notably, two prominent historians of Mormon women's history have acknowledged poems as significant historical sources. As reason for publishing the complete poetic works of Eliza R. Snow—dubbed Zion's poetess by Joseph Smith—Jill Mulvay Derr and Karen Lynn Davidson write, "More than her letters, discourses, or journals, her poems are comprehensive in their scope and as immediate as snapshots in their depiction of Mormon culture" (xv–xvi). Further, they argue Snow's poetry "is singular for its social, historical, and linguistic record of the first six decades of Mormonism" (xvi). Derr and Davidson's work is notable for its recovery of Snow's work; however, it is an anthology rather than an argumentative text illustrating the validity of their claim, and unfortunately, few historians have yet to make use of this valuable resource. Google Scholar, for instance, lists only five articles or books that cite this collection of poetry. Jill Mulvay Derr and Karen Lynn Davidson, eds., *Eliza R. Snow: The Complete Poetry* (Provo, UT: Brigham Young University Press, 2009).

5. For information on American scholars' dismissal of poetry, see Mary Loeffelholz, *From School to Salon: Reading Nineteenth-Century American Women's Poetry* (Princeton, NJ: Princeton University Press, 2004), 2; Joseph Harrington, "Why American Poetry Is Not American Literature," *American Literary History* 8 (Fall 1996): 496–515.

6. Janet Gray, *She Wields a Pen: American Women Poets of the Nineteenth Century* (Iowa City: University of Iowa Press, 1997), xxix. See also Paula Bernat Bennett, *Nineteenth-Century American Women Poets: An Anthology* (Malden, MA: Wiley-Blackwell, 1998), xxxv.

7. For more information, see Jonathan Culler, *Theory of the Lyric* (Cambridge, MA: Harvard University Press, 2015), 5; Shira Wolosky, "The Claims of Rhetoric: Toward a Historical Poetics (1820–1900)," *American Literary History* (2003): 14–15.

8. Michael C. Cohen, *The Social Lives of Poems in Nineteenth-Century America* (Philadelphia: University of Pennsylvania Press, 2015), 10.

9. For more on sentimentality as the dominant rhetorical mode, see Bennett, *Nineteenth-Century American Women Poets*, xxxviii. For more on women's dominant place in the literary marketplace, see Gray, *She Wields a Pen*, xxx; Patricia Okker, *Our Sister Editors: Sarah J.*

Hale and the Tradition of Nineteenth-Century American Women Editors (Atlanta: University of Georgia Press, 2008), 6–37.

10. Okker, *Our Sister Editors*, 6.

11. Gray, *She Wields a Pen*, xxxii.

12. Cheryl Walker, *American Women Poets of the Nineteenth Century: An Anthology* (New Brunswick, NJ: Rutgers University Press, 1992), xxvii.

13. Elizabeth A. Petrino, *Emily Dickinson and Her Contemporaries: Women's Verse in America 1820–1885* (Hanover, NH: University Press of New England, 1998), 207.

14. For more information, see Petrino, *Emily Dickinson*, 12–20; Walker, *American Women Poets*, xxvi–xxviii; Paula Bernat Bennett, *Poets in the Public Sphere: The Emancipatory Project of American Women's Poetry, 1800–1900* (Princeton, NJ: Princeton University Press, 2003), 5.

15. For more information, see Bennett, *Poets in the Public Sphere*; Wolosky, "The Claims of Rhetoric," 16.

16. For more information on how literary works bridged public and private worlds and allowed women to reach large audiences and personalize complex political and social situations, see Mary Chapman and Angela Mills, *Treacherous Texts: U.S. Suffrage Literature, 1846–1946* (New Brunswick, NJ: Rutgers University Press, 2011), 4–12.

17. For more information, see Cohen, *Social Lives of Poems*, 10, 156, 200; Wolosky, "Poetry and Public Discourse," 18.

18. For more information, see Petrino, *Emily Dickinson*, 210.

19. Cohen, *Social Lives of Poems*, 186, 159–63, 200.

20. For more information on how poetry's foregrounding of formal artifice and individual emotion has traditionally made historians skeptical of its ability to give an accurate portrayal of history or individuals, see Loeffelholz, *From School to Salon*, 2; Harrington, "Why American Poetry Is Not American Literature," 496–515.

21. Gary Grieve-Carlson, *Poems Containing History: Twentieth-Century American Poetry's Engagement with the Past* (Lanham, MD: Lexington Books, 2013), 7.

22. Louisa Lula Greene, "A Utah Ladies' Journal," *Woman's Exponent* 1, no. 1 (June 1, 1872): 8.

23. Greene, "A Utah Ladies' Journal," 8.

24. Greene, "A Utah Ladies' Journal," 8.

25. Carol Cornwall Madsen, "'Remember the Women of Zion': A Study of the Editorial Content of the *Woman's Exponent*, a Mormon Woman's Journal, 1872–1914" (master's thesis, University of Utah, 1977).

26. For historical background on the *Exponent*, see Sherilyn Cox Bennion, "The *Woman's Exponent*: Forty-Two Years of Speaking for Women," *Utah Historical Quarterly* 44, no. 3 (Summer 1976): 226–39; Carol Cornwall Madsen, *An Advocate for Women: The Public Life of Emmeline B. Wells, 1870–1920* (Provo, UT: BYU Studies, 2006), 34–66. See also Madsen, "'Remember the Women of Zion.'"

27. The one notable exception to this is Susanna Morrill's work that uses poetry from the *Exponent* and other nineteenth-century LDS periodicals to make her arguments. See Susanna Morrill, *White Roses on the Floor of Heaven: Mormon Women's Popular Theology, 1880–1920* (New York: Routledge, 2006).

28. For more information, see Jill Mulvay Derr, "The Lion and the Lioness: Brigham Young and Eliza R. Snow," *BYU Studies* 40, no. 2 (2001): 62–63.

29. Derr and Davidson, *Eliza R. Snow*, xix.

30. Claudia Stokes, *The Altar at Home: Sentimental Literature and Nineteenth-Century American Religion* (Philadelphia: University of Pennsylvania Press, 2014), 143.

31. On American journalistic poems, see Wolosky, "Claims of Rhetoric," 17.

32. Barbara Welter, "The Cult of True Womanhood: 1820–1860," *American Quarterly* 18, no. 2 (Summer 1966): 151–74; Frances Cogan, *All American Girl: The Ideal of Real Womanhood in Mid-Nineteenth-Century America* (Atlanta: University of Georgia Press, 1989).

33. For more on the centrality of women's relationships to one another, see the seminal work of Caroll Smith-Rosenberg, "The Female World of Love and Ritual: Relations between Women in Nineteenth-Century America," *Signs* 1, no. 1 (Autumn 1975): 1–29.

34. M. L. M., "Affection," *Woman's Exponent* 12, no. 23 (May 1, 1884): 179.

35. Lula Greene Richards, "To Sister Emma P. Toone," *Woman's Exponent* 17, no. 24 (May 15, 1889): 192.

36. Emily Hill Woodmansee, "A Demonstration of Respect," *Woman's Exponent* 8, no. 19 (March 1, 1880): 145.

37. Morrill, *White Roses*, 7.

38. In addition to previous sources cited, see also Jill Mulvay Derr, "'Strength in Our Union': The Making of Mormon Sisterhood," in *Sisters in Spirit: Mormon Women in Historical and Cultural Perspective*, ed. Maureen Ursenbach Beecher and Lavina Fielding Anderson (Urbana and Chicago: University of Illinois Press, 1987), 153–207.

39. Cohen, *Social Lives of Poems*, 198; see also Wolosky, "Claims of Rhetoric," 18.

40. Marianna Stratford and Nellie Beecroft, "A Tribute of Love [for Maria D. Chambers]," *Woman's Exponent* 22, no. 13 (March 1, 1894): 104.

41. See Lori D. Ginzberg, *Women and the Work of Benevolence: Morality, Politics, and Class in the 19th-Century United States* (New Haven, CT: Yale University Press, 1990), 1–10; Debra Bernardi and Jill Annette Bergman, "Introduction: Benevolence Literature by American Women," in *Our Sisters' Keepers: Nineteenth-Century Benevolence Literature by American Women*, ed. Jill Annette Bergman, Debra Bernardi, and Sarah E. Chinn (Tuscaloosa: University of Alabama Press, 2009), 1–22.

42. Ellis R. Shipp, "Half a Century," *Woman's Exponent* 18, no. 6 (August 15, 1889): 45.

43. Shipp, "Half a Century," *Woman's Exponent* 18, no. 6 (August 15, 1889): 45.

44. Sarah J. Tarbet, "In Memoriam For [Ann H. Davis]," *Woman's Exponent* 12, no. 12 (November 15, 1883): 96.

45. Marian Adams Gudmensen, "Past and Future," *Woman's Exponent* 39, no. 5 (November 1910): 40.

46. Discussing how this occurred in America at large Cohen explains, "[American ballads] also helped to *make* Americans by providing a set of songs that *were* American, in both their content and form, so that a person might *become* American by identifying with the song." Cohen, *Social Lives of Poems*, 196.

47. Cohen, *Social Lives of Poems*, 60–61.

48. Cohen, *Social Lives of Poems*, 61.

49. Most famously, Harriet Beecher Stowe; see Jane Tompkins, "Sentimental Power: Uncle Tom's Cabin and the Politics of Literary Power," in *Sensational Designs: The Cultural Work of American Fiction, 1790–1860* (New York: Oxford University Press, 1985), 122–46.

50. For many good examples of this, see the different essays in Maureen Ursenbach Beecher and Lavina Fielding Anderson, eds., *Sisters in Spirit: Mormon Women in Historical and Cultural Perspective* (Urbana and Chicago: University of Illinois Press, 1987).

51. Derr, "'Strength in Our Union,'" 172–73; Maureen Ursenbach Beecher, "The Eliza Enigma," *Dialogue: A Journal of Mormon Thought* 11, no. 1 (Spring 1978): 31, 38.

52. M. L. M., "Affection," 179.

53. Emmeline B. Wells, "Quest and Message," *Woman's Exponent* 38, no. 10 (May 1910): 75.

54. L. L. Greene Richards, "A Remembered Exhortation," *Woman's Exponent* 23, nos. 3 and 4 (August 1 and 15, 1894): 171.

55. B. B. [Emmeline B. Wells], "A Tribute of Respect," *Woman's Exponent* 3, no. 17 (February 1, 1875): 130.

56. Ellen Jakeman, "The Lady Pioneers," *Woman's Exponent* 19, no. 7 (September 15, 1890): 51.

57. Emily Hill Woodmansee, "The Pioneer Mothers," *Woman's Exponent* 9, no. 20 (March 15, 1881): 151.

58. Hannah T. King, "Isabella," *Woman's Exponent* 21, no. 7 (October 1, 1892): 49.

59. Lydia Alder, "The Last Letter," *Woman's Exponent* 28, no. 24 (May 15, 1900): 130.

60. E. T., "Number Nine," *Woman's Exponent* 18, no. 16 (January 15, 1890): 121.

61. Stuart Parker, "The Hermeneutics of Generosity: A Critical Approach to the Scholarship of Richard Bushman," *Journal of Mormon History* 38, no. 3 (Summer 2012): 12–27.

62. For examples of this, see August Joyce Crocheron, "Patriot Mothers," *Woman's Exponent* 11, no. 11 (November 1, 1882): 83; Woodmansee, "The Pioneer Mothers," 151; Annie Wells Cannon, "Mother," *Woman's Exponent* 40, no. 7 (March 1912): 49.

63. Other poignant examples of this are Lu Dalton, "Afraid," *Woman's Exponent* 17, no. 18 (February 1, 1890): 130; Augusta Joyce Crocheron, "Lines to an Infant," *Woman's Exponent* 8, no. 6 (August 15, 1879): 43.

64. For an explanation of why poems create greater transference than prose, see Culler, *Theory of the Lyric*, 134, 350–52.

65. John Coffey and Alister Chapman, "Introduction: Intellectual History and the Return of Religion," in *Seeing Things Their Way: Intellectual History and the Return of Religion*, ed. Alister Chapman, John Coffey, and Brad S. Gregory (Notre Dame, IN: University of Notre Dame Press, 2009), 16.

66. Donald A. Yerxa, "Introduction: Historical Inquiry and Thinking Today," in *Recent Themes in Historical Thinking: Historians in Conversation*, ed. Donald A. Yerxa (Columbia: University of South Carolina Press, 2008), 1.

67. Richard Lyman Bushman, *Joseph Smith: Rough Stone Rolling; a Cultural Biography of Mormonism's Founder* (New York: Alfred A Knopf, 2005), xxii.

68. Morrill, *White Roses*, 79, 81.

69. Lydia D. Alder, "A Vision," *Woman's Exponent* 27, nos. 3 and 4 (July 1 and 15, 1898): 11.

70. Hannah T. King, "Lord Thou Knowest!" *Woman's Exponent* 12, no. 6 (August 15, 1883): 43.

71. For more information, see Dorothy Brewerton, Carolyn Gorwill, and Leonard Reed, *The Songstress of Dernford Dale: The Life of Poetess, Diarist and Latter-day Saint Hannah Tapfield King* (n.p.: privately published, 2011), 133–38; Leonard Reed, "'As a Bird Sings': Hannah Tapfield King, Poetess and Pioneer," *BYU Studies Quarterly* 51, no. 3 (2012): 113–15.

72. Hannah Tapfield, "Salt Lake Endowment House Records," Book H, 353, quoted in Jeffery Ogden Johnson, "Determining and Defining 'Wife': The Brigham Young Households," *Dialogue: A Journal of Mormon Thought* 20, no. 3 (Fall 1987), 69.

73. King, "Lord Thou Knowest!," 43.

74. This letter is found in Brigham Young, Office files 1832–1878, Incoming General Correspondence, LDS Church History Library, Salt Lake City, UT, quoted in Brewerton, Gorwill, and Reed, *Songstress of Dernford Dale*, 137.

75. Brewerton, Gorwill, and Reed, *Songstress of Dernford Dale*, 108–9, 119–20.

76. For the most thorough treatment of Snow's poem, see Jill Mulvay Derr, "The Significance of 'O My Father' in the Personal Journey of Eliza R. Snow," *BYU Studies* 36 (1996–1997): 98–100.

77. "Discourse by President Wilford Woodruff, October 8, 1893 (in Salt Lake)," *Millennial Star* 56 (April 9, 1894): 229, quoted in Derr, "Significance of 'O My Father,'" 98.

78. Boyd Jay Petersen, "'Redeemed from the Curse Placed upon Her': Dialogic Discourse on Eve in the *Woman's Exponent*," *Journal of Mormon History* 40, no. 1 (2014): 157.

79. Morrill, *White Roses*, 4.

80. Morrill, *White Roses*, 13.

81. For more information on this incident, see Derr, "The Lion and the Lioness," 88–90.

82. Eliza R. Snow, "My Sister, Mrs. Leonora A. Morley," *Woman's Exponent* 1, no. 5 (August 1, 1872): 35.

83.

Her noble spirit lives and dwells above.
The casket rests—The pure component part,
Th' eternal portion of the human form,
In life combined with the gross element,
Sleeps in the bosom of our mother Earth,
Secure from nature's changing processes—
Despite decomposition's complex skill.
But the gross, earthly substance, that which is
Both tangible to mortal sight and touch—
Formed with affinities that downward tend
Strengh'ning our hold on this our lower life,
Clinging to earth as like adheres to like
This, soon as life becomes extinct, by dint
Of one of nature's fundamental laws,
The law of restitution, has commenced,
And separates till all is disengaged—
Till every particle shall be restored
Back to its native element, to be
Transformed in infinite varieties
To new creations and in other forms—
Through every grade of life and being here
From earth and herbage up to brute and man—
From land to land—from clime to clime transferred;
Leaving the pure unchanging element
(When all that is corruptible has been
Dissolved and passed away) to rest—to sleep
Until the glorious resurrection morn

84. Lydia D. Alder, "Birthday Greetings," *Woman's Exponent* 22, no. 17 (May 15, 1894): 131.

85. L. L. Greene Richards, "A Thread of Thought," *Woman's Exponent* 29, nos. 6 and 7 (August 15, and September 1, 1900): 27.

86. Mary A. Freeze, "To Julia," *Woman's Exponent* 38, no. 9 (April 1910): 67.

87. Richards, "A Thread of Thought," 27. See also Crocheron, "Lines to an Infant," 43; E. T., "Number Nine," 121.

88. Lula [L.L. Greene Richards], "Ourselves," *Woman's Exponent* 10, no. 18 (February 15, 1882): 137.

89. Morrill, *White Roses*, 171.

90. Tanner, "To Mrs. Emily Scott," 139.

Chapter Six

Aesthetic Evangelism, Artistic Sisterhood, and the Gospel of Beauty

Mormon Women Artists at Home and Abroad, circa 1890–1920

Heather Belnap Jensen

Tucked in the pages of a 1920 issue of the *Relief Society Magazine* is a short and stirring piece titled "The Gospel of Beauty." Author Alice Merrill Horne, one of the most ardent art advocates the state of Utah and the Latter-day Saints (LDS) Church has produced, made a bold claim for cultural authority:

> If God spoke to Emma Smith concerning music and art, should not we, the recipients of benefits, from that "turning of the key" be glad to preach the Gospel of beauty? Eliza R. Snow heard the music and sang. She blessed me with a message of what I should do when I was but a little child. In the presence of Sisters Zina, Bathsheba, Rachel Grant, E. B. Wells, and a dozen others I could name, she blessed me to bring forward a work which no one else could do and which would bring great joy in its accomplishment. That call has never since ceased.

With this blessing and charge, Merrill Horne pursued her lifelong mission of promoting art and beauty and did so with unparalleled vision and indefatigable energy. She also issued a clarion call to her fellow sisters of the Mormon faith to recommit to their God-given duty to serve as its guardians, writing, "Let us take up again this study of art in our society with the hope that the Gospel of Beauty may dispel much of the ugliness which grips the race. Remembering always that it is our privilege to flood the world with the beautiful and good."[1]

In early twentieth-century Utah, several Mormon women eagerly assumed the sacred obligation of cultivating the visual arts and refining aesthetic sensibilities, forming an informal artistic sisterhood at home and abroad to facilitate this noble undertaking.[2] Establishing art institutions in the Intermountain West; producing art-related curriculum for the LDS women's auxiliaries; fashioning civic, school, and Church art collections; and authoring countless texts on art were part of a committed missionary effort to spread this aesthetic message. Individuals such as Alice Merrill Horne, Mary Teasdel, Rose Hartwell, and other women in the nascent art community of Mormon Utah infused their work with a sense of spirituality and higher purpose that transcended the mere practice of one's trade. They assumed the role of protector of the eternal flames of beauty and declared it their spiritual calling, even birthright, to proselytize and preside over the holy realms of art and culture, becoming, as contemporary William C. Brownell termed it, "aesthetic evangelists."[3]

Unlike the male Mormon art missionaries, who were given an official calling as Church representatives to travel to Paris in 1890 for art training, these women neither received an ecclesiastical mandate or financial support to continue their studies abroad nor were they given Church-sponsored commissions, such as painting temple murals.[4] However, these women believed they were uniquely positioned to foster the arts among their people and that, with their special blessings and gifts, they were called upon to magnify and consecrate their artistic capacities to the edification of the Saints. This shared vision united them in an unofficial, but equally important, art mission—one that required tremendous personal initiative and inner conviction, for they were not fulfilling a short-term ecclesiastical assignment but, rather, were committing to a way of life.

Central to this mission was a rigorous art education and the forging of female alliances, both of which were frequently accomplished while in Europe. These experiences enhanced their authority in the arena of art and aesthetics, thereby further qualifying them for this work. While there, they also formed strong bonds of collegiality and found profitable models for professional female networks by virtue of their single-sex modes of education, habitation, and sociability. And so these Mormon women went abroad, becoming "pioneers in reverse," with these cosmopolitan spaces—and particularly Paris—becoming their seminary for not only art but also for social politics. When they returned, they fashioned a female art collective akin to those established by the band of Mormon art missionaries and to the artistic brotherhoods that undergirded the modern art world, and that bore the distinct imprint of the LDS Church's well-established women's organizations in which they were already deeply invested.

This artistic sisterhood and its enterprises were informed by and in turn formative to the phenomena of culture's feminization, the sacralization of art, and aesthetic evangelism. As Kathleen McCarthy notes in her important study *Women's Culture: American Philanthropy and Art, 1830–1930*, "One of the most enduring American notions is that women are the national cultural custodians, and always have been."[5] Over the course of the nineteenth century, "culture," broadly defined, had become increasingly valenced as feminine.[6] Women were celebrated for their innate morality, sensitivity to beauty in art and nature, and ability to foster these virtues in those within their spheres of influence. As protectors and purveyors of the realm of the ideal, they were heralded as angels of art.[7] While in antebellum America women's participation in the art world was generally circumscribed within the domestic sphere, their reach began expanding at the turn of the century. Capitalizing on the cultural sanctioning of women's engagement with philanthropy, which had served as the primary means for middle- and upper-class women to perform public roles in the nineteenth century, they began to wed their commitment to art and beauty with philanthropic endeavors outside the home, thereby becoming agents in the American art scene.[8]

This cultural guardianship emerged at a time in which the young nation embarked on its "sacralization" of art and culture. The late nineteenth-century endeavors to create canons, establish institutions, and set standards of aesthetic taste were ways in which genteel Americans attempted to differentiate themselves from the popular classes (and to some extent from the Europeans and their traditions).[9] It was conjoined with, and indeed a by-product of, Protestant evangelism.[10] At this time, the aesthetic and the religious became somewhat coterminous. Witness Henry James's fictional art patron Roderick Hudson, who declared that "the office of art is second only to that of religion," or *Scribner's Monthly* declaring that the development of artistic taste "may be compared with what the religious call a 'growth in grace.' There is such a thing as 'the witness of the spirit,' in art as in religion."[11] The porosity of the boundaries between the spiritual and the aesthetic—realms then gendered as female—was one of the means by which women could assume a degree of religious authority.[12] And so with this national movement championing art's capacity to transform communities, coupled with a rich theological tradition celebrating the beauty of the earth and humankind's eternal creative impulse, it is of no surprise that Mormon Utah experienced an aesthetic turn and that women were among its most ardent evangelists.[13]

Women of the LDS faith eagerly embraced these positions, viewing themselves not so much as keepers of the flame of civilization but, rather, as its igniters, for Utah and Mormon communities in the American West were newly formed.[14] A more expansive attitude toward women's roles in the civic and social spheres was enabled by somewhat unique elements in the state of Utah and within turn-of-the-century LDS Church culture. For example, the realities of frontier life meant that prescribed gendered divisions of labor were untenable. Furthermore, in Mormon Utah, where men would leave their families to preach for years at a time, Church members were instructed by their leaders to take on whatever responsibilities necessary to develop their communities. Women were urged to study medicine, mind shops, become bookkeepers, and take on other professional roles, and thus it would seem the cult of domesticity held less sway here (at least in the years prior to World War I) than in more established communities in the United States.[15] Moreover, this period witnessed concerted efforts by the LDS Church to mainstream Mormonism within American society; this included eschewing the controversial practice of polygamy and embracing the two-party political system, among other measures, to "de-peculiarize" the Saints of the West.[16] Emphasizing the Mormons' shared values with middle-class, Protestant Americans was another means, and the LDS Church's appreciation for the beautiful and commitment to cultivating the arts was certainly consonant with these national trends.[17] Alice Merrill Horne, the *grande dame* of the Utah art scene, maintained that "the women of 'The Valley' were ladies of culture, refinement and spirituality . . . hungering for the beautiful."[18]

Importantly, these Mormon women artists and art advocates used the organs of the women's auxiliaries of the Church—the Relief Society and Young Ladies' Mutual Improvement Association—to promote the development of aesthetic ideals within their faith and civic communities and to lay claim for women the province of the arts. Unlike other areas of the United States, where women's cultural activities were decidedly domesticated, Mormon Utah proved unusually hospitable to women's participation in the public art scene. Especially critical to this enterprise were the Church-sponsored publications, including the *Woman's Exponent*, the *Relief Society Magazine*, and the *Young Woman's Journal*. The magazines, whose staffs were predominantly female, served the dual purpose of providing instruction for Mormon women and young girls and demonstrating to those outside the faith how members were in most respects like the nation's middling classes in their values and practices.[19] Philosophical discussions of art, biographies of artists, exhibition reviews, and a plethora of art-related material, whose scope ranged from the historical and international to the local and contemporary, filled the pages of these periodicals. They also printed numerous pieces devoted specifically to women artists and women's responsibility to valorize art and beauty in their homes and communities.[20] The sheer volume of this kind of material indicates that the realm of art was deemed the LDS woman's rightful sphere to nurture and protect.

Women's fulfillment of this vocation did not mean standing guard over sacred shrines; rather, it required activity and engagement within the public sphere. For those with artistic aspirations, it meant making pilgrimage to the Mecca of the art world: Paris. Between 1890 and 1920, at least a dozen Mormon women went to Paris to study the visual arts and become more effective emissaries of "culture, refinement and spirituality."[21] In the late 1890s, Rose Hartwell and Mary Teasdel journeyed separately to enroll in the Académie Julian. Lara Rawlins Cauffmann, May Jennings Farlow, and Myra Sawyer joined their LDS artist-sisters on the Continent. Over the course of the next two decades, Louise Richards Farnsworth, Florence Ware, Lu Deen Christensen, Alice Merrill Horne, and others would follow suit, each spending some time abroad, and with Paris as a required destination. While there, they were immersed in the art spaces to which American expatriates gravitated, such as the Louvre, the art Salon, Whistler's studio, Monet's Giverny, and Normandy. Unsurprisingly, they also frequented those places in the city fashioned especially for American women, such as the American Girls' Club and boarding houses in the Latin Quarter.

Paris was a beacon of light to all art devotees, even a city set on a hill, and in the late nineteenth century, serious American artists in particular believed it compulsory that they not only make pilgrimage to view its masterpieces but also conduct sustained training in the center of the art world. Those with means began traveling to Paris to avail themselves of the newly opened studios for women offering comparable training to that given to men.[22] By the turn of the century, there were boarding houses, reading rooms, clubs, and other organizations fashioned exclusively for American women artists, including the American Students' Home and American Girls' Club. And hence a colony of sorts was established where female students shared expenses and expertise as they made their way away from home.[23]

Mary Teasdel came to this colonized Paris in 1898 determined to learn the principles of "true art," as she called it. Born into a privileged Salt Lake City family, she was afforded an excellent education and studied art at the University of Utah, the National Academy of Design, and the Art Students League in New York.[24] As her biographer noted, her determination to become a serious artist required some sacrifice, and so, "looking forward to the day when she might undertake her life's work she began to religiously save what she might have spent (as her girl associates did) for pleasure."[25] This devotion allowed her to spend three years studying art in France, which she did with her companion and fellow Utah artist May Jennings Farlow. Once in Paris, she enrolled in the same school where the male LDS art missionaries had studied, the Académie Julian, which had pioneered an art education for women on par with that given to men,[26] as well as in the studio of perhaps the most esteemed American artist of the period, James McNeill Whistler. Both studios served as important sites in the production of female networks of sociability and professionalism.

A lengthy article in the *Young Woman's Journal* on Teasdel's Paris days emphasized the importance of personal initiative and a support system of women in order to achieve artistic success. Before going to France, the artist spent a winter in the art studios of New York, staying with "a true friend, Cora Hooper, now Mrs. Ernst Eldredge."[27] With her companion from Utah and other women art students she met along the way, Teasdel navigated the foreign frontier of the Paris art scene. Merrill Horne, the author of this article, asks her young readers:

> Have you a rosy picture of student life in Paris and the art studios there? Forget them! The studios are dirty and barren. . . . The studios for women are a counterpart of those for men, but for women the tuition is double. . . . There are three

periods of study, morning, afternoon, and evening. A serious student could not get along with only one period. Miss Teasdel took four hours in the morning and three hours—from seven to ten—in the evening.[28]

The training regimen during the summer was no less rigorous: Teasdel joined with eight or ten other women art students in hiring a teacher and letting a house in the countryside, and then walking at least six miles a day with her companions to gather material for the two sketches she produced daily without fail.[29]

When the young Mormon woman artist returned to Utah "with the determination of one following her chosen vocation,"[30] as one reporter aptly said, she was well positioned to advocate for the advancement of the arts in her church and civic communities. The local press had followed Teasdel's time abroad with much enthusiasm,[31] and her homecoming was a triumphant one. This accomplished artist was immediately inundated with speaking invitations and requests to join various arts organizations, including the newly formed Utah Art Institute (of which she would become president in 1902). Within a few years of her return, Teasdel authored an art manifesto of sorts for the *Young Woman's Journal* titled "True Art: Harmony, Beauty, and Eternal Fitness." The essay is infused with LDS beliefs about beauty being a reflection of God and a powerful instrument for spreading his word.[32] She began this essay by quoting the poet Robert Browning, who says, "For—don't you mark we are made so that we love first when we see them painted—things we have passed perhaps a hundred times nor cared to see; and so they are better, painted, better to us which is the same thing. *Art was given for that—God uses us to help each other, so leading our minds out.*"[33]

At the core of Teasdel's aesthetic belief is her conviction of its divine nature. She proclaims, "Art is infinite in its various expressions and should enter every part of our lives because art means harmony, beauty and the eternal fitness of things."[34] Her manifesto reflects Whistler's tutelage, for the high priest of Aestheticism preached a "belief in the power of a pure art to transform the world,"[35] and he maintained that the individual's ability to recognize an object's intrinsic and autonomous beauty intimated spiritual acumen. Obtaining such powers of discernment "requires some study and search," Teasdel emphasized, but was a worthy goal.[36] She included in this essay reproductions of two paintings she had studied at the Louvre, Ernest Meissonier's *Young Woman Singing* and Elisabeth Vigée-Lebrun's *Self Portrait with Daughter*, as exemplary works. These paintings, which feature women developing their artistic talents and embracing the role of motherhood, reinforced the notion that culture was women's rightful realm.

Similar to her religiously themed writings about art,[37] Teasdel's paintings were oriented toward motifs of the beautiful and the good. Her *Mother and Child* (1901; see figure 6.1), which was awarded best in show at the 1902 Utah

Art Institute's exhibition, features a French peasant woman holding a sleeping baby while gazing tranquilly out the window at the quaint village beyond.
Reflecting Teasdel's training in the latest stylistic approaches, with its simpli-
fied forms and reduced color palette, the subject also shows an awareness of
her audience. It was featured as the frontispiece for the November 1902 issue

Figure 6.1. Mary Teasdel, *Mother and Child*, 1901. Oil on canvas, 37 × 30.5 inches,
State of Utah Fine Art Collection.

of the *Young Woman's Journal* with the following explanatory note: "The mother is a French peasant. The scene is Miss Teasdel's studio, at the sea coast at Bologne [*sic*]. Through the open window, we catch a glimpse of a little cathedral. Peace is in the air, and altogether the picture is exquisite in feeling. The artist is a Utah girl who has devoted much time in the perfecting of her talent."[38] With its valorization of maternity, domesticity, and piety, *Mother and Child* would have resonated with its Mormon Utah viewers.

But it was the world of nature that appealed most to Teasdel, and once home, she primarily painted scenes of the Wasatch mountains and other picturesque sites in the Salt Lake Valley. With Teasdel's painting *Apple Blossoms* (1930; see figure 6.2), she ably translated her study of French art and landscape to the treatment of local sites. Under her deft hand, an ordinary apple tree becomes majestic, and its radiant blossoms, made more lifelike through thick daubs of pinkish-white paint, flit across and animate the surface. Rather than paint the highly masculinized subject of the rugged American frontier, Teasdel painted small-scale landscapes and domestic scenes that would be accessible to those in her community and train their eye to see beauty in the everyday.

Like her sister-artist Mary Teasdel, Rose Hartwell (Whiteley) was also attuned to the mission of cultural refinement.[39] Her discussion of the value

Figure 6.2.   Mary Teasdel, *Apple Blossoms*, 1930. Oil on canvas, dimensions unknown, Smithfield Public Library.

of studying art shifted the focus away from her own creations and toward the merit of other artists. Hartwell writes, "You ask what my appreciation of art means to me. It means this, that if I could never do anything worthy of mention myself, I should never regret the study I have given art in order to appreciate the art in others."[40] For the many readers who would have neither the opportunities to travel nor the artistic successes that she did, such advice intimates the intrinsic value of study of objects of beauty and aligns nicely with the broader mission of these Mormon women artists.

Letters home from Rose Hartwell, which were published in the *Young Woman's Journal*, were similar to those from Mary Teasdel in that they emphasized the demands of art-student life in Paris.[41] While abroad, Hartwell's work regimen was strict; for the first two years, she worked only on drawing from eight in the morning until five in the evening every day except Saturday, when she took the afternoon off to visit the museums and galleries. It appears that Hartwell was like the majority of American art students in Paris who, in the words of Emily Burns, assumed "the proverbial Puritan's cloak . . . exhibiting a steadfast work ethic and moral code"[42] and eschewed bohemian life.

The informal network of American women artists traveling and abroad shaped the course of Hartwell's education. She writes of crossing the Atlantic with a group of "very intelligent women" from Chicago touring the cathedrals of Great Britain.[43] Once in Paris, she met a young American woman who advised her to go to the Académie Vitti instead of the Académie Julian (where the male Mormon missionary artists had trained) to get more individualized instruction.[44] Hartwell found this advantageous, especially as the Vitti was near the American Girls' Club, a much-valued resource and haven for women studying in Paris.[45] There, she writes:

> I could get help and advice about things I did not understand. I am very glad that I followed her advice and soon began to feel quite at home, for there seemed to be more Americans and English in the "quarter" and in the "Vitti" than French. There I met an English girl who afterward became a very dear friend and with whom I spent the first six years of my European life. We took apartments, kept house together, and traveled together constantly.[46]

The "English girl" whom she referred to here was most likely Myra Louise Sawyer, another artist who hailed from Utah and who was a key member of this Mormon artistic sisterhood. In a posting that emphasized the Utah contingency of women artists, the *Salt Lake Herald* reported, "Miss Myra Sawyer, who spent the summer in Holland, is now in Paris, where she will spend the entire winter studying painting under noted masters. Miss Sawyer spent several days recently as the guest of Miss Kimball and Miss Hartwell, who are also in Paris, where they have been students of art and music for the past two years."[47] Within the year, she was displaying her paintings at the American Girls' Club; in 1912, her art was featured in the American Society's show in Paris. Sawyer was eager to explore the art scene outside of the city and joined Hartwell on her trips to Spain, Italy, Belgium, and the Netherlands. The two even spent one summer painting in Giverny, home of the painter Claude Monet.[48]

From Sawyer's portraits, executed in the style of Edouard Manet, to her *French Landscape* (1900; see figure 6.3), her art has a marked foreign streak. Like scores of other American artists, including the male Mormon art missionaries, she drew inspiration from Monet's iconic series of haystacks. In *French Landscape*, Sawyer juxtaposed mounds of golden grain against the cottages of a charming French village, whose rooftops formally echo the haystacks. The bright green strip of the grass below and hazy blue sky above serve to enliven this picturesque landscape. This humble approach, wherein the viewer is gently reminded of the beauty of the everyday, surely appealed to audiences in the largely agrarian state of Utah.

As with the paintings of Teasdel and Sawyer, Hartwell's artworks suggest a negotiation of her upbringing in Mormon Utah with her experiences and art training abroad. Her large-scale *Frugal Meal* (1903; see figure 6.4) features a

Figure 6.3. Myra Louise Sawyer, *French Landscape*, 1900. Oil on canvas, 17.88 × 23.75 inches, Springville Museum of Art.

Figure 6.4.   Rose Hartwell (1861–1917), *The Frugal Meal,* 1903. Oil on canvas, 79.125 × 63.25 inches, Brigham Young University Museum of Art, 1941.

family of four shown in a modest dining room, its terra-cotta-colored stucco walls decorated with a few vases, some drying herbs, and a small religious painting of St. Anthony holding a baby.[49] The parents and children are shown gathered, their heads slightly bowed, around a small table crowded with plates of pasta. It is humble fare, but a sense of plenitude and well-being pervades the space. And the light that filters through the adjacent window shines brightest on the standing woman and her brilliant white blouse. It is she who serves as the painting's focal point and who presides over this scene. Hartwell has endowed this everyday scene, one surely inspired by her long sojourn in southern Italy, with a sense of sanctity, and it is of little surprise that this painting, which celebrates the virtues of humility, piety, and family, was so well received back home.

Hartwell's painting *Nursery Corner* (1910; see figure 6.5) also elevates woman and her work, giving it dignity and grace. In its artfully decorated room covered with plum-red striped wallpaper sits a woman in a rocking chair with an infant lying on her lap. In front of her is a cradle, which anchors the composition. Painted in sage green, adorned with scarlet flowers, and laid with white linens, it is perhaps a subtle reference to Christ's holy manger. The color harmonies and innovative use of space found in Hartwell's *Nursery Corner* are striking, as is its quiet lyricism. Like her painting *Frugal Meal*, there is something almost reverential to this artwork. In sum, Hartwell's paintings effectively preach the values of these Mormon women artists.

Figure 6.5.   Rose Hartwell (1861–1917), *Nursery Corner*, c. 1910. Oil on canvas, 23.75 × 28.25 inches, Brigham Young University Museum of Art, 1941.

Although Hartwell believed in the power of art, she was a private person by nature and so less gregarious in her missionary efforts. In fact, Merrill Horne would chide her in the pages of the *Young Woman's Journal* for not advancing the sisterhood of Utah women artists: "Miss Hartwell, who pioneered the way for women to study art abroad, has shown very little of her work at exhibitions at home."[50] After this gentle but public rebuke, she began to show her works more often in local exhibits.[51] But Hartwell was clearly more comfortable as an expatriate, even field missionary, one could say. In one of her published letters, she promotes the importance of travel, noting, "In Paris and Florence I am more at home than in Salt Lake City. To me, travel seems as necessary to one's education as books, and it is through travel only that one gets clear and concise, yes, and independent, ideas. . . . Paris is the greatest educator of all the cities I have visited."[52] Hartwell's travels had given her worldly experience, and she had more success abroad than any other Utah woman artist.[53] She also did well commercially back home.[54] Rose Hartwell remained an unassuming but committed advocate for the development of the arts in Utah until her untimely death in 1917.

Mormon women artists' experiences working, living, and socializing almost exclusively with other women while abroad—and the rehearsal of their activities in Church publications—influenced the fashioning of the artistic sisterhood back home. In the European art world, where gender segregation in the public sphere was more pronounced, this meant working in women-only studios, living in *pensions* geared for single American women, and participating almost exclusively in women's professional and social clubs. These ranged from the association of sixty-odd women art students at the American Girls' Club, which organized an annual exhibition and sale each December,[55] to the almost 500-member Union des Femmes Peintres et Sculpteurs (Union of Women Painters and Sculptors), whose lobby to allow the admittance of women to the state-sponsored École des Beaux-Arts (School of Fine Arts) had just recently met with success.[56] Letters and interviews about Mormon women artists' time in Europe show that female relationships were critical to their personal and professional development. As Jane Mayo Roos notes in her study of women artists in nineteenth-century France, "female bonding seems to be a much over-looked phenomenon in the development of serious women artists, and although male teachers and colleagues certainly provided encouragement and support, the presence of women allies could go a long way toward countering the gender prejudices of the period."[57] And the expertise gained while studying abroad dovetailed beautifully with existing foundations and frameworks of the LDS Church's women's auxiliary organizations, which facilitated the construction of a female-centric culture of art and refinement in Mormon Utah at the turn of the century.

Mary Teasdel, Myra Sawyer, Rose Hartwell, and their "sisters of the brush"[58] came back from their studies abroad prepared to both assume prominent leadership roles in civic and ecclesiastical organizations in Utah and to mobilize the lessons they had learned about artistic sisterhoods at home. Soon after her return from her three-year stint in France, Mary Teasdel was appointed by Governor Wells as director of the newly formed Utah Art Institute and within the year became its president, with Edna Wells Sloan as secretary and Alice Merrill Horne as treasurer ("all places of trust and requiring executive responsibility," it was noted in the *Woman's Exponent*).[59] Myra Sawyer was appointed to the institute's governing board in 1907; she also served as the chair of the fine arts department of the Utah Federation of Women's Clubs and in 1935 was appointed as the fine arts chair of the Western Federation of Women's Club.[60] Teasdel, along with Sawyer and Hartwell, was among the ten founding members of the Association of Salt Lake Artists, formed in 1913.[61] The Mormon women artists also served on juries for art competitions ranging from the Utah State Fair to the annual Utah Art Institute competition. Of note is that there existed greater gender parity in these juries than one might expect. For example, the 1901 Utah Art Institute annual exhibition jury included six men and four women.[62] The extensive involvement of these women in the development of the state's art institutions was unusual in comparison to the developed art scenes back East.[63] But as Phil Kovinick has demonstrated, the number of art schools and organizations in the western United States increased significantly between 1893 and 1930, with women frequently playing major roles.[64]

At the helm of this unofficial art mission was Alice Merrill Horne, described as "the First Lady in Art in the State of Utah" (see figure 6.6).[65] A tireless promoter of women's sacred role in preaching the gospel of art and of her responsibility to cultivate her talents to that end, she dedicated her life to this calling. What was said of sister artist Mabel Frazer applied equally well to her, "Her religion and her art took precedence over everything else in her life; she couldn't be bothered with anyone or anything else."[66]

While a full account of Merrill Horne's art missionary work stands outside the bounds of this chapter, a cursory gloss over some of her accomplishments will sufficiently illustrate her devotion to "the Gospel of Beauty."[67] Having become a state legislator for the express purpose of introducing legislation to advance the arts, she authored the landmark Bill 124, the so-called Utah Art Bill of 1899, which created the first art institute in the United States. Subsequently, she was appointed the first president of the Utah Art League, and the institute's art holdings were christened the Alice Art Collection in her honor. In 1902, Merrill Horne was called to the LDS Church's General Relief Society Board, and in this capacity she developed an art curriculum for this organization. In her positions as a former state

Figure 6.6.   Alice Merrill Horne, c. 1890. Fox & Symons, photographers, LDS Church History Library, Utah.

legislator and representative of the Relief Society, Merrill Horne pontificated upon the virtues of cultivating the arts in an address delivered to the International Council of Women, which met in Berlin in 1904.[68] Additionally, she founded the Utah Art Colony in 1920 and in this role mounted over one hundred exhibits and put together at least thirty-nine collections of Utah artists for schools and civic groups.[69] Merrill Horne's accomplishments in the art world of Mormon Utah are legion. Susa Young Gates perhaps said it best when she wrote to her, saying, "You . . . have done more to promote and preserve the love of the beautiful in the hearts of our Utah citizens than any woman in the church or in the state. Indeed, I feel that your influence reaches out all over the West."[70]

Alice Merrill Horne's appreciation for the Old World and its treasures, for the beauty of nature, and for the virtues of art were encouraged in her youth, and so she was prepared to preside over this sisterhood. As a young child, she was brought to live in Salt Lake City with her grandmother, Bathsheba W. Smith, an accomplished artist who had traveled across the plains with her treasured watercolors and who had given Alice her initial art training.[71] Young Alice was also allowed to sort through boxes of pictures her grandfather, George A. Smith, had collected from his trips to Europe. When she was fifteen years old, she began drawing classes with George Ottinger and later continued her studies at the University of Utah with J. T. Harwood and Herman Haag, and even took private lessons from Mary Teasdel.[72] Merrill Horne records a pivotal moment in her training: "Mr. Harwood returned from Paris with his painting and opened classes. A friend of mine, Hattie Richards, was drawing from a Venus de Melos cast. From that hour I became a devotee to art."[73] In the next decade, she began to find ways to travel throughout the United States, with visits to museums and exhibitions as mainstays of her itinerary. In 1915, Teasdel and Merrill Horne traveled together to the San Francisco exposition for the purpose of not only studying but also speaking to the curators about bringing some of the paintings to Salt Lake City "under the auspices of the Relief Society."[74] When she was invited to represent Utah at the 1904 International Council of Women in Berlin, Merrill Horne conducted a bit of a Grand Tour of Europe, where finally she was able to worship in person the objects she had known only from books and magazines. At that very women's congress, she gave two speeches, and "one subject, art, was a request," she informed her readers.[75] Apparently her great accomplishments in the sacralization of art on the frontiers of the American West had drawn national and international interest, and in Berlin she had a grand forum in which to pontificate.

Perhaps Merrill Horne's most influential evangelizing was in poetry and prose, however. She authored dozens of essays, features, notices, and poems on art and aesthetics, most of which were published in LDS Church publications. One of her poems, "At My Easel," captures her deep-seated conviction in the sacred act of creating art, as evidenced in the stanzas below:

A new strange light veils all without,
My brushes call.
Beauty invokes the mystical:
I seize the canvas, paint
Poor things inanimate
To make them live.
Feelings my sense on my soul hath wrought
Must never wholly be forgot.
. . .
A sweeter meaning in the scene I learn:
Some hidden truth I feel with fervor burn
Into my heart, my soul! Intelligence!
Intelligence, God's glory!
Glory be to Thee
For *Thine the gifted be!*[76]

Merrill Horne's writings on art and beauty were expanded upon and published in her magnum opus, the first art book published in Utah, *Devotees and Their Shrines: A Handbook of Utah Art* (1914).[77] The invocation of religion in the book's title situates the local art community as a sacred one, where artists understand that they were consecrated to create holy works worthy of being worshipped by the devout.[78] "All who serve art, no matter in what medium they work, be it canvas, marble, plaster, wood, metal or textile, are of one family, consecrated to one end: to make the world beautiful," the author intones.[79]

The importance of studying abroad to becoming a devotee of art is a leitmotif in this text. One of the sections of the book is titled "Winners of Honors Abroad," where she discussed the lives and art of those who studied in Paris, heralding their awards and honors, appending "Paris Salon" or "Autumn Salon" (for the *Salon d'automne*) to the illustrated works of Utah art exhibited there. Indeed, special emphasis was given in *Devotees and Their Shrines* to those Utah artists who had traveled, trained, and exhibited in Paris—their biographies are the lengthiest and most laudatory. Moreover, she constantly referenced French art and its institutions and includes illustrations of masterpieces of the Louvre, such as the *Venus de Milo*, the *Nike of Samothrace*, and the *Mona Lisa* are scattered (with captions that make it clear to the reader that Merrill Horne had seen these in person). It becomes obvious that for those dedicated to the visual arts, a pilgrimage to Paris was an absolute necessity. In sum, this text is a critical linchpin to the story of Mormon Utah art, wherein aesthetic vision and artistic values were established, institutions and practices formulated, and the cult of the artist and Gospel of Beauty articulated.

Laden with religious terminology, syntax, and rhetorical strategy, Merrill Horne's *Devotees and Their Shrines* served as a kind of scriptural source for the LDS art scene and one that put women at its center as subjects and as audience.[80] It included biographies and illustrated art works of many local women artists. It celebrated the accomplishments of Mormon women who had trained abroad, won awards, and assumed significant leadership positions within the Utah art world, thus encouraging the continuation of Mormon women's engagement in the arts and the reification of women in the cultural sphere. Furthermore, women were its primary readership, for it was drafted as a manual for a Relief Society program of study on art, architecture, and landscape that Merrill Horne developed and implemented in 1914–1915.[81] And it was a female alliance that enabled this program, it seems; Merrill Horne intimated that this curriculum was adopted because her grandmother, the LDS Church's acting General Relief Society president, had endorsed it.[82] Its board lauded *Devotees*, remarking that it "has been widely circulated, and has reached thousands of women who have been lifted up by its teachings into the realm of harmony and loveliness."[83] Merrill Horne put the number of readers at forty thousand.[84] Moreover, the text was adopted in the schools of Utah, where it "has been widely read, still maintaining its place as a most inspiring reference book," as reported some thirty-plus years after its initial publication.[85]

Alice Merrill Horne was the primary figure in the Mormon artistic sisterhood that emerged at the turn of the century, and as suggested in the narrative that opened this chapter, she ardently believed that she was called of God to direct this sacred task. Indeed, she had firsthand experiences in her youth and young adulthood that demonstrated the power of women's collectives, as suggested by the full account of the blessing she had received from an LDS Church matriarch. Merrill Horne records:

> Eliza R. Snow sat on the other side of the room. I stood up when there was a moment's pause and asked her to bless me for I was ill, that if she would do it I knew I would recover my good health. Sister Snow stood up and reached her hand toward me and spoke to me in an unknown tongue but I knew she was blessing me. I felt myself lift up and strength came into my limbs and I knew then I was in health. Zina D. Young arose and said that she had received the interpretation of the tongue among other things. She said I would be healed to the desire and faith I had expressed and that I would live to do a work that no one else would be prepared to do. I forgot that I had been ill and grew strong and active.[86]

In her published account of this blessing in the *Relief Society Magazine*, she reminded her readers that this experience

> induced me to bring forward a law in the third State Legislature for the promotion of fine arts; and when asked [in the Relief Society Committee] to suggest a

study for our year's work, I knew what it was to be. You all know the response. Every passing cloud, each hill-line, each patch of color, became charged with a message of beauty to a great multitude of observing and loving women.[87]

In order to accomplish this mission, Merrill Horne nurtured a female network of artists, collectors, and supporters. She spent her days legislating for art institutions, delivering speeches on the virtues of the arts to ladies' clubs and to international conferences of women, and organizing art shows in Utah schools and businesses (and this sometimes meant having her eleven-year-old son drive her around the Salt Lake Valley, their motorcar loaded to the hilt with paintings).[88] Merrill Horne wrote letters of encouragement and lent financial support to local artists—it is even said that she gave money to young artists to study abroad—and performed the role of art agent in her later years. When she sent artists their commission checks, she would append a poem she had written, titled "My Prayer," which captures her unwavering commitment to this mission and her desire to have these artists see their work as a purposeful, holy vocation. The final stanza reads:

The spark was struck in me,
Help me to keep it white
That my one little candle light
May cross the path at darkest night
That a gifted lonely one must scale,
And turn his thought within
To work a mighty miracle.
His skill of line, its wondrous grace
Might take hold the people, lift the race;
Perchance a brave new renaissance,
Bowed by an arch-feigned suppliance
Shall no longer be concealed,
When a master shall stand revealed
For our own day, and for our time.
May it be mine, I pray
May it be mine.[89]

Strengthened by their conviction in the sanctity of their aesthetically oriented endeavors and emboldened by the authority and expertise they gained from their pioneer adventures across the Atlantic, these women were active, visionary, and vocal in their commitment to cultivating the arts among their people.[90] They used the organs of the women's auxiliaries of the LDS Church—the Relief Society and Young Ladies' Mutual Improvement Association—to promote these lofty aesthetic ideals in their various spheres of influence. In a 1914 issue of the *Young Woman's Journal*, Emmeline B. Wells all but guaranteed LDS women's forthcoming ascendency in the visual arts:

We predict, therefore, for the young women of today, greater excellence in literature and the arts than has been attained by their mothers, or by their sex elsewhere. It is doubtful if the women of any other church have done as much in these lines as has already been accomplished by the women of the Church of Jesus Christ of Latter-day Saints.[91]

This prognostication was followed by essays in the same publication authored by Mabel Frazer detailing her vision of an ideal Mormon aesthetic and urging the young women readers to "with your own hands lay a part of the foundation for the last great art development of the world, the art of 'Mormonism.'"[92] With unbounded optimism for the future of art in Mormon Utah and sincere belief in the destined role women were to play in its development, these Mormon women artists, art educators, and art advocates thus fashioned a space in which they could assert authority and power.

NOTES

Early versions of this chapter were delivered as part of a panel, "Mormon Migrations: Travels to Nauvoo, Salt Lake City, and Paris," at the 2013 conference of the Nineteenth-Century French Studies Association, as well as at the 2016 LDS Church History Symposium, *Beyond Biography: Sources and Contexts for Mormon Women's History.* I would like to thank the other panelists and participants in these sessions for their useful feedback, as well as the editors of this volume for their careful reading and excellent suggestions for refining the chapter. This chapter is part of a larger book project tentatively titled *Artistic Frontiers: Mormon Women Artists Abroad, 1880–1945,* which has been generously supported by both a BYU Women's Initiative grant as well as a Charles Redd Center for Western Studies grant.

1. Alice Merrill Horne, "The Gospel of Beauty," *Relief Society Magazine* 7, no. 4 (1920): 202–3.

2. The development of a vibrant local arts culture was due in no small part to the efforts of these individuals. For an overview of women and the arts in Utah, see Raye Price, "Utah's Leading Ladies of the Arts," *Utah Historical Quarterly* 38, no. 1 (1970): 65–85; and Martha Sonntag Bradley-Evans, "Women in the Arts: Evolving Roles and Diverse Expressions," in *Women in Utah History: Paradigm or Paradox?*, eds. Patricia Lyn Scott and Linda Thatcher (Logan: Utah State University Press, 2005), 324–59.

3. *"Take care of the art-schools.* It is to these schools that one looks, both for accomplishment of good work and for the dissemination of aesthetic taste. Out of these schools should come, not only artists, but aesthetic evangelists." William C. Brownell, "The Art Schools of New York," *Scribner's Monthly* 16, no. 6 (October 1878): 765.

4. For additional information on the Paris Art Mission, see William C. Seifrit, "Letters from Paris," *Utah Historical Quarterly* 54, no. 2 (Spring 1986): 179–202; Linda Jones Gibbs, *Harvesting the Light: The Paris Art Mission and Beginnings of Utah Impressionism,* published in conjunction with the exhibition at the Museum of Church History and Art (Salt Lake City, UT: Church of Jesus Christ of Latter-day Saints, 1987); and Jeffery D. Andersen, "Portrait of the 1890–1892 LDS Paris Art Mission: An Andragogical Perspective" (PhD diss., University of Idaho, 2006); and Rachel Cope, "'With God's Assistance I Will Someday Be an Artist': John B. Fairbanks's Account of the Paris Art Mission," *BYU Studies* 50, no. 3 (2011): 133–59.

5. Kathleen D. McCarthy, *Women's Culture: American Philanthropy and Art, 1830–1930* (Chicago: University of Chicago Press, 1991), xi.

6. For more on this development, consult Ann Douglas, *The Feminization of American Culture* (New York: Alfred A. Knopf, 1977).

7. Bailey Van Hook, *Angels of Art: Women and Art in American Society, 1876–1914* (University Park: Pennsylvania State University Press, 1996), 210.

8. See McCarthy, "Culture and Gender in Antebellum America," in *Women's Culture*, 3–36.

9. This sacralization was a complex and uneven process and was inextricably linked to such developments as the professionalization of the arts and attempt to impose order on the pluralistic society of the Gilded Age. For more on this process, see Lawrence W. Levine, *Highbrow/Lowbrow: The Emergence of Cultural Hierarchy in America* (Cambridge, MA: Harvard University Press, 1988); and Paul DiMaggio, "Cultural Entrepreneurship in Nineteenth-Century Boston: The Creation of an Organizational Base for High Culture in America," *Media, Culture, and Society* 4, no. 1 (1982): 33–50.

10. For women's roles in American evangelism, see Catherine A. Brekus, *Strangers and Pilgrims: Female Preaching in America, 1740–1845* (Chapel Hill: University of North Carolina Press, 1998); and Barbara Leslie Epstein, *The Politics of Domesticity: Women, Evangelism, and Temperance in Nineteenth-Century America* (Middletown, CT: Wesleyan University Press, 1981).

11. Quoted in Levine, *Highbrow/Lowbrow*, 150.

12. For more on the redistribution of gendered religious authority in the field of culture, see Claudia Stokes, *The Altar at Home: Sentimental Literature and Nineteenth-Century Religion* (Philadelphia: University of Pennsylvania Press, 2014).

13. For the relationship between liberal religion and the visual arts in American culture during this period, see Sally M. Promey, "Visible Liberalism: Liberal Protestant Taste Evangelism, 1850 and 1950," in *Religion in North America: American Religious Liberalism*, ed. Leigh E. Schmidt and Sally M. Promey (Bloomington: Indiana University Press, 2012), 76–96.

14. In turn-of-the-century Utah, there was very little differentiation between church and state, and this was particularly true in its cultural arenas. For example, one of the prizes of the Utah Art Institute was having one's artwork grace the cover for the *Young Woman's Journal*, as mentioned in the newspaper coverage of its annual exhibition. See "Art Exhibit Attracts Many Visitors to Display at Provo," *Salt Lake Herald*, September 21, 1902, 7.

15. For example, Mormon women in early Utah founded its first hospital and went back East to secure medical degrees, ran several journals and magazines, and created and managed the state's largest mercantile company and a homegrown silk industry.

16. See Thomas G. Alexander, *Mormonism in Transition: A History of the Latter-day Saints, 1890–1930* (Champaign: University of Illinois Press, 1986; repr. Salt Lake City, UT: Greg Kofford Books, 2012); and Lawrence Foster, *Women, Family, and Utopia: Communal Experiments of the Shakers, the Oneida Community, and the Mormons* (Syracuse, NY: Syracuse University Press, 1991).

17. See James L. Haseltine, "Mormons and the Visual Arts," *Dialogue: A Journal of Mormon Thought* 1, no. 2 (1966): 17–34.

18. Alice Merrill Horne, *Devotees and Their Shrines: A Hand Book of Utah Art* (Salt Lake City, UT: Deseret News, 1914), 24.

19. The mission of the *Woman's Exponent* proclaimed that Mormon women "are engaged in the practical solution of some of the greatest social and moral problems of the age." *Woman's Exponent* 1, no. 12 (November 15, 1872): 96, as quoted in Stokes, *The Altar at Home*, 157.

20. See, for example, Lillian B. Connelly, "Women in Art," *Young Woman's Journal* 23, no. 11 (1912): 622–25; and Alfred Lambourne, "Women in Art," *Young Woman's Journal* 32, no. 6 (1921): 347–53.

21. In 1889, Harriet Richards Harwood went abroad, studying art in Europe as the fiancée and then wife of the most esteemed Utah artist of the generation, J. T. Harwood. While not a member of the LDS religion, she was good friends with many of the Mormon women artists, and her journey was inspirational to them.

22. For an introduction to this phenomenon, see Jo Ann Wein, "The Parisian Training of American Women Artists," *Woman's Art Journal* 2, no. 1 (Spring/Summer 1981): 41–44; and Kirsten Swinth's "Illustrious Men and True Companionship: Parisian Study," in *Painting Professionals: Women Artists & the Development of Modern American Art, 1870–1930*, ed. Kirsten Swinth (Chapel Hill: University of North Carolina Press, 2001), 37–62.

23. See Emily C. Burns, "Revising Bohemia: The American Artist Colony in Paris, 1890–1914," in *Foreign Artists and Communities in Modern Paris, 1870–1914: Strangers in Paradise*, ed. Karen L. Carter and Susan Waller (Burlington, VT: Ashgate Press, 2015), 97–110.

24. For an overview of Teasdel's time in the City of Light, consult Martha S. Bradley, "Mary Teasdel: Yet Another American in Paris," *Utah Historical Quarterly* 58, no. 3 (Summer 1990): 244–60.

25. Alice Merrill Horne, "Mary Teasdel: The Utah Impressionistic Painter," *Young Woman's Journal* 21, no. 3 (March 1910): 131.

26. For additional information on this subject, read Catherine Fehrer, "Women at the Académie Julian," *Burlington Magazine* 136, no. 1100 (November 1994): 752–57; and Gabriel P. Weisberg and Jane R. Becker, eds., *Overcoming All Obstacles: The Women of the Académie Julian* (New Brunswick, NJ: Rutgers University Press, 1999).

27. Merrill Horne, "Mary Teasdel," 132.

28. Merrill Horne, "Mary Teasdel," 133.

29. Merrill Horne, "Mary Teasdel," 135.

30. "Miss Teasdel Returns: Salt Lake Young Lady Who Has Been Abroad," *Salt Lake Tribune*, October 15, 1900.

31. In 1899, Teasdel had three ivory miniatures displayed, becoming the first woman (and third person) from Utah to have art shown at the Paris Salon, and the following year, her painting *Little Boy* was accepted for the United States exhibition at the World's Fair in the City of Light—Utah's only painter on display. Examples of press notices that highlight her triumphs abroad include "Utah Artist's Success: Miss Mary Teasdel Has Work Accepted in Paris," *Salt Lake Tribune*, March 3, 1900; and "Successful Utah Artist," *Salt Lake Tribune*, March 4, 1900.

32. Mary Teasdel, "True Art: Harmony, Beauty and Eternal Fitness," *Young Woman's Journal* 15, no. 1 (January 1904): 14.

33. Robert Browning, quoted in Teasdel, "True Art," 14. Emphasis mine.

34. Teasdel, "True Art," 14.

35. Kathleen Pyne, "Whistler and the Religion of Art," in *Art and the Higher Life: Painting and Evolutionary Thought in Late Nineteenth-Century America* (Austin: University of Texas Press, 1996), 85.

36. Teasdel, "True Art," 16.

37. See also Mary Teasdel, "Michael [sic] Angelo's 'David,'" *Young Woman's Journal* 12, no. 3 (March 1901): 159–60.

38. "Mother and Babe," *Young Woman's Journal* 13, no. 11 (November 1902): 522.

39. Hartwell was not a practicing member of the LDS Church for most of her life. She did, however, remain a cultural Mormon and retain some of her Mormon sensibilities, proudly reporting that when witnessing a grape pressing in Italy, she only partook of fresh wine that had not yet fermented. Carmen Rose de Jong Anderson, "Nine Rosabel Hartwell Whiteley (1861–1917)," Rose Hartwell Curatorial File, 1n2, Brigham Young University Museum of Art.

40. Hartwell quoted in Alice Merrill Horne, "Rose Hartwell—the Utah Colorist," *Young Woman's Journal* 22, no. 3 (1911): 129–30.

41. Merrill Horne, "Rose Hartwell—the Utah Colorist," 127–32.

42. Emily Burns, "Puritan Parisians: American Art Students in Late Nineteenth-Century Paris," in *A Seamless Web: Transatlantic Art in the Nineteenth Century*, ed. Cheryll L. May and Marian Wardle (Newcastle-upon-Tyne, UK: Scholars Press, 2014), 124.

43. Merrill Horne, "Rose Hartwell," 129.

44. Hartwell, as quoted in Merrill Horne, "Rose Hartwell," 129.

45. For additional information on this institution, see Marie Caudill Dennison, "The American Girls' Club in Paris: The Propriety and Impudence of Art Students, 1890–1914," *Woman's Art Journal* 26, no. 1 (Spring/Summer 2005): 32–37.

46. Hartwell, as quoted in Merrill Horne, "Rose Hartwell," 127.

47. "Society," *Salt Lake Herald-Republican*, September 26, 1909, 5.

48. See Vern G. Swanson, Richard S. Olpin, and William C. Seifrit, *Utah Painting and Sculpting* (Salt Lake City, UT: Gibbs Smith Publishers, 1997), 106.

49. This "Italian family scene," as it was described, was prominently placed in the Salt Lake Commercial Club before joining the collection. See Merrill Horne, *Devotees*, 65. This is confirmed in the notice "Salt Lake Painter Is Successful in Paris," *Salt Lake Tribune*, April 9, 1911, 10.

50. Merrill Horne, "Rose Hartwell," 127.

51. Hartwell exhibited at the State Fair of 1913 and at the inaugural exhibit of the Associated Artists of Salt Lake City of that same year, at a free exhibit at 41 South State in 1914 and at the Utah Art Institute in 1916 and 1917.

52. Quoted in Merrill Horne, *Devotees*, 71.

53. Hartwell had more works accepted to the Paris Salon than any other woman artist from Utah. Of the five works she sent to the Salon, four were admitted. She was the only Utah woman artist who received notice in the French press. See "Le Salon de la Société nationale des Beaux-Arts," *Journal des débats politiques et littéraires* 110 (April 10, 1912): n.p. The assertion that Hartwell exhibited her work in other European venues is made in *Utah since Statehood: Historical and Biographical*, vol. 3 (Salt Lake City, UT: S. J. Clarke Publishing, 1919), 1025. Utah newspapers state that she sold work to European buyers. See "Salt Lake Painter Is Successful in Paris," 10; and "Honors for Utah Artist: Her Painting Exhibited," *Salt Lake Tribune*, June 25, 1911, 11. To date, I have not been able to substantiate either of these claims.

54. Merrill Horne, "Rose Hartwell," 128. Hartwell's Salon painting of 1903 (now lost) commanded the unheard-of sum of $1,000 when it was sold back home.

55. Caro Lloyd, "The Club for American Girls Studying in Paris," *Outlook* 50, no. 2 (July 14, 1894): 61.

56. For information on this collective, see Tamar Garb, "Revising the Revisionists: The Formation of the Union des Femmes Peintres et Sculpteurs," *Art Journal* 48, no. 1 (Spring 1989): 63–70.

57. Jane Mayo Roos, "Girls 'n' the 'Hood: Female Artists in Nineteenth-Century France," in *Artistic Brotherhoods in the Nineteenth Century*, ed. Laura Morowitz and William Vaughan (Burlington, VT: Ashgate Press, 2000): 169.

58. For a discussion of how women capitalized on their segregated social and psychic positions in the late nineteenth-century French art world, see Tamar Garb, *Sisters of the Brush: Women's Artistic Culture in Late Nineteenth-Century Paris* (New Haven, CT: Yale University Press, 1994).

59. A. M. H. [Alice Merrill Horne], "Items about Art," *Woman's Exponent* 31, nos. 5–6 (August 1 and 15, 1902): 17.

60. "Miss Sawyer Appointed," *Inter-Mountain Republican*, October 25, 1907, 5; and "Western Clubs Group Appoints Salt Laker," *Salt Lake Telegram*, October 16, 1935, 24.

61. See "Salt Lake Artists Form Association," *Salt Lake Telegram*, December 8, 1913, 10. All of the founding artists had studied in Paris.

62. "Art Judges Are Named," *Salt Lake Tribune*, November 22, 1901.

63. McCarthy, *Women's Culture*, preface. See also Laura R. Prieto, *At Home in the Studio: The Professionalization of Women Artists in America* (Cambridge, MA: Harvard University Press, 2001).

64. Phil Kovinick, *The Woman Artist in the American West, 1860–1960* (North Orange County, CA: Muckenthaler Cultural Center, 1976), 1–2.

65. Alice Merrill Horne Letters 1944–1947, Genevieve Lawrence Papers, ACC1110, box 1, folder 2, Marriott Library Special Collections, University of Utah.

66. See http://smofa.org/files/lesson_plan_packets/lkk6wkrz.pdf.

67. Some useful sources on this extraordinary woman are Harriet Horne Arrington, "Alice Merrill Horne, Art Promoter and Early Utah Legislator," *Utah Historical Quarterly* 58, no. 3 (Summer 1990): 261–76; and "Alice Merrill Horne," *Dedication and Name of 22 Buildings* (Provo, UT: Brigham Young University, May 26, 1954), 50–51.

68. Merrill Horne's address was cited in Marie Stritt, *Der Internationale Frauen-Kongress in Berlin 1904* (Berlin: Verlag von Carl Kabel, n.d.), 251–52; and Frau Eliza Ichenhaeuser, *Bilder vom Internationalen Frauen-Kongress 1904* (Berlin: Druck und Verlag von August Scherl, n.d.), 23.

69. The organization had mounted 129 free exhibitions, hung exhibitions in over 40 different schools, and placed 30 art collections in public schools. See *Art Strands* 1 (July 1931): 22. The number of collections grew to 39 by 1942, according to *Art Strands*, Ella Quayle Van Cott Memorial Number (1942): 2–3.

70. Quoted in *Art Strands* 2 (July 1932): 5.

71. *Art Strands* 1 (July 1931): 10–12. Of all her grandmother's possessions, this was the most cherished: "The most wonderful of all were Grandma's box of watercolors and her book of drawings—heads, copies of Gainsborough and others. The box of watercolors brought from England by an old friend and presented to Grandma just before the pioneers left for Utah. They were used in the camps of the Saints and had its place in their wagon crossing the plains. Sundays were all so long but many a tedious hour grew charmed when the watercolors were brought out—for Grandma would not let me play but I could paint or draw on Sunday." See Alice Merrill Horne Family History Record 1912–1935, Bathsheba W. Smith Collection, 1842–1948, MS 20701, box 2, folder 1, 166, Church of Jesus Christ of Latter-day Saints Church History Library, Salt Lake City, UT, https://dcms.lds.org/delivery/DeliveryManagerServlet?dps_pid=IE8079755.

72. While she had yearned to go to college back East and become a writer, her grandmother did not approve. Merrill Horne records, "I nursed my disappointment and fell to thinking that had I been a boy I could have followed my desires and being a woman I had to be hedged in and handicapped." Alice Merrill Horne Family History Record, 193.

73. Alice Merrill Horne Family History Record, 271. She would later win a silver medal for her drawing of the *Venus de Melos*.

74. "Brought to Zion," *Salt Lake Tribune*, September 25, 1915, n.p.

75. Alice Smith Merrill Horne Biography, Dorothy Shepherd van Stripiaan Papers, MS 281, box 1, folder 1, Marriott Library Special Collections, University of Utah.

76. Merrill Horne, *Devotees*, 39.

77. Jill Mulvay notes that her engagement in the civic arts scene meant her impact was felt on many members of the LDS Church, but it was especially exercised by her numerous publications on art. See her "Three Mormon Women in the Cultural Arts," *Sunstone* 1 (Spring 1976): 29–39.

78. The title may have been inspired by Helen Noe's 1901 poem "Art's Devotees," published in *Munsey's Magazine* 25 (June 1901): 391, as referenced in Levine, *Highbrow/Lowbrow*,

211–12. The final stanza reads: "With steadfast eyes, with white, set, fearless faces, / We reach unto the laurel leaves of art; / And rather those green garlands of the Graces, / Than ships at sea, than wealth of field and mart!"

79. Merrill Horne, *Devotees*, 117.

80. In fact, this text should be viewed as an offshoot of the evangelical print culture. See Candy Gunther Brown, *Word in the World: Evangelical Writing, Publishing, and Reading in America, 1789–1880* (Chapel Hill: University of North Carolina Press, 2004).

81. Advertisements for purchase of the book were placed in the *Woman's Exponent* throughout 1916, stating that it is "this book from which the lessons on architecture for 1916 are assigned." The cost was $1.25, payable to Mrs. Alice Merrill Horne.

82. Merrill Horne characterizes her grandmother as "a forward thinking person so that when a high position was given her in her more advanced years she was willing to try new things and was glad to allow the younger women to propose and suggest new topics and new avenues for her 'oldest organization among women,'—the Relief Society." Alice Merrill Horne Family History Record, 164–65.

83. "Mrs. Alice Merrill Horne," *Relief Society Magazine* 4, no. 1 (1917): 10.

84. Alice Smith Merrill Horne Biography.

85. "In Memoriam—Alice Merrill Horne," *Relief Society Magazine* 35, no. 12 (1948): 816.

86. Alice Merrill Horne Family History Record, 177.

87. Merrill Horne, "The Gospel of Beauty," 202–3.

88. Lola Beatlebrox, *Alice Merrill Horne, 1868–1948* (Salt Lake City, UT: Salt Lake City Art Council, 2007).

89. Alice Merrill Horne, "My Prayer," *Art Strands*, Ella Quayle Van Cott Memorial Number (1942): 13.

90. Erika Doss, a prominent historian of American art, claims that "the art associations that emerged in Utah provided sustenance mostly for male artists, and thereby helped institutionalize Latter-day Saints ideology." This conclusion is problematic on several counts. First, women were heavily involved in the founding and developing of these associations. Second, this statement also presumes that only male artists could be engaged in the construction and reproduction of the LDS Church's system of values—and that LDS ideology is solely patriarchal. See Erika Doss, "I *Must* Paint: Women Artists of the Rocky Mountain Region," in *Independent Spirits of the American West, 1890–1945*, ed. Patricia Trenton (Los Angeles: University of California Press, 1995), 216.

91. Emmeline B. Wells, "Thoughts and Remembrances," *Young Woman's Journal* 25, no. 10 (October 1914): 606.

92. See Mabel Frazer, "Art Appreciation," *Young Woman's Journal* 26, no. 12 (1915): 755; and Mabel Frazer, "The Art Value of Bee-Hive Symbolism," *Young Woman's Journal* 31, no. 10 (1920): 559.

Chapter Seven

Leah Dunford Widtsoe, Alice Merrill Horne, and the Sacralization of Artistic Taste in Mormon Homes, circa 1900

Josh E. Probert

The Mormon home was, along with the Southern plantation home, one of the most contested topics in nineteenth-century America. The travel writer W. F. Rae demonstrated this when in 1871 he wrote, a "home in the English and American sense of the word has no existence among the Latter-day Saints of the Great Salt Lake."[1] At the time Rae made this remark, most Mormons lived in modest or even rustic houses that were sparsely furnished. But frontier living conditions were only one part of the problem. The practice of polygamy—or "celestial marriage," as the Saints preferred to call it—was the major problem. The image of multiple wives inhabiting one house or plural wives living with their children in their own houses with periodic visits from their husband was an affront to the Victorian cult of domesticity. In short, the nineteenth-century Mormon home was uncivilized.

By the turn of the twentieth century, Latter-day Saints had an opportunity for the broader American public to reappraise the cultural orthodoxy of their homes. The church had largely abandoned plural marriage and, simultaneously, redefined celestial marriage as a monogamous union.[2] At the same time, many Latter-day Saints were living in larger, nicer homes than those their parents and grandparents had constructed in earlier generations. Nevertheless, church leaders knew that they still had a lot of work to do in order to measure up to national standards of domestic refinement. Elder John Henry Smith, a Mormon apostle, expressed this awareness when, during the April 1899 general conference, he said, "There are many people that question there being in this western country a people who have the arts of civilization. They regard us in a measure as savages." While the cultural stigma of polygamy had begun to dissipate, the perceived lack of material refinement remained. Because of this cultural deficit, Smith urged members of the Church to redouble their efforts to construct and furnish houses that would earn them the cultural approbation he desired. He boldly informed the Saints that "there shall be no slackening" in this project, and he went on to express hope that they would have the financial "means necessary for the adornment and beautifying of our homes."[3] If church members would follow this guidance and spend the money necessary to improve their living conditions, the Mormon home, and by inference the Mormon people, would finally be deemed civilized.

Leah Dunford Widtsoe (1874–1965) and Alice Merrill Horne (1868–1948) acted as self-appointed leaders in the Mormon pursuit of domestic refinement and cultural reintegration. Widtsoe was a progressive reformer who had been trained in domestic science at the Pratt Institute in Brooklyn and had taught at Brigham Young Academy.[4] Horne was a painter, trained at the Art Institute of Chicago, who promoted the arts in Utah through her own gallery, as a member of the Utah State House of Representatives, and as a member of the Relief Society General Board.[5] Between 1899 and 1902, both of these prominent women published a series of articles on domestic architecture and interior design in the *Young Woman's Journal*, the monthly magazine of the Young Ladies' Mutual Improvement Association.[6] In 1899, Widtsoe published a series titled "Studies in Household Art."[7] In 1902, she published twelve lengthy illustrated articles titled "Furnishing the Home."[8] In 1901, between Widtsoe's two series, Alice Merrill Horne published two substantial illustrated articles titled "Suggestions on Artistic Home Building."[9] The articles expounded on the topics of stylistic vocabularies, interior furnishings, and timesaving workspaces. Some essays focused entirely on one item, such as wallpaper, carpet, or curtains, while others focused on an entire area of the house, such as the dining room, bedrooms, or bathrooms.

The anxiety over social respectability demonstrated in Widtsoe's and Horne's essays was as much about socially aspirational Mormons wanting to accept themselves as it was about having outsiders accept them. Their rhetoric looked both inward and outward in search of usable ingredients for a turn-of-the-century Mormon identity. Church leaders had pivoted outward toward national integration by abandoning polygamy and obtaining statehood for Utah during the 1890s, but the pivot was never a singular or complete one. Just as the Saints' separation from the Babylon of American society in preparation for the Second Coming at midcentury had been selectively partial, so too the reintegration into the American mainstream at the end of the century was selectively partial. A fervent belief that the Second Coming of Christ would occur during their lives was one of the inward-looking beliefs that the Saints held onto, and this belief made the Saints' pursuit of genteel living a matter more consequential than conspicuous consumption.

ENVIRONMENTAL DETERMINISM

The essays in the *Young Woman's Journal* evidence how fully the Victorian belief in the moral power of the built environment had saturated Mormon culture. This belief held that by surrounding people with objects of good taste, those people would, in turn, become tasteful themselves. Objects facilitated what an 1899 marketing pamphlet from Tiffany Studios called "an unconscious education."[10] Genteel furnishings, for example, contained "polish," "finish," "softness," and "refinement"—all cognate characteristics of a genteel person.[11] Conversely, Horne wrote, shoddy houses would create "shoddy people."[12] Yet the influence of objects upon people extended to traits far weightier than posture and decorum. Aesthetically respectable homes would, the authors promised, produce morally respectable people. In one of Widtsoe's essays, she succinctly summarized the belief system: "Our daily surroundings not only shape character but make character."[13] Horne went even further when she said, "Homes built on artistic lines have an abiding influence for honesty, refinement, and spirituality."[14] For both women, spirituality was not confined to the internal workings of the mental realm. It was both materialist and idealist. The physical universe was, to them, a highly active force that exerted a powerful, even coercive, type of non-sentient agency upon its inhabitants. Therefore, seemingly inconsequential things like wallpaper, carpet, and clocks became items of moral significance.

The guidance that Widtsoe and Horne dispensed was a provincial version of the nationally disseminated advice of popular authors and designers such as Candace Wheeler, Edith Wharton, and Ogden Codman Jr.[15] Widtsoe made her borrowings from these sources transparent by citing them in her essays and by including a list of books for further reading. On the educational value of the living room, she quoted art and design critic Clarence Cook, who said, "I look upon this living-room as an important agent in the education of life."[16] And she used the following quote from Candace Wheeler as an epigraph for an article on curtains and pictures: "A perfectly furnished house is a crystallization of the culture, the habits, and the tastes of the family, and not only expresses but makes character."[17]

In looking to elite tastemakers for design guidance, Widtsoe and Horne sacralized genteel culture. They granted power to non-Mormons to shape Mormon identity by looking to them for guidance as to what the Mormon home should be. While Mormon leaders had long castigated Babylon as irredeemably fallen, Widtsoe and Horne made living up to its cultural codes of material refinement necessary to being a fully realized Mormon. The social capital necessary to attain a communal identity of refinement was not available in Utah. Members of the Church had to look back to that Babylon from which they had fled in order to create their uniquely Mormon identity—an example of what Terryl Givens calls the "election-versus-exile" paradox of Mormon culture.[18] The discourse of artistic taste was a particular type of knowledge-as-power that Widtsoe and Horne deployed in order to reposition Mormons in the American imagination.[19]

Because objects shaped character, the logic naturally followed that domestic furnishings also reflected the character of the family to others—Mormon and non-Mormon, neighbor and visitor. Furnishings acted as indices of the education, taste, and character of a family, hence the importance of a well-appointed parlor.[20] But a house exerted its influence on people in every room, not just in the parlor. "The modern view of house building," Widtsoe wrote, "is one that favors building rooms to be lived in, instead of rooms to be shown off at stated periods."[21] In fact, a parlor could be deceptive to a family's character, as it was a designated space of public performance. In an 1895 sermon titled "The House Beautiful," the Unitarian minister William Channing Gannett advised his congregation, "Petition to see a friend's own room before feeling that you really know that friend." The private bedroom was a better "index of one's taste, of one's culture, and of a good deal of one's character" because it was a private, personal space.[22]

ARTISTIC TASTE AND THE BEAUTY OF EFFICIENCY

Horne and Widtsoe were concerned not just with taste but with a particular type: "artistic taste." This is reflected in Horne's title, "Suggestions on Artistic Home Building," and in Widtsoe's assertions that home furnishing was "an art" and that "good taste" was the first necessity in furnishing an "artistic home."[23] But what exactly did artistic taste mean? The phrase, which became popular during the mid-nineteenth century, was so commonly used that a precise definition is elusive.[24] Nevertheless, it denoted an aesthetic sensibility that stood over and against that of factory-made, commercially marketed products—what the apostle of aestheticism Oscar Wilde called "those ugly things made by machinery."[25] Many viewed artistic taste as a humanistic antidote to the stultifying environments of an increasingly mechanized capitalist order. The words "art" and "artist," which first made their appearance in the seventeenth century, signified a gifted type of inspiration that could not be explained by economic forces or by scientific deductions.[26] Artistic objects evinced human originality and the touch of the maker's hand.

The rhetoric of the integration of art and life had its roots in the writings of John Ruskin, the designers of the South Kensington School, and the British leaders of the Arts and Crafts movement.[27] Horne and Widtsoe made generous use of their writings. Horne, for example, echoed William Morris's dictum that all objects should be "useful and beautiful" in defining the type of artistic design she extolled.[28] Both women expressed concern for the "truthfulness" and "simplicity" of domestic furnishings and recommended looking to nature for design inspiration. Horne praised "honest taste" and enjoined her readers to "put a premium on honest construction."[29] They promised that these characteristics, which British design reformers had earlier espoused, would be made manifest in the character of those living amid furnishings possessing them. Widtsoe stressed that honest, dignified furniture produced honest, dignified children. "How necessary that a child's surroundings which are so potent a factor in his character-building be full of harmony, dignity, and truthfulness!" she asserted.[30]

While Widtsoe and Horne described artistic taste in terms of the ineffable, the spiritual, and the beautiful, they also paradoxically framed it as scientific, rational, and efficient. Their rhetoric identified the house as a closed system of productivity and thus as amenable to the nascent field of scientific management, which was concerned with increasing the efficiency of factories.[31] A house should be "a healthy organism," Widtsoe wrote. Through "intelligent manipulation and care of the household belongings," this could be accomplished.[32] She advised that a housewife should get rid of anything "that requires a useless expenditure of living energy." An efficient home should have pure water, plenty of sunlight, ample ventilation, and provision for waste disposal.[33] A home should be a haven of health and repose; and only artistically designed interiors that worked as a unified system of efficiency and beauty could produce these ends.

Because the kitchen was where women spent a lot of their time, the authors were particularly concerned that Mormon women bring their kitchens into alignment with the dictates of artistic efficiency. Horne bragged that her kitchen was "the pleasantest and most artistic room in the house" not just because of its color scheme but because it was efficiently arranged. The time she spent reaching for cooking dishes and food ingredients was minimal because she had designed the kitchen in order to optimize workflow. Horne argued that the layout of the kitchen emitted an influence on the nature of the cook and, therefore, on the nature of her work. Horne rhetorically asked her readers, "Is it logical to hope to appeal to the artistic side and have the [food preparation and other kitchen work] well done, when the surroundings only appeal to the coarser nature?"[34] Such thinking blurred the romantic delineation between art and science. A woman could be a great cook, according to Horne's logic, only if she worked in a great kitchen.

Clutter and uncleanliness, as well as excessive storage, were also inartistic. "Sideboards, shelves, cupboards, wardrobes, and all such furniture built in walls" were easier to keep clean, Horne stated. Furthermore, built-in furniture could "be made much more artistic than is movable furniture, with the added advantage of never being in the way."[35] But even more important, built-in furniture would have a palliative effect on those using it. "This very element will give the repose we so much desire in our homes—the restfulness that is better than pepsin for indigestion and that serves as a balm to disordered nerves." Relatedly, a compact kitchen plan would save "physical and nervous energy as well as mental force on the part of the housekeeper.[36] The soothing influence of artistic furnishings and efficient layouts exuded therapeutic effects on the health as well as the character of those using them. In fact, according to Horne, built-in furniture was just as effective as oral medications in treating neurasthenia, the epidemic of late nineteenth-century urbanites.[37]

Widtsoe and Horne expected readers to take their advice seriously not just because they were church leaders but because they were experts on the topic. They were professional interior decorators—a profession that first emerged in the 1870s.[38] And they demonstrated their professional *bona fides* through their command of the literature, their academic training, and their public lives. Widtsoe invoked the authority of "sociologists and men of science" to declare that "one of the most potent factors in the rise of a great and mighty nation is the existence of the home in which is enshrined all the pure, noble traits of human nature."[39] This professionalization of housekeeping of which Widtsoe and Horne were a part originated in the mid-nineteenth century in the advice literature of reformers like Catherine Beecher and became institutionalized in higher education by academics like Ellen Swallow Richards and Melvil Dewey. The discipline of domestic science, which later became home economics, sought to make housewives more efficient in the home and more effective consumers in the marketplace.[40] Domestic science received much attention in Mormon women's circles, in the pages of the *Young Woman's Journal*, and in the pages of other Mormon women's literature. Widtsoe's mother, Susa Young Gates, had been a founder of the National Home Economics Organization and had introduced domestic science classes at the Brigham Young Academy (later University). She also edited the *Young Woman's Journal* until 1901.[41] Widtsoe succeeded her mother at the Brigham Young Academy and became head of the Department of Domestic Sciences in 1897.[42]

WOMEN AS PIOUS CONSUMERS

The design and decorating advice that Widtsoe and Horne dispensed in the pages of the *Young Woman's Journal* was progressive in nature but still deeply rooted in the mid-nineteenth-century Victorian cult of domesticity. Because of the economic realignments brought about by industrialization and professionalization, many men worked away from the home by the turn of the twentieth century. With men going to work in urban centers, women were most often left home. There they were to create comfortable, religious refuges from the ills of modern urban life. At the same time, they were to create spaces of cultured refinement that favorably mapped the family onto the social landscape.[43]

Such a weighty responsibility required women to become intimately involved with all the physical aspects of their houses. Leah Widtsoe said as much when she told her readers, "If there is one thing in that whole house from the lowest stone to the topmost shingle about which she is indifferent or ignorant, then it is impossible for her to become the Mistress of that home."[44] As these comments make clear, women were to be familiar with the structural and functional aspects of domestic architecture. But the public performance of being the "mistress" of the house was based on what people saw. They looked for what Widtsoe and Horne called "a woman's touch" in the furnishings and decor. Houses were filled with what Jackson Lears calls "the iconography of female experience."[45] The pervasiveness of this gendered aesthetic is evident when contrasted with the smoking rooms and billiard rooms designated specifically for men in upper-class houses. But for the large majority of houses, the woman's touch was to be seen throughout, and both men and women identified this touch as something inherent to women's nature. It was an aptitude, they said, that men did not naturally possess.

Yet despite the rhetoric of women's aesthetic sensibilities being "natural" or "innate," essays like Widtsoe's and Horne's demonstrate that these sensibilities were a socially constructed part of the separation of male and female spheres— an ideology that crystallized during the mid-nineteenth century that still held great power at the turn of the century. In previous eras, men, not women, had played a large, even leading, role in the design and furnishing of home interiors (think Jefferson and Monticello). Furthermore, if women had such an innate gift for design and decor, why were most of them, in the opinion of Widtsoe and Horne, doing it wrong? This tension reframes the essays in the *Young Woman's Journal* as debates among Mormon women as to how they should and should not carry out their domestic duties.

Widtsoe presented women's primary role in creating artistic, efficient homes as an empowering opportunity to Mormon women. The need was for "more convenient and artistic houses than are now built," she declared. "It is upon women that this responsibility largely rests."[46] The man might have the right of proposing ideas, but "since this is to be the woman's domain, she may have the right of disposing."[47] Women needed to study the principles of artistic design and efficient arrangement; they also needed to become effective consumers who could adroitly select fabrics, colors, and furnishings. Here, too, Widtsoe participated in a wider discourse, not coincidentally tied to the rise of women's magazines, where consumption had been firmly gendered as a largely female enterprise.[48] The impression that a domestic interior created for visitors was particularly important to Mormon women because women's identities were more contingent upon interiors than men's were.[49]

When religious progressives like Widtsoe and Horne tethered taste to moral character, they made capitalist consumption an act of religious devotion, a practice that one scholar calls "pious consumption."[50] Indeed, a few years before Widtsoe and Horne published their articles, the *Young Woman's Journal* published a regular feature titled "Our Shopping Department." This column—written by Widtsoe's mother, Susa Young Gates, who was then editor of the magazine—was an advertising strategy to raise revenue for the publication. The column employed the popular method of editorial puffery to promote goods and merchandisers, but it also sought to guide readers in becoming better consumers.[51] "We are all anxious to become the best of wives and mothers, and consequently the best shoppers," Gates asserted, and then went on to dispense advice about how one should behave in city shops. One should politely ask for goods as if the clerk were "the President of the Church" and say "please" and "thank you." Shoppers should not spend cash at other merchants while holding debt with a neighboring one. And haggling over prices was in the worst of taste. "Wherein we fail to be ladies, we fail just so much in being or living up to our religion," she concluded.[52] In their later articles, Widtsoe and Horne focused more on the products, rather than the process, of shopping, but in either case, the assumptions were the same: women were the primary consumers, and their behavior and choices would demonstrate their refined status.

CLASS, WEALTH, AND THE PARADOX OF SIMPLICITY

Horne's and Widtsoe's rhetoric implicitly made spiritual refinement contingent upon the acquisition of wealth. Horne told her readers to look to "wealthy France" as a repository of "artistic work" and that in order for the Latter-day Saints to achieve similar heights of aesthetic achievement, "Nothing will 'do' if it is not the best we can give."[53] Closer to home, she recommended the McCune mansion in Salt Lake City to her readers as a "work of architectural art." Completed in 1901 at a cost of $1 million, the twenty-one-room Shingle Style house was "built to supply all the needs and comforts of a home."[54] Horne presented Elizabeth McCune to her readers as an exemplar of her vision for what Mormon women could become. McCune could "claim the honor for this architectural work of art," Horne wrote, as she was largely responsible for the house's design and its implementation. So credited was McCune as the creative force behind the house that, upon her death, Susa Young Gates titled her tribute "Memorial to Elizabeth Claridge McCune, Missionary, Philanthropist, Architect."[55]

The mansion's interior, which included a ballroom and a banquet room, featured wood-paneled walls, some incorporating satin-brocade fabric and Russian leather paneling (see figure 7.1).

Figure 7.1.   This parlor in the Alfred W. and Elizabeth McCune house exemplifies a late nineteenth-century "artistic" interior. Furnished in the French taste, it emulated the most fashionable interiors of the American bourgeoisie. Furnishings included plaster-cast ceiling ornament, gilded French furniture with tapestry panels, elaborate window treatments, silk wall panels, marble statuary, matching gas-and-electric light fixtures, and an "art glass" lamp on the center table—all furnishings that were far out of financial reach for most Mormons at that time. Utah State Historical Society.

For the woodwork, the McCunes imported oak from England, red mahogany from Santo Domingo, and white-grained mahogany from South Africa. Other elements included art glass windows, marble and onyx fireplaces, and an abundance of decorative painting that took an artist two years to complete.[56] Horne's readers may have wondered whether they shared the same definition of the term "simplicity" with her while reading her praise of the "simple" interiors that the McCune house possessed. This standard of living was completely unrealistic for most Mormon women. While many lived in modest though respectable homes, plenty still lived in rustic conditions (see figure 7.2).

The recommendations for fabrics, furnishings, carpets, colors, decorations, and room layout presented an unattainable constellation of objects by virtue of the sheer quantity, to say nothing of quality and cost. The experience of Lydia Jasperson Moore (1873–1941) evidences the very real financial dispari-ties among turn-of-the-century Mormons. Recalling her early married years in

Figure 7.2 .   This photograph of an unknown Mormon woman and child, taken around 1900, evidences the crude houses that some Latter-day Saints lived in at the turn of the twentieth century. The log structure was furnished with a grain-painted pine lounge and chest of drawers, an oilcloth-covered Eastlake table, a patchwork quilt, a simple kerosene lamp, and a calendar, a poster, and pages from an illustrated book of animals nailed along the wall for decoration. Utah State Historical Society.

Payson, Utah, a settlement some sixty miles south of Salt Lake City, Moore recalled, "I always worked hard and had but little to do with. I piled up boxes and put a curtain in front which had to serve as a wardrobe. How did I wish for a dresser or something with drawers or shelves, but never got it until after my last child was born in 1911. Then we got a second hand dresser and bed to match, which was appreciated."[57] With only stacked boxes for storage to work with, Moore lacked the basic material resources necessary to perform the arts of civilization, as Elder Smith advocated, or to attend to the finer points of artistic taste, as Widtsoe and Horne were encouraging. Eking out a basic subsistence preoccupied her time. Yet her aside that the dresser and bed "matched" when she obtained them reveals the power that even this small modicum of material respectability could have in enhancing the sensory experience of her domestic world. She didn't own an entire matching bedroom set, to say nothing of a matching suite of parlor furniture. But she was able to approximate or paraphrase the ideal and demonstrate a measure of vernacular gentility.[58]

Widtsoe and Horne attempted to bridge the dissonance between the refined living conditions they promoted and the financial constraints of many of their readers, women of the Church like Lydia Moore in Payson. They did so by claiming that obtaining and performing artistic taste was not predicated on wealth. Widtsoe, for example, told her readers that wealth is very often the "chief enemy" of artistic taste. "Expensive things," she said, "are by no means always artistic."[59] True enough, but expensive things had a far greater chance of being artistic than inexpensive things. And most women of the Church did not risk overdoing their interiors, as critics sometimes faulted the nouveau riche for doing, because they did not have the money to even try.[60]

Horne similarly gestured in the direction of sensitivity to those with modest means. "It is not so much the cost of the house, but the way in which it is kept, that makes the home artistic," she insisted. Any house could be beautiful as long as it was "sweet and clean."[61] Employing a term often used by national authors, Horne proclaimed "simplicity" as a sign of good taste—"the highest expression of art."[62] But here again, Horne's illustrations and examples belied her protestations of simplicity. The "cottage" home whose plan she described in detail presupposed modern conveniences like plumbing and a bathroom and called for a kitchen, dining room, pantry, sitting room, and (though she did not enumerate them specifically) multiple bedrooms. Although Horne's idea of a cottage was not as overblown as the "cottages" of Newport, Rhode Island, and Bar Harbor, Maine, it was nevertheless a romanticized ideal that required significant financial means to realize.

PREPARING FOR THE NEW JERUSALEM

The spiritual influence borne by the built environment made cultural progress tantamount to spiritual progress. Leah Widtsoe's architectural aspirations for the Leah Latter-day Saints would culminate in the construction of the New Jerusalem in Jackson County, Missouri. She framed her first series of articles, "Studies in Household Art," as a tutorial in preparation for the millennial event. In the following passage that must be quoted at length to fully understand her thinking, Widtsoe demonstrates one way in which Mormon reintegration was highly selective:

> One of the most glorious conceptions of the Latter-day Saints is that of the possession of the New Jerusalem by the faithful children of God. They look forward to it with the most profound anticipation: the magnificent temples and houses of worship; the many public buildings, planned and executed with the skill and power of which man has never been capable on this earth; and the homes that are to be homes in very deed, luxurious and glorious abodes for eternal spirits where refinement and purified desire will direct the use of the eternal riches and materials out of which these buildings are to be constructed. And the gardens,

groves and walks, combined with the many beautiful buildings will produce an eternal city, the splendor and grandeur of which has never been conceived on this earth. Who is to design and build this glorious City of Promise? The faithful Saints of God. Are they preparing themselves for this mighty labor? Do they concern themselves with the artistic and appropriate arrangement of the homes and cities they own now that they may be the better prepared to build the City Beautiful they hope to possess in a happy future?[63]

Widtsoe's New Jerusalem was a beatified version of an American city full of artistic taste—a spiritualized version of the "City Beautiful" campaign then in high gear throughout the United States.[64] The celestial city's houses would be constructed in the most fashionable styles with characteristics that complimented those of the people living in them. In Widtsoe's vision, these were "to be homes in very deed," physical enclosures in which spirit parents would raise spirit children who would be perpetually exposed to exquisitely tasteful objects that would shape children's character in the same way the objects of Latter-day Saint homes were shaping character in the present. Indeed, refinement was a necessary characteristic of millennial life. Exalted taste would lead to exalted environments, luxurious and glorious abodes for eternal spirits where refinement and purified desire would direct the use of the eternal riches and materials out of which these eternal environments were to be constructed.

Widtsoe's millenarian vision was an outgrowth of authoritative discourse then current within the Mormon community. In 1897, Church president Wilford Woodruff told audiences that the final winding-up scene was imminent, God was going to bring his wrath down upon the earth, and that many of the Saints he preached to "would see the savior." After Woodruff's death in 1898, President Lorenzo Snow continued to stoke the millennial fervor. He taught, "Christ will come before long" and that Church members' consecrated donations would provide the money needed to purchase the temple site and adjacent properties. In July 1899—four months after Leah Widtsoe recruited the young women of the Church to prepare themselves for temple design and construction—President Snow promised Church leaders, "If you live 10 or 15 yrs more or less[,] perhaps Less, we are going back to Jackson Co." The next year, in November 1900, he taught, "There are many here now under the sound of my voice, probably a majority who will have to go back to Jackson County and assist in building the temple."[65] Widtsoe did not want Mormon women to be sidelined when these events transpired, watching men alone design, construct, and furnish the New Jerusalem. If the women of the Church arrived in Missouri possessing expertise in the principles and practices of architecture and interior design, they would also be deeply involved in the design, construction, and furnishing of Zion.

However glorious and equitable the millennial day would prove to be, its future promise provided a way to justify the pursuit of a materialistic, even inequitable society in the here and now. Although Horne assured her readers,

"A log cabin is beautiful if the hearth is clean and the kettle bright," nobody envisioned the New Jerusalem as a city of log cabins with dirt floors and gingham curtains.[66] Instead, as Widtsoe wrote, the holy city was to be populated with buildings of "splendor and grandeur." The Mormon community's pivot away from its separatist roots and egalitarian vision made this compromise possible. Both Horne and Widtsoe were certain that the aesthetic reformation of the Church was both necessary and justified. Yet just under the surface of their advice, there remained anxiety about whether pursuing worldly standards of gentility was, in fact, fully compatible with their heritage.

The pursuit of artistic taste stood in tension with the dual traditions of republican frugality and Mormon insularity. The urge to claim "simplicity" and moral weight for these pursuits was one way of mitigating this dissonance. Another possibility, as Elder Smith's comments had suggested, was to view the material improvement of the community as evidence of divine favor. Widtsoe took this tack in one of her pieces, responding to a hypothetical reader who bemoaned that she lived in a two-room house and did not see how all this decorating advice could apply to her. Widtsoe asserted that "the Lord is blessing this people" and intends that "His children shall reap the benefits of these blessings, if they will keep His commandments." Furthermore, she said, "Nothing that points out a better way should be ignored even though we see no immediate way of obtaining the ideal we read about." And if readers felt dissatisfied with their lives after reading her advice, Widtsoe put the onus on them for failing to understand the broader principles being taught. She insisted that her articles were "meant to encourage and help the readers, not to make them dissatisfied with what they have."[67]

Nevertheless, the tensions were irresolvable as long as Zion remained embedded within the economic and social structures of turn-of-the-century America and Latter-day Saints' incomes varied widely. The Saints were left to negotiate these tensions while looking forward to the day when they would inhabit the "luxurious and glorious abodes" in the New Jerusalem, buildings that Mormon women would help design and construct.[68] Perhaps the Latter-day Saints would have to wait until then to both realize their egalitarian ideals and at the same time receive the cultural esteem they so deeply desired.

NOTES

1. W. F. Rae, *Westward by Rail: The New Route to the East* (New York: D. Appleton and Company, 1871), 122, cited in Christine Talbot, "The Church Family in Nineteenth-Century America: Mormonism and the Public/Private Divide," *Journal of Mormon History* 37, no. 4 (Fall 2011): 219.

2. On the cultural accommodations of turn-of-the-century Mormonism, see Thomas G. Alexander, *Mormonism in Transition: A History of the Latter-day Saints, 1890–1930* (Urbana:

University of Illinois Press, 1986); Grant Underwood, "Re-visioning Mormon History," *Pacific Historical Review* 55 (August 1986): 403–26; and Ethan R. Yorgason, *Transformation of the Mormon Culture Region* (Urbana: University of Illinois Press, 2003).

3. John Henry Smith, Untitled address, *Conference Report*, April 1899, 101.

4. Widtsoe went on to research and teach at Brigham Young University, the Agricultural College of Utah, and the University of Utah in partnership with her husband, John A. Widtsoe, who served as president of both the Agricultural College and the University of Utah. See Virginia F. Cutler, *A Twenty-One Gun Salute for Leah Dunford Widtsoe* (Logan: College of Family Life, Utah State University, n.d.); Mary Jane Woodger, "Leah Widtsoe: Pioneer in Healthy Lifestyle Family Education," *Journal of Family and Consumer Sciences* 92, no. 1 (2000): 50–54; and "Death Takes Widtsoe, 91, LDS Writer," *Salt Lake Tribune*, June 9, 1965.

5. On Alice Merrill Horne, see Harriet Horne Arrington, "Alice Merrill Horne: Art Promoter and Early Utah Legislator," in *Worth Their Salt: Notable but Often Unnoted Women of Utah*, ed. Colleen Whitley (Logan: Utah State University Press, 1996), 170–87.

6. The journal was the monthly magazine of the Young Ladies' Mutual Improvement Association (YLMIA), the Church's organization for young women ages fourteen and up. While fourteen was explicitly designated as the lower age limit for membership in the YLMIA, no upper limit was specified. Much of the magazine's content was directed toward young married women, presumably in their late teens and early twenties.

7. Leah E. Widtsoe, "The Home," *Young Woman's Journal* 10, no. 1 (January 1899): 38–41; Leah E. Widtsoe, "Studies in Household Art I: A Glance at the History of Architecture," *Young Woman's Journal* 10, no. 2 (February 1899): 87–91; Leah E. Widtsoe, "Studies in Household Art II: Roman Architecture," *Young Woman's Journal* 10, no. 4 (April 1899): 170–74.

8. Leah Dunford Widtsoe, "Furnishing the Home," *Young Woman's Journal* 13, no. 1 (January 1902): 25–29; "Furnishing the Home II: Basement, Cellar, Laundry," *Young Woman's Journal* 13, no. 2 (February 1902): 85–88; "Furnishing the Home III: Color," *Young Woman's Journal* 13, no. 3 (March 1902): 124–27; "Furnishing the Home IV: Color (Continued)," *Young Woman's Journal* 13, no. 4 (April 1902): 179–81; "Furnishing the Home V: About Carpets and Wall Papers," *Young Woman's Journal* 13, no. 5 (May 1902): 205–11; "Furnishing the Home VI: About Curtains and Pictures," *Young Woman's Journal* 13, no. 6 (June 1902): 274–77; "Furnishing the Home VII: Decoration and Furnishing in General," *Young Woman's Journal* 13, no. 7 (July 1902): 322–26; "Furnishing the Home VIII: Kitchen and Pantry," *Young Woman's Journal* 13, no. 8 (August 1902): 367–72; "Furnishing the Home IX: The Dining Room and Sitting Room," *Young Woman's Journal* 13, no. 9 (September 1902): 421–24; "Furnishing the Home: The Entrance Hall," *Young Woman's Journal* 13, no 10 (October 1902): 467–72; "Furnishing the Home: Bedrooms and Bathrooms," *Young Woman's Journal* 13, no. 11 (November 1902): 514–16; "Furnishing the Home XII: The Two-Roomed House," *Young Woman's Journal* 13, no. 12 (December 1902): 566–73.

9. Alice Merrill Horne, "Suggestions on Artistic Home Building," *Young Woman's Journal* 12, no. 3 (March 1901): 121–25; "Suggestions on Artistic Home Building II," *Young Woman's Journal* 12, no. 4 (April 1901): 169–73.

10. Tiffany Studios, *Portfolio of the Work of Tiffany Studios* (New York: Tiffany Studios, 1899), 1.

11. Katherine C. Grier, *Culture and Comfort: People, Parlors, and Upholstery, 1850–1930* (Rochester, NY: Strong Museum, 1988), 5–8, 140, and 147. The origins of this ideology and its influence in eighteenth- and nineteenth-century America are discussed in Richard Lyman Bushman, *The Refinement of America: Persons, Houses, Cities* (New York: Knopf, 1992).

12. Horne, "Suggestions on Artistic Home Building II," 172.

13. Widtsoe, "Furnishing the Home," 27.

14. Horne, "Suggestions on Artistic Home Building," 125.

15. A sampling of these authors' publications includes Candace Wheeler, *Principles of Home Decoration* (New York: Doubleday, Page & Co., 1903); Edith Wharton and Ogden Cod-

man Jr., *The Decoration of Houses* (New York: Charles Scribner's Sons, 1898). On the cultural power of elite architects, artists, and designers during the late nineteenth century, see Russell Lynes, *The Tastemakers* (New York: Grosset and Dunlap, 1949).

16. Widtsoe, "The Entrance Hall," 468.

17. Widtsoe, "About Curtains and Pictures," 274. On Wheeler, see Amelia Peck and Carol Irish, *Candace Wheeler: The Art and Enterprise of American Design, 1875–1900* (New York: Metropolitan Museum of Art; New Haven, CT: Yale University Press, 2001). Although the sources that Widtsoe and Horne drew upon were contemporary ones, the moralistic strain of domestic furnishing originated decades earlier. Catherine Beecher, for example, wrote in 1869 that the "aesthetic element . . . contributes much to the education of the entire household in refinement, intellectual development, and moral sensibility." Catherine E. Beecher and Harriet Beecher Stowe, *The American Woman's Home* (1869; facsimile of the first edition, Hartford, CT: Harriett Beecher Stowe Center, 1975), 84. Beecher allowed that aesthetics were subordinate to "the requirements of physical existence" and should not absorb more expenditure than "means of higher moral growth"; nonetheless, her association of home decoration with moral refinement helped lay influential groundwork for the more explicit discussions like Widtsoe's and Horne's.

18. Terryl Givens explores this paradox in *People of Paradox: A History of Mormon Culture* (New York: Oxford University Press, 2007), 53–64.

19. On taste as a form of social capital, see Pierre Bourdieu, *Distinction: A Critique of Social Taste* (Cambridge, MA.: Harvard University Press, 1984). An excellent case study is Leora Auslander, *Taste and Power: Furnishing Modern France* (Berkeley: University of California Press, 1996).

20. On parlor culture, see Grier, *Culture and Comfort*; Thad Logan, *The Victorian Parlour: A Cultural Study* (Cambridge: Cambridge University Press, 2010); Louise L. Stevenson, *The Victorian Homefront: American Thought and Culture, 1860–1880* (New York: Twayne Publishers, 1991).

21. Widtsoe, "The Entrance Hall," 468.

22. William Channing Gannett, *The House Beautiful* (Boston: James H. West, 1895), 22–23.

23. Widtsoe, "Furnishing the Home," 25, 27.

24. Martha Crabill McClaugherty, "Creating the Artistic Home, 1868–1893," *Winterthur Portfolio* 18, no. 1 (Spring 1983): 1–26.

25. Kevin H. F. O'Brien, "'The House Beautiful': A Reconstruction of Oscar Wilde's American Lecture," *Victorian Studies* 17, no. 4 (June 1974): 404.

26. On the discursive transition from artisan to artist, see Larry Shriner, *The Invention of Art: A Cultural History* (Chicago: University of Chicago Press, 2001). Horne later authored a series of articles in the *Young Woman's Journal* profiling several Utah artists: "James T. Harwood—the Strenuous Utah Artist," *Young Woman's Journal* 21, no. 1 (January 1910): 14–19; "John Hafen, the Utah Landscapist," *Young Woman's Journal* 21, no. 2 (February 1910): 87–92; "Mary Teasdel: The Utah Impressionistic Painter," *Young Woman's Journal* 21, no. 3 (March 1910): 130–37; "Utah's Sculptor, Mahonri M. Young," *Young Woman's Journal* 21, no. 4 (April 1910): 196–204; "The Utah Painter—Lee Greene Richards," *Young Woman's Journal* 21, no. 5 (May 1910): 262–70; "Cyrus Edwin Dallin," *Young Woman's Journal* 21, no. 9 (September 1910): 491–97.

27. On the nineteenth-century design reform movement, see George P. Landow, *The Aesthetic and Critical Theories of John Ruskin* (Princeton, NJ: Princeton University Press, 1971); Owen Jones, *On the True and the False in the Decorative Arts: Lectures Delivered at Marlborough House, June 1852* (London, 1863); Charles Locke Eastlake, *Hints on Household Taste* (London: Longmans, Green and Co., 1868); Michael Snodin and John Styles, *Design and the Decorative Arts, Victorian Britain, 1837–1901* (London: V&A Publications, 2004); Wendy Kaplan, *The Arts and Crafts Movement in Europe and America* (London: Thames & Hudson, 2004).

28. Horne, "Suggestions on Artistic Home Building II," 171. On Morris, see Diane Waggoner, ed., *The Beauty of Life: William Morris and the Art of Design* (New York: Thames & Hudson, 2003).

29. Horne, "Suggestions on Artistic Home Building," 172–73.

30. Widtsoe, "Furnishing the Home," 27.

31. On scientific management and the ethos of efficiency in the early twentieth century, see Samuel Haber, *Efficiency and Uplift: Scientific Management in the Progressive Era, 1890–1920* (Chicago: University of Chicago Press, 1964); and Daniel Nelson, *Frederick W. Taylor and the Rise of Scientific Management* (Madison: University of Wisconsin Press, 1980).

32. Leah Dunford Widtsoe, "The Home," *Young Woman's Journal* 10, no. 1 (January 1899): 39.

33. Widtsoe, "Furnishing the Home," 29. Widtsoe would elaborate in greater detail on time-saving practices at length in her book, *Labor Saving Devices for the Farm Home* (Logan: Utah Agricultural Experiment Station, 1912).

34. Horne, "Suggestions on Artistic Home Building II," 169.

35. Horne, "Suggestions on Artistic Home Building II," 170.

36. Horne, "Suggestions on Artistic Home Building II," 169–70.

37. On neurasthenia, see David G. Schuster, *Neurasthenic Nation: America's Search for Health, Happiness, and Comfort, 1869–1920* (New Brunswick, NJ: Rutgers University Press, 2011).

38. Edwin G. Burrows and Mike Wallace, *Gotham: A History of New York City to 1898* (New York: Oxford University Press, 1999), 1080.

39. Widtsoe, "Furnishing the Home," 26.

40. On the history of domestic science, see Carolyn M. Goldstein, *Creating Consumers: Home Economists in the Twentieth Century* (Chapel Hill: University of North Carolina Press, 2012); and Megan J. Ellis, *Stir It Up: Home Economics in American Culture* (Philadelphia: University of Pennsylvania Press, 2010).

41. Susa Young Gates, "Hail and Farewell," *The Young Woman's Journal* 40, no. 10 (October 1929): 675–78.

42. "Death Takes Widtsoe, 91, LDS Writer."

43. This dual purpose of both culture and comfort is the interpretive framework of Grier, *Culture and Comfort*. On Victorian domesticity, see Barbara Welter, "The Cult of True Womanhood, 1820–1860," *American Quarterly* 18, no. 2 (1966): 151–74; and Glenna Matthews, *"Just a Housewife": The Rise and Fall of Domesticity in America* (New York: Oxford University Press, 1989).

44. Widtsoe, "The Home," 39.

45. Jackson Lears demonstrates how Victorian interiors contained "the iconography of female experience." Jackson Lears, "Beyond Veblen: Rethinking Consumer Culture in America," in *Consuming Visions: Accumulation and Display of Goods in America, 1880–1920*, ed. Simon J. Bronner (New York: W. W. Norton, 1989), 87.

46. Widtsoe, "Furnishing the Home," 26.

47. Widtsoe, "The Home," 38–39.

48. On the gendering of commerce and the commercialization of gender, see the introduction to Helen Damon-Moore, *Magazines for the Millions: Gender and Commerce in the Ladies' Home Journal and the Saturday Evening Post, 1880–1910* (Albany: State University of New York Press, 1994), 1–13.

49. Beverly Gordon, "Woman's Domestic Body: The Conceptual Conflation of Women and Interiors in the Industrial Age," *Winterthur Portfolio* 31, no. 4 (Winter 1996): 281–301.

50. Lori Merish, "'The Hand of Refined Taste' in the Frontier Landscape: Caroline Kirkland's 'A New Home, Who'll Follow?' and the Feminization of American Consumerism," *American Quarterly* 45, no. 4 (December 1993): 487.

51. On the background of the Shopping Department columns, see Lisa Olsen Tait, "Between Two Economies: The Business Development of the *Young Woman's Journal*, 1889–1900," *Journal of Mormon History* 38, no. 4 (Fall 2012): 18–23.

52. [Susa Young Gates], "Our Shopping Department," *Young Woman's Journal* 2, no. 8 (May 1891): 385.

53. Horne, "Suggestions on Artistic Home Building II," 172–73.

54. Horne, "Suggestions on Artistic Home Building," 124–25.

55. Susa Young Gates, *Memorial to Elizabeth Claridge McCune, Missionary, Philanthropist, Architect* (Salt Lake City, UT: n.p., 1924).

56. National Register of Historic Places Inventory—Nomination Form, Alfred W. McCune Mansion, June 13, 1974.

57. Robert L. Menlove, ed., *Spring Lake, 1856–2000* (Spring Lake, 2000), 39.

58. Andrea Radke-Moss provides a helpful history of vernacular gentility among settlers of the Great Plains with similar financial constraints as Moore in Andrea G. Radke, "Refining Rural Spaces: Women and Vernacular Gentility in the Great Plains, 1880–1920," *Great Plains Quarterly* 24 (Fall 2004): 227–48.

59. Widtsoe, "Furnishing the Home," 28.

60. The millionaire artist and interior furnisher Louis Comfort Tiffany expressed concern for the tacky flaunting of wealth when he wrote the following in 1910: "For beauty in the home has little or nothing to do with the amount of money spent; extravagance does not produce beauty; and many of our richest people, like some of our poor people, have not yet come to see the value of good taste. . . . In fact, money is frequently an absolute bar to good taste, for it leads to show and over-elaboration." Louis C. Tiffany, "The Gospel of Good Taste," *Country Life in America* 19, no. 2 (November Mid-Month, 1910): 105.

61. Horne, "Suggestions on Artistic Home Building," 122.

62. Horne, "Suggestions on Artistic Home Building," 123.

63. Widtsoe, "Studies in Household Art I," 87.

64. William H. Wilson, *The City Beautiful Movement* (Baltimore: Johns Hopkins University Press, 1989).

65. All of the quotes in this paragraph come from Dan Erickson, *As a Thief in the Night: The Mormon Quest for Millennial Deliverance* (Salt Lake City, UT: Signature Books, 1998), 214–18, and Thomas G. Alexander, *Mormonism in Transition: A History of the Latter-day Saints, 1890–1930* (Urbana: University of Illinois Press, 1986), 288–89. Revelations to Joseph Smith had designated Jackson County, Missouri, as the "center place" for the city of the New Jerusalem, the millennial capital of Zion. See Doctrine and Covenants 57:3. Latter-day Saints had been driven from Missouri by mob violence in the 1830s but continued to believe that they would one day return and "redeem" Zion in conjunction with the Second Coming of Jesus Christ.

66. Horne, "Suggestions on Artistic Home Building," 122.

67. Widtsoe, "The Two-Roomed House," 566–67.

68. Widtsoe, "Studies in Household Art I," 87.

Chapter Eight

Double Jeopardy in Pleasant Grove

The Gender and Cultural Challenges
of Being a Danish Mormon Missionary
Grass Widow in Territorial Utah

Julie K. Allen

"I must in truth say that I understand what it means to be deprived of a good and loving father and provider and he who was my support. I always felt so secure when you were with me and I hope that God, who is in Heaven, will grant that day unto me again and I will then learn to appreciate it more than before."

—Mine Jørgensen to her husband, Hans, June 30, 1881

In the spring of 1881, when the Danish Mormon convert-immigrant Hans Jørgensen was called to serve as a Latter-day Saint (LDS) missionary in his native Denmark, he left his wife, Wilhelmine Marie Jacobsen Bolvig (cited hereafter simply as Mine), to fend for herself and their five children on a farm in Pleasant Grove, Utah. During the nearly three years Hans was away, from April 1881 to November 1883, they wrote to each other several times a month, in Danish.[1] The extensive preserved correspondence between Mine and Hans Jørgensen—comprising roughly two hundred letters—documents not only the emotional trial of being separated and the economic hardship of his absence and ministry but also how Mine, as a Danish Mormon woman in territorial Utah, navigated a society in which both her female gender and her Danish cultural identity isolated her from mainstream economic and social networks. In her letters to her husband over the course of his mission, Mine documents how she coped with the dual challenges of being a missionary "grass widow"[2] and a foreigner on the periphery of Utah society by enlarging the scope of her accustomed gender role and relying on a network of fellow Danes to meet her family's needs.

Hans and Mine Jørgensen's correspondence spans the entire length of Hans's mission and deals with a range of mundane and profound topics. It begins with a postcard from Ogden on April 19, 1881, reporting Hans's safe arrival there, and ends with a brief letter from Castle Garden in New York, dated Novem-

185

Figure 8.1. Portrait of Wilhelmine Marie Jacobsen Bolvig
Jørgensen, ca. 1882, reproduced by permission of Mary Lambert, Salt Lake City, Utah.

ber 8, 1883, where Hans and the company of 353 Danish immigrants he and
twenty other returning elders had escorted across the Atlantic went through
immigration prior to embarking on the week-long rail journey from New York
to Salt Lake City. While Hans generally reports on the events of his mission
and interactions with members, other missionaries, and his own family back in
Denmark, Mine addresses a wide range of topics related to the challenges she
faced and worried about—she admonishes her husband not to take a second
wife, laments the difficulty of farming in the heat, reports her fears that her
sons will be mistreated at school because of their father's absence, gives thanks
for the generous assistance of some neighbors, and complains about another
neighbor's apparent attempt to extort money from her. The majority of the

letters focus on the emotional and economic toll that Hans's absence inflicted on the family—their mutual loneliness, longing for each other, and feelings of inadequacy; her struggles to keep the farm operational; his reliance on Church members' charity; Hans's constant fears for his children's health and education—but they also reveal how Mine grew into a more competent, self-reliant individual as she moved out of her gendered and cultural comfort zone to tackle challenges her husband would otherwise have handled.

Mine Jørgensen's story offers an important enhancement to the traditional Mormon history focus on the challenges and triumphs of English-speaking male missionaries in the mission field, which have been documented in accounts such as Andrew Jenson's *History of the Scandinavian Mission*.[3] Missionary wives' experiences are not visible in conference meeting notes or mission logs but emerge from personal documents such as diaries and letters. Mine's letters, which paint a vivid picture of how missionary service affected the women left behind, complete this narrative by reminding us that the men's missionary service would have been impossible without their wives' willingness to assume responsibilities that were unconventional in terms of nineteenth-century American gender roles, from running a farm to negotiating labor contracts to defending her family's honor. Mine's letters challenge popular, romanticized images of angelic pioneer Mormon women by giving readers access to a complex, whole person, who struggles to reconcile her faith in the gospel she had embraced as a child with the myriad problems she faced as a result of her husband's prolonged absence in the service of the LDS Church. Living her adopted faith day by day on a farm as a single parent for three years in a country where she was a foreigner by birth and language required at least as much courage and endurance of Mine as crossing the ocean from Denmark to join the Saints in Utah must have. During Hans's mission, Mine's personal journey lacked the measurable milestones of physical travel that her husband recorded in his letters. Instead, it is traceable through the chronology of her letters, in which she records the passage of time—through seasons of planting and harvest, the growth of her children, the length of time her husband has been away, and her anticipation of his return. Mine, as her husband called her, or "Minnie," as she is known to her descendants, left few tangible traces of her existence in frontier Utah, but her letters provide valuable insights into the facts of her life and the nature of the overlapping communities to which she belonged.

The significance of Mine's narrative of her life as a woman, mother, wife, and convert to the LDS Church is enhanced by the element of cultural negotiation necessitated by her Danish nationality and immigrant status. The language of Hans's and Mine's letters has rendered them inaccessible to many historians, but their meticulous documentation of her interactions with the Danish Mormon community in Pleasant Grove reveals both how much Mine's Danish cultural identity shaped her experience of pioneer Utah and how central her ethnic network was to her family's spiritual and physical well-being. While Mine does not reflect explicitly on her situation as a Danish woman in an American town, her letters illuminate ways in which questions of acculturation and integration affected her personally; how her relationship to the LDS Church was constrained by language, gender, and geography; and how the Danish community in Pleasant Grove functioned much like a parish back in Denmark would have. Mine's letters describe how she navigates her membership in a Danish Mormon pioneer community that existed parallel to the larger population of English-speaking Mormon pioneers, revealing how distinct ethnic communities within the LDS Church in territorial Utah provided additional networks of support, based on a similar linguistic identity, common cultural norms, and shared history for Danish Mormon missionary grass widows like Mine.

GRASS WIDOWS AND THE GENDER DYNAMICS OF UTAH FARM LIFE

"The wheat is now ripe and people are working as hard as they can to harvest it. We have lovely wheat, corn, and potatoes. Everything is decked out and enjoying life, as we should also, for life is quite short, in a certain sense, and we ought to always be happy and content since we are in truth doing so well, but there is always so much that tries to disrupt our joy and tempt us with this or that and sometimes get us in a bad mood. I know that nothing which comes from that direction should be given room in us, but it is not easy to be as good as one ought."

—Mine to Hans, August 1, 1882

Hans's and Mine's life stories are quite typical for nineteenth-century Danish Mormon convert-immigrants. Four years apart in age, both Hans and Mine had been born in Denmark, joined the LDS Church in the early 1860s, and immigrated to Utah shortly thereafter, although Hans served a three-year mission in Denmark, from 1864 to 1867, before emigrating by steamship via England. They met in Utah, became engaged on April 5, 1871, and were married on March 4, 1872, in Salt Lake City by Daniel H. Wells. Their first child, Henson, was born in November 1872, followed by three more boys, Lorenzo, Daniel, and George, in 1874, 1876, and 1878, respectively, and their first daughter, Wilhelmine Severine, whom they called "little Minnie," in 1880. From the early 1870s until their deaths in the 1910s, they lived on a farm in Pleasant Grove, where they raised crops, including wheat, alfalfa, oats, potatoes, hay, apples, peaches, and apricots, as well as sheep, cows, and pigs.

Life on a frontier homestead, though more rewarding than the near-serfdom Hans had left behind in Denmark, was difficult, and cash money hard to come by, so a mission call entailed considerable economic strain. Hans worked on the Pleasant Valley railroad in the fall of 1879 to obtain the cash necessary to replace his team of horses, which had died in 1875. Although the winter of 1879–1880 was a difficult one, Hans was able to maintain his livestock and, together with his brother-in-law Lauritz Jacobsen, to farm more than forty acres of his neighbors' land in addition to running his own farm. In his letter to Church president John Taylor accepting his mission call in early 1881, Hans explains, "My circumstances . . . are not the very best; that is, my family has up to the present had to rely on my labours for support, and shal [*sic*] therefore miss me, when my team is sold and I am gone. Nevertheless I will go at your request."[4] Before leaving on his mission, Hans obtained his US citizenship and sold his horses, harness, neck yoke, and doubletree to his neighbor Christian Olsen for $65, noting in his diary that this sum represented "about halfe of what it was worth, but I was obliged to sell it at almost any figure as time drawed nearer, when I had to leave. It was a hard task for me to part with my team, for I had considerable bodder [*sic*] to get it in 1879."[5] Hans left on his mission before daybreak on April 17, 1881, and did not return home until the evening of November 16, 1883, exactly two years and seven months later, less twelve hours, as Hans noted in his diary entry that day.[6]

Mine supported Hans's decision to accept a mission call and frequently expresses her confidence in him and her desire that he fulfill an honorable mission, but she also recognized that his mission service entailed dangers for both her husband and herself. She worried about his poverty, reliance on the kindness of strangers, and exposure to the elements, as well as more intangible dangers. In her letter of June 10, 1881, she encourages Hans to resist the temptation to fall back into the sinful, secular life of his countrymen:

> People seem to want to cheer me up and say that I have a good and honest husband and that you were a good missionary last time and that they are sure that you will be one this time. May their words be and become true. Many a good man has fallen when he has gone back, but do not let that be your fate. I pray to God to prevent it! Come back as an honest and honorable man.

Mine's concern for Hans's temporal and spiritual well-being pervades her letters, but a comment in her letter dated December 28, 1882—"Wouldn't you rather remain there a few more years than come home to all of the work and toil that you are accustomed to here at home?"—makes it clear that she was also aware of the reduced physical strain of mission life in comparison with frontier farming, perhaps because she had been shouldering much of that burden in his absence. In her letters, she generally minimizes the problems she and the children are dealing with, whether it be illness and accidents or lack of supplies, in hopes of sparing Hans distress and not distracting him from his work. He seems to have read between the lines, however, as a comment in one of his letters from late 1882 reveals: "I know that you do not usually complain, even if the world is going against you, but I hope anyway that you do not suffer want for I would not desire this. Tell me when you write if you have a cow that gives milk or not and if the children have adequate shoes." While the physical challenges Mine faced were significant, the psychological ones seem to be the hardest for her to bear.

Hans's prolonged absence forced Mine to redefine her role in her family and community. Her second letter to Hans, dated May 17, 1881, reveals how Hans's departure had destabilized their customary division of gender roles and responsibilities by requiring Mine to attempt to fulfill, however inadequately, certain fatherly duties toward her children:

> Now I must be as both Father and Mother to these small ones. I feel as though they are being done a disservice. They say so often that if Papa just were home, then he would also take care of them just as they see others take their children around with them.

This passage represents Mine's first attempt to articulate which aspects of Hans's responsibilities she felt inadequate to assume—in this case, taking the children to destinations outside the home, which was not within Mine's normal scope of activities. Up to this point, her world had been a small one, centered on her home, and her mobility had been limited, by preference and social norms, to attending Church meetings and visiting neighbors. As she explains to Hans on October 25, 1882, "A quiet life is all that I desire. I go to [church] meetings as often as I can, but otherwise the home is my place, so people who speak the truth cannot say that I run around in town." Nevertheless, her husband's absence forced Mine to tackle unfamiliar new tasks—although some, including organizing her children's formal education, she simply postponed until his return when the obstacles proved too great.

As a grass widow and temporarily single mother, Mine faced considerable challenges just keeping her family sheltered and fed. She was at a severe economic disadvantage in Hans's absence, not just because of the loss of his labor and its returns but also because of her own inability—due to her gender, her limited English skills, her responsibilities to her children, and prevailing social norms—to earn her own living. Like every pioneer woman, Mine had always had a great deal of work to do, but most of it was unpaid domestic tasks within the home, such as cooking, baking, washing, ironing, milking the cows, gathering eggs, hauling water, rearing children, and the like. Although many Scandinavian women, particularly in midwestern communities, were highly involved in the agricultural production of their family farms, the general trend after 1865, as farm families oriented their production more for the market than for their own consumption, was toward male labor.[7] During the nine years of their marriage thus far, Mine had apparently not been accustomed to helping with the outdoor labor on the farm, nor had Hans expected it of her, but the work had to be done in his absence and there was no money to hire outside help. In one early letter, dated May 17, 1881, Mine rejoices that a recent rainstorm has freed her from the need to water the crops. She explains: "I had started on it, but the work was too hard for me. You know, of course, that I have not been used to working outside since I became your wife, which is why it is so hard for me that I must now do so."

Instead of complaining about the situation, however, Mine approached it with determination and creativity. In her May 17 letter, she makes a suggestion that reveals how her childhood in Denmark informed her sense of the possibilities open to her: "What would you say if I let the children go to strangers and let somebody live in the house and I went out to earn money? Being both the man and the woman seems so sad to me." Mine's suggestion of fostering out the children and going into domestic service was a fairly common practice among poor or unmarried women in Denmark at the time, similar to "baby farming" in the United Kingdom and Australia in the same period.[8] Many Scandinavian American women worked as maids and housekeepers, particularly in cities such as Minneapolis and Chicago. Mine's proposal would have ensured the family's financial stability during Hans's absence by providing a steady wage and would have spared Mine the hard physical labor of farming, as well as solving her dilemma of trying to fulfill both her own and her husband's responsibilities. Hans's own parents had both been in service most of their lives; they had been unable to marry because of financial constraints, so his mother had had to put Hans in foster care from a very young age.

Although he had been very fond of his foster parents, Hans reacted very strongly against Mine's proposal, suggesting, in his letter on June 14, 1881, that someone else had put the idea into Mine's head, and explaining his strenuous objections to it: "I do not like your idea of sending the children out to live with strangers so that you can go into service, like poor women do in this country [Denmark]." Hans's initial objection reveals that if Mine were to seek gainful employment, it could harm their social status, which they had worked hard—particularly through immigration and homesteading—to attain. Historian Miriam Murphy explains that, although half of all workers employed in American factories in the mid-nineteenth century were women, the question over wage earning exacerbated the divide between upper-class women "who no longer needed to contribute their wage labor to ensure the financial security of home and family; [and] poorer women—especially widows, free blacks, immigrants, and rural women who moved to the cities in search of jobs."[9] Although Mine was, for all practical purposes, financially situated like a widow, her husband did not want her to suffer the loss of social standing that she would incur by getting a job.

Hans's second objection concerns the negative effects of such a scheme on their children, which reflects his own possibly emotionally difficult childhood experiences in foster care, as well as an emerging domestic code that

defined women's roles in terms of nurturing children, providing emotional
support to their husbands, and guarding society's moral values.[10] In the same
letter, he cautions Mine against proceeding with her plan, invoking both his
legal and emotional authority over her:

> If you will listen to me as your husband and as him whom you love most, please
> don't do it, for you must remember that you are our poor children's mother and
> if they live among strangers, no matter who they are, they will not be as happy
> when they are with you. It is also a good medicine for causing children to forget
> their mother and sometimes to come to despise her, so if you have not already
> taken this step, please let it go and do not think of it any more. . . . If you are in
> a strange place and have sent the children away from you, then I would ask you
> to come home and gather them to you once again.

Hans's response aligns with the predominant view in American society at the
time that equated female wage earners with selfishness and family neglect,[11]
regardless of the economic realities of a woman's situation or the emotional
strain on children caused by their family's desperate financial straits. The
number of women working outside the home increased rapidly in the latter
half of the nineteenth century, in Utah as elsewhere in America, but in Pleasant Grove in the early 1880s, the idea that Mine should seek outside employment was anathema to her husband. Despite the fact that he had left his family
for extended periods in the past to work on the railroad and to fulfill his missionary obligations, Hans was convinced that Mine's children would resent
and come to despise her, should she leave them to find work. Hans's fear and
emotional agitation come through quite clearly in the letter, so much so that
Mine took offense and claimed, in her next letter, dated July 7, 1881, that the
whole idea had been a joke, not something to be taken seriously.

  With the possibility of paid employment thus closed to her, Mine simply
made the best of her situation, despite her inexperience with farming, and
tried to maintain a positive attitude, as the quote from her letter on August
1, 1882, at the beginning of this section confirms. Somewhat to her own
surprise, Mine began to feel pride in her own accomplishments on the farm
and in the respect this earned her within the community. On July 7, 1881,
after Hans had been gone for three months, she reports, in a rather self-
congratulatory tone,

> I have watered all of our things myself and everything looks very good. . . .
> The little bit of corn that I planted is so tall that I haven't seen anything as tall
> around here. The potatoes also look very good and the trees have such big green
> tops that you can hardly believe how lovely they look. The alfalfa is tall enough
> to cut again. . . . There has been plenty of water, as you know, and I have been
> generous with the watering. People say that I am not such a bad farmer.

As challenging as Hans's absence was for her, Mine was gradually able to see her deprivation as an opportunity for personal growth. On August 16, 1881, she announces the fruits of her labor, both tangible and intangible: "In the past few days, we have had rainy weather. You can believe that I am glad that I got our wheat harvested and also threshed. There were 62 bushels. That wasn't so bad for a new farmer like me." It is difficult to say whether Mine is more impressed with the sixty-two bushels or with the fact that she had managed to produce them on her own, but in either case, she recognized that she had done as well as any of her male neighbors. She continued to run the farm for the next two years, keeping Hans updated on the progress of their crops and who had helped her with plowing, planting, and harvesting each year.

AMONG THE DANES IN PLEASANT GROVE

"I am happy and I have plenty to eat and I also have a little firewood and good people have promised me some more."

—Mine to Hans, October 25, 1881

"Peter Selebak gave us 12 hundred pounds of coal and Peter Jenson gave us just as much. Those 2 are always good to us. Andru Larson gave us a load of firewood and we received a load of the same from Moroni Prat. Alma Iversen Horton brought it from the mill."

—Mine to Hans, November 7, 1881

Although Mine's pride on the momentous occasion of her first independent harvest was both justified and understandable, it is important to remember that she had not been left entirely to her own devices but had access to various social and ecclesiastical support networks that were crucial to her and her family's well-being, including members of her immediate family, neighbors, ethnic community, and local Church leaders. Of course, there were times when no assistance was forthcoming in times of need, as she complains in her letter of July 17, 1881:

Now it is the busy harvest time. There is almost not a single person to get to help bind for they would rather go out and work on the railroad than in the grain but I will surely get the wheat harvested. I would think that people would be ashamed to let it stay standing when I have watered it myself the whole time.

The scarcity of cash money in pioneer communities made working on the railroad attractive for many local men, as Hans himself had done on several occasions, but the lack of available assistance put Mine in a difficult situation that irritated her, not least because of the risk that all of her labor would be wasted. For the most part, however, Mine was fortunate to receive considerable assistance from neighbors and friends with all manner of tasks, from shed construction and plastering to watering and harvesting her crops.

As part of a large Scandinavian (predominantly Danish) Mormon immigrant community, Mine had access to a substantial network of support, which seems to have functioned on a labor barter system. Since Hans had participated in this system before his departure, Mine had credit to draw upon as necessary for physically demanding tasks that needed completion in Hans's absence. While this system reflected the collectivism of early Mormon society, it may also have drawn on the immigrants' experiences in Denmark, where, until the early nineteenth century, the arable land in rural villages was farmed cooperatively and, in the latter half of the nineteenth century, cooperative dairies, slaughterhouses, and retail endeavors emerged to allow individual farmers to share the cost and risk of commercial endeavors. Contributions and deductions seem to have been minutely documented, presumably in order to ensure that no one abused the system. Hans repeatedly urges Mine, as in his letter of June 1, 1881, to "write it down when someone gives you something or does any work for us, so that we can keep it in fond memory." She does so quite faithfully, commenting in one letter on June 10, 1881, about the plastering and whitewashing that had been done: "Peter Maurits did the work in return for the two days of work you did for him. He says he is willing to pay back the rest if there is something he can help me with. He was willing; as soon as I asked him about it, he came." A few days later, on June 14, in response to Mine's letter about watering the crops, Hans scolds, "It did not make me happy to hear that you have begun to water; I thought that Jeppe would have been good enough to keep his promise and water when it became necessary. I promised to repay him just as many days if he would just do that." On November 20, 1881, as the weather began to worsen, she reports, "You wanted to know if I had gotten the firewood shed up—Jørgen Nielsen set it up immediately after you left. He plastered the walls with adobe and laid boards across the top of it." All this help kept her family warm and safe but could not replace the loss of her husband. She notes with some sadness on September 25, 1881, "The heat is now over and the cold has come, but my husband will not be coming to bring me firewood," echoing her melancholy complaint of August 16, "I feel now as before that they did me an injustice who took my husband from me."

Mine frequently mentions getting assistance from various neighbors, but the most frequently recurring assistance is provided by Christian Peter Larsen, known as Peter Selebak, after the name of the farm in Denmark where he had been born. On September 25, 1881, Mine reports, "Peter Selebak is the man assigned to help me. The bishop most likely doesn't think of me any more often than his night cap does." While the use of the phrase "assigned to help" suggests that Peter Selebak may have been tasked with seeing to her welfare by the local congregation, her rather provocative aside about the bishop's indifference suggests that Peter Selebak's dedication to his task transcended his sense of ecclesiastical duty. In addition to being countrymen and fellow Saints, Mine and Peter came from the same part of Denmark, near Hjørring in northern Jutland, which might have given them the bond of a shared regional identity and dialect. While it is unlikely they had known each other in Denmark, Peter Selebak proved to be Mine's most loyal supporter in her husband's absence, driving in her grain, bringing her coal and firewood, plowing her fields, harvesting her wheat and alfalfa, and driving her to Salt Lake City for a friend's daughter's wedding. She mentions him no less than thirty times in her letters, always with gratitude and words of praise for his kindness to her family. Even when other neighbors pitch in to help out, it is often at Peter Selebak's instigation. On March 17, 1883, for example, Mine writes, "On March 12, I got our wheat sown in between the trees and in the areas where we had corn and potatoes last year. Peter Selebak, Charliy Warnak and Lauritz plowed and sowed, while Moritz Andrus brought fertilizer. It was Peter who arranged for it to be done. He is always the one who looks out for my welfare. He is a good man." Peter's assistance did not falter even when he suffered his own personal tragedies, including the loss of his (likely) plural wife Charlotte Christine Johnson in January 1882 from childbed fever and the death of his infant child in June 1883.

From Mine's letters, it is clear that the members of her support network, from Peter Selebak and Jørgen Nielsen to Christiane Hansen and Marie Warnick, were almost exclusively Scandinavian, rather than being drawn equally from both the Scandinavian and Anglo-American populations of Pleasant Grove. Non-Scandinavian residents of Pleasant Grove or other towns in Utah are hardly mentioned in her letters, with the exception of Moroni Llewellyn Pratt, who gave Mine a load of firewood in the fall of 1881. Unlike the town of Ephraim in Sanpete County, which was 90 percent Scandinavian in 1880,[12] Pleasant Grove was almost evenly divided between Scandinavian and Anglo-American settlers in 1881. While the majority of Pleasant Grove's residents listed on the 1880 US Census were Utah-born children (930 in total), their parents came in almost equal numbers from the British Isles and Scandinavia, with 238 Danes, 83 Swedes, and 11 Norwegians (332 total) versus 307 English, 23 Scottish, 5 Irish, and 2 Welsh (337 total). The remainder of the population (153 people) hailed from twenty-three states and four foreign countries.

Founded in 1850 by twenty-nine families of American Mormons,[13] Pleasant Grove would eventually become the town with the highest concentration of Scandinavians per capita in Utah County, as the tide of Scandinavian immigration to Utah rose.[14] Between 1850 and 1900, more than thirty thousand Danes joined the LDS Church, more than half of whom subsequently immigrated to

Utah, where they settled from Sanpete County in central Utah to Cache County in the north, often alongside many other Danes and Scandinavians. Danish Mormon immigration began with fairly small groups but quickly scaled up to a mass movement. The first group of twenty-eight Danish Mormon emigrants left Copenhagen in early 1852, less than two years after the arrival of the first Mormon missionaries in Denmark. Accompanied by Erastus Snow, who had been involved in the conversion of many of these early Danish Mormons, they crossed the plains in ox-drawn covered wagons and arrived in Salt Lake City, Utah, on October 16, 1852. The Danish LDS newspaper *Skandinaviens Stjerne* (Scandinavia's star) reported of the emigrants, "They are all alive and well satisfied and they urge their friends to follow them."[15]

The report in *Skandinaviens Stjerne* was intended to dispel fears among prospective immigrants about the hazards of the journey and conditions in Salt Lake, but it also shows how the Danish Mormons began to carve out a cultural space for themselves within the Mormon settlements. William Mulder notes that many of the immigrants settled in the Second Ward parish of Salt Lake City, which soon came to be known as "Little Denmark."[16] They were joined a year later, in 1853, by a second group of Danish converts led by another of the first missionaries to Denmark, John Forsgren. Following the direction of President Brigham Young, many members of Forsgren's company went south to the high country of Sanpete County, where they established the towns of Spring City, known as "New Denmark"; Manti; and Ephraim. Companies of Danish immigrants continued to arrive in Utah at regular intervals for the next four decades, tapering off in frequency and size after the 1870s. As the Utah territory filled up with settlers, additional Scandinavian communities emerged, such as Elsinore, in Sevier County; Logan, in Cache County; and Pleasant Grove, in Utah County.

In contrast to the planned Scandinavian settlements in Sanpete and Sevier Counties, Pleasant Grove seems to have become a Scandinavian cultural center almost by accident. One day's wagon ride south of Salt Lake City with plentiful grass and water, Pleasant Grove was, at first, merely an ideal stopping place for settlers on their way to the designated Scandinavian settlements farther south in Sanpete County, but it soon became an attractive alternative to the latter, especially as resident Scandinavians recruited their countrymen from wagon trains passing through the area. The first two Scandinavian families in the area, Iver Nicholas and Catherine Williams Iverson and Rasmus and Ingerline Petersen, came to Pleasant Grove from Salt Lake City after the arrival of the US Army in 1858, followed by four more Scandinavian families by 1860. Pleasant Grove became an incorporated city in 1855 but was not officially opened for homesteading by the US Federal Land Office until 1869,[17] at which point many squatters were allowed to claim or purchase the lands they had already settled and improved, while later settlers, including most of the later-coming Scandinavians, had to settle on unclaimed lands outside of town in the area known as the North Fields.

As the pace of emigration from Scandinavia increased over the course of the 1860s, a steady stream of Scandinavian immigrants arrived in Pleasant Grove, such that the 1870 territorial census listed 35 Scandinavian families in town, rising to 110 Scandinavian families by the 1880 federal census. Not only did local Scandinavians recruit other Nordics—for example, Swedish settler Paul Anderson's invitation to the Danish brothers Charles and August Warnick, as they camped nearby one night in 1866, to stay on, since "this was as good a place as we would find in Sanpete"[18]—but returning missionaries from Scandinavia also invited new Scandinavian converts to settle in their hometown, as Nicholas Iverson did for Andrew Jenson,[19] a Danish convert-immigrant who later became an assistant LDS Church historian.

Unlike mainstream Scandinavian immigration to the United States, Danish Mormon emigration was not primarily motivated by economic conditions in either the homeland or the new land but by ideological conviction. As Mulder explains, "The Danes, proverbially reluctant to sail out farther than they could row back and traditionally considered poor pioneers, nevertheless, as Mormons, left their homeland in years of actual prosperity to become hardy grass-roots settlers well beyond the frontier of Scandinavian occupation in the United States."[20] One of the unique aspects of the Mormon migration from Scandinavia was, as Mulder's book title *Homeward to Zion* indicates, the way in which the move to Utah as Zion was pitched as a spiritual homecoming that preempted the convert-emigrants' ethnic solidarity. Harald Jensen Kent notes that messages from the LDS Church to Danish converts published in *Skandinaviens Stjerne* invite them to "come home" to Zion. "It is important to remember," Kent cautions, "that this 'come *home*' means that these people, who have never before left their fatherland, should call Utah, which is entirely foreign to them, their 'home' and hurry there."[21] By way of illustration, one Danish Mormon hymn, "O Herre Lad Mig Komme Frem" (O Lord, please grant that I arrive) taught new converts to think of "Zion's land" as "my home beloved."[22] In this way, Danish Mormons were conditioned to form an emotional bond with their new home that would ease their transition from Denmark and strengthen their sense of belonging to their new culture and society.

Danish Mormon converts' decision to emigrate thus entailed more than simply the change of geographic location and language; it required instead a complete social reorientation—and did so without the driving force of economic hardship, relying on the ideological conviction of the emigrant, as well as the bonds with other Danish convert-emigrants. Despite popular perceptions that Danish Mormon convert-emigrants tended to be drawn from the poorest members of society, many prosperous Danes also converted and chose to emigrate in order to join with the Saints in Utah. The communal orientation of the Church, which encouraged well-off emigrants to sponsor poorer ones, as well as loans available from the Church's Perpetual Emigration Fund, made it possible for people to emigrate who would not have had the financial resources to do so on their own. The theological dimension of Danish Mormon immigration thus overrode both the economic and cultural considerations that shaped most other Danish immigration to the United States, facilitating the emigration of people who may not otherwise have been motivated to emigrate or have been able to afford the costs of the journey. At the same time, however, Danish Mormon immigrants faced many of the same challenges that other Danish Americans did with regard to language preservation, intermarriage, and maintenance of cultural traditions, from folk songs to sweet soups. Despite their desire to be part of the Zion community, many Danish immigrants cherished their native culture and did not want to abandon it entirely, despite their geographic distance from Denmark.

Although many Danish Mormons assimilated rapidly into English-speaking settlements in Utah, large numbers of Danish Mormon immigrants chose to settle in predominantly Scandinavian communities, where they could continue to speak Danish in the course of their everyday lives, intermarry with other Scandinavians, and express their Danish cultural identity in both explicit and implicit ways. Jennifer Eastman Attebery has documented the presence of such cultural identity markers among Danish Mormons in forms as diverse as self-descriptions in American letters and the celebration of Scandinavian holidays in Utah,[23] for example, while Rachel Gianni Abbott has shown how the material culture legacy of Scandinavian Mormons, which encompasses both objects that they brought with them from the old country and objects that they produced in their new homeland, confirms their efforts to maintain their cultural heritage despite some inevitable modifications and adaptations.[24] In addition to maintaining some of their own Danish traits, Danish Mormon settlers in Utah contributed to shaping the character of the state itself and thereby perpetuated aspects of Danish culture in their new homeland.

The communal nature of many aspects of pioneer society in Utah bears a strong resemblance to such Danish traditions as cooperative economic enterprises and communal settlements. Abbott's research shows that the "Mormons were indeed communal in many more aspects than other Americans; though they were pioneers in moving westward into unsettled territory, they created a rather insular community."[25] Likewise, Davis Bitton contends that Mormon collectivism conflicted with laissez-faire economic practices of the late nineteenth century in the United States,[26] whereas Mormon village settlement patterns resemble traditional (pre–land reform) Scandinavian villages, with homes clustered together and farms outside the village, rather than individual homesteads on separate farms. It may be impossible to determine whether such features of pioneer life in Utah were inspired by Danish

Mormons, either directly or indirectly, but their presence suggests that Danish Mormons may have found certain customs and values in their new homeland to be familiar to their old one.

While LDS Church leaders expected and promoted assimilation in order to create a cohesive community out of immigrants from the Eastern United States, Great Britain, Germany, Scandinavia, and many other countries, Danish Mormons, like other Scandinavian Mormons elsewhere in Utah, were able to assert and maintain their cultural specificity in many ways, including holding church services in their native language, organizing Scandinavian choirs and theatrical productions, and celebrating Danish national holidays, including Midsummer Day, a Winter Festival, and Constitution Day (June 5). They organized annual Christmas Day programs at least as early as 1876 and as late as 1916, held New Year's Eve parties in the United Order Hall, and were well known for the "Grand Scandinavian Balls" held in the Clark and Orpheus Halls, where traditional Danish buns and coffee were served.[27] Beginning in 1890, to celebrate the fortieth anniversary of the commencement of LDS proselytizing in Denmark in 1850, an annual two-day Scandinavian reunion was convened in Pleasant Grove, attracting more than a thousand people each year, including prominent Scandinavian Church leaders such as the Danish apostle Anthon H. Lund, in the 1910s and 1920s with meetings, outings, and concerts.[28] Several Danish-language newspapers, such as *Bikuben* and *Utah Posten*, facilitated communication between the far-flung centers of Danish Mormon settlement within Utah, while pan-Scandinavian organizations commemorated events such as the fiftieth anniversary of the arrival of the first LDS missionaries in Denmark. The four-day jubilee celebration in 1900 featured distinguished Scandinavian Mormon speakers—including Anthon H. Lund and the painter C. C. A. Christensen—a commemorative volume of reminiscences and illustrations, an evening concert, an outdoor carnival, and a group outing to the bathing resort Saltair, on the Great Salt Lake.[29] The numerical superiority of Danish Mormons among Scandinavian Mormon settlers in Utah made them such an important constituency that a group of Swedish Mormons, led by Otto Rydman, protested in 1904 that the Danish Mormons received preferential treatment from the LDS Church.

Although Church leaders strongly encouraged new immigrants to learn English—"the language of God, the language of the Book of Mormon, the language of the Latter Days," as President Brigham Young described it[30]—as quickly as possible, the Church did not enforce an "English only" policy but maintained instead, as Lynn Henrichsen and George Bailey have documented, a "flexibly, linguistically pluralistic" attitude toward foreign language usage in Church contexts.[31] For more than eighty years, Scandinavian immigrants were permitted to hold auxiliary Scandinavian-language meetings to help them transition to life in Utah "until they should acquire a sufficient knowledge of the English language to keep pace with the rest of the Saints."[32] While all of Pleasant Grove was officially encompassed in a single ward (until 1890, when it was divided into three), Rasmus Petersen was called already in 1858 to preside over a local Scandinavian congregation in Pleasant Grove, which position he held until his death in 1890. These meetings were held in homes, the schoolhouse, and in local church buildings on Sunday afternoons, and settlers traveled in from far-flung farms to attend meetings. In the mid-1870s, these meetings were so well attended that three Scandinavian districts were established for winter meetings, to be held on Wednesday evenings, in the north, east, and northwest of town in an area known as "Little Denmark."[33] Linguistic assimilation rates were very high among Scandinavians in Utah, particularly in the second generation, so many settlers were able to move freely between the Scandinavian and English-speaking congregations, such as Hans's missionary colleague Andrew Jenson, who reported that he had "attended equal numbers of Scandinavian and English-speaking meetings in town during the interim [1875–1879] between his two missions."[34] Others, including some women who had fewer opportunities to practice their English skills outside the home, felt uncomfortable in English-language meetings or simply enjoyed hearing and speaking their native language.

Constrained by a lack of transportation, limited fluency in English, and the need to care for her small children, Mine Jørgensen did not attend church services regularly for many years, but when she was able to go to a meeting, she generally preferred Scandinavian-language services, where she would meet people that she knew. Regardless of the language of worship, she clearly felt very much a part of the LDS Church and was devoted to its teachings. Her letters reveal that she found that the expansion of her horizons as a result of her husband's absence (and her daughter Minnie's lengthening legs) also extended to her activity in the Church. On February 4, 1883, she reports to Hans,

> Otherwise I am feeling very well and am happy to be united with the people who live in Utha [*sic*], even though things are not always as they should be here. After all, it is only ourselves that we can try to improve. I attend meetings more frequently than I have since you've known me. My baby is so big that she can walk the whole way.

Mine occasionally reports attending both English and Danish meetings, for example, in her letter of September 9, 1883, and she tried to attend semiannual church-wide General Conference meetings held in Salt Lake City whenever possible. In April 1882, for example, she was thrilled to hear "Brother Jon Tieler and several of the Twelve speak," as she reports to Hans in a letter of April 12, and wished "with all my heart that I could be able to live according to even a part of the doctrines they gave us." Mine's letters make it clear that she felt included within the theological community of the LDS Church, but they also confirm that the social community in Pleasant Grove was not ethnically integrated in this early period despite its religious homogeneity.

Mine's letters suggest, as much by what they don't say about her English-speaking neighbors as what they do, that her interactions with the larger, non-Scandinavian Mormon community in Utah were informed and often constrained by her outsider status as part of a linguistic and ethnic minority. While immigrants were a welcome, even essential, part of Utah's successful settlement, non-English-speaking immigrants were noticeably different enough from their Anglo-American neighbors in dress, habits, and speech that they could not assimilate immediately or completely into their new communities, despite the bond of shared religious beliefs. Ruby Warnick recalls "the particular kind of language spoken in our part of town, a mixture of Swedish, Norwegian, Danish, and broken English, made for a lot of hilarity."[35] In contrast to this rosy memory, Beth Olson reports that the language barrier between the population groups and nationalistic feelings on both sides caused friction between the groups, with the Anglo-American settlers mocking the Scandinavians' dress, foods, language, and mannerisms.[36] This division is evidenced in the marriage patterns in town: although intermarriage rates between Anglo-American and Scandinavian residents of Pleasant Grove rose dramatically between 1880 and 1900 (from eleven in 1880 to thirty-one in 1900), the majority of marriages involving Scandinavians in Pleasant Grove were contracted with other Scandinavians (seventy-eight in 1880 and eighty-seven in 1900).[37] The children of these mixed marriages could sense the social hierarchies. Local resident Grace F. Boulter, born to an English father and Swedish mother, recalled that she "always felt like papa's folks, being English, were better than the Swedish people. In fact, most people looked down on those who spoke broken English."[38] These social barriers ensured that Scandinavians in Pleasant Grove lived alongside but separate from their Anglo-American neighbors well into the twentieth century, despite the official LDS Church insistence on assimilation for Mormon convert-immigrants and the immigrants' desire to live in harmony with their fellow believers.

ACCOMMODATING MORMON DOCTRINES

"Now my good husband, I hope that you have happily reached the land of your birth and I pray that the Lord's hand and blessing will rest upon you, that you will be able to accomplish a good work and return clean and untainted. I have heard that the young sisters there cling to a man from Zion like grapevines cling to an apple tree, even though they know that he has a wife in Zion who is sitting and waiting for the day when her husband will return again and be her joy and comfort. I think that if such a one were to entice my husband to promise her marriage upon his return, then I could never forgive her, no matter who she is, even though I know that we are all weak and imperfect and often make mistakes and ought to forgive each other, but such a day would come so close to my heart that I cry at the thought of it. Now, good Jørgensen, don't be angry at this. I hope you are man enough to resist such chains and come home as a faithful servant of the Lord."

—Mine to Hans, May 17, 1881

In contrast to Danish Lutheran immigrants, who settled in predominantly Protestant or secular American communities, Danish Mormons' efforts to blend elements of their Danish cultural identity with a new American one had to take the norms of Mormon culture and the expectations of the LDS Church into account. These negotiations contributed to certain accommodations that other Danish Americans had no need to consider making, such as risking imprisonment in order to defend the doctrine of polygamy or giving their children Mormon-inflected names such as Erastus and Nephi. As a result, the question of cultural identity maintenance and/or transformation is a complicated one with regard to the Danish Mormon community. Those accounts of Utah history that mention the many thousands of Danish immigrants to Utah generally take it for granted that the converts abandoned their Danish heritage in favor of their new identity as Mormons and Americans. The initial decision to join the LDS Church and adopt its belief system already represented a major shift in the subjects' cultural identity, both in terms of self-perception and perception by outsiders.

When immigrating to Utah, Danish Mormon converts added an additional layer of cultural identity by adopting American customs, language, and citizenship, but this new national identity competed at times with the immigrants' identity as Mormons—for example, when the US federal government passed laws outlawing the Mormon practice of polygamy. When Pastor H. C. Rørdam had accused the Mormon community in Vendsyssel, in northern Jutland, of practicing polygamy in 1854, an editorial in *Skandinaviens Stjerne* responded with a vehement denial, noting that "it would be a violation of the law of this land."[39] Yet although most Danish Mormons prided themselves on being law-abiding citizens, both in the old country and the new, the percentage of Scandinavian Mormons who served jail time for violating the Edmunds-Tucker Anti-Polygamy Act of 1887 was even higher than the percentage of Scandinavians actually involved in plural marriages, since it was regarded as an honor to be imprisoned for the sake of one's beliefs.[40]

This demonstrated willingness to accommodate and embrace Mormon doctrine did not mean, however, that all Scandinavian Saints were equally enthusiastic about all doctrinal points. One area in which Danish Mormon immigrants, despite the Church's official policies of assimilation and temperance, modified certain aspects of Mormon culture to accommodate their culturally determined habits and preferences, was with regard to the Mormon code of health known as the Word of Wisdom, which forbids the use of alcohol, tobacco, and coffee. A flexible interpretation of the Word of Wisdom was by no means limited to Scandinavians, to be sure, but folkloric accounts emphasize how the Danes in the heavily Scandinavian community of Elsinore, for example, prided themselves on their home-brewed beer and regarded coffee as a necessity of civilized life. Folklorist Thomas Cheney recounts how a second-generation Danish immigrant, Brother Swenson, who held responsible positions of authority in the Church but was known to drink coffee regularly, was asked by a visiting Church leader from Salt Lake whether he used coffee. Brother Swenson replied simply, "The Word of Wisdom never bothers me."[41] Anthon H. Lund's Norwegian bride Sarah Peterson, whose father had been among the Norwegian converts to Mormonism in the Fox River Valley in Illinois in the 1840s, allegedly extracted a promise from him before their marriage that he would allow her to continue "indulging her Scandinavian fondness for coffee and tea." Her second stipulation was that he would never take a second wife.[42]

The passage from Mine's letter quoted at the beginning of this section reveals a similar hesitancy about the practice of plural marriage, as well as a tacit acknowledgment that many other Danish women did not share her hesitation. Her resistance is not directed toward the LDS Church leadership or the doctrine itself, but toward the women in Denmark who might view her husband as an available marriage prospect. Her allusion to herself, in her letter of May 17, 1881, barely a month after her husband's departure, as "a wife in Zion who is sitting and waiting for the day when her husband will return again and be her joy and comfort" emphasizes her emotional partnership with her husband, while her metaphor of young Danish women as "grapevines cling[ing] to an apple tree" suggests the danger of a parasitic or at least suffocating dependency. Unlike Sanie Petersen Lund, she does not demand an outright promise that Hans would not take a second wife, but she implores him to "resist such chains" and speculates on the difficulty she would have, in such an event, forgiving the woman who had "entice[d] my husband to promise her marriage upon his return." Whatever his feelings toward Church doctrine, Hans respected Mine's concerns and reassured her, in his letter of June 14, 1881, "No man is overwhelmed by love and proposals of marriage unless he himself desires it in his heart; therefore if I or any other man from America wants to keep himself pure and seeks the Lord's assistance in this, it can easily be done." He did not ever take a plural wife.

Mine's attitude toward polygamy was not uniformly negative, but she does take note of problems that the practice caused within her own community. In many of her letters, Mine comments nonjudgmentally on men and women entering into plural marriages, such as the news, on June 10, 1881, that

"Niels Peter Larson Number 2 has married Ane Ekerhoi as his second wife."
One situation that seemed to disturb her involved her neighbor Peter Johan-
sen, who arranged to pay for a Danish girl's immigration with the apparent
expectation that she would marry him upon arrival. The only Peter Johnson
in Pleasant Grove listed in the 1880 US Census, born in Denmark in 1836,
already had a wife, Christiana, and six children, the youngest of whom was
two years old in 1881. Mine urged Hans not to involve himself in the matter,
though he seemed unperturbed by it. On August 11, 1881, he explains,

> Regarding Peter Johnson and the girl, you must not be anxious about it, for it
> was arranged between him and me before I left. I can tell you that she could
> have been married here, for she showed me a proposal she had received from
> another at the same time, but when a girl has kept her covenants for more than
> 6 years, she would be dumb to give her hand to the first best. If they can't be
> reconciled to each other, then the world is large enough for each of them to go
> their own way. I feel no remorse in that area, for I did it with the best intentions.

Mine's worries that the matter would not be as straightforward as Hans expected
proved to be justified. After Peter fixed up his house in anticipation of the girl's
arrival in September, she changed her mind and moved to Salt Lake City instead.
A few weeks later, on October 7, Mine wrote to Hans, "Peter is to be married
tomorrow, but not to Marie." As her final commentary on this matter, she admonishes Hans in her next letter, "Never have anything to do with such matters
as you did, specifically with the girl who was sent for Peter's money. It was so
sad that he should send his money for such a one." Mine's sympathies lay with
Peter Johnson, not the Danish girl, but she clearly disapproved of the quid pro
quo deal Peter had worked out to get himself a second wife.

Although Mine was never involved in a plural marriage, she felt the effects
of the conflict brewing between the US government and the LDS Church
that would culminate in the Edmunds Act of 1882 and the Edmunds-Tucker
Act of 1887. The former was signed into law by President Chester A. Arthur
on March 23, 1882, and revoked polygamists' right to vote, serve on a jury,
or hold political office. Although women were not prosecuted under these
acts, the anti-polygamy activists who descended on Utah caused an uproar
in Mormon communities, including Pleasant Grove. On September 12, 1882,
Mine wrote to Hans:

> Today is the 12th and for the first time in my life, I have been required to give
> an oath. Our new judges continue to try to destroy us and no one who has more
> than one wife is allowed to vote, but I could answer freely that I don't belong to
> a polygamist. I wonder what they will do with us now. I do hope that they will
> let us stay here a while yet, or else people like us will be left behind.

As Hans's only wife, Mine was not in any legal danger, nor was her husband (unlike his friend and fellow missionary Christian Fjeldsted, who had to go into hiding upon his return from Denmark), but the persecution of her fellow Church members disrupted her life and caused her to fear for her future. Her remarks to Hans reflect her fear of being driven out of Utah and the worry that "people like us," presumably immigrants, would be "left behind." Whatever her differences of opinion with the Church about plural marriage, Mine felt a deep loyalty and connection to the Mormon faith and people.

CONCLUSION

Mine Jørgensen's correspondence with her missionary husband not only documents her individual situation as a woman separated from the man she loved and struggling to provide for her family but also illuminates the broader gender and cultural challenges that colored her experiences as a Danish Mormon missionary grass widow in territorial Utah. In terms of her personal history, Mine comes to life in her letters as a woman passionately in love with her husband, proud of her own resourcefulness, devoted to her children, grateful for the kindnesses of her neighbors, ashamed of her own shortcomings, and much more. In his early letters, Hans asks for a photograph of his wife, so he could "go to it and see my beloved as she looked when I first won her love," but Mine's letters themselves provide an in-depth, nuanced portrait of the smart, generous, brave, caring, outspoken woman she was, in a time and place that were physically, socially, and emotionally challenging. She did not accept all Mormon doctrine and practices without question, but she strove sincerely to fulfill her covenants and obligations as a member of the LDS Church.

Taken as a representative example of a missionary wife's experiences, Mine's letters reveal how the practice in territorial Utah of calling married men on foreign missions placed a tremendous economic and emotional burden on their wives, while simultaneously providing them with opportunities for personal growth and empowerment. Mine's struggles during her husband's absence were shared by thousands of other grass widows across the Utah territory, most of whom did not leave as detailed and candid an account of their struggles and triumphs. The everyday details of life that Mine's letters reveal, from harvesting wheat and alfalfa to hitching rides with neighbors to attend weddings far from home and worrying about polygamy and her children's education, enrich the histories of Utah pioneer women and the early LDS Church that are often painted with a broader and more idealistic or sentimental brush.

In addition to fleshing out her own biography and illuminating the challenges faced by missionary wives, Mine's story is also highly relevant to contemporary Mormonism's efforts to accommodate the increasingly multi-cultural population of the LDS Church. Mine's letters paint a picture of the Scandinavian Mormon frontier community to which she belonged—one in which she was constrained by gender expectations and linguistic barriers but sustained by the generosity of neighbors and their shared enthusiasm for their adopted faith. Far from her native land and isolated from the dream of America, which many of her countrymen sought, Mine was connected by bonds of faith, language, heritage, and mutual assistance—as well as some of the culturally determined obstacles to belief that they had to navigate—to other Scandinavians who had chosen to follow the call to come and build Zion, generally more so than to the English-speaking neighbors alongside whom she lived in a sometimes awkward but generally placid mutual indifference. Her cultural identity as a Danish Mormon enhanced her spiritual and material endeavors, rather than detracting from them, while the assistance of the local Danish Mormon labor network enabled her to contribute to the success of the Utah territory, even when deprived of her husband's financial and physical support. In contrast to the long-standing tendency of regarding all early Utah settlers as an undifferentiated cultural unit, Mine's letters offer the possibility of recovering a more nuanced history of how the non-English-speaking convert-immigrants on the periphery of territorial Utah society related to the core population. Such models of the historical coexistence of devout Mormons from many different cultural traditions may prove useful as the LDS Church strives to encompass the cultural plurality of global Mormonism in the twenty-first century.

NOTES

1. I translated the entire correspondence between Hans and Mine between 2004 and 2007 at the request of their great-granddaughter, Mary Lambert.
2. Although the definition of this term has undergone several shifts, it is most commonly used to describe a woman whose husband is temporarily absent.
3. Andrew Jenson, *History of the Scandinavian Mission* (Salt Lake City, UT: Deseret News Press, 1927).
4. Hans Jørgensen, *Daybook 1845–1883* (Salt Lake City, UT: privately printed, 1996), 101.
5. Jørgensen, *Daybook*, 103.
6. Jørgensen, *Daybook*, 281.
7. Lori Ann Lahlum, "Women, Work, and Community in Rural Norwegian America," in *Norwegian American Women: Migration, Communities, and Identities*, ed. Betty A. Bergland and Lori Ann Lahlum (Minneapolis: Minnesota Historical Society Press, 2011), 85.
8. Ruth Ellen Homrighaus, "Baby Farming: The Care of Illegitimate Children in England, 1860–1943" (PhD diss., University of North Carolina at Chapel Hill, 2003).
9. Miriam B. Murphy, "Gainfully Employed Women, 1896–1950," in *Women in Utah History: Paradigm or Paradox?*, ed. Patricia Lyn Scott and Linda Thatcher (Logan: Utah State University Press, 2005), 184.

10. Murphy, "Gainfully Employed," 184.

11. Alice Kessler-Harris, *Out to Work: A History of Wage-Earning Women in the United States* (New York: Oxford University Press, 1982), 22.

12. Albert C. T. Antrei and Allen D. Roberts, *A History of Sanpete County* (Salt Lake City: Utah State Historical Society, 1999), 367.

13. Beth R. Olson, "Chronological History of Pleasant Grove, Utah 1850–2000," in *Pleasant Grove Sesquicentennial History*, ed. Beth R. Olson and Mildred Sutch (Provo, UT: Stevenson's Supply/ Pleasant Grove City Corporation, 2000), 1:21.

14. Olson, "Chronological History," 58.

15. William Mulder, *Homeward to Zion: The Mormon Migration from Scandinavia* (Minneapolis: University of Minnesota Press, 1957), 157.

16. Mulder, *Homeward to Zion*, 157.

17. Olson, "Chronological History," 40.

18. "Charles Peter Warnick," in *Our Pioneer Heritage*, 20 vols., ed. Kate B. Carter (Salt Lake City: Daughters of Utah Pioneers, 1958–1977), 10:58–63.

19. Olson, "Chronological History," 59.

20. Mulder, *Homeward to Zion*, x.

21. Harald Jensen Kent, *Danske Mormoner* (Copenhagen: Udvalget for Utahmissionen, 1913), 6.

22. Rochelle Wright and Robert L. Wright, *Danish Emigrant Ballads and Songs* (Carbondale: Southern Illinois University Press, 1983), 152.

23. Jennifer Eastman Attebery, *Up in the Rocky Mountains: Writing the Swedish Immigrant Experience* (Minneapolis: University of Minnesota Press, 2007).

24. Rachel Gianni Abbott, "The Scandinavian Immigrant Experience in Utah, 1850–1920: Using Material Culture to Interpret Cultural Adaptation" (PhD diss., University of Alaska–Fairbanks, 2013).

25. Abbott, "Material Culture," 28.

26. Davis Bitton, "A Reevaluation of the Turner Thesis and Mormon Beginnings," *Utah Historical Quarterly* 34, no. 4 (October 1966): 331.

27. Olson, "Chronological History," 61–62.

28. Olson, "Chronological History," 62.

29. Andrew Jenson, *The Autobiography of Andrew Jenson* (Salt Lake City, UT: Deseret News Press, 1938), 415.

30. Quoted in Lynn E. Henrichsen and George Bailey, "'No More Strangers and Foreigners': The Dual Focus of the LDS Church Language Program for Scandinavian Immigrants," *Mormon Historical Studies* 11 (Fall 2010): 2, 28.

31. Henrichsen and Bailey, "LDS Church Language Program," 39.

32. Andrew Jenson, "Pleasant Grove First Ward Records, Utah Stake" (Salt Lake City, UT: LDS Church Archives, 1900).

33. Olson, "Chronological History," 59.

34. Olson, "Chronological History," 59.

35. Ruby Radmall Warnick, "The Life and Times of Coffee Oscar Olson," typed manuscript, vertical file (Pleasant Grove, UT: Pleasant Grove City Library, n.d.), 1.

36. Olson, "Chronological History," 60.

37. Misty Armstrong, "The Assimilation of Scandinavian Immigrants in Pleasant Grove, Utah, 1880–1900," *Genealogical Journal* 27, nos. 3–4 (1999): 125.

38. Grace F. Boulter, oral history, interviewed by Marsha Martin, 1983, L. Tom Perry Special Collections, Brigham Young University, Provo, UT.

39. Jørgen Würtz Sørensen, *Rejsen til Amerikas zion: den danske mormonudvandring før århundredeskiftet* (Aalborg, Denmark: Forlaget Fenre, 1985), 37.

40. Mulder, *Homeward to Zion*, 241.

41. Thomas Cheney, "Scandinavian Immigrant Stories," *Western Folklore* 18, no. 2 (April 1959): 104.

42. Jennifer Lund, "Out of the Swan's Nest: The Ministry of Anthon H. Lund, Scandinavian Apostle," *Journal of Mormon History* 29, no. 2 (2003): 84.

Chapter Nine

Kings and Queens of the Kingdom

Gendering the Mormon Theological Narrative

Benjamin E. Park

"[Women] will awake one fine morning and rise up an unfettered being, bound only by the law of God and her own pure nature[.] [T]hose awful words and their still more awful meaning: 'Thy desire shall be to thy husband and he shall rule over thee,' will have been cancelled because the curse is ful-filled and the judge opens the door and bids the captive go free, and she walks forth a free, unfettered being in her primal advent in the garden of Eden."[1]

Those are the words of Hannah Tapfield King, a British convert to Mormon-ism in the nineteenth century who was descended from quasi-aristocracy yet forfeited her fortune and cultural esteem to join the Church of Jesus Christ of Latter-day Saints (LDS) and migrate to Utah in the 1850s. She wrote the passage in the midst of Mormon women's push for suffrage during the 1870s. It is part of her radical reinterpretation of the Garden of Eden scene in which Eve is valorized for making a tough decision that, while destined to denigrate women in their mortality, promised a restoration of female empowerment and freedom in the eternities. King's words are indicative of a robust theology cultivated by a number of women in territorial Utah during the period. Yet while it was written by a Mormon, and embraced by many other Mormons still, historians who are conceptualizing a Mormon historical theology do not typically engage its message when constructing a narrative of LDS thought. This chapter is, in part, an extended exercise in asking, "Why not?"

The terms historians choose to employ to frame how they approach a topic often reveal gendered assumptions. When a scholar references "Mormon the-ology" in particular, or even Christian theology in general, it is immediately assumed that they are speaking of male constructions of religious imagina-tion. If a scholar's subject matter focuses on the thought of women, it is often specified as "female theology."[2] "Mormon theology," historically speaking, typically refers to the writings of men such as Joseph Smith, Parley Pratt, or James Talmage. The recent *Columbia Sourcebook of Mormons in the United States*, for instance, features twelve documents in the section on "Mormon Theology," none of which were written by women.[3] The writings of Eliza R. Snow, Annie Clark Tanner, and Maxine Hanks, on the other hand, are housed in the "Sexuality and Gender" section, along with those by men. The editors explain that because "the church is led by a male priesthood, women's voices are principally found in the social and cultural, rather than theological, sections," which typifies the connection between authority and theological vision.[4] The theological sphere is envisioned as a patriarchal space.

This compartmentalization is representative not only of the field of Mormon history but also the general approach to historical theology. That is, even while the subfield of women's history is encouraged, it is often compartmentalized from broader Mormon narratives and frameworks. What Paul Harvey and Kevin Schultz said about religion within twentieth-century American history can similarly be said about women in Mormon history, and especially Mormon historical theology: it is "everywhere" in that specialized work in the field has proliferated at an astounding rate, but it is still "nowhere" in that it has been relegated as marginal and contained.[5] Women's history becomes a methodological ghetto, unable to make any real revision to synthetic narratives. Only through the integration into broader synthetic stories can our historical narratives become less exclusive and more representative. Otherwise, only those specifically interested in women's history will encounter the lessons of the subfield.

This chapter is both historiographical and provocative in nature and seeks to point to future roads for historians to traverse and questions for scholars to answer. Following a general overview of how historians of Mormon thought have dealt with—or, in many cases, avoided dealing with—theology produced by women, it will posit reasons for this androcentric framing as well as point toward potential methodological avenues for more integrative synthetic approaches. Rather than merely carving space for the history of women in Mormon thought, we must conceive of ways in which female voices both constructed and transformed the history itself. And finally, this chapter will offer one example of such a study that seeks to blend both male and female voices into a Mormon theological narrative of the Nauvoo period. Throughout, this chapter also attempts to demonstrate how this Mormon example provides important lessons for theological, intellectual, and religious history more broadly, as it identifies how to integrate a broader array of voices and frameworks into broader synthetic narratives.

* * *

Historical theology has long been a popular topic in the field of Mormon history, likely because of the cultural significance of demonstrating ideological change over time as well as the unique divergences from broader Christian traditions. Early treatments emphasized theological ruptures throughout the nineteenth century and relied primarily on ecclesiastical thinkers.[6] More recently, scholars have offered increasingly nuanced interpretations that have emphasized intellectual continuities as well as cultural intersections.[7] The period-centric approaches have often been framed around themes that privileged men's voices: the founding period has revolved around male mysticism and folkloric practices,[8] the territorial period has focused on theocracy and the patriarchal defenses of polygamy,[9] and the transition period has emphasized institutional evolution and priesthood development.[10]

Even the most recent, persuasive, and successful overviews of the origins of Mormon thought have perpetuated these gendered frameworks. Samuel Brown's treatment of early Mormon death theologies relies primarily on men, aside from sections on women like Eliza R. Snow, whose elegiac poems add passion to his main protagonists' prose.[11] Terryl Givens's magisterial overview of the foundations of Mormon thought gives little space to female voices, save for a chapter on the concept of a Mother in Heaven.[12] (Indeed, turning to women only to explain particularly gendered principles, of course, reaffirms gendered divisions with regard to synthetic narratives.) A particularly sophisticated approach that integrates both gendered voices is found in Christine Talbot's *A Foreign Kingdom*, which uses Mormon men and women to elucidate how the LDS tradition grappled with the concept of polygamy and the division of public and private. Yet even Talbot's book separates voices of female suffragists into their own chapter, separate and distinct from the patriarchal politics personified by men.[13] This is not to say such an approach is flawed—indeed, Talbot's own framing device necessitated such a division—but it points to this broader issue of compartmentalization and highlights the fact that we still need a more synthetic image.

At the heart of most work on Mormon theology is a central assumption: theology is an exclusively male sphere. This is reflected even in the numerous works on the religious imagination of Mormon women, as they then have to classify their work as "female theology" and contextualize it within the context of other women. To speak of a male Mormon theology is to be redundant. This was, in part, a result of the New Mormon History movement's convergence with women's studies, a disciplinary approach that was nobly dedicated to resurrecting female voices. Much of the feminist awakening that is reflective in Mormon history during the 1970s and 1980s stands as a hallmark to this methodological intervention. But the academy's shift from "women's history" to "gender studies" has destabilized even those frameworks. Rather than isolating female actors within their own spheres, scholars are now more attuned to breaking apart gendered boundaries in general. This requires integrating both "male" and "female" actors and voices within the same analytical structure.[14]

Sadly, though certainly not unexpectedly, academic analysis of Mormon women's religious imagination and theology has not received the same degree of attention as that given to the more general categories of women's history and thought. There are definite exceptions, however, like Susanna Morrill's *White Roses on the Floor of Heaven: Mormon Women's Popular Theology, 1880–1920*, which looks at how women constructed theological worlds through their literary explorations.[15] Others, including Boyd Peterson, Lisa Tait, and Amy Easton-Flake, have produced excellent works that reclaim the theological tradition of Mormon women in territorial Utah.[16] And there is a proliferation of biographical work that, in part, explores the mental world of prominent figures like Eliza R. Snow and Emmeline B. Wells.[17] Mormon women's history has certainly not lacked quantity and quality when it comes to assessing their theological imagination. Yet biographies often perpetuate a denominational and marginalized context, and much of this work remains isolated and unincorporated when it comes to synthetic treatments of a Mormon period, moment, or theme. These works on the mind of Mormon women often remain segregated from larger narratives of Mormon theology in general.

This problem within Mormon historiography mirrors issues of the broader field of American religious history, as the major scholarly overviews of the nation's theological trajectories have focused on male voices.[18] Indeed, the best works on women's religious imaginations have remained isolated within subfield genres, denominational studies, and biographies.[19] Mormon historians, then, are largely following a long-established historiographical tradition of separate spheres. Yet dissecting why historians of Mormonism have maintained this separatist approach, and how such a methodology might be overcome, adds much to the scholarship on American religious thought. Within the discipline of religious studies, the focus on ideas allows the integration of various voices in the attempt to delineate thematic tensions and processes; within the subdiscipline of intellectual history, the cultural turn has required the broadening of the source base.[20] This has pushed scholars to ask questions concerning how nontraditional voices that fall outside the category of elite white men both contributed to and transformed the thought culture around them. Taking these historiographical developments together, the examination of religious ideas necessitates a rethinking of methodological approach. The Mormon case study offers an acute example.

* * *

There are often methodological considerations behind these gendered frameworks. In the Mormon historiographical sphere, the separation between male and female theology is often based on the belief that the two fields are typically seen as oppositional. That is, male voices are seen as constructing the mainstream orthodoxy, and women are tasked with filling in the gaps.

Throughout the nineteenth century, Mormonism flowed through a patriarchal culture that privileged male status and reaffirmed priesthood authority. Mormon women were left to construct a theological vision that validated their own experience in the face of patriarchal control. It makes sense, then, to acknowledge this division within an imminently present power structure. Some have even concluded that modern-day gendered politics necessitates the construction of a reactionary female message that strikes against lingering cultural control—that is, a theological vision that pushes back against the dominant patriarchal structure.[21]

Yet seeing Mormon female theology as merely a reaction to patriarchal culture masks the fact that female voices should be seen as central to shaping Mormonism's theological narrative writ large. This principle is true in most historical studies—as Anne Braude famously put it, "Women's history *is* American religious history"[22]—but it is especially true when dealing with the Mormon theological tradition. All religious beliefs contain logical leaps and theological gaps, but the unsystematic nature of Mormonism made the faith particularly prone to the necessity for supplemental modes of theological discourse. LDS leaders mostly eschewed formal religious training, often refused to engage intellectual contemporaries, and rejected the necessity of a systematic theology. The populist impulse of frontier leaders did not equate to methodical treatises.[23] And the marginalized ecclesiastical and ministerial roles for women limited female participation. Therefore, the porous, inconsistent, and sporadic nature of Mormon doctrine in general, and of the role of women in particular, provided space into which alternative and, at times, competing forms of thought could be birthed. The male and female theological traditions within Mormonism were two sides of the same coin that spun in unison—the one could not exist without the other.

Put in other words, separating Mormon women's theology from institutional and male voices perpetuates the orthodoxy of patriarchal tradition—that men are the core, and women the margins. Such a perspective is short-sighted. The abstract rumination of Eliza R. Snow, the gentle poetry of Ruth May Fox, or the theodical reflections of Helen Mar Kimball Whitney are just as fundamentally "Mormon" as the systematic vision of Parley Pratt, the legalistic discourse of Orson Spencer, or the domineering pronouncements of Brigham Young, even as they were challenging traditional boundaries. Perhaps more than seeing them as merely reactionary, or an orthodoxy and periphery, we can rather see them as dialogic, a give-and-take tug-of-war that shaped the boundaries and stakes for both sides of the divide. We have yet to reconstruct a "Mormon" theological discourse that synthesizes gendered voices, even as careful and provocative scholarship exists within each particular sphere. And as a result, our traditional narratives of Mormon history and Mormon thought remain exclusively dictated by and focused on men and male interests.

But can these two fields speak to each other? In order for them to do so, there are at least three issues that would have to be addressed. First, and perhaps most substantially, the very boundaries of *theology* would have to be revised. Traditionally speaking, the term has referred to a systematic intellectual construction delivered through prose and, implicitly, written from a position of authority. This categorization has, of course, already been challenged within the Mormon tradition given the eclectic and inchoate nature of LDS thought—not to mention the rugged, amateurish, and inconsistent nature of nineteenth-century Mormon authors. But even within the LDS theological tradition, certain modes of discourse and particular expectations for authors have substantially narrowed potential inclusions. While the Pratt Brothers, Orson Hyde, and a host of other male writers were able to dictate pages upon pages of religious precepts, similar avenues for women—who also held serious thoughts regarding the religious world around them—were restricted. And when it was possible for elite authors like Eliza R. Snow to produce their own theological work, the reception was likely constricted due to issues of gendered authority. In a Victorian period in which domestic spheres were often trumpeted and reaffirmed, this was far from solely a Mormon problem.

Indeed, the medium, tone, and parameters of female religious expression grate against the typically constricted confines of Mormon theological discourse. Thus, the traditional boundaries of Mormon theology necessitate revision. Scholars of American religious history have already demonstrated how this can be done through the cultivation of religious worldviews—arguably the real product at the end of the theological process.[24] Sentimental poetry, discursive correspondence, didactic literature—all these genres are potent avenues through which to understand theological imagination.[25] Similar methodological transformations have already taken place in the world of intellectual history as the cultural turn has necessitated a much broader inclusion of voices and mediums in order to posit more diverse thought about worlds of the past. Susanna Morrill's work has shown, for instance, how Mormon women's writing unveils an ideological world of creation, compassion, and cultivation—ideas that they believed centralized their role within the Mormon cosmos and attached their ideas to a broader American culture. And now to better incorporate those crucial insights into the broader synthetic picture, scholars of Mormon thought will need to expand the horizons of what we term "Mormon theology."[26]

The second issue to be addressed is one of contextualization. The reason male and female theologies work so well in isolation is because they fit within the conceptual frameworks imagined and invoked by modern-day historians. For Mormon women in particular, their voices are isolated so that scholars can understand the interior conditions of the Mormon patriarchal structure; the role of these women is to reveal the confrontation with and adaptation of their immediate cultural surroundings.[27] This denominational focus is crucial to restoring the parochial dimensions of Mormon development, but it does little to transcend the artificially gendered framing created in the past and perpetuated in the present.

One solution to this problem is to broaden the context of study. When Mormon women are no longer understood as particular players within the Mormon patriarchal structure, but as examples—along with Mormon men—of a much larger spectrum of cultural change, they are freed for new conceptual contexts. That is, when the Mormon patriarchal tradition remains the subject, then women and men will obviously be relegated as either competing objects or mere complementary bodies. But if the "subject" of study is something much more encompassing—for example, the late-Victorian assault on death culture, the implementation of millennial belief, or the contestation of authority—the "objects" become much more malleable and usable for a host of new topics.[28] As is often the case, once freed from denominational boundaries, historical actors become much less restricted by traditional gendered spheres.[29]

This expanded focus does not necessarily have to be a historical or cultural context, as it could also include a more strictly theoretical tension. For instance, both male and female voices could be integrated into a narrative of Mormon theology based on power. Such a concept may seem quixotic at first, given the patriarchal structure of Mormonism that would seem to imply the privileging of priesthood authority, but that doesn't necessarily have to be the case.[30] Indeed, the general bifurcation of male and female theologies within the Mormon tradition has masked a subtle yet substantive discourse of power embedded within much of Mormon women's dialogue concerning expanded rights. For instance, Ida Peay argued in the pages of the *Woman's Exponent* (1913) that male dominance came from men "wrest[ing] from Eve's daughters their God-given rights [of] dominion, hence this modern war which woman-kind is waging to obtain them back again. This struggle," she insisted, "is surely divinely instituted and will ultimately succeed" because humanity's success depended on it.[31] Women's subservience, another Mormon author argued, "never was a divine wish or expectation." Rather, it "was only a mundane retrogression that must first be checked before woman can attain her God-given position [of] strict equality with . . . man."[32] This interplay of power within ecclesiastical, political, and domestic spheres is just one avenue that could integrate a variety of gendered voices.

The third issue regarding synthetic narratives is mostly concerned with guiding metaphors and framing structures. To make sense of historical discursive trajectories, scholars invoke interpretive categories that are often self-contained and self-referential. For the territorial Utah period, for instance, that of "kingdom" is most common given that theocracy was the red herring for those decades.[33] Such a conceptual framing assumes, of course, an institutional and patriarchal power. For women, framing metaphors are often taken from the domestic or natural sphere, like the divine feminine or eternal mothering.[34] These types of potent metaphors are indeed crucial to understand the immediate context, purpose, and products that resulted within these gendered spheres. But do they work when we attempt to present a more synthetic picture?

Mormonism posited a gendered theology that was simultaneously divergent from and a reflection of their surrounding culture, and both men and women struggled to dictate their place within a rapidly changing world. To reconstruct that ideological space requires not only the presence of male and female voices but also frameworks that integrate both in ways that do not subsume one into the other. Indeed, it is not only important to seek to *include* female voices, then, but also to choose governing focuses that highlight their importance and acknowledge their fundamental contributions. Devising a framework that privileges women's voices as much as men's is a crucial dilemma for not only the next generation of Mormon studies but also religious history writ large.

* * *

One possible organizational prism through which to take a more integrative look at Mormon thought is redemption. By *redemption*, I mean an attempt to view the present as a probationary and transformative period in which religion serves as an instigative agent to bring about change and sanctification. That is, redemption is a social as much as a spiritual idea. Such a concept is quite universal for religious movements—especially in the nineteenth century—but that universal dimension is actually crucial in that it allows more interreligious comparisons. It is also eclectic enough to capture men and women as equal participants in a much broader cultural yearning. For example, Brigham Young's patriarchal domineering and Emmeline Wells's subtle providentialism can be seen as two concomitant strains of angst toward a democratized culture that lacked societal structure and protection. Young's response was to introduce a rigid patriarchal hierarchy based in polygamy, dominion, and adoption, while Wells's was to cultivate a religious message that worked to reform the world. "We believe in redemption from the curse placed upon woman" in Eden, she declared to a group of non-Mormons. "If you ask why," Wells continued, "we tell you it is a part of our religion."[35] "The mission of the Latter-day Saints," similarly wrote Harriet Cook Young, "is to reform abuses which have for ages corrupted the world."[36] These responses may seem diametrically opposed, but they are both based in a desire to transcend societal misgivings for perceived minority slights.

One period in which Mormons were especially keen to redeem society was during their Nauvoo sojourn between 1839 and 1846. Joseph Smith's final years were spent building up a religious city-state, settled on the banks of the

Mississippi River, where God's elect could flee a gentile world bound for destruction. The Saints desired Nauvoo to be a sacred refuge where divine law ordered society, church, and everyday life. And women played an important role in shaping this vision of a godly community. Yet because most did not have access to the press—which was controlled by ecclesiastical leaders and filled with the words of male authorities—they were left to express their redemptive message through different mediums, including institutional meetings like the Relief Society as well as private discussions like written correspondence. Incorporating these sources into narratives of theological development offers a richer and more exhaustive view of Mormon Nauvoo's radical vision.

Perhaps the moment of perfect coalescence was in early 1842, when for a period of a few months Mormons sought to organize the world according to the pattern of heaven. "The New year has been ushered in," Smith wrote a few days after the start of the year, and "a new order had begun." With the roots of God's empire taking hold, it was time for "the God of heaven . . . to restore the ancient order of his Kingdom unto his servants & his people." This order included social, religious, and political dimensions. Indeed, it was meant to unify God's people into a community heretofore unforeseen, including "those things, which the ancient prophets and wise men desired to see . . . but [died] without beholding it." The Mormons in Nauvoo were to establish "a kingdom of Priests & Kings to God & the Lamb forever." In the midst of America's democratic chaos, it was time for Smith and his followers to establish the foundations for a new social order.[37]

This new social order was implemented through a series of theological, fraternal, organizational, ritual, and familial innovations. These revisions to the structure of society were not only extensions of previous experiences but also built upon a new scriptural translation project that came to be known as the Book of Abraham, which introduced how the order of heaven was to operate. "Now the lord had shewn unto me, Abraham," the scriptural text proclaimed, "the intelligences that were organized before the world was." Those "noble and great ones" will be made "rulers." This scriptural text laid the groundwork for the social redemptive project Smith and other leaders introduced over the final years of Smith's life. The fallen world had lost its true order, and it could be redeemed only through a reorganization of its inhabitants according to the pattern of the priesthood. These principles were then disseminated through new organizations and practices that promoted unity, encouraged morality, policed misconduct, and maintained secrets. They were also translated into a new ritualistic system that routinized radical belief and made tangible esoteric salvific promises, as well as actualized through the formation of new family structures, including the scandalous—and secret—polygamous unions. In short, the first six months of 1842 witnessed the organizing principles of Mormonism's new social order, the visible branches of the theological and political seeds already planted. They were a direct repudiation of and challenge to a particular version of America's democratic society.[38]

Simultaneously with the Book of Abraham appearing in the newspaper *Times and Seasons*, and only a couple of days after the introduction of freemasonry as a critical center of the city's social life, the Relief Society was organized in the upper room of Joseph Smith's store. Though originally envisioned by its founders to be a group focused on offering support for the crew building the Nauvoo Temple, it was quickly redirected, according to Smith, "under the priesthood after the pattern of the priesthood." Besides merely providing materials for men working on the temple, the women were to form a governing and policing society that would root out iniquity, build solidarity, and prepare the women for further integration through temple rites. The organization would be a crucial institution in the Mormon theological quest to redeem society.[39]

The antebellum period was rife with women's organizations that were designed to reform America's culture and restore the nation's dignity. As the early republic witnessed a division between public and private spheres as a way to retain politics as a purely male arena and stall appeals for female suffrage, women were increasingly seen as guardians of virtue and protectors of the hearth. This cult of domesticity forced women to find avenues of influence outside of traditional organizations, which they did through the formation of reform movements. As the moral center of their homes, women could logically be regarded as the moral conscience of the nation, which validated their activities to transform society. Most of these female-led societies were focused on reforming asylums or attacking alcoholism, and many were rooted in religious sensibilities. In an empire of liberty where Andrew Jackson's government made clear that the nation's morality was outside the boundaries of its power and prerogatives, religious women served as saviors for a fallen people. Even if the Mormon women believed these other societies were corrupted, their Nauvoo organization was rooted in these broad cultural trends.[40]

Yet it would be a mistake to couch these reform efforts as merely a woman's project. Across the nation, there was such a loud call for societal redemption that it became known as the Age of Reform—abolitionists, suffragists, utopians, and many others believed that religious militarization was needed to transform the culture into its promised millenarian glory. This was a cultural project that drew theologians from both genders—like Theodore Parker in the north and the Grimké sisters in the south—in the quest to cultivate a spiritual view of humanity aimed at redeeming it from its fallen condition.[41] Within Nauvoo, the city council was devoted to rooting out societal ills through the revocation of liquor licenses, removal of vagrants, and promised punishment for adultery and fornication.[42] The entire city was focused on the reformation of its inhabitants, yet as a religious city-state it was especially keen to draw from a theological defense for this mission.

The Relief Society's organization brought many opportunities for the women involved to be part of this project. Joseph Smith charged them "to administer in that authority which is confer'd on them."[43] As Mormonism was in part founded in response to the moral degradation of the world, the Society offered women a chance to envision ways to regulate their community's culture and actions. The women were to "provoke the brethren to good works," a common adage of America's female-led reform efforts, but also improve society through "correcting the morals and strengthening the virtues of the female community."[44] This commitment to policing female behavior highlighted their belief in humanity's fallen nature and a pledged responsibility on behalf of the religious leadership to identify and reprove transgressors. In a disestablished culture where the state had no power to punish sin, it was left to voluntary organizations like the Relief Society—and, indeed, the Mormon Church—to provide stability and structure. Emma Smith declared that "this day was an evil day" and that "there is as much evil in this [city] as in any other place." She wished that their society "were pure before God," and therefore the sisters could "not be careful enough" in their quest "to expose iniquity."[45] It was their right—even their obligation—to maintain virtue in their City of God. The first published report of the Society in the *Times and Seasons* explicitly connected their reforming impulse to overcoming the tragedies they experienced in Missouri.[46]

The nature of this religious authority was crucial and reflected both Mormonism's developing theological pattern and the Saints' understanding of how the world operated. Joseph Smith instructed the women that "the Society should move according to the ancient Priesthood" and that "he was going to make of this Society a kingdom of priests a[s] in Enoch's day—as in Paul['s] day."[47] After speaking to the Relief Society a month later, he recorded in his journal that he explained to the Relief Society "how the Sisters would come in possession of the priviliges & blesings [*sic*] & gifts of the priesthood."[48] Decades later, Eliza R. Snow explained that the Relief Society was "an organization that cannot exist without the Priesthood, from the fact that it derives all its authority and influence from that source."[49] The term *priesthood* possessed multiple and potent meanings in early Mormonism, and significantly it can be understood only within the context of both male and female perspectives. During the movement's first decade, the term mostly referred to ecclesiastical offices (separated into classes like "deacons," "priests," and "elders") as well as ritual authority (including the right to perform baptisms). But these parameters were quickly expanded and radically revised during the Nauvoo period to something that included more than just clerical positions and ordinances but, rather, an all-encompassing notion of cultural belonging and societal order. That is, the priesthood not only structured and dictated the Saints' community through offices and practices but also defined the relationship between the Saints and the rest of the world. So when Smith told the Society they were to "move according to the ancient priesthood," he explained that such a charge meant they "should be a select Society separate from all the evils of the world, choice, virtuou[s] and holy." To be a "kingdom of priests" like Enoch's and Paul's communities implied establishing a refuge from the wicked world where God's laws could be kept even while Babylon burned. This expansive definition of "priesthood," and the Relief Society that was now contained within it, served as a theological boundary between the saved and the damned, a Godly kingdom located within yet set apart from the anarchic American republic.[50]

An organization like the Relief Society was one prominent way for women to participate in the theological project of societal redemption, but it was far from the only option. Individual women also articulated visions of redemption in private correspondence with family, which is one arena where women could more fully—if often unsystematically—outline their religious vision. Zilpha Baker Cilly Williams was one female convert to Mormonism who worked to synthesize these broader theological tensions in her private writings. Born in New Hampshire in 1813, she married Almond McCumber Williams in 1833 and converted to Mormonism less than a decade later. While on her way to Nauvoo in 1841, she wrote her cousin, Eliza Cilley, to calm her fears concerning her conversion. "I am not surprised that my Aunt and you should be startled with the idea of joining the Mormons," she wrote. Yet the letter gave her the opportunity to explicate a theological defense for her faith.

"The time has been when it was a disgrace to be a true follower of Christ," Williams told her family, and "it may be again but what of it we count all things for loss for his sake happy are we." The recent convert outlined the fallen nature of American society, the false path of American ministers, and the apostate nature of religious belief prevalent in the nation. "The Latter day saints reject the common plan of spiritualizing the bible," Williams explained; instead, Mormons understood the radical role biblical beliefs should play in establishing a political order. She offered a "word of caution" to her kin not to take Mormonism's message lightly, "lest haply [they] be found to fight against God," whose redemptive power "can overthrow" the entire society. Williams did not claim to her family that conversion to Mormonism wasn't a major transformation; rather, she reinforced the strict separation between the LDS community and the gentile world, and claimed that their refusal to join the fold possessed deep consequences. Her letter, written on the road to Nauvoo, expressed the bold nature of Mormonism's attempt to overturn—to redeem—the entire landscape.[51] Four years later, after witnessing the death of her beloved prophet, Williams was even more forthright: "This nation have rejected the gospel[,] slain the prophets and now if they will learn the truth they must come here for the judgements of God will be poured out in quick succession upon this nation till it is trembled under his hand." The Kingdom of God made no compromises.[52]

Williams was far from the only woman in Nauvoo defending her conversion to family. Flora Drake, about five years Williams's junior, was similarly forced to respond to a mother, sisters, and a cousin who believed she was abducted from her home, not allowed to correspond with family, and was even married to Joseph Smith. Frustrated, Drake responded, "I have nothing to write to you that would be interesting to you," but "if I was writing to a Mormon I could find enough that would be interesting to them but to you it would not." Mormonism had completely realigned her vision of how the world operated and how people related to one another. "In Mormonism," she explained, "we attend to spiritual things and leave Temporal things to [those outside the Church] who are about organizing themselves into [corporations]." She explained that the gentile world had corrupted God's true principles but that Smith had taught the principles necessary to redeem society and gather the elect. Mormonism transformed her vision to allow her to see what mattered and what did not, as well as how to separate the two.[53]

In many ways, Zilpha Williams and Flora Drake echoed the calls for separation from the fallen world proclaimed by their male counterparts. The Quorum of the Twelve Apostles published a proclamation to the world's rulers in 1845, for instance, which denounced the apostate religions that had led the earth to near ruin, and posited Mormonism as the only tool that could still redeem society. The restored gospel, they declared, is "sent forth to renovate the world—to enlighten the nations—to cover the earth with light, knowledge, truth, union, peace and love."[54] That same year, Heber C. Kimball proposed to a gathered conference that they "withdraw fellowship from the Gentiles [entirely]." The motion passed unanimously, and the clerk noted, "Now they are disfellowshipt."[55] These sentiments were expressed both publicly and privately. As Louisa Follett noted in her diary after a prolonged visit to family outside of Nauvoo, "I have left Babalon [*sic*] for the last time."[56] The cultural division was both deep and significant.

The theological appeal to a fallen world, necessary redemption, and required separation has been well covered by Mormon historians. Yet by adding the female voices like those of Flora Drake and Zilpha Williams it becomes clear that these principles had a poignant domestic dimension as well. Apostles spoke of displacing corrupt kingdoms and apostate nations, while the theological defenses penned by women emphasized familial separation. The Mormon gospel was to redeem society, but it was also a two-edged sword that divided the worthy from the unworthy within individual families. Indeed, that division was part of the redemptive process, as Mormonism's sacralized society required the eviction of unclean persons, even if they were parents, siblings, or cousins. That may sound ironic for a religious movement that became centered on the power of eternal family units, but in the 1840s, the path for familial redemption was found as much through exclusion as

through sealing. Indeed, even as Zilpha Williams warned her father of ev-
erlasting punishment and isolation if he refused baptism, she asked him for
the names of her "Grand parents [and] many of my uncles aunts and cousins
[that] are dead" so that "the redemption of Zion" and her family could be
secured in "the temple of the Lord."[57]

These issues of family, union, and redemption were complex theological
questions posed to Mormons, male and female, during a crucial period of
the Church's development. The ritual, cultural, and intellectual developments that took place while the Saints were gathered in Nauvoo—where they
sought to reform society, escape the gentile world, and introduce salvific and
consanguineous ordinances—can be fully understood only when framed in a
way that integrates both male and female voices. Redeeming the world, as
was Mormonism's mission, introduced a theological project that required all
hands on deck. And highlighting the men and women who participated in
that work during the Church's earliest decades exhibits the multiple prisms
through which the project was understood.

* * *

Returning to Hannah Tapfield King, the introduction of more inclusive
methodological frameworks promises many opportunities. Late in life, King
composed a poem that explicitly looked forward to a day when women
gained equal status with men, a moment seen as the culmination of the Mormon tradition. Co-opted for my purposes, it is a passionate and prescient—if
purple-prosed—call for a better integration of women's voices into theological traditions in general.

'Tis a foretaste of that which in future will be,
A mirror upheld in which visions we see!
A picture presented—a realm of the soul,
Releasing the spirit from mortal control!

How we hunger, and listen to voices like these,
That come in the flowers, that come in the trees,
That come in the cataract roaring and wild,
That has often our soul of its sorrow beguiled![58]

The Mormon theological project was, at its heart, a reflection of the cultural
context from which it was birthed. To fully understand its broad parameters
and lasting legacy, it is important to integrate the many voices involved. The
attempt to better contextualize Mormonism's unique religious message, then,
is an attempt to better elaborate the work of theology in general.

Scholars of intellectual history have lately pushed for broader inclusion
into narratives of America's ideological development. Similarly, historians of

American religions have pushed to integrate female voices into narratives of national development. One way to bridge these two issues is the field of historical theology, a sphere where thought, culture, and practice intersect. Mormonism provides an especially potent example for this kind of analysis, as both the priesthood structure and lived reality of the LDS faith, especially in the nineteenth century, established both strict gender divisions and frequent boundary transgressions. That is, the Mormon gendered experience embodies the paradoxes of American religious life. Charting how these women both accommodated and expanded these barriers gives context and meaning not only to the parochial community they cultivated but also to the society from which Mormonism itself was birthed.

NOTES

1. Hannah Tapfield King, "Epistolary Fragment," *Woman's Exponent*, November 1, 1884.

2. See, for instance, Maxine Hanks, ed., *Women and Authority: Re-emerging Mormon Feminism* (Salt Lake City, UT: Signature Books, 1992); Susanna Morrill, *White Roses on the Floor of Heaven: Mormon Women's Popular Theology, 1880–1920* (New York: Routledge, 2006); Boyd Jay Peterson, "'Redeemed from the Curse Placed upon Her': Dialogic Discourse on Eve in the *Woman's Exponent*," *Journal of Mormon History* 40, no. 1 (2014): 135–74.

3. Terryl L. Givens and Reid L. Neilson, eds., *The Columbia Sourcebook of Mormons in the United States* (New York: Columbia University Press, 2014), 1–51.

4. Givens and Neilson, *Columbia Sourcebook*, xvii.

5. Kevin M. Schultz and Paul Harvey, "Everywhere and Nowhere: Recent Trends in American Religious History and Historiography," *Journal of the American Academy of Religion* 78, no. 1 (March 2010): 129–62.

6. See, for instance, Thomas G. Alexander, "The Reconstruction of Mormon Doctrine: From Joseph Smith to Progressive Theology," *Sunstone* 5, no. 4 (July–August 1980): 24–33. For a more recent example, see Charles R. Harrell, *"This Is My Doctrine": The Development of Mormon Theology* (Salt Lake City, UT: Greg Kofford Books, 2011).

7. See Stephen C. Taysom, *Shakers, Mormons, and Religious Worlds: Conflicting Visions, Contested Boundaries* (Bloomington: Indiana University Press, 2010); Matthew B. Bowman, "The Crisis of Mormon Christology: History, Progress, and Protestantism," *Fides et Historia* 40, no. 2 (Fall 2008): 1–27.

8. See John L. Brooke, *Refiner's Fire: The Making of Mormon Cosmology, 1644–1844* (New York: Cambridge University Press, 1994); D. Michael Quinn, *Early Mormonism and the Magic World View* (Salt Lake City, UT: Signature Books, 1987); Jan Shipps, "The Reality of the Restoration and the Restoration Ideal in the Mormon Tradition," in *The American Quest for the Primitive Church*, ed. Richard T. Hughes (Urbana: University of Illinois Press, 1988), 181–95.

9. See, for instance, Ronald W. Walker, Richard E. Turley, and Glen W. Leonard, *Massacre at Mountain Meadows: An American Tragedy* (New York: Oxford University Press, 2008), 6–40; Leonard J. Arrington, *Great Basin Kingdom: An Economic History of the Latter-day Saints, 1830–1900* (Cambridge, MA: Harvard University Press, 1958).

10. See Thomas G. Alexander, *Mormonism in Transition: A History of the Latter-day Saints, 1890–1930* (Urbana: University of Illinois Press, 1986).

11. Samuel M. Brown, *In Heaven as It Is on Earth: Joseph Smith and the Early Mormon Conquest of Death* (New York: Oxford University Press, 2012), 276, 284, 292.

12. Terryl L. Givens, *Wrestling the Angel: The Foundations of Mormon Thought: Cosmos, God, Humanity* (New York: Oxford University Press, 2015), 106–11. One notable moment of gendered integration is where Givens deals with theosis on pages 285–86. For a cogent critique of this lack of gendered issues in Givens's analysis, see Seth Perry, "A Mother Where?," *Los Angeles Review of Books*, April 29, 2015.

13. Christine Talbot, *A Foreign Kingdom: Mormons and Polygamy in American Political Culture, 1852–1890* (Urbana: University of Illinois Press, 2013), 63–82.

14. For the influence of women's history on Mormon scholarship, see Laurel Thatcher Ulrich, "Mormon Women in the History of Second-Wave Feminism," *Dialogue: A Journal of Mormon Thought* 43, no. 2 (Summer 2010): 45–63. The resulting work on the thought of Mormon women is both quantitatively broad and qualitatively deep. See, for example, Maureen Ursenbach Beecher, "Three Women and the Life of the Mind," *Utah Historical Quarterly* 43, no. 1 (Winter 1975): 26–40; and Maureen Ursenbach Beecher, "The 'Leading Sisters': A Female Hierarchy in Nineteenth Century Mormon Society," *Journal of Mormon History* 9 (1982): 25–39. For the methodological shift to gender studies, see Louise A. Tilly, "Gender, Women's History, and Social History," *Social Science History* 13, no. 4 (Winter 1989): 439–62.

15. Morrill, *White Roses*.

16. See Peterson, "Redeemed from the Curse Placed upon Her"; Lisa Olsen Tait, "The *Young Woman's Journal*: Gender and Generations in a Mormon Women's Magazine," *American Periodicals* 22, no. 1 (2012): 51–71; Amy Easton-Flake, "Biblical Women in the *Woman's Exponent*: Nineteenth-Century Mormon Women Interpret the Bible," in *The Bible in Family Life*, ed. Philip Goff, Aruthru E. Farnsley II, and Peter J. Thuesen (New York: Oxford University Press, 2017), 89–100.

17. See, for example, Jill Mulvay Derr, "The Significance of 'O My Father' in the Personal Journal of Eliza R. Snow," *BYU Studies* 36, no. 1 (1996–1997): 84–126; Carol Cornwall Madsen, *An Advocate for Women: The Public Life of Emmeline B. Wells, 1870–1920* (Provo, UT: Brigham Young University Press, 2005); Mary Lythgoe Bradford, "The Odyssey of Sonia Johnson," *Dialogue: A Journal of Mormon Thought* 14, no. 2 (Summer 1981): 14–26; Maureen Ursenbach Beecher, "Each in Her Own Time: Four Zinas," *Dialogue: A Journal of Mormon Thought* 26, no. 2 (Summer 1993): 119–35.

18. Mark A. Noll, *America's God: From Jonathan Edwards to Abraham Lincoln* (New York: Oxford University Press, 2002); E. Brooks Holifield, *Theology in America: Christian Thought from the Age of the Puritans to the Civil War* (New Haven, CT: Yale University Press, 2003).

19. See Ann Braude, *Radical Spirits: Spiritualism and Women's Rights in Nineteenth-Century America*, 2nd ed. (Bloomington: Indiana University Press, 2001); Evelyn Brooks Higginbotham, *Righteous Discontent: The Women's Movement in the Black Baptist Church, 1880–1920* (Cambridge, MA: Harvard University Press, 1994); Glendyne R. Wergland, *Sisters in the Faith: Shaker Women and Equality of the Sexes* (Boston: University of Massachusetts Press, 2011); Catherine A. Brekus, *Sarah Osborn's World: The Rise of Evangelical Christianity in Early America* (New Haven, CT: Yale University Press, 2013). For an exception to this trend, see Catherine L. Albanese, *A Republic of Mind and Spirit: A Cultural History of American Metaphysical Religion* (New Haven, CT: Yale University Press, 2008), which integrates both male and female voices.

20. See Leigh E. Schmidt, "Religious History and the Cultural Turn," in *A Companion to American Cultural History*, ed. Karen Halttunen (Malden, MA: Blackwell Publishing, 2008), 406–15. David D. Hall, "Backwards to the Future: The Cultural Turn and the Wisdom of Intellectual History," *Modern Intellectual History* 9, no. 1 (2012): 171–84.

21. For an example, see Catherine A. Brekus, "Mormon Women and the Problem of Historical Agency," *Journal of Mormon History* 37, no. 2 (Spring 2011): 59–87.

22. Ann Braude, "Women's History *Is* American Religious History," in *Retelling U.S. Religious History*, ed. Thomas A. Tweed (Berkeley: University of California Press, 1997), 87–107.

23. See Benjamin E. Park, "(Re)Interpreting Early Mormon Thought: Synthesizing Joseph Smith's Theology and the Process of Religious Formation," *Dialogue* 44, no. 2 (Summer 2012): 59–88.

24. See Ted A. Smith, "Redeeming Critique: Resignations to the Cultural Turn in Christian Theology and Ethics," *Journal of the Society of Christian Ethics* 24, no. 2 (Fall/Winter 2004): 89–113; Hall, "Backwards to the Future."

25. See, for example, Claudia Stokes, *The Altar at Home: Sentimental Literature and Nineteenth-Century American Religion* (Philadelphia: University of Pennsylvania Press, 2014).

26. For example, Laurel Thatcher Ulrich's "An American Album, 1857," *American Historical Review* 115, no. 1 (February 2010): 1–25, demonstrates how women's beliefs concerning marriage and family amplified tensions of union and disunion on the eve of the American Civil War.

27. See, for example, Talbot, *Foreign Kingdom*.

28. My use of the terms *objects* and *subjects* comes from Patrick Q. Mason, *The Mormon Menace: Violence and Anti-Mormonism in the Postbellum South* (New York: Oxford University Press, 2011). For more on this historiographical shift, see Benjamin E. Park, "'Reasonings Sufficient': Joseph Smith, Thomas Dick, and the Context(s) of Early Mormonism," *Journal of Mormon History* 38, no. 3 (Summer 2012): 210–24.

29. For the status of denominational study in religious studies currently, see Laurie F. Maffly-Kipp, "The Burdens of Church History," *Church History* 82, no. 2 (June 2013): 353–67.

30. For an example of a study on discursive power that privileges women's voices, see R. Marie Griffith, *God's Daughters: Evangelical Women and the Power of Submission* (Berkeley: University of California Press, 1997).

31. Ida S. Peay, "Taking a Stand for the Right," *Woman's Exponent*, June 1, 1913.

32. D. P. Felt, "A Man's Advice about Woman Suffrage," *Woman's Exponent*, November 15, 1891.

33. See, for instance, David L. Bigler and Will Bagley, *The Mormon Rebellion: America's First Civil War, 1857–1858* (Norman: University of Oklahoma Press, 2011), 10–30.

34. See Morrill, *White Roses*.

35. Emmeline B. Wells, "Why a Woman Should Desire to Be a Mormon," *Woman's Exponent*, December 1, 1907.

36. Harriett Cook Young, "Minutes of a Ladies Mass Meeting, January 6, 1870," in *The First Fifty Years of Relief Society: Key Documents in Latter-day Saint Women's History*, ed. Jill Mulvay Derr et al. (Salt Lake City, UT: Church Historian's Press, 2016), 326.

37. "Joseph Smith Journal, January 6, 1842," in *Joseph Smith Papers: Journals*, ed. Andrew W. Hedges, Alex D. Smith, and Richard Lloyd Anderson, vol. 2, *December 1841–April 1843* (Salt Lake City, UT: Church Historian's Press, 2011), 25–26.

38. "The Book of Abraham," *Times and Seasons*, March 15, 1842. See Kathleen Flake, "Ordering Antinomy: An Analysis of Early Mormonism's Priestly Offices, Councils and Kinship," *Religion and American Culture* 26, no. 2 (Summer 2016): 139–83.

39. Sarah M. Kimball, "Autobiography" (1883), in *Women of Covenant: The Story of the Relief Society*, ed. Jill Mulvay Derr, Janath Russell Cannon, and Maureen Ursenbach Beecher (Salt Lake City, UT: Deseret Book, 1992), 26.

40. See Lori D. Ginzberg, *Women and the Work of Benevolence: Morality, Politics, and Class in the Nineteenth-Century United States* (New Haven, CT: Yale University Press, 1990); Lori D. Ginzberg, *Women in Antebellum Reform* (New York: Wiley-Blackwell, 2000).

41. See Daniel Walker Howe, *What Hath God Wrought: The Transformation of America, 1815–1848* (New York: Oxford University Press, 2007), 570–612; T. Gregory Garvey, *Creating the Culture of Reform in Antebellum America* (Athens: University of Georgia Press, 2006).

42. John S. Dinger, ed., *The Nauvoo City and High Council Minutes* (Salt Lake City, UT: Signature Books, 2011), 11, 36, 81.

43. Nauvoo Relief Society Minute Book, April 28, 1842, 36, LDS Church History Library, accessed May 2016, josephsmithpapers.org. A major component of this conferral related to healing of the sick. See Jonathan A. Stapley and Kristine Wright, "Female Ritual Healing in Mormonism," *Journal of Mormon History* 37, no. 1 (Winter 2011): 1–85.

44. Nauvoo Relief Society Minute Book, March 17, 1842, 47.

45. Nauvoo Relief Society Minute Book, May 17, 1842, 48. Much of this language regarding secrecy and iniquity related to the practice of polygamy.

46. "Ladies' Relief Society," *Times and Seasons*, April 1, 1842.

47. Nauvoo Relief Society Minute Book, March 31, 1842, 22.

48. "Joseph Smith Journal, April 28, 1842," in *Joseph Smith Papers: Journals*, 2:52.

49. Eliza R. Snow, "Female Relief Society" (1868), in Derr et al., eds., *First Fifty Years*, 271.

50. For the evolving definition of *priesthood*, see Jonathan A. Stapley, "Women and Mormon Authority," in *Women and Mormonism: Historical and Contemporary Perspectives*, ed. Kate Holbrook and Matt Bowman (Salt Lake City: University of Utah Press, 2016), 101–20.

51. Zilpha Baker Cilley Williams to Eliza Cilley, December 5, 1841, LDS Church History Library, Salt Lake City, UT.

52. Williams to Samuel Cilley, July 13, 1845, LDS Church History Library, Salt Lake City, UT.

53. Flora Drake to "Dear Brother and Sister," October 24, 1844, LDS Church History Library, Salt Lake City, UT. Flora's mother expressed her fear that Joseph Smith was reading all her letters in Betsy Haydon to Flora Drake, April 23, 1842, and Heydon to Flora Drake, August 1842. Flora is asked if she became a plural wife of Joseph Smith in Helen Mar Heydon to Flora Drake, April 7, 1844. These letters are in the LDS Church History Library.

54. *Proclamation of the Twelve Apostles of the Church of Jesus Christ, of Latter-day Saints. To All the Kings of the World* (New York, 1845), 5.

55. "Speech Delivered by Heber C. Kimball," *Times and Seasons*, July 15, 1845.

56. Louisa T. Follett Diary, June 4, 1845, LDS Church History Library, Salt Lake City, UT.

57. Williams to Samuel Cilley, July 13, 1845, LDS Church History Library, Salt Lake City, UT.

58. Hannah Tapfield King, "Silent Voices," *Woman's Exponent*, March 15, 1883.

Chapter Ten

Individual Lives, Broader Contexts

Mormon Women's Studies and the Refashioning of American History and Historiography

R. Marie Griffith

In recent years, scholars of Mormon history have enthusiastically and increasingly reached out to historians of other, non-Mormon subjects to initiate interchanges that have proven enormously rewarding and productive. These conversations spur us to think more deeply about the Mormon tradition—not in isolation from but in relation to other traditions in American life and history.

In her important and influential 1997 article, "Women's History *Is* American Religious History," Ann Braude analyzes the ways in which attention to women, as nearly always the majority participants in American religious congregations and institutions, would upend three motifs long invoked to structure the narrative of American religious history. Braude argues that those three themes—declension, feminization, and secularization—"can be said to have happened only if they are understood as referring not to demographic shifts but rather to anxieties caused by the belief that such shifts were occurring or the fear that they might occur."

> In each case, the term expresses nostalgia for a world that never existed, a world in which men went to church and were as moved as women by what they heard there, a world in which the clergy felt they had precisely as much public influence as they should. Perhaps it is not women who have sentimentalized American Protestantism, but rather the male clergy who have cherished a romantic notion of a patriarchal past.[1]

Braude's critique has been exceedingly effective: when was the last time you heard a respected American religious historian use "declension," "feminization," or even "secularization" as a grand historical narrative? While the presence of women may yet not be a key theme in all our scholarship, the socially expected greater religiousness of women is certainly a fact that everyone

227

knows has deeply mattered to the shaping of religion and culture in the United States over time.

This chapter pushes Braude's argument one step forward by exploring how and in what ways Mormon women's history can work to refashion the broader narratives historians tell about American religious history. I will touch briefly on some formative works from other subfields that were field changing to American *women's* religious history as well as American religious history writ large, and suggest why and how new work on Mormon women can gain greater traction in those far-ranging fields. New scholarship on Mormon women can, should, and will have much more expansive implications to the wider historical enterprise.

* * *

Scholarship is an inexorably collective enterprise, and any field of inquiry is crucially shaped by prior generations of scholarship and by a number of genres. There are, for example, very closely detailed monographic primary source analyses of specific local topics: a sketch of an important place or event during a consequential historical moment—the settlement of Jamestown, Virginia, in the early 1600s, or the Battle of Chickamauga during the Civil War; the presidential campaign of John F. Kennedy in a nation still wary of Catholics, or the early stirrings of second-wave feminism. There are also biographies of prominent public figures—Jonathan Edwards, Joseph Smith, Frederick Douglass, Emma Goldman, Dorothy Day, Zora Neale Hurston, Alfred Kinsey—and, more recently, biographical studies of less publicly or nationally prominent but powerfully representative persons or collectives—Sarah Osborne, Martha Ballard, Sally Hemings, the Oneida community, Heaven's Gate. There are invaluable, and painstakingly assembled, collections of significant primary source documents, such as the superb collection, hot off the press, that Laurel Thatcher Ulrich has called "the most important work to emerge from the Mormon press in the last fifty years": *The First Fifty Years of Relief Society: Key Documents in Latter-day Saint Women's History*.[2] There are obsessively researched narrative volumes published by smallish nonprofit university presses, religious presses, self-publishing outfits, and others that may earn only tiny but devoted audiences, and there are grandiose tomes aimed at the masses and published by for-profit trade presses that may, in some cases at least, sacrifice scholarly precision for influence.

These and countless other types of research and writing efforts contribute over time to our richer knowledge of history: we would not want to do away with either the fine-grained, narrow studies of specific topics or the broader brushstroked analyses, the vital primary source collections or the sometimes offbeat, theory-heavy meditations on the rhetorical and discursive strategies embedded in such primary sources. The varied genres can seem to be at cross purposes, but in fact they are mutually beneficial ventures, and both scholars and serious non-scholarly readers can and do use all these literary types in service to deeper and wider understanding of our collective social and cultural past. The innumerable subfields within the wider category of American religious history—American Catholicism, Judaism, evangelicalism, Mormonism, African American religion, missions, women and religion, and increasingly Islam, to name but a few—are all populated with myriad studies across a wide spectrum from specialized monographs to reference works to primary source collections to synthetic scholarly accounts to popular treatments that sell. And each, in its own meaningful way, enables the general growth of our understanding of historical subjects and subcultures from the vantage of our own particular moment and context.

* * *

Now and again, this spectrum is ruptured by what we can call a crossover book: a scholarly analysis generated from within a specific subfield that manages to transcend its own local subfield audience and reverberate across a range of other fields. Examples of such classic historical analyses include Natalie Zemon Davis, *The Return of Martin Guerre*; Carlo Ginzburg, *The Cheese and the Worms*; Martin Jay, *The Dialectical Imagination*; Nell Irvin Painter, *Exodusters*; Robert Darnton, *The Great Cat Massacre*; Nancy Cott, *The Bonds of Womanhood*; Albert J. Raboteau, *Slave Religion*; Thomas Kuhn, *The Structure of Scientific Revolutions*; and Caroline Walker Bynum, *Holy Feast and Holy Fast.*[3] Or think of the philosophical and analytic contributions of keenly observant theoreticians such as John Rawls, Michel Foucault, Julia Kristeva, Jean Elshtain, bell hooks, and Cornel West.

While the list of works whose influence exploded far beyond its originating intellectual context could stretch on endlessly, I'd like to hone in on subfields within American religious history, and even more locally to sub-subfields within the academic arena of American *women's* religious history since 1980 or so. What are the books, in the last thirty-five years, that have crossed over from their own specific, local context to reshape patterns of thinking and analysis across the full range of American women's religious history and American religious history much more generally? Who are the authors who have managed to generate field-changing interpretations of gender and religion in US history, and what about their work has been field changing?

The list would have to begin with Robert Orsi and his first two books: *The Madonna of 115th Street*, originally published in 1985, and *Thank You, St. Jude*, originally published in 1996. Orsi's work broke out of the ghetto of American Catholic studies and persuaded scholars of other subfields to think differently about their own subjects. *The Madonna of 115th Street* is, at first glance, a close study of Italian Harlem from 1880 to 1950 and how the annual *festa* of the Madonna of 115th Street "both influenced and reflected the lives of the celebrants." However, those who have read the book know that it is far more than that: the book is about immigrant rage and assimilation, about family dynamics and especially young women's struggles against the patriarchal authority structuring Italian Catholic culture during that era, about prayer and healing during desperate times, about women willingly dragged by their hair down the aisles of musty churches, licking the dirty stone floor all the way—is this abuse or empowerment or something else altogether? It is about pain, it is about the deep hope inspired by faith, the hunger for God and connection with others, and it is riveting in its acuity as well as its empathy.[4]

Thank You, St. Jude draws as its basic source the letters that women wrote and still write to a Catholic shrine. Yet, more deeply, it draws out the performance of female submission to the patron (male) saint of hopeless causes while women simultaneously wield an underlying and seemingly terrifying influence as bearers of babies and the primary caregivers of children, the fundraisers of parish life, the overseers of community morals, and the shapers of female (and male) culture within American Catholicism. The subjects and themes Orsi delineated were (and are) simultaneously local and very specifically American Catholic, on the one hand; yet, on the other, they are broadly representative, applicable, almost even universal in their depicted needs and fears, their loves and loathings, their suffering and courage. In these ways, such very specific Catholic women have, through Orsi's astonishingly persuasive analysis, been generative of wide-ranging questions across numerous religious and cultural contexts.[5]

Orsi's classic books focus on lived theology and practice, religion as relationship (with God, with saints, with others), religion in the streets and in the *domus* (or home), in holy shrines, in the weeping letters of hopeless women begging St. Jude for help and healing. Both books read deeply into the longing at the heart of Catholic women's culture, the tension over gender roles that overt compliance and submission try to mask, and the work of prayer and ritual. And both books engendered dramatic shifts in how scholars of American religion across subfields thought about gender, power, and religious life in their own settings. Orsi, more than any other single scholar, gave us the rubric "lived religion" that academics across the far-reaching discipline of religious studies—not to mention many in history, anthropology, and sociology—have grappled with ever since.

I consider Orsi's *Madonna* and *Jude* books to be *the* most important crossover books in American women's religious history to date. They are by no means the only ones, however. Other crossover books of note include Ann Braude's *Radical Spirits* (1989), a model for analyzing the power of religion—not just Reformed Protestantism but Spiritualism—in the advancement of social reform and women's rights in nineteenth-century America. Braude lifted Spiritualism out of the ghetto in which it had been studied and forever away from the presumption that it was quirky and offbeat, and that these marginal women—seers and mediums—were no fit subject for scholarship. Braude taught us through carefully crafted empirical analysis that female trance speakers of the nineteenth century became, as her dust jacket summarizes, "the first large group of American women to speak in public," and she beautifully explicated the complexities of their religious worldview as well as the grief and deep feelings of loss animating the desire to speak with the dead.[6] Beryl Satter's own crossover book, published a decade later, the groundbreaking *Each Mind a Kingdom: American Women, Sexual Purity, and the New Thought Movement, 1875–1920*, is unthinkable without the foundational example of Braude; likewise are Kathi Kern's irreplaceable 2001 book, *Mrs. Stanton's Bible*, as well as Leigh Eric Schmidt's 2005 book, *Restless Souls: The Making of American Spirituality*. Satter, Kern, and Schmidt's books too have crossed over well beyond their own subgenres of New Thought and related spiritual currents, making a tangible difference in how scholars from other subfields—and serious non-scholarly readers, too—conceptualize the lives of their own religious subjects and their own histories.[7]

Historians and anthropologists of African American women and religion have produced several particularly influential crossover books. In 1991, the late Karen McCarthy Brown published *Mama Lola*, her landmark analysis of a Vodou priestess in Brooklyn and the remarkable gender bending that Mama Lola's leadership entailed and produced. Evelyn Brooks Higginbotham's *Righteous Discontent* (1993) crossed over genres even more influentially, with its extraordinary analysis of the ways in which African American Baptist women between 1880 and 1920 built the church into a powerful force for social and political change, "the most effective vehicle by which men and women alike, pushed down by racism and poverty, regrouped and rallied against emotional and physical defeat." Judith Weisenfeld's *African American Women and Christian Activism* (1997) followed Higginbotham and made its own valuable contributions to this analysis. Later ethnographies, notably, Marla Frederick's 2003 *Between Sundays: Black Women and Everyday Struggles of Faith* and Carolyn Rouse's 2004 *Engaged Surrender: African American Women and Islam*, evinced powerful analyses of black women in different religious settings making sense of their own lives and transforming their religious cultures as well as their wider communities. All these books crossed over in important ways to fields far beyond their own and have been quite influential across scholarly disciplines, as well as reaching serious non-scholarly readers.[8]

One could keep going: Karla Goldman's 2000 book, *Beyond the Synagogue Gallery*, showed scholars that American Jewish women had their own unique religious history and whose analysis added much to the general picture of American women's lives. Margaret Lamberts Bendroth's 1993 book, *Fundamentalism and Gender, 1875 to the Present*; my own book,

God's Daughters: Evangelical Women and the Power of Submission, originally published in 1997; and (outside the American field) Saba Mahmood's *Politics of Piety: The Islamic Revival and the Feminist Subject*, originally published in 2005, have each found audiences beyond the fundamentalist, evangelical, and Islamic worlds of scholarship, among scholars wanting to think more about the complex power dynamics embedded in certain forms of professed female submission to male authority, as well as the disciplinary regimens of conservative religious traditions and how women may manage to turn these to their own ends, creating liberal subjectivity, autonomy, and even "agency" in unexpected places. And I daresay that many of us whose work may have crossed over in small or larger ways found inspiring influences in earlier classic crossovers: for me, Orsi, Braude, and McCarthy Brown were authors I turned to again and again for models of thick description and analysis, as were Natalie Davis and Caroline Bynum. Thankfully, all these individuals also have been extraordinarily gracious as teachers, mentors, and tireless supporters of younger generations of scholars; that generosity, too, has aided more scholarly writers in working hard to write books that will be read, debated, critiqued, and extensively used across disciplinary fields.[9]

I have lingered on these crossover examples and their influence at some length in order to consider what Mormon women as a historical case study can add to or change about these models. For as fertile as Mormon historical studies have been in recent years—and the output is truly stunning in terms of both quantity and quality—the crossover books that have come out of this subfield have not yet touched the genre of American women's religious history.

Some of the important and wonderful crossover books that have emerged out of Mormon studies over the past three decades include John Brooke's *The Refiner's Fire: The Making of Mormon Cosmology, 1644–1844*, which has been enormously influential in the scholarly study of early modern magic and alchemy and is also read widely beyond. Sarah Barringer Gordon's *The Mormon Question: Polygamy and Constitutional Conflict in Nineteenth-Century America* (2002) and Kathleen Flake's *The Politics of American Religious Identity*, on the seating of Senator Reed Smoot (2004), explore the question of whether being LDS would disqualify believers from participation in the political process and American politics at the highest levels. Terryl Givens's *The Viper on the Hearth* (1997) and Patrick Mason's *The Mormon Menace* (2011) elaborated on the demonization of Mormons in US history (like the demonization of Catholics and Masons). Richard Bushman's 2005 biography of Joseph Smith is widely read (or at least skimmed!) and widely acclaimed.[10] But we have not yet seen a crossover book on Mormon women—doubtless in large part because, as a subfield of Mormon studies, this area of inquiry is still a relatively young subfield. It will surely happen, and soon, so it is instructive to think about the qualities of a crossover book on Mormon women. How might a book on Mormon women open up female devotion or ritual life in LDS communities the way that Orsi's books have done for Catholic women? How might we better understand the complexities of female leadership in officially male-governed religious structures in the way that Higginbotham's book revealed the experience of African American Baptist women? Can a book illuminate the Mormon renderings of death and the profoundly human desire to overcome death in ways similar to what Braude's book did for the countless Americans drawn to Spiritualism?

Speaking not only as a scholar but as a classroom teacher who has repeatedly taught Orsi, Higginbotham, Braude, and other crossover authors for more than two decades in women and American religion classes, I must say that this lack of a crossover text on LDS women makes it difficult to know what to teach in my women and American religion classes. There are wonderful Mormon feminist analyses, nonfeminist personal narratives, accounts of women leaving the Church and accounts of women returning, novels by or about women, and other primary sources that I have and do use, but frankly, in a class that tries to cover a range of religious traditions in the United States, these LDS primary sources on their own do not work as compellingly for undergraduates as the crossover texts I have described, perhaps because they feel so specifically LDS without connecting thematically to works in other fields. We need a book that compels students to fall in love with Mormon women's lives and to really grasp these lives in larger historical context, the way Orsi and others get students to fall in love with and grasp the social and cultural contexts of Catholics, Jews, African American Baptists, and even white evangelicals in American life and history. There is also no outstanding crossover book for Muslim American women, by the way, but we'll save that discussion for another time.

* * *

How would such a crossover book best be structured, and what would its content and analysis be? As a scholar outside of Mormon studies, it seems to me that the very subjects Mormon studies scholars have been writing about for years can work beautifully for the sort of crossover book for which I'm calling. An easy example might be the themes of missionization and globalization, surely some of the most significant and fascinating dimensions of the LDS tradition, absolutely unequaled in our time by other groups. What happens on the ground when Mormons successfully missionize a culture that is structured by an extremely patriarchal system? The LDS tradition is patriarchal in its own specific way, of course, but in many ways it also topples patriarchal norms and reshapes gender roles and expectations: what happens, then, to gender in the mission field?

Elizabeth Brusco taught us a great deal about such a topic in her excellent 1995 book, *The Reformation of Machismo: Evangelical Conversion and*

Gender in Colombia. To quote from the very apt and succinct book jacket description, Brusco analyzes how

> the asceticism required of evangelicals (no drinking, smoking, or extramarital sexual relations are allowed) redirects male income back into the household, thereby raising the living standard of women and children. This benefit helps explain the appeal of evangelicalism for women and questions the traditional assumption that organized religion always disadvantages women. Brusco also demonstrates how evangelicalism appeals to men by offering an alternative to the more dysfunctional aspects of machismo.

Brusco does not argue simplistically that evangelicalism overturns deeply embedded Colombian habits of machismo, but her analysis greatly helps us see the nuanced transformations that do occur, both domestically and to some degree socially, when evangelicals missionize successfully there.[11] I wonder what patterns Mormon mission work, in countless global contexts, have likewise shifted, reinforced, or transformed in terms of local gender norms.

* * *

Finally, if we want to think in terms of scholarly crossover work, we'll want to think about what is unique to Mormon women's experience, and what is shared; so let me offer some of my own reflections as an interested outsider to the study of Mormon women. It is quite clear from the long history of religion and society in the United States that an emphasis on women's leadership capabilities has grown steadily over time, if sometimes in a "two steps forward, one step back" fashion. Many historians who are interested in this phenomenon have referred to it as "liberation," the assumption being that as women have become better educated, better informed, more affluent, and more dissatisfied with their lot in society, they have broken the chains of religion, or at least the chains of conservative religion. Feminist liberation theology is all about reimagining God, church, liturgy, and service in female-centered terms, or at least terms that do not oppress half of the human population.

But not all religious groups follow the liberation model. There are many communities throughout the nation (and the world) in which majorities of women remain faithful to their tradition even as they work gradually for significant if sometimes incremental changes in how they are perceived and what roles they may fulfill. Evangelical and Pentecostal women may exemplify this narrative in part, as do many faithful Roman Catholic women; but the evangelical and Pentecostal community is markedly splintered and disunified, while the broader American Catholic community contains nearly as many disaffected female critics of the tradition's all-male celibate priesthood as it does steady, quiet changers from within. There are both similarities and differences between Mormon women and these other communities—evangelical, Pentecostal, Roman Catholic—and I would like to suggest the possibility that a key difference pertains to the specific, habitual ways in which Mormon women are shaped by a culture of female solidarity, friendship, and care—networks within which many have also come to think in new ways about the powerfulness of womanhood, gender roles, and multiple forms of leadership and influence.

I believe that we could define this as a process of discovering and claiming agency, if a very different sort than what may be advocated in feminist liberation theology. But we could also think of it as something else, something like "the power of solidarity"—that term sounds banal, rather like a slogan from a 1970s consciousness-raising group, but I mean it in very strong terms (indeed, terms that LDS women themselves have used): the power of friendship, of sisterhood, of connectedness, of standing together while caring for others. Think of the tasks women in the Relief Society were charged with from the start: saving souls, relieving the poor, building the kingdom of God. And think of the ways that we learn, from the extraordinary collection of documents collected and published in *The First Fifty Years of Relief Society*, how these networks enabled LDS women to expand their public roles, their public speaking and writing, the ways Relief Society women mobilized against antipolygamy legislation and worked, in the words of this collection's editors, "to transform the national image of Latter-day Saint women from downtrodden and abused to proactive and empowered."[12]

Mormon women have provided these and many other extraordinary examples of what we might think of as "changing the system from within," nowhere more importantly than the realm of gender roles and expectations. While some disaffected members have left the LDS Church for others that allow women to ascend to the highest positions of leadership, far more Mormon feminists have remained solidly within the Church and worked steadily for satisfying roles within the Church and family. Growing numbers of Mormon women scholars are bringing new and fresh perspectives to the study of Mormon women's history, and Mormon men are also increasingly engaged in such work—this fact alone is very different from evangelical women's studies and highlights something itself about gender and Mormons. Further, the Mormon studies scholarly community has increasingly reached out to non-Mormon studies scholars to participate in, and learn from, this significant body of work. These efforts at recovery and retelling the history of Mormon women from a whole range of perspectives exemplify one crucial piece of this "change from within" model to which I refer.

* * *

To conclude, let me simply leave you with a few thoughts about what I think are the vital characteristics of crossover books, for anyone who may aspire to write such a book for Mormon women's history or to help advise a student to write one. First, crossover books do not, of course, assume an audience of sub-field specialists; they attempt to connect with important themes and ideas and rubrics across fields—in this case, I would say "lived religion" remains full of analytic promise, but there are many others. Crossover authors must read widely across subfields, so that they know what the key questions are. Second, crossover books deal deeply with emotional registers that may not always be comfortable for a tradition's leaders to muse about publicly: they are often about the pain of feeling oneself simultaneously devoted to a tradition and yet in some way ambivalent about it, or frustrated with some dimension of it, or chafing at the rules or simply finding oneself unable to uphold the rules. Hagiography doesn't cross over, nor does literature aimed at conversion. Third, crossover books deal with multiple layers of experience, from the most inward heart experience to domestic life to social networks to politics; indeed, they try to draw connections across these realms and show how the heart affects politics, and how politics transforms the heart. Finally, crossover books deal with complexity and do not shy away from hard questions; a critic could call this "airing one's dirty laundry in public." For the crossover scholar, however, the aim is simply getting at the deep truths embedded in one setting that will speak to and resonate with the deep truths embedded in others.

NOTES

1. Ann Braude, "Women's History *Is* American Religious History," in *Retelling U.S. Religious History*, ed. Thomas Tweed (Berkeley: University of California Press, 1997), 96.

2. Jill Mulvay Derr, Carol Cornwall Madsen, Kate Holbrook, and Matthew J. Grow, eds., *The First Fifty Years of Relief Society: Key Documents in Latter-day Saint Women's History* (Salt Lake City, UT: Church Historian's Press, 2016). Note: Ulrich quotation comes from first edition dust jacket.

3. Caroline Walker Bynum, *Holy Feast and Holy Fast: The Religious Significance of Food to Medieval Women* (Berkeley: University of California Press, 1988); Nancy F. Cott, *The Bonds of Womanhood* (New Haven, CT: Yale University Press, 1997); Robert Darnton, *The Great Cat Massacre: And Other Episodes in French Cultural History* (New York: Basic Books, 2009); Natalie Zemon Davis, *The Return of Martin Guerre* (Cambridge, MA: Harvard University Press, 1983); Carlo Ginzburg, *The Cheese and the Worms: The Cosmos of a Sixteenth-Century Miller*, trans. Anne C. Tedeschi and John Tedeschi (Baltimore: Johns Hopkins University Press, 1992); Martin Jay, *The Dialectical Imagination: A History of the Frankfurt School and the Institute of Social Research, 1923–1950* (Berkeley: University of California Press, 1996); Thomas S. Kuhn, *The Structure of Scientific Revolutions: 50th Anniversary Edition* (Chicago: University of Chicago Press, 2016); Nell Irvin Painter, *Exodusters: Black Migration to Kansas after Reconstruction* (New York: W. W. Norton, 1992); Albert J. Raboteau, *Slave Religion: The "Invisible Institution" in the Antebellum South* (Oxford: Oxford University Press, 2004).

4. Robert A. Orsi, *The Madonna of 115th Street: Faith and Community in Italian Harlem, 1880–1950* (1985; repr., Hartford, CT: Yale University Press, 2010); quote from original paperback cover.

5. Robert A. Orsi, *Thank You, St. Jude: Women's Devotion to the Patron Saint of Hopeless Causes* (1996; repr., Hartford, CT: Yale University Press, 1998).

6. Ann Braude, *Radical Spirits: Spiritualism and Women's Rights in Nineteenth-Century America*, 2nd ed. (Bloomington: Indiana University Press, 2001).

7. Beryl Satter, *Each Mind a Kingdom: American Women, Sexual Purity, and the New Thought Movement, 1875–1920* (Berkeley: University of California Press, 2001); Kathi Kern, *Mrs. Stanton's Bible* (Ithaca, NY: Cornell University Press, 2001); Leigh Eric Schmidt, *Restless Souls: The Making of American Spirituality*, 2nd ed. (Berkeley: University of California Press, 2012).

8. Evelyn Brooks Higginbotham, *Righteous Discontent: The Women's Movement in the Black Baptist Church, 1880–1920* (Cambridge, MA: Harvard University Press, 1993), publisher book description; Marla F. Frederick, *Between Sundays: Black Women and Everyday Struggles of Faith* (Berkeley: University of California Press, 2003); Carolyn Rouse, *Engaged Surrender: African American Women and Islam* (Berkeley: University of California Press, 2004).

9. Margaret Lamberts Bendroth, *Fundamentalism and Gender, 1875 to the Present*, rev. ed. (Hartford, CT: Yale University Press, 1996); Karla Goldman, *Beyond the Synagogue Gallery: Finding a Place for Women in American Judaism* (Cambridge, MA: Harvard University Press, 2001); R. Marie Griffith, *God's Daughters: Evangelical Women and the Power of Submission* (1997; repr., Berkeley: University of California Press, 2000); Saba Mahmood, *Politics of Piety: The Islamic Revival and the Feminist Subject* (2005; repr., Princeton, NJ: Princeton University Press, 2011).

10. John L. Brooke, *The Refiner's Fire: The Making of Mormon Cosmology, 1644–1844* (Cambridge: Cambridge University Press, 1996); Sarah Barringer Gordon, *The Mormon Question: Polygamy and Constitutional Conflict in Nineteenth-Century America* (Charlotte: University of North Carolina Press, 2002); Kathleen Flake, *The Politics of American Religious Identity: The Seating of Senator Reed Smoot, Mormon Apostle* (Charlotte: University of North Carolina Press, 2004); Terryl Givens, *The Viper on the Hearth: Mormons, Myths, and the Construction of Heresy*, updated ed. (Oxford: Oxford University Press, 2013); Patrick Mason, *The Mormon Menace: Violence and Anti-Mormonism in the Postbellum South* (Oxford: Oxford University Press, 2011); Richard Lyman Bushman, *Joseph Smith: Rough Stone Rolling* (New York: Vintage, 2007).

11. Elizabeth E. Brusco, *The Reformation of Machismo: Evangelical Conversion and Gender in Colombia* (1995; repr., Austin: University of Texas Press, 2011).

12. Derr et al., eds., *First Fifty Years of Relief Society*, xxxvi.

Bibliography

INTRODUCTION

Aalders, Cynthia Yvonne. "Writing Religious Communities: The Spiritual Lives and Manuscript Cultures of English Women, 1740–90." PhD thesis, Trinity College, University of Oxford, 2014.

Braude, Ann. "Women's History *Is* American Religious History." In *Retelling U.S. Religious History*, edited by Thomas A. Tweed, 87–107. Berkeley: University of California Press, 1997.

Brooks, Joanna, Rachel Hunt Steenblik, and Hannah Wheelwright, eds. *Mormon Feminism: Essential Writings.* New York: Oxford University Press, 2016.

Brown, Samuel. *In Heaven as It Is on Earth: Joseph Smith and the Early Mormon Conquest of Death.* New York: Oxford University Press, 2012.

Cope, Rachel. "John B. Fairbanks: The Man behind the Canvas." Master's thesis, Brigham Young University, 2003.

——. "'With God's Assistance I Will Someday Be an Artist': John B. Fairbanks's Account of the Paris Art Mission." *Brigham Young University Studies* 50, no. 3 (2011): 133–59.

Daynes, Kathryn. *More Wives Than One: Transformation of the Mormon Marriage System, 1840–1910.* Urbana: University of Illinois Press, 2001.

Derr, Jill Mulvay, Carol Cornwall Madsen, Kate Holbrook, and Matthew J. Grow. *The First Fifty Years of Relief Society: Key Documents in Latter-day Saint Women's History.* Salt Lake City, UT: Church Historian's Press, 2016.

Flake, Kathleen. *The Politics of Religious Identity: The Seating of Senator Reed Smoot, Mormon Apostle.* Chapel Hill: University of North Carolina Press, 2004.

Garrett, Matthew. *Making Lamanites: Mormons, Native Americans, and the Indian Student Placement Program, 1947–2000.* Salt Lake City: University of Utah Press, 2016.

Gordon, Sarah Barringer. *The Mormon Question: Polygamy and Constitutional Conflict in Nineteenth-Century America.* Chapel Hill: University of North Carolina Press, 2002.

Hall, Dave. *A Faded Legacy: Amy Brown Lyman and Mormon Women's Activism, 1872–1959.* Salt Lake City: University of Utah Press, 2015.

Hemphill, C. Dallett. *Siblings: Brothers and Sisters in American History.* New York: Oxford University Press, 2011.

Holbrook, Kate, and Matthew Bowman, eds. *Women and Mormonism: Historical and Contemporary Perspectives*. Salt Lake City: University of Utah Press, 2016.

James Austin Cope and Florence Fairbanks Cope Family Papers. L. Tom Perry Special Collections Library, Harold B. Lee Library, Brigham Young University, Provo, UT.

Lawrence, Anna M. *One Family under God: Love, Belonging, and Authority in Early Transatlantic Methodism*. Philadelphia: University of Pennsylvania Press, 2011.

Mack, Phyllis. *Heart Religion in the British Enlightenment: Gender and Emotion in Early Methodism*. Cambridge: Cambridge University Press, 2008.

Madsen, Carol Cornwall. *An Advocate for Women: The Public Life of Emmeline B. Wells, 1870–1920*. Provo, UT: Brigham Young University Press, 2005.

———. *Emmeline B. Wells: An Intimate History*. Salt Lake City: University of Utah Press, 2017.

Orsi, Robert. *The Madonna of 115th Street: Faith and Community in Italian Harlem*. New Haven, CT: Yale University Press, 1985.

Reeder, Jennifer, and Kate Holbrook, eds. *At the Pulpit: 185 Years of Discourses by Latter-day Saint Women*. Salt Lake City, UT: Church Historian's Press, 2017.

Stapley, Jonathan. "Adoptive Sealing Ritual in Mormonism." *Journal of Mormon History* 37, no. 3 (2011): 53–118.

Tadmor, Naomi. *Friends and Family in Eighteenth-Century England: Household, Kinship, and Patronage*. Cambridge: Cambridge University Press, 2001.

Tanner, Annie Clark. *A Mormon Mother: An Autobiography by Annie Clark Tanner*. Salt Lake City, UT: Tanner Trust Fund, University of Utah Library, 1991.

Ulrich, Laurel Thatcher. *A House Full of Females: Plural Marriage and Women's Rights in Early Mormonism, 1835–1870*. New York: Knopf, 2017.

Wilson, Lisa. *A History of Step Families in Early America*. Chapel Hill: University of North Carolina Press, 2014.

CHAPTER ONE

Alexander, Thomas G. "Historiography and the New Mormon History: A Historian's Perspective." *Dialogue: A Journal of Mormon Thought* 19 (Fall 1986): 25–49.

Allen, James B., and Glen M. Leonard. *The Story of the Latter-day Saints*. 2nd ed. Salt Lake City, UT: Deseret Book, 1992.

Anderson, Lavina Fielding, ed. *Lucy's Book: A Critical Edition of Lucy Mack Smith's Family Memoir*. Salt Lake City, UT: Signature Books, 2001.

Arrington, Leonard J., and Davis Bitton. *The Mormon Experience: A History of the Latter-day Saints*. Urbana: University of Illinois Press, 1992.

Arrington, Leonard J., Susan Arrington Madsen, and Emily Madsen Jones. *Mothers of the Prophets*. Salt Lake City, UT: Deseret Book, 1992.

Barrett, Ivan J. *Heroines of the Church*. Provo, UT: Brigham Young University, 1964.

Bartholomew, Rebecca. *Audacious Women: Early British Mormon Immigrants*. Salt Lake City, UT: Signature Books, 1995.

Bashore, Melvin L. "Index to Books in the Noble Women's Lives Series." Salt Lake City, UT: Historical Department, LDS Church History Library, 1979.

Beck, Julie B. "Preserving the Heritage of Latter-day Saint Women." Presented at the Church History Symposium, June 3, 2016. https://history.lds.org/article/preserving-the-heritage-of-latter-day-saint-women.

Beecher, Maureen. *The Personal Writings of Eliza Roxcy Snow*. Logan: Utah State University Press, 2000.

Beecher, Maureen Ursenbach. "Under the Sunbonnets: Mormon Women with Faces." *BYU Studies* 16, no. 4 (October 1, 1976): 471–84.

Beecher, Maureen Ursenbach, and Lavina Fielding Anderson, eds. *Sisters in Spirit: Mormon Women in Historical and Cultural Perspective*. Urbana: University of Illinois Press, 1987.

Best, Christy. *Guide to Sources for Studies of Mormon Women in the Church Archives*. Salt Lake City, UT: Historical Department of the Church of Jesus Christ of Latter-day Saints, 1976.

Bitton, Davis. *Guide to Mormon Diaries & Autobiographies*. Provo, UT: Brigham Young University Press, 1977.

Black, Susan Easton, and Mary Jane Woodger, eds. *Women of Character: Profiles of 100 Prominent LDS Women*. American Fork, UT: Covenant Communications, 2011.

Bowman, Matthew. *The Mormon People: The Making of an American Faith*. New York: Random House, 2012.

Bradley, Martha Sonntag. *Pedestals and Podiums: Utah Women, Religious Authority and Equal Rights*. Salt Lake City, UT: Signature Books, 2005.

———, ed. *Plural Wife: The Life Story of Mabel Finlayson Allred*. Logan: Utah State University Press, 2012.

Bradley, Martha Sonntag, and Mary Brown Firmage Woodward. *4 Zinas: A Story of Mothers and Daughters on the Mormon Frontier*. Salt Lake City, UT: Signature Books, 2000.

Bradley-Evans, Martha S. *Pedestals and Podiums: Utah Women, Religious Authority, and Equal Rights*. Salt Lake City, UT: Signature Books, 2005.

Brands, H. W. *The Devil We Knew: Americans and the Cold War*. New York: Oxford University Press, 1993.

Braude, Ann. "Women's History *Is* American Religious History." In *Retelling U.S. Religious History*, edited by Thomas A. Tweed, 87–107. Berkeley: University of California Press, 1997.

Brekus, Catherine A. "Mormon Women and the Problem of Historical Agency." *Journal of Mormon History* (Spring 2011): 59–87.

Brooks, Joanna. *The Book of Mormon Girl: Stories from an American Faith*. Lexington, KY: Free Press, 2012.

Brooks, Joanna, Rachel Hunt Steenblik, and Hannah Wheelwright, eds. *Mormon Feminism: Essential Writings*. New York: Oxford University Press, 2016.

Brooks, Juanita. *Quicksand and Cactus: A Memoir of the Southern Mormon Frontier*. Logan: Utah State University Press, 1992.

Brown, S. Kent, Donald Q. Cannon, and Richard H. Jackson, eds. *Historical Atlas of Mormonism*. New York: Simon & Schuster, 1994.

Burgess-Olson, Vicky. *Sister Saints*. Provo, UT: Brigham Young University Press, 1978.

Bushman, Claudia. "Edward W. Tullidge and *The Women of Mormondom*." *Dialogue* 33, no. 4 (Winter 2000): 15–26.

———, ed. *Mormon Sisters: Women in Early Utah*. 2nd ed. Logan: Utah State University Press, 1997.

Bushman, Claudia, and Caroline Kine, eds. *Mormon Women Have Their Say: Essays from the Claremont Oral History Collection*. Salt Lake City, UT: Greg Kofford Books, 2013.

Butler, Jon. "Jack-in-the-Box Faith: The Religion Problem in Modern American History." *Journal of American History* 90 (March 2004): 1357–478.

Cannon, Peter. "The Mormons: Saints or Sinners?" *Social Studies Review*, no. 3 (Winter 1990): 9–10.

Carmack, Noel A., and Karen Lynn Davidson, eds. *Out of the Black Patch: The Autobiography of Effie Marquess Carmack, Folk Musician, Artist, and Writer*. Logan: Utah State University Press, 1999.

Carter, Kate B., comp. *Heart Throbs of the West*. Salt Lake City: Daughters of Utah Pioneers, 1939–1951.

———, comp. *Our Pioneer Heritage*. Salt Lake City: Daughters of Utah Pioneers, 1958–1977.

———, comp. *Treasures of Pioneer History*. Salt Lake City: Daughters of Utah Pioneers, 1952–1957.

The Church of Jesus Christ of Latter-day Saints. *Daughters in My Kingdom: The History and Work of Relief Society*. Salt Lake City, UT: Church of Jesus Christ of Latter-day Saints, 2011.

———. *Our Heritage*. Salt Lake City, UT: Church of Jesus Christ of Latter-day Saints, 1996.

Cohen, Lizabeth. *A Consumer's Republic: The Politics of Mass Consumption in Postwar America*. New York: Alfred A. Knopf, 2003.

Coontz, Stephanie. "The Challenge of Family History." *OAH Magazine of History* 15, no. 4 (Summer 2001).

Cope, Rachel. "The Unexplored Drama within the Drama." *Journal of Mormon History* 35, no. 3 (Summer 2009): 195–200.

Correspondence between Rev. Abraham De Witt, Pastor of Rock Church, Cecil Co., Md. and Miss Sarah Stageman, One of His Flock, regarding the Principles and Faith of the Church of Jesus Christ of Latter-day Saints. Philadelphia: Bicking & Guilbert Printers, 1849.

Cott, Nancy F., and Drew Gilpin Faust. "Recent Directions in Gender and Women's History." *OAH Magazine of History* 19, no. 2 (March 2005): 4.

Crawley, Peter. *A Descriptive Bibliography of the Mormon Church*. 3 vols. Provo, UT: Brigham Young University Religious Studies Center, 2005.

Cross, Mary Bywater. *Quilts & Women of the Mormon Migrations: Treasures of Transition*. Nashville, TN: Rutledge Hill Press, 1997.

Crowther, Duane S., and Jean Decker Crowther, eds. *The Joy of Being a Woman: Guidance for Meaningful Living by Outstanding LDS Women*. Bountiful, UT: Horizon, 1972.

Daughters in My Kingdom: The History and Work of Relief Society. Salt Lake City, UT: Church of Jesus Christ of Latter-day Saints, 2011.

Davidson, Karen Lynn, and Jill Mulvay Derr. *Eliza: The Life and Faith of Eliza R. Snow*. Salt Lake City, UT: Deseret Book, 2014.

Daynes, Kathryn M. *More Wives Than One: Transformation of the Mormon Marriage System, 1840–1910*. Urbana: University of Illinois Press, 2001.

Derr, Jill Mulvay, Janath Russell Cannon, and Maureen Ursenbach Beecher. *Women of Covenant: The Story of Relief Society*. Salt Lake City, UT: Deseret Book, 1992.

Derr, Jill Mulvay, Carol Cornwall Madsen, Kate Holbrook, and Matthew J. Grow, eds. *The First Fifty Years of Relief Society: Key Documents in Latter-day Saint Women's History*. Salt Lake City, UT: Church Historian's Press, 2016.

DeSimone, Linda, ed. *Exposé of Polygamy: A Lady's Life among the Mormons, Fanny Stenhouse*. Logan: Utah State University Press, 2008.

Dew, Sheri L. *Women and the Priesthood: What One Mormon Woman Believes*. Salt Lake City, UT: Deseret Book, 2013.

Easton-Flake, Amy, and Rachel Cope. "A Multiplicity of Witnesses: Women and the Translation Process." In *The Coming Forth of the Book of Mormon: A Marvelous Work and a Wonder*, edited by Dennis L. Largey, Andrew H. Hedges, John Hilton III, and Kerry Hull, 133–53. Provo, UT: Brigham Young University Religious Studies Center, 2015.

Ellsworth, S. George. *The History of Louisa Barnes Pratt: Mormon Missionary Widow and Pioneer*. Logan: Utah State University Press, 1998.

Erekson, Keith A. *Everybody's History*. Amherst: University of Massachusetts Press, 2012.

Eubank, Sharon. "This Is a Woman's Church." Presented at the FairMormon Conference, Provo, UT, August 8, 2014. https://www.fairmormon.org/fair-conferences/2014-fairmormon-conference/womans-church.

Flake, Chad J., and Larry W. Draper, eds. *A Mormon Bibliography, 1830–1930: Books, Pamphlets, Periodicals, and Broadsides Relating to the First Century of Mormonism.* 2nd ed. 2 vols. Provo, UT: Brigham Young University Religious Studies Center, 2004.

"Frequently Asked Questions, History—Daughters in My Kingdom." https://www.lds.org/callings/relief-society/messages-from-leaders/news-and-announcements/frequently-asked-questions.

Froiseth, Jennie Anderson, ed. *The Women of Mormonism; or, The Story of Polygamy as Told by the Victims.* Detroit: C. G. G. Paine, 1882.

Fuller, Metta Victoria. *Mormon Wives: A Narrative of Facts Stranger Than Fiction.* New York: Derby & Jackson, 1856.

Gaddis, John Lewis. *We Now Know: Rethinking Cold War History.* New York: Oxford University Press, 1997.

Garr, Arnold K., Donald Q. Cannon, and Richard O. Cowan, eds. *Encyclopedia of Latter-day Saint History.* Salt Lake City, UT: Deseret Book, 2000.

Gates, Susa Young. *Heroines of Mormondom.* Salt Lake City, UT: Juvenile Instructor Office, 1884.

——. *History of the Young Ladies' Mutual Improvement Association of the Church of Jesus Christ of Latter-day Saints, from November 1869 to June 1910.* Salt Lake City, UT: Deseret News, 1911.

——. *Lydia Knight's History.* Salt Lake City, UT: Juvenile Instructor Office, 1883.

Gates, Susa Young, and Leah Eudora Dunford Widstoe. *Women of the "Mormon" Church.* Independence, MO: Zion's Printing and Publishing Company, 1928.

General Board of Relief Society. *A Centenary of Relief Society, 1842–1942.* Salt Lake City, UT: General Board of Relief Society, 1942.

Givens, Terryl L. *The Viper on the Hearth: Mormons, Myths, and the Construction of Heresy.* New York: Oxford University Press, 1997.

Godfrey, Kenneth W., Audrey M. Godfrey, and Jill Mulvay Derr. *Women's Voices: An Untold History of the Latter-day Saints, 1830–1900.* Salt Lake City, UT: Deseret Book, 1982.

Gordon, Margaret E. P., and Claudia L. Bushman. *Pansy's History: The Autobiography of Margaret E. P. Gordon, 1866–1966.* Logan: Utah State University Press, 2011.

Gordon, Sarah Barringer. "'Our National Hearthstone': Anti-polygamy Fiction and the Sentimental Campaign against Moral Diversity in Antebellum America." *Yale Journal of Law & the Humanities* 8 (Summer 1996): 295–350.

Hall, Dave. *A Faded Legacy: Amy Brown Lyman and Mormon Women's Activism, 1872–1959.* Salt Lake City: University of Utah Press, 2015.

Hanks, Maxine, ed. *Women and Authority: Re-emerging Mormon Feminism.* Salt Lake City, UT: Signature Books, 1992.

Harris, Amy. "Converting Mormon History." *Journal of Mormon History* 35, no. 3 (Summer 2009): 226–29.

Hartshorn, Leon R., ed. *Remarkable Stories from the Lives of Latter-day Saint Women.* Salt Lake City, UT: Deseret Book, 1974.

Hatch, Charles M., and Todd M. Compton, eds. *A Widow's Tale: The 1884–1896 Diary of Helen Mar Kimball Whitney.* Logan: Utah State University Press, 2003.

Holbrook, Kate, and Matthew Burton Bowman, eds. *Women and Mormonism: Historical and Contemporary Perspectives.* Salt Lake City: University of Utah Press, 2016.

Jepson, Ring. *Among the Mormons: How an American and an Englishman Went to Salt Lake City, and Married Seven Wives Apiece; Their Lively Experience, a Peep into the Mysteries of Mormonism.* San Francisco, CA: San Francisco News Company, 1879.

Jessop, Carolyn, with Laura Palmer. *Escape.* New York: Broadway Books, 2007.

Johnson, Janiece L., and Jennifer Reeder, eds. *The Witness of Women: Firsthand Experiences and Testimonies from the Restoration.* Salt Lake City, UT: Deseret Book Company, 2016.

Kane, Elizabeth Wood. *Twelve Mormon Homes Visited in Succession on a Journey through Utah to Arizona.* Philadelphia: William Wood, 1874.

Kimball, James N., and Kent Miles. *Mormon Women: Portraits and Conversations.* Salt Lake City, UT: Handcart Books, 2009.

Krakauer, Jon. *Under the Banner of Heaven: A Story of Violent Faith.* New York: Doubleday, 2003.

Launius, Roger. "The 'New Social History' and the 'New Mormon History': Reflections on Recent Trends." *Dialogue: A Journal of Mormon Thought* 27, no. 1 (Spring 1994): 109–27.

LeBaron, Anna, and Leslie Wilson. *The Polygamist's Daughter: A Memoir.* Carol Stream, IL: Tyndale House Publishers, 2017.

Lyman, Edward, Susan Ward Payne, and S. George Ellsworth, eds. *No Place to Call Home: The 1807–1857 Life Writings of Caroline Barnes Crosby, Chronicler of Outlying Mormon Communities.* Logan: Utah State University Press, 2005.

Madsen, Carol Cornwall. *An Advocate for Women: The Public Life of Emmeline B. Wells, 1870–1920.* Provo, UT: Brigham Young University Press, 2005.

——, ed. *Battle for the Ballot: Essays on Woman Suffrage in Utah, 1870–1896.* Logan: Utah State University Press, 1997.

——. *Emmeline B. Wells: An Intimate History.* Salt Lake City: University of Utah Press, 2017.

——. "'Feme Covert': Journey of a Metaphor." *Journal of Mormon History* 17 (1991): 43–61.

Madsen, Carol Cornwall, and Susan Staker Oman. *Sisters and Little Saints: One Hundred Years of Primary.* Salt Lake City, UT: Deseret Book, 1979.

Madsen, Carol Cornwall, and David J. Whittaker. "History's Sequel: A Source Essay on Women in Mormon History." *Journal of Mormon History* 6 (1979): 123–45.

Mansbridge, Jane J. *Why We Lost the ERA.* Chicago: University of Chicago Press, 1986.

McBaine, Neylan, ed. *Sisters Abroad: Interview from the Mormon Women Project.* Englewood, CO: Patheos Press, 2013.

——. *Women at Church: Magnifying LDS Women's Local Impact.* Salt Lake City, UT: Greg Kofford Books, 2014.

Milewski, Melissa Lambert, ed. *Before the Manifesto: The Life Writings of Mary Lois Walker Morris.* Logan: Utah State University Press, 2007.

Mintz, Steven. "Does the American Family Have a History? Family Images and Realities," *OAH Magazine of History* 15, no. 4 (Summer 2001).

——. "Teaching Family History: An Annotated Bibliography." *OAH Magazine of History* 15, no. 4 (Summer 2001).

Nash, Brittany Chapman, and Richard E. Turley, eds. *Fearless in the Cause: Remarkable Stories from Women in Church History.* Salt Lake City, UT: Deseret Book, 2016.

Newell, Linda King, and Valeen Tippetts Avery. *Mormon Enigma: Emma Hale Smith, Prophet's Wife, "Elect Lady," Polygamy's Foe, 1804–1879.* Garden City, NY: Doubleday, 1984.

Nielson, Carol Holindrake. *The Salt Lake City 14th Ward Album Quilt, 1857: Stories of the Relief Society Women and Their Quilt.* Salt Lake City: University of Utah Press, 2004.

Paddock, Mrs. A. G. *Saved at Last from among the Mormons.* Springfield, OH: Mast, Crowell, and Kirkpatrick, 1894.

Peterson, Janet, and LaRene Gaunt. *Elect Ladies: Presidents of the Relief Society.* Rev. ed. Salt Lake City, UT: Deseret Book, 1990.

——. *Keepers of the Flame: Presidents of the Young Women.* Salt Lake City, UT: Deseret Book, 1993.

Petree, Sandra Ailey, ed. *Recollections of Past Days: The Autobiography of Patience Loader Rozsa Archer.* Logan: Utah State University Press, 2006.

Pidgin, Charles Felton. *The House of Shame: A Novel.* New York: Cosmopolitan Press, 1912.

Plewe, Brandon S., ed. *Mapping Mormonism: An Atlas of Mormon History.* Provo, UT: Brigham Young University Press, 2014.

Quinn, D. Michael. "Editor's Introduction." In *The New Mormon History: Revisionist Essays on the Past*. Salt Lake City, UT: Signature Books, 1992.

Reeder, Jennifer, and Kate Holbrook, eds. *At the Pulpit: 185 Years of Discourses by Latter-day Saint Women*. Salt Lake City, UT: Church Historian's Press, 2017.

Roberts, B. H. *A Comprehensive History of the Church of Jesus Christ of Latter-day Saints*. 6 vols. Salt Lake City, UT: Deseret News Press, 1930.

———. *History of the Church*. Salt Lake City, UT: Deseret News, 1902.

Scott, Patricia Lyn, and Maureen Ursenbach Beecher. "Mormon Women: A Bibliography in Process, 1977–1985." *Journal of Mormon History* 12 (1985): 113–27.

Smart, Donna T., ed. *Mormon Midwife: The 1846–1888 Diaries of Patty Bartlett Sessions*. Logan: Utah State University Press, 1997.

Smith, Bonnie G. "Gender and the Practices of Scientific History: The Seminar and Archival Research in the Nineteenth Century." *American Historical Review* 100 (1995): 1150–76.

Smith, George A. *The Rise, Progress and Travels of the Church of Jesus Christ of Latter-day Saints*. Salt Lake City, UT: Deseret News Office, 1869.

Snyder, LuAnn Faylor, and Phillip A. Snyder, eds. *Post-Manifesto Polygamy: The 1899–1904 Correspondence of Helen, Owen and Avery Woodruff*. Logan: Utah State University Press, 2009.

Spafford, Belle S. *A Woman's Reach*. Salt Lake City, UT: Deseret Book, 1974.

Stegner, Wallace. *The Gathering of Zion: The Story of the Mormon Trail*. New York: McGraw-Hill, 1964.

Terry, Keith, and Ann Terry. *Eliza: A Biography of Eliza R. Snow*. Santa Barbara, CA: Butterfly Publishing, 1981.

Thatcher, Linda, comp. *Guide to Women's History Holdings at the Utah State Historical Society Library*. Salt Lake City: Utah State Historical Society Library, 1985.

Tullidge, Edward W. *The Women of Mormondom*. New York: Tullidge and Crandall, 1877.

Turley, Richard E., Jr., and Brittany A. Chapman, eds. *Women of Faith in the Latter Days*. 3 vols. Salt Lake City, UT: Deseret Book, 2011–2014.

Ulrich, Laurel Thatcher. *A House Full of Females: Family and Faith in 19th-Century Mormon Diaries*. New York: Alfred A. Knopf, 2017.

Walch, Tad. "Women Hired by LDS Church History Department Making Huge Strides in Mormon Women's History." DeseretNews.com, February 7, 2016. http://www.deseretnews.com/article/865647165/Women-hired-by-LDS-Church-History-Department-making-huge-strides-in-Mormon-womens-history.html?pg=all.

Wall, Elissa, and Lisa Pulitzer. *Stolen Innocence: My Story of Growing Up in a Polygamous Sect, Becoming a Teenage Bride, and Breaking Free of Warren Jeffs*. New York: Harper, 2009.

Ward, Kyle. *Not Written in Stone: Learning and Unlearning American History through 200 Years of Textbooks*. New York: New Press, 2010.

Ward, Maurine Carr, ed. *Winter Quarters: The 1846–1848 Life Writings of Mary Haskin Parker Richards*. Logan: Utah State University Press, 1996.

Wariner, Ruth. *The Sound of Gravel: A Memoir*. New York: Flatiron Books, 2016.

Wells, Emmeline B. "Self-Made Women." *Woman's Exponent* 9 (March 1, 1881): 148.

Whitfield, Stephen J. *The Culture of the Cold War*. 2nd ed. Baltimore: Johns Hopkins University Press, [1991] 1996.

Whitley, Colleen, ed. *Worth Their Salt: Notable but Often Unnoted Women of Utah*. Logan: Utah State University Press, 1996.

———. *Worth Their Salt, Too: More Notable but Often Unnoted Women of Utah*. Logan: Utah State University Press, 2000.

Whitney, Orson F. *History of Utah, Comprising Preliminary Chapters on the Previous History of Her Founders, Accounts of Early Spanish and American Explorations in the Rocky Mountain Region: The Advent of the Mormon Pioneers, the Establishment and Dissolution of the*

Provisional Government of the State of Deseret, and the Subsequent Creation and Development of the Territory. Salt Lake City, UT: G. Q. Cannon & Sons Co., 1892.

Wikert, Kathryn Webb. "Home to Iowa: Letters from the Western Trails." *Iowa Heritage Illustrated* 84, no. 1 (Spring 2003): 30–46.

"Women in Church History: A Research Guide," March 3, 2016. https://history.lds.org/article/women_in_church_history_research_guide.

Woodger, Mary Jane, and Paulette Preston Yates. *Courtships of the Prophets: From Childhood Sweethearts to Love at First Sight.* American Fork, UT: Covenant Communications, 2015.

CHAPTER TWO

Andrew Jenson Biographical Files. LDS Church History Library, Salt Lake City, UT.

Bellin, Joshua David. "'A Little I Shall Say': Translation and Interculturalism in the John Eliot Tracts." In *Reinterpreting New England Indians and the Colonial Experience*, edited by Colin G. Calloway and Neal Salisbury, 52–83. Boston: Colonial Society of Massachusetts, 2003.

Berkhofer, Robert F., Jr. *The White Man's Indian: Images of the American Indian from Columbus to the Present.* New York: Knopf, 1978.

Blackhawk, Ned. *Violence over the Land: Indians and Empires in the Early American West.* Cambridge, MA: Harvard University Press, 2006.

Bragdon, Kathleen J. *Native People of Southern New England, 1500–1650.* Tulsa: University of Oklahoma Press, 1996.

Brigham Young Office Files. LDS Church History Library, Salt Lake City, UT.

Brooks, James F. *Captives and Cousins: Slavery, Kinship, and Community in the Southwest Borderlands.* Chapel Hill: University of North Carolina Press, 2002.

Brooks, Juanita, ed. *On the Mormon Frontier: The Diary of Hosea Stout, 1844–1861.* Vol. 2. Salt Lake City: University of Utah Press, 1964.

Bross, Kristina, and Hilary E. Wyss. *Early Native Literacies in New England: A Documentary and Critical Anthology.* Amherst: University of Massachusetts Press, 2008.

Brown, James S. *Giant of the Lord: Life of a Pioneer.* Salt Lake City, UT: Bookcraft, 1960. First published in 1902.

Carmack, Sharon DeBartolo. "Family Legends and Myths: Watching Out for Red Flags." Accessed June 8, 2016. http://www.genealogy.com/articles/research/90_carmack.html.

Clark, Ella E., and Margot Edmunds. *Sacagawea of the Lewis & Clark Expedition.* Berkeley: University of California Press, 1979.

Codman, John. *The Round Trip by Way of Panama.* New York: G. P. Putnam's Sons, 1879.

Cogley, Richard W. "John Eliot and the Origins of the American Indians." *Early American Literature* 21 (1986–1987): 210–25.

Columbia River Fishing and Trading Company Accounts at Fort Hall from 1834 to 1837. Transcription. Accessed May 29, 2017. www.xmission.com/~drudy/mtman/html/fthall/index.html.

Daughters of Utah Pioneers Obituary Scrapbook for James L. Daley. Accessed May 29, 2017. http://search.ancestry.com/cgi-bin/sse.dll?_phsrc=SIM5&_phstart=successSource&usePUBJs=true&indiv=1&db=obit&gss=angs-d&new=1&rank=1&msT=1&gskw=James%20L.%20Daley&MSAV=1&MSV=0&uidh=u1c&pcat=34&fh=0&h=3835&recoff=&ml_rpos=1.

Daynes, Kathryn M. *More Wives Than One: Transformation of the Mormon Marriage System, 1840–1910.* Champaign: University of Illinois Press, 2001.

DeLay, Brian. *War of a Thousand Deserts: Indian Raids and the U.S.-Mexican War, 1846–1848.* New Haven, CT: Yale University Press, 2009.

Deloria, Philip J. *Playing Indian.* New Haven, CT: Yale University Press, 1998.

Dibble, Charles E. "The Mormon Mission to the Shoshoni Indians." *Utah Humanities Review* 1 (January/April/July 1947): 53–73, 166–77, 279–93.

Divorce decree for Polly Ward Donley and Upton Donley, June 27, 1879, Utah State Archives.

Evans, Stephen F. "'Open Containers': Sherman Alexie's Drunken Indians." *American Indian Quarterly* 25, no. 1 (Winter 2001): 46–72.

Faragher, John Mack. "The Custom of the Country: Cross-Cultural Marriage in the Far Western Fur Trade." In *Western Women, Their Land, Their Lives*, edited by Lillian Schlissel, Vicki Ruiz, et al. Albuquerque: University of New Mexico Press, 1988.

Farmer, Jared. *On Zion's Mount: Mormons, Indians, and the American Landscape.* Cambridge, MA: Harvard University Press, 2008.

Fremont, John Charles. *Report of the Exploring Expedition to the Rocky Mountains in the Year 1842, and to Oregon and North California in the Years 1843–'44.* N.p.: Readex Microprint, 1966. First published in 1845.

Gowans, Fred, and Eugene Campbell. *Fort Supply: Brigham Young's Green River Experiment.* Provo, UT: Brigham Young University Press, 1976.

Graham, Rev. John. *Annals of Ireland.* London, 1817.

Green, Rayna. "The Pocahontas Perplex: The Image of Indian Women in American Culture." *Massachusetts Review* 16, no. 4 (1975): 698–714.

Hafen, Leroy R. "Elijah Barney Ward." In *The Mountain Men and the Fur Trade of the Far West*, edited by Leroy R. Hafen and Ann W. Hafen, 7:343–51. Spokane, WA: A. H. Clark, 2002.

Hämäläinen, Pekka. *The Comanche Empire.* New Haven, CT: Yale University Press, 2008.

Hebard, Grace. *Sacajawea: Guide and Interpreter of Lewis and Clark.* Glendale, CA: A. H. Clark, 1933.

Henkel, Jacqueline M. "Represented Authenticity: Native Voices in Seventeenth-Century Conversion Narratives." *New England Quarterly* (March 2014): 5–45.

Horne, Esther Burnett, with Sally MacBeth. *Essie's Story: The Life and Legacy of a Shoshone Teacher.* Lincoln: University of Nebraska Press, 1998.

Idaho Death Index, 1890–1964. Accessed May 29, 2017. http://search.ancestry.com/cgi-bin/sse. dll?_phsrc=SIM16&_phstart=successSource&usePUBJs=true&indiv=1&db=IdahoDeathIn dex&gss=angs-d&new=1&rank=1&msT=1&gsfn=Polly&gsfn_x=1&gsln=Williams&gsln_ x=1&msddy=1947&msdpn__ftp=Idaho,%20USA&msdpn=15&msdpn_PInfo=5-%7C0%7 C1652393%7C0%7C2%7C0%7C15%7C0%7C0%7C0%7C0%7C0%7C&MSAV=1&MSV =0&uidh=u1c&pcat=34&fh=0&h=169276&recoff=8%2010&ml_rpos=1.

Isaac Bullock Diary. LDS Church History Library, Salt Lake City, UT.

Jackson, Donald, ed. *Letters of the Lewis and Clark Expedition with Related Documents, 1783–1854.* Vol. 2. Urbana: University of Illinois Press, 1978.

Jenson, Andrew. *Latter-day Saint Biographical Encyclopedia.* Vol. 4. Salt Lake City, UT: Andrew Jenson History Co., 1901.

Johnson, Thomas H., with Helen S. Johnson. *Also Called Sacajawea: Chief Woman's Stolen Identity.* Long Grove, IL: Waveland Press, 2008.

Jones, Sondra. *The Trial of Don Pedro Leon Lujan: The Attack against Indian Slavery and Mexican Traders in Utah.* Salt Lake City: University of Utah Press, 2000.

Kessler, Donna J. *The Making of Sacagawea: A Euro-American Legend.* Tuscaloosa: University of Alabama Press, 1996.

Kitchen, Richard Darrell. *Mormon-Indian Relations in Deseret: Intermarriage and Indenture, 1847 to 1877.* PhD diss., Arizona State University, 2002.

Kosmider, Alexia. "Strike a Euroamerican Pose: Ora Eddleman Reed's 'Types of Indian Girls.'" *American Transcendental Quarterly* 12, no. 2 (June 1998): 109–32.

Magee, Pennie L. "What Ever Happened to Sacagawea? The Debate between Grace Hebard (1861–1936) and Blanche Schroer (1907–1998)." *Heritage of the Great Plains* 37, no. 1 (2004): 27–39.

Mancall, Peter C. *Deadly Medicine: Indians and Alcohol in Early America*. Ithaca, NY: Cornell University Press, 1995.

Marsh, James B. *Four Years in the Rockies; or, The Adventures of Isaac P. Rose of Shenango Township, Lawrence County, Pennsylvania*. New Castle, PA: W. B. Thomas, 1884.

Mihesuah, Devon A., ed. *Natives and Academics: Researching and Writing about American Indians*. Lincoln: University of Nebraska Press, 1998.

Miller, Courtney. "Cherokee Misconceptions, Part 7: The Cherokee Princess," December 26, 2013. Accessed June 8, 2016. http://nativeamericanantiquity.blogspot.com/2013/12/cherokee-misconceptions-part-7-cherokee.html.

Neihardt, John G. *Black Elk Speaks*. Albany: State University of New York Press, 2008. First published in 1932.

Nelson, W. Dale. *Interpreters with Lewis and Clark: The Story of Sacagawea and Toussaint Charbonneau*. Denton: University of North Texas Press, 2003.

O'Brien, Jean M. *Dispossession by Degrees: Indian Land and Identity in Natick, Massachusetts, 1650–1790*. Cambridge: Cambridge University Press, 1997.

Ogden 1st Ward Manuscript History and Historical Reports. LDS Church History Library, Salt Lake City, UT.

Ogden 1st Ward Relief Society Minutes. LDS Church History Library, Salt Lake City, UT.

Oxendine, Jamie K. "My Grandmother Was a Cherokee Indian Princess." Accessed June 8, 2016. http://www.powwows.com/2011/11/18/my-grandmother-was-a-cherokee-indian-princess/#ixzz49i7wjIzg.

"Papers Pertaining to Chief Baziel." LDS Church History Library, Salt Lake City, UT.

Parry, Mae. "The Northwestern Shoshone: Utah's Native Americans." Accessed July 22, 2016. http://historytogo.utah.gov/people/ethnic_cultures/the_history_of_utahs_american_indians/chapter2.html.

Pearce, Roy Harvey. *Savagism and Civilization: A Study of the Indian and the American Mind*. Baltimore: Johns Hopkins University Press, 1965. First published in 1953.

Peterson, John Alton. *Utah's Black Hawk War*. Salt Lake City: University of Utah Press, 1998.

Plane, Ann Marie. *Colonial Intimacies: Indian Marriage in Early New England*. Ithaca, NY: Cornell University Press, 2000.

Preuss, Charles. *Exploring with Fremont: The Private Diaries of Charles Preuss, Cartographer for John C. Fremont on His First, Second, and Fourth Expeditions to the Far West*. Translated and edited by Erwin G. and Elisabeth K. Gudde. Norman: University of Oklahoma Press, 1958.

Price, John S. "Mormon Missions to the Indians." In *History of Indian-White Relations*, edited by Wilcomb A. Washburn, 459–63. Vol. 4 of *Handbook of North American Indians, Northeast*, edited by Bruce G. Trigger. Washington, DC: Smithsonian Institution, 1978.

Probate Court Civil and Criminal Case Registers of Actions, 1868–1887. Utah State Archives.

Pulsipher, John. "A Short Sketch of the History of John Pulsipher." Provo, UT: L. Tom Perry Special Collections, Harold B. Lee Library, Brigham Young University.

Ramsey, Colin. "Cannibalism and Infant Killing: A System of 'Demonizing' Motifs in Indian Captivity Narratives." *Clio* 24, no. 1 (Fall 1994): 55–68.

Reeve, Paul. *Religion of a Different Color: Race and the Mormon Struggle for Whiteness*. New York: Oxford University Press, 2015.

Reynolds, Sir Joshua. *The Discourses of Sir Joshua Reynolds*. London, 1842.

Richter, Daniel K. *Facing East from Indian Country: A Native History of Early America*. Cambridge, MA: Harvard University Press, 2001.

———. *Ordeal of the Longhouse: The Peoples of the Iroquois League in the Era of European Colonization*. Chapel Hill: University of North Carolina Press, 1992.

———. "Whose Indian History?" *William and Mary Quarterly*, 3rd ser., 50, no. 2 (April 1992): 379–93.

Sage, Rufus B. *Rufus B. Sage: His Letters and Papers, 1836–1847.* 2 vols. Far West and the Rockies Historical Series, 1820–1875, edited by Leroy R. Hafen and Ann W. Hafen. Glendale, CA: Arthur H. Clark Company, 1956.

Sanderson, Henry Weeks. "History of Henry Weeks Sanderson." Typescript copy of original, 1916. L. Provo, UT: Tom Perry Special Collections, Harold B. Lee Library, Brigham Young University.

Scharff, Virginia. *Twenty Thousand Roads: Women, Movement, and the West.* Berkeley: University of California Press, 2002.

Schultz, Duane. *Over the Earth I Come: The Great Sioux Uprising of 1862.* New York: St. Martin's Press, 1992.

Selley, April. "'I Have Been, and Ever Shall Be, Your Friend': *Star Trek, The Deerslayer* and the American Romance." *Journal of Popular Culture* 20, no. 1 (Summer 1986): 89–104.

Sides, Hampton. *Blood and Thunder: The Epic Story of Kit Carson and the Conquest of the American West.* New York: Anchor Books, 2006.

"A Sketch of the History of a Company of Elders . . . on the Shoshone Mission." LDS Church History Library, Salt Lake City, UT.

Skousen, Christina. "Toiling among the Seed of Israel: A Comparison of Puritan and Mormon Missions to the Indians." Master's thesis, Brigham Young University, 2005.

Slaughter, Thomas P. *Exploring Lewis and Clark: Reflections on Men and Wilderness.* New York: Alfred A. Knopf, 2003.

Sleeper-Smith, Susan. *Indian Women and French Men: Rethinking Cultural Encounter in the Western Great Lakes.* Amherst: University of Massachusetts Press, 2001.

Slotkin, Richard. *Regeneration through Violence: The Mythology of the American Frontier, 1600–1860.* Middletown, CT: Wesleyan University Press, 1973.

Smith, George D., ed. *An Intimate Chronicle: The Journals of William Clayton.* Salt Lake City: Signature Books, 1995.

Stuart, Joseph Alonzo. *My Roving Life: A Diary of Travels and Adventures by Sea and Land, during Peace and War.* Auburn, CA, 1895.

Swagerty, William R. "Marriage and Settlement Patterns of Rocky Mountain Trappers and Traders." *Western Historical Quarterly* 11, no. 2 (April 1980): 159–80.

Talbot, Theodore. *The Journals of Theodore Talbot, 1843 and 1849–52: With the Fremont Expedition of 1843 and with the First Military Company in Oregon Territory, 1849–52.* Edited by Charles H. Carey. Portland, OR: Metropolitan Press, 1931.

Thompson, Stith. *The Folktale.* Berkeley: University of California Press, 1977. First published in 1946.

Tonkin, Elizabeth. *Narrating Our Pasts: The Social Construction of Oral History.* Cambridge: Cambridge University Press, 1992.

Van Kirk, Sylvia. *Many Tender Ties: Women in Fur-Trade Society, 1670–1870.* Norman: University of Oklahoma Press, 1980.

"Why Your Great-Grandmother Wasn't a Cherokee Princess." Accessed June 8, 2016. http://www.native-languages.org/princess.htm.

Wiget, Andrew. "Father Juan Greyrobe: Reconstructing Tradition Histories, and the Reliability and Validity of Uncorroborated Oral Tradition." *Ethnohistory* 43, no. 3 (Summer 1976): 459–82.

———. "Truth and the Hopi: An Historiographic Study of Documented Oral Tradition concerning the Coming of the Spanish." *Ethnohistory* 29, no. 3 (Summer 1982): 181–99.

Wyss, Hilary E. *Writing Indians: Literacy, Christianity, and Native Community in Early America.* Amherst: University of Massachusetts Press, 2000.

Young, Zina D. H. *"A Weary Traveler": The 1848–50 Diary of Zina D. H. Young.* Edited by
    Marilyn Higbee. Honors thesis, Brigham Young University, 1992.

CHAPTER THREE

Baugh, Alexander L. *A Call to Arms: The 1838 Mormon Defense of Northern Missouri.* Provo,
    UT: Joseph Fielding Smith Institute for Latter-day Saint History and BYU Studies, 2000.
——. "'Silence, Ye Fiends of the Infernal Pit!': Joseph Smith's Incarceration in Richmond, Mis-
    souri, November 1838." *Mormon Historical Studies* 13, nos. 1–2 (Spring/Fall 2012): 135–59.
Beecher, Maureen Ursenbach, ed. *Personal Writings of Eliza R. Snow.* Logan: Utah State Uni-
    versity Press, 2000.
Beecher, Maureen Ursenbach, Linda King Newell, and Valeen Tippetts Avery. "Emma and
    Eliza and the Stairs." *Brigham Young University Studies* 22, no. 1 (Winter 1982): 87.
Block, Sharon. *Rape & Sexual Power in Early America.* Chapel Hill: University of North
    Carolina Press, 2006.
Bolles, Edmund Blair. *Remembering and Forgetting: An Inquiry into the Nature of Memory.*
    New York: Walker, 1988.
Brownmiller, Susan. *Against Our Will: Men, Women, and Rape.* New York: Simon & Schuster,
    1975.
Collier, Fred C., ed. *The Office Journal of President Brigham Young: 1858–1863, Book D.*
    Hanna, UT: Collier's Publishing, 2006.
Davidson, Karen Lynn. *Our Latter-day Hymns: The Stories and the Messages.* Rev. ed. Salt
    Lake City, UT: Deseret Book, 2009.
Dougall, Lily. *The Mormon Prophet.* New York: D. Appleton and Company, 1899.
"Eliza Roxie Snow Smith: A Tribute of Affection." *Woman's Exponent* 16 (December 15,
    1887): 109.
Fish, Joseph. *The Life and Times of Joseph Fish, Mormon Pioneer.* Edited by John H. Krenkel.
    Danville, IL: Interstate Printers & Publishers, 1970.
Gentry, Leland Homer. "A History of the Latter-day Saints in Northern Missouri from 1836 to
    1839." PhD diss., Brigham Young University, 1965.
Gentry, Leland Homer, and Todd M. Compton. *Fire and Sword: A History of the Latter-day
    Saints in Northern Missouri, 1836–39.* Salt Lake City, UT: Greg Kofford Books, 2011.
Givens, Terryl L., and Matthew J. Grow. *Parley P. Pratt: The Apostle Paul of Mormonism.* New
    York: Oxford University Press, 2011.
Grua, David W. *Surviving Wounded Knee: The Lakotas and the Politics of Memory.* Oxford:
    Oxford University Press, 2016.
Halbwachs, Maurice. *The Collective Memory.* Translated by Francis J. Ditter Jr. and Vida Yazdi
    Ditter. New York: Harper Colophon Books, 1980.
——. *On Collective Memory.* Edited and translated by Lewis A. Coser. Chicago: University
    of Chicago Press, 1992.
Hales, Brian C. "Emma Smith, Eliza R. Snow, and the Reported Incident on the Stairs." *Mor-
    mon Historical Studies* 10, no. 2 (Fall 2009): 63–76.
Henry, Nicola. *War and Rape: Law, Memory, and Justice.* New York: Routledge, 2011.
Hodgkin, Katharine, and Susannah Radstone, eds. *Contested Pasts: The Politics of Memory.*
    Routledge Studies in Memory and Narrative. London: Routledge, 2003.
Jessee, Dean C., and David J. Whittaker. "The Last Months of Mormonism in Missouri: The
    Albert Perry Rockwood Journal." *BYU Studies* 28, no. 1 (Winter 1988): 5–41.Johnson, Clark
    V., ed. *Mormon Redress Petitions: Documents of the 1833–1838 Missouri Conflict.* Provo,
    UT: Religious Studies Center, Brigham Young University, 1992.

Johnson, Janiece. "In Search of Punishment: Mormon Transgressions and the Mountain Meadows Massacre." PhD diss., School of History, University of Leicester, 2014.

Johnstun, Joseph. "A Victim of the 1838 Mormon-Missouri War: The Life and Tragedy of Hannah Kinney Johnstun." Paper presented at Mormon History Association Conference, Independence, MO, May 2010.

Joseph Smith: Prophet of the Restoration. Directed by T. C. Christensen and Gary Cook. Salt Lake City, UT: Church of Jesus Christ of Latter-day Saints, 2005. DVD. https://www.lds.org/media-library/video/2011-03-01-joseph-smith-the-prophet-of-the-restoration?category=feature-films&lang=eng.

Kammen, Michael. "Commemoration and Contestation in American Culture: Historical Perspectives." *Amerikastudien/American Studies* 48, no. 2 (2003): 185–205.

———. *Mystic Chords of Memory: The Transformation of Tradition in American Culture.* New York: Knopf, 1991.

Kester, Matthew. *Remembering Iosepa: History, Place, and Religion in the American West.* Oxford: Oxford University Press, 2013.

Kimball, Sarah Granger, ed. *World's Fair Ecclesiastical History of Utah.* Salt Lake City, UT, 1893.

Kunz, Rhea Allred. *Voices of Women Approbating Celestial or Plural Marriage.* Vol. 2, *Treasured Memories.* Draper, UT: Review and Preview Publishers, 1985.

LeSueur, Stephen C. *The 1838 Mormon War in Missouri.* Columbia: University of Missouri Press, 1987.

Lund, Gerald. *The Work and the Glory.* Vol. 4, *Thy Gold to Refine.* Salt Lake City, UT: Deseret Book, 2006.

Praise to the Man. Directed by T. C. Christensen and Gary Cook. Salt Lake City, UT: Excel Entertainment, 2005. DVD. https://www.lds.org/media-library/video/2006-05-01-joseph-smith-prophet-of-the-restoration-2002-version.

Pratt, Parley P. *Autobiography of Parley Parker Pratt.* Chicago: published for Pratt Bros., 1888.

Radke-Moss, Andrea G. "'I Hid [the Prophet] in a Corn Patch': Mormon Women as Healers, Concealers, and Protectors in the 1838 Mormon-Missouri War." *Mormon Historical Studies* 15, no. 1 (Spring 2014): 25–40.

Reading, Anna. *The Social Inheritance of the Holocaust: Gender, Culture and Memory.* New York: Palgrave Macmillan, 2002.

Roberts, B. H. *The Missouri Persecutions.* Salt Lake City, UT: George Q. Cannon & Sons, 1900.

Rubin, D. C., ed. *Autobiographical Memory.* Cambridge: Cambridge University Press, 1986.

Smith, Bathsheba W. Autobiography. Typescript. L. Tom Perry Special Collections, Harold B. Lee Library, Brigham Young University.

Snow, Eliza R. *Poems, Religious, Historical, and Political, also Two Articles in Prose.* Vol. 1. Liverpool, England: Franklin D. Richards, 1856; Salt Lake City, UT: Latter-day Saints' Printing and Publishing Establishment, 1877. http://archive.org/stream/PoemsReligiousHistoricalAndPolitical/poemsreligioushi01snow_djvu.txt.

Son, Elizabeth W. *Embodied Reckonings: Comfort Women, Performance, and Transpacific Redress.* Ann Arbor: University of Michigan Press, forthcoming.

———. "Memorializing Loss." Paper presented at the Histories of Violence Symposium, Northwestern University, Evanston, IL, April 27, 2013.

Sturken, Marita. *Tangled Memories: The Vietnam War, the AIDS Epidemic, and the Politics of Remembering.* Berkeley: University of California Press, 1997.

Taves, Ann. *Religious Experience Reconsidered: A Building Block Approach to the Study of Religion and Other Special Things.* Princeton, NJ: Princeton University Press, 2009.

Taysom, Steve C. *Shakers, Mormons, and Religious Worlds: Conflicting Visions, Contested Boundaries.* Bloomington: Indiana University Press, 2011.

Thelen, David. "Memory and American History." *Journal of American History* 75 (March 1989): 1117–29.

Turley, Richard E., and Janiece Johnson, eds. *Mountain Meadows Massacre: Complete Legal Papers*. 2 vols. Norman: University of Oklahoma Press, 2017.

Walker, Ronald W., Richard E. Turley Jr., and Glen M. Leonard. *Massacre at Mountain Meadows*. Oxford: Oxford University Press, 2008.

Whitney, Orson F. *Life of Heber C. Kimball: An Apostle, the Father and Founder of the British Mission*. 3rd ed. Salt Lake City, UT: Bookcraft, 1940.

Wilson, Harry Leon. *The Lions of the Lord: A Tale of the Old West*. Illustrated by Rose Cecil O'Neill. Boston: Lothrop Publishing, 1903.

Zerubavel, Eviatar. *Time Maps: Collective Memory and the Shape of the Past*. Chicago: Chicago University Press, 2004.

CHAPTER FOUR

Aalders, Cynthia. "'Your Journal, My Love': Constructing Personal and Religious Bonds in Eighteenth-Century Women's Diaries." *Journal of Religious History* 39, no. 3 (September 2015): 386–98.

Adair, Richard. *Courtship, Illegitimacy, and Marriage in Early Modern England*. Manchester: Manchester University Press, 1996.

Alexander, Thomas G. "Wilford Woodruff and the Mormon Reformation of 1855–57." *Dialogue: A Journal of Mormon Thought* 25, no. 2 (Summer 1992): 25–38.

Bailey, Joanne. *Unquiet Lives: Marriage and Marriage Breakdown in England, 1660–1800*. Cambridge: Cambridge University Press, 2003.

Beecher, Maureen Ursenbach, and Lavina Fielding Anderson, eds. *Sisters in Spirit: Mormon Women in Historical and Cultural Perspective*. Urbana: University of Illinois Press, 1992.

Bennett, Richard. "Wilford Woodruff and the Rise of Temple Consciousness among the Latter-day Saints, 1877–84." In *Banner of the Gospel: Wilford Woodruff*, edited by Alexander C. Baugh and Susan Easton Black, 233–50. Provo, UT: Religious Studies Center, Brigham Young University; Salt Lake City, UT: Deseret Book, 2010.

Bergera, Gary. "The Earliest Eternal Sealings for Civilly Married Couples Living and Dead." *Dialogue: A Journal of Mormon Thought* 35 (Fall 2002): 41–66.

Bloxham, V. Ben, James R. Moss, and Larry C. Porter. *Truth Will Prevail: The Rise of the Church of Jesus Christ of Latter-day Saints in the British Isles, 1837–1987*. Salt Lake City, UT: Church of Jesus Christ of Latter-day Saints, 1987.

Browett, Elizabeth [Elizabeth Johnstun]. Correspondence with Brigham Young and Wilford Woodruff, May 1856. CR 12341. Brigham Young Incoming Correspondence, 1839–1877. Box 25. Folder 1. Images 46–48. LDS Church History Library, Salt Lake City, UT.

Brown, Lisel G. "'Temple pro Tempore': The Salt Lake City Endowment House." *Journal of Mormon History* 34, no. 4 (Fall 2008): 1–68.

Brown, Richard. *Society and Economy in Modern Britain 1700–1850*. New York: Routledge, 1991.

Brown, Samuel M. "Early Mormon Adoption Theology and the Mechanics of Salvation." *Journal of Mormon History* 37, no. 3 (Summer 2011): 3–52.

———. "Early Mormon Chain of Belonging." *Dialogue: A Journal of Mormon Thought* 44, no. 1 (Spring 2011): 1–52.

Campbell, Eugene Edward. "The Mormon Gold Mining Mission of 1849." *BYU Studies* 1, no. 2 (1959–1960): 19–31.

Carlsruh, Dan, and Eve Carlsruh, eds. *Layton, Utah: Historic Viewpoints, Kaysville-Layton Historical Society*. Salt Lake City, UT: Moench Printing, 1985.

The Church of Jesus Christ of Latter-day Saints. *Early Church Information File* (Card Index). Browett Entries. Microfilm 1750663. Family History Library, Salt Lake City, UT.

Compton, Todd. "'Remember Me in My Affliction': Louisa Beaman and Eliza R. Snow Letters, 1849." *Journal of Mormon History* 25, no. 2 (1999): 51–53.

Coontz, Stephanie. *The Social Origins of Private Life: A History of American Families, 1600–1900*. New York: Verso, 1988.

Crawford, Patricia. *Parents of Poor Children in England, 1580–1800*. Oxford: Oxford University Press, 2010.

Davidoff, Leonore. *Thicker Than Water: Siblings and Their Relations, 1780–1920*. Oxford: Oxford University Press, 2011.

Daynes, Kathryn. *More Wives Than One: Transformation of the Mormon Marriage System, 1840–1910*. Urbana: University of Illinois Press, 2001.

Egan, Ferol. "Incident at Tragedy Springs: An Unsolved Mystery of the California Trail." *American West* 8, no. 1 (1971): 36–39.

Flake, Kathleen. "The Development of Early Latter-day Saint Marriage Rites, 1831–53." *Journal of Mormon History* 41, no. 1 (January 2015): 77–102.

Fleming, Stephen J. "The Religious Heritage of the British Northwest and the Rise of Mormonism." *Church History* 77, no. 1 (March 2008): 73–104.

Garrett, H. Dean. "Rebaptism." In *Encyclopedia of Mormonism*, edited by Daniel H. Ludlow. New York: Macmillan, 1992.

Godfrey, Audrey M. "Colonizing the Muddy River Valley: A New Perspective." *Journal of Mormon History* 22, no. 2 (Fall 1996): 120–42.

Harris, Amy. *Siblinghood and Social Relations in Georgian England: Share and Share Alike*. Manchester: Manchester University Press, 2012.

Harris, Darryl. *Life History of Robert Harris, Jr., and Hannah Maria Eagles Harris, Daniel Browett, Elizabeth Harris Browett*. Idaho Falls, ID: self-published, 2002.

Harline, Paula Kelly. *The Polygamous Wives Writing Club: From the Diaries of Mormon Pioneer Women*. Oxford: Oxford University Press, 2014.

Hartley, William G. "Council Bluffs/Kanesville, Iowa: A Hub for Mormon Settlements, Operations, and Emigration, 1846–1852." *John Whitmer Historical Association Journal* 26 (2006): 17–47.

Hartman, Mary S. *The Household and the Making of History: A Subversive View of the Western Past*. Cambridge: Cambridge University Press, 2004.

Hartog, Hendrik. *Man and Wife in America: A History*. Cambridge, MA: Harvard University Press, 2000.

Hill, Bridget. *Servants: English Domestics in the Eighteenth Century*. Oxford: Clarendon Press, 1996.

Hyde, Myrtle Stevens. *Orson Hyde: The Olive Branch of Israel*. Salt Lake City, UT: Agreka Books, 2000.

Hyde, Orson. Correspondence with Martha Rebecca Browett, 1859. Romania Jeanette Hyde Woolley Collection. MS 9681. Folder 2. LDS Church History Library, Salt Lake City, UT.

Hyer, Paul. "Sealing: Temple Sealings." In *Encyclopedia of Mormonism*, edited by Daniel H. Ludlow. New York: Macmillan, 1992. http://eom.byu.edu/index.php/Sealing#Sealing:_Temple_Sealings.

Irving, Gordon. "The Law of Adoption: One Phase of the Development of the Mormon Concept of Salvation, 1830–1900." *BYU Studies* 14, no. 3 (Spring 1974): 291–314.

Jensen, Richard J., and Malcolm Thorp. *Mormons in Early Victorian Britain*. Salt Lake City: University of Utah Press, 1989.

Kenney, Scott G., ed. *Wilford Woodruff's Journal 1833–1898*. Vol. 1. Midvale, UT: Signature Books, 1983–1985.

Kuper, Adam. *Incest and Influence: The Private Life of Bourgeois England*. Cambridge, MA: Harvard University Press, 2009.

Levy, Barry. *Quakers and the American Family: British Settlement in the Delaware Valley*. Oxford: Oxford University Press, 1988.

McClellan, Rolander Guy. *The Golden State: A History of the Region West of the Rocky Mountains: Embracing California, Oregon, Nevada, Utah, Arizona, Idaho, Washington Territory, British Columbia, and Alaska, from the Earliest Period to the Present Time . . . with a History of Mormonism and Mormons*. N.p.: W. Flint, 1876.

Morgan, S. Philip. "Late Nineteenth- and Early Twentieth-Century Childlessness." *American Journal of Sociology* 97, no. 3 (November 1991): 784–85.

Muldrew, Craig. *The Economy of Obligation: The Culture of Credit and Social Relations in Early Modern England*. Houndmills, England: Palgrave, 1998.

O'Day, Rosemary. *The Family and Family Relationships, 1500–1900: England, France, and the United States of America*. New York: St. Martin's, 1994.

Perry, Ruth. *Novel Relations: The Transformation of Kinship in English Literature and Culture, 1748–1818*. Cambridge: Cambridge University Press, 2004.

Peterson, Paul H. "The Mormon Reformation of 1856–1857: The Rhetoric and Reality." *Journal of Mormon History* 15 (January 1989): 549–87.

Ricketts, Norma Baldwin. *The Mormon Battalion: U.S. Army of the West, 1846–1848*. Logan: Utah State University Press, 1996.

Roberts, B. H. *Comprehensive History of the Church*. Vol. 3. Salt Lake City, UT: Church of Jesus Christ of Latter-day Saints, Deseret New Press, 1930.

Sarti, Raefaella. "Forum: Domestic Service since 1750." *Gender and History* 18, no. 2 (August 2006): 187–98.

Skolnick, M., et al. "Mormon Demographic History I: Nuptiality and Fertility of Once-Married Couples." *Population Studies* 32, no. 1 (March 1978): 5–19.

Smith, Joseph. *History of the Church of Jesus Christ of Latter-day Saints*. Vol. 4. Salt Lake City, UT: Deseret Book, 1978.

Stapley, Jonathan A. "Adoptive Sealing Ritual in Mormonism." *Journal of Mormon History* 37, no. 3 (Summer 2011): 53–117.

Tadmor, Naomi. *Family and Friends in Eighteenth-Century England: Household, Kinship, and Patronage*. Cambridge: Cambridge University Press, 2001.

Thorp, Malcolm. "Religious Backgrounds of Mormon Converts in Britain, 1837–1852." *Journal of Mormon History* 4 (1977): 51–66.

Tobler, Ryan. "'Saviors on Mount Zion': Mormon Sacramentalism, Mortality, and the Baptism for the Dead." *Journal of Mormon History* 39, no. 4 (Fall 2013): 182–238.

Turley, Richard E. "The Latter-day Saint Doctrine of Baptism for the Dead." BYU Family History Fireside, 2001. https://cfhg.byu.edu/pdf/firesides/2001-11-09.pdf.

Ulrich, Laurel Thatcher. *A House Full of Females: Plural Marriage and Women's Rights in Early Mormonism, 1835–1870*. New York: Knopf, 2017.

———. "Runaway Wives, 1830–1860." *Journal of Mormon History* 42, no. 2 (April 2016): 1–26.

Vandenberg-Daves, Jodi. *Modern Motherhood: An American History*. New Brunswick, NJ: Rutgers University Press, 2014.

Whittaker, David J. "East of Nauvoo: Benjamin Winchester and the Early Mormon Church." *Journal of Mormon History* 21, no. 2 (1995): 31–83.

Wilkinson, Carol. "The Restoration of the Gadfield Elm Chapel." In *Regional Studies in Latter-day Saint Church History: The British Isles*, edited by Cynthia Doxey, Robert C. Freeman, Richard Neitzel Holzapfel, and Dennis A. Wright, 41–59. Provo, UT: Religious Studies Center, Brigham Young University, 2007.

CHAPTER FIVE

Alder, Lydia D. "Birthday Greetings." *Woman's Exponent* 22, no. 17 (May 15, 1894): 131.

———. "The Last Letter." *Woman's Exponent* 28, no. 24 (May 15, 1900): 130.

———. "A Vision." *Woman's Exponent* 27, nos. 3 and 4 (July 1 and 15, 1898): 11.

B. B. [Emmeline B. Wells]. "A Tribute of Respect." *Woman's Exponent* 3, no. 17 (February 1, 1875): 130.

Beecher, Maureen Ursenbach. "The Eliza Enigma." *Dialogue: A Journal of Mormon Thought* 11, no. 1 (Spring 1978): 31–43.

Beecher, Maureen Ursenbach, and Lavina Fielding Anderson, eds. *Sisters in Spirit: Mormon Women in Historical and Cultural Perspective*. Urbana and Chicago: University of Illinois Press, 1987.

Bennett, Paula Bernat. *Nineteenth-Century American Women Poets: An Anthology*. Malden, MA: Wiley-Blackwell, 1998.

———. *Poets in the Public Sphere: The Emancipatory Project of American Women's Poetry, 1800–1900*. Princeton, NJ: Princeton University Press, 2003.

Bennion, Sherilyn Cox. "The *Woman's Exponent*: Forty-Two Years of Speaking for Women." *Utah Historical Quarterly* 44, no. 3 (Summer 1976): 226–39.

Bernardi, Debra, and Jill Annette Bergman. "Introduction: Benevolence Literature by American Women." In *Our Sisters' Keepers: Nineteenth-Century Benevolence Literature by American Women*, edited by Jill Annette Bergman, Debra Bernardi, and Sarah E. Chinn, 1–22. Tuscaloosa: University of Alabama Press, 2009.

Brewerton, Dorothy, Carolyn Gorwill, and Leonard Reed. *The Songstress of Dernford Dale: The Life of Poetess, Diarist and Latter-day Saint Hannah Tapfield King*. N.p.: privately published, 2011.

Bushman, Richard Lyman. *Joseph Smith: Rough Stone Rolling; a Cultural Biography of Mormonism's Founder*. New York: Alfred A Knopf, 2005.

Cannon, Annie Wells. "Mother." *Woman's Exponent* 40, no. 7 (March 1912): 49.

Chapman, Mary, and Angela Mills. *Treacherous Texts: U.S. Suffrage Literature, 1846–1946*. New Brunswick, NJ: Rutgers University Press, 2011.

Coffey, John, and Alister Chapman. "Introduction: Intellectual History and the Return of Religion." In *Seeing Things Their Way: Intellectual History and the Return of Religion*, edited by Alister Chapman, John Coffey, and Brad S. Gregory, 1–23. Notre Dame, IN: University of Notre Dame Press, 2009.

Cogan, Frances. *All American Girl: The Ideal of Real Womanhood in Mid-Nineteenth-Century America*. Atlanta: University of Georgia Press, 1989.

Cohen, Michael C. *The Social Lives of Poems in Nineteenth-Century America*. Philadelphia: University of Pennsylvania Press, 2015.

Crocheron, August Joyce. "Lines to an Infant." *Woman's Exponent* 8, no. 6 (August 15, 1879): 43.

———. "Patriot Mothers." *Woman's Exponent* 11, no. 11 (November 1, 1882): 83.

Culler, Jonathan. *Theory of the Lyric*. Cambridge, MA: Harvard University Press, 2015.

Dalton, Lu. "Afraid." *Woman's Exponent* 17, no. 18 (February 1, 1890): 130.

Derr, Jill Mulvay. "The Lion and the Lioness: Brigham Young and Eliza R. Snow." *BYU Studies* 40, no. 2 (2001): 62–63.

———. "The Significance of 'O My Father' in the Personal Journey of Eliza R. Snow." *BYU Studies* 36 (1996–1997): 98–100.

———. "'Strength in Our Union': The Making of Mormon Sisterhood." In *Sisters in Spirit: Mormon Women in Historical and Cultural Perspective*, edited by Maureen Ursenbach Beecher and Lavina Fielding Anderson, 153–207. Urbana and Chicago: University of Illinois Press, 1987.

Derr, Jill Mulvay, and Karen Lynn Davidson, eds. *Eliza R. Snow: The Complete Poetry*. Provo, UT: Brigham Young University Press, 2009.

E. T. "Number Nine." *Woman's Exponent* 18, no. 16 (January 15, 1890): 121.

Freeze, Mary A. "To Julia." *Woman's Exponent* 38, no. 9 (April 1910): 67.

Ginzberg, Lori D. *Women and the Work of Benevolence: Morality, Politics, and Class in the 19th-Century United States*. New Haven, CT: Yale University Press, 1990.

Gray, Janet. *She Wields a Pen: American Women Poets of the Nineteenth Century*. Iowa City: University of Iowa Press, 1997.

Greene, Louisa Lula. "A Utah Ladies' Journal." *Woman's Exponent* 1, no. 1 (June 1, 1872): 8.

Grieve-Carlson, Gary. *Poems Containing History: Twentieth-Century American Poetry's Engagement with the Past*. Lanham, MD: Lexington Books, 2013.

Gudmensen, Marian Adams. "Past and Future." *Woman's Exponent* 39, no. 5 (November 1910): 40.

Harrington, Joseph. "Why American Poetry Is Not American Literature." *American Literary History* 8 (Fall 1996): 496–515.

Jakeman, Ellen. "The Lady Pioneers." *Woman's Exponent* 19, no. 7 (September 15, 1890): 51.

Johnson, Jeffery Ogden. "Determining and Defining 'Wife': The Brigham Young Households." *Dialogue: A Journal of Mormon Thought* 20, no. 3 (Fall 1987): 57–70.

King, Hannah T. "Isabella." *Woman's Exponent* 21, no. 7 (October 1, 1892): 49.

———. "Lord Thou Knowest!" *Woman's Exponent* 12, no. 6 (August 15, 1883): 43.

Loeffelholz, Mary. *From School to Salon: Reading Nineteenth-Century American Women's Poetry*. Princeton, NJ: Princeton University Press, 2004.

Lula [L. L. Greene Richards]. "Ourselves." *Woman's Exponent* 10, no. 18 (February 15, 1882): 137.

M. L. M. "Affection." *Woman's Exponent* 12, no. 23 (May 1, 1884): 179.

Madsen, Carol Cornwall. *An Advocate for Women: The Public Life of Emmeline B. Wells, 1870–1920*. Provo, UT: BYU Studies, 2006.

———. "'Remember the Women of Zion': A Study of the Editorial Content of the *Woman's Exponent*, a Mormon Woman's Journal, 1872–1914." Master's thesis, University of Utah, 1977.

Morrill, Susanna. *White Roses on the Floor of Heaven: Mormon Women's Popular Theology, 1880–1920*. New York: Routledge, 2006.

Okker, Patricia. *Our Sister Editors: Sarah J. Hale and the Tradition of Nineteenth-Century American Women Editors*. Atlanta: University of Georgia Press, 2008.

Parker, Stuart. "The Hermeneutics of Generosity: A Critical Approach to the Scholarship of Richard Bushman." *Journal of Mormon History* 38, no. 3 (Summer 2012): 12–27.

Petersen, Boyd Jay. "'Redeemed from the Curse Placed upon Her': Dialogic Discourse on Eve in the *Woman's Exponent*." *Journal of Mormon History* 40, no. 1 (2014): 135–74.

Petrino, Elizabeth A. *Emily Dickinson and Her Contemporaries: Women's Verse in America 1820–1885*. Hanover, NH: University Press of New England, 1998.

Reed, Leonard. "'As a Bird Sings': Hannah Tapfield King, Poetess and Pioneer." *BYU Studies Quarterly* 51, no. 3 (2012): 113–15.

Richards, L. L. Greene. "A Remembered Exhortation." *Woman's Exponent* 23, nos. 3 and 4 (August 1 and 15, 1894): 171.

———. "A Thread of Thought." *Woman's Exponent* 29, nos. 6 and 7 (August 15, and September 1, 1900): 27.

Richards, Lula Greene. "To Sister Emma P. Toone." *Woman's Exponent* 17, no. 24 (May 15, 1889): 192.

Scott, Emily. "To Mary J. Tanner." *Woman's Exponent* 12, no. 15 (January 1, 1884): 11.

Shipp, Ellis R. "Half a Century." *Woman's Exponent* 18, no. 6 (August 15, 1889): 45.

Smith-Rosenberg, Caroll. "The Female World of Love and Ritual: Relations between Women in Nineteenth-Century America." *Signs* 1, no. 1 (Autumn 1975): 1–29.

Snow, Eliza R. "My Sister, Mrs. Leonora A. Morley." *Woman's Exponent* 1, no. 5 (August 1, 1872): 35.

Stokes, Claudia. *The Altar at Home: Sentimental Literature and Nineteenth-Century American Religion.* Philadelphia: University of Pennsylvania Press, 2014.

Stratford, Marianna, and Nellie Beecroft. "A Tribute of Love [for Maria D. Chambers]." *Woman's Exponent* 22, no. 13 (March 1, 1894): 104.

Tanner, Mary J. "I'll Lay by the Harp." *Woman's Exponent* 12, no. 12 (November 15, 1883): 91.

———. "To Mrs. Emily Scott." *Woman's Exponent* 12, no. 18 (February 15, 1884): 139.

Tarbet, Sarah J. "In Memoriam For [Ann H. Davis]." *Woman's Exponent* 12, no. 12 (November 15, 1883): 96.

Tompkins, Jane. "Sentimental Power: Uncle Tom's Cabin and the Politics of Literary Power." In *Sensational Designs: The Cultural Work of American Fiction, 1790–1860,* 122–46. New York: Oxford University Press, 1985.

Walker, Cheryl. *American Women Poets of the Nineteenth Century: An Anthology.* New Brunswick, NJ: Rutgers University Press, 1992.

Wells, Emmeline B. "Quest and Message." *Woman's Exponent* 38, no. 10 (May 1910): 75.

Welter, Barbara. "The Cult of True Womanhood: 1820–1860." *American Quarterly* 18, no. 2 (Summer 1966): 151–74.

Wolosky, Shira. "The Claims of Rhetoric: Toward a Historical Poetics (1820–1900)." *American Literary History* (2003): 14–21.

Woodmansee, Emily Hill. "A Demonstration of Respect." *Woman's Exponent* 8, no. 19 (March 1, 1880): 145.

———. "The Pioneer Mothers." *Woman's Exponent* 9, no. 20 (March 15, 1881): 151.

Yerxa, Donald A. "Introduction: Historical Inquiry and Thinking Today." In *Recent Themes in Historical Thinking: Historians in Conversation,* edited by Donald A. Yerxa, 1–6. Columbia: University of South Carolina Press, 2008.

CHAPTER SIX

Alexander, Thomas G. *Mormonism in Transition: A History of the Latter-day Saints, 1890–1930.* Champaign: University of Illinois Press, 1986. Reprinted, Salt Lake City, UT: Greg Kofford Books, 2012.

"Alice Merrill Horne." *Dedication and Naming of 22 Buildings,* 50–51. Provo, UT: Brigham Young University, 1954.

Alice Merrill Horne Family History Record 1912–1935. Bathsheba W. Smith Collection, 1842–1948. MS 20701. Box 2. Folder 1. LDS Church History Library, Salt Lake City, UT. https://dcms.lds.org/delivery/DeliveryManagerServlet?dps_pid=IE8079755.

Alice Merrill Horne Letters 1944–1947. Genevieve Lawrence Papers. ACC1110. Box 1. Folder 2. Marriott Library Special Collections, University of Utah.

Alice Smith Merrill Horne Biography. Dorothy Shepherd van Stripiaan Papers. MS 281. Box 1. Folder 1. Marriott Library Special Collections, University of Utah.

Andersen, Jeffery D. "Portrait of the 1890–1892 LDS Paris Art Mission: An Andragogical Perspective." PhD diss., University of Idaho, 2006.

Anderson, Carmen Rose de Jong. "Nine Rosabel Hartwell Whiteley (1861–1917)." Rose Hartwell Curatorial File, 1n2. Brigham Young University Museum of Art.

Arrington, Harriet Horne. "Alice Merrill Horne, Art Promoter and Early Utah Legislator." *Utah Historical Quarterly* 58, no. 3 (Summer 1990): 261–76.

"Art Exhibit Attracts Many Visitors to Display at Provo." *Salt Lake Herald*, September 21, 1902, 7.

"Art Judges Are Named." *Salt Lake Tribune*, November 22, 1901.

Art Strands. Ella Quayle Van Cott Memorial Number (1942): 2–3.

Art Strands 1 (July 1931): 22.

Art Strands 2 (July 1932): 5.

Beatlebrox, Lola. *Alice Merrill Horne, 1868–1948*. Salt Lake City, UT: Salt Lake City Art Council, 2007.

Bradley, Martha S. "Mary Teasdel: Yet Another American in Paris." *Utah Historical Quarterly* 58, no. 3 (Summer 1990): 244–60.

Bradley-Evans, Martha Sonntag. "Women in the Arts: Evolving Roles and Diverse Expressions." In *Women in Utah History: Paradigm or Paradox?*, edited by Patricia Lyn Scott and Linda Thatcher, 324–59. Logan: Utah State University Press, 2005.

Brekus, Catherine A. *Strangers and Pilgrims: Female Preaching in America, 1740–1845*. Chapel Hill: University of North Carolina Press, 1998.

"Brought to Zion." *Salt Lake Tribune*, September 25, 1915.

Brown, Candy Gunther. *Word in the World: Evangelical Writing, Publishing, and Reading in America, 1789–1880*. Chapel Hill: University of North Carolina Press, 2004.

Brownell, William C. "The Art Schools of New York." *Scribner's Monthly* 16, no. 6 (October 1878): 761–81.

Burns, Emily C. "Puritan Parisians: American Art Students in Late Nineteenth-Century Paris." In *A Seamless Web: Transatlantic Art in the Nineteenth Century*, edited by Cheryll L. May and Marian Wardle, 123–46. Newcastle-upon-Tyne, UK: Scholars Press, 2014.

———. "Revising Bohemia: The American Artist Colony in Paris, 1890–1914." In *Foreign Artists and Communities in Modern Paris, 1870–1914: Strangers in Paradise*, edited by Karen L. Carter and Susan Waller, 97–110. Burlington, VT: Ashgate Press, 2015.

Connelly, Lillian B. "Women in Art." *Young Woman's Journal* 23, no. 11 (1912): 622–25.

Cope, Rachel. "'With God's Assistance I Will Someday Be an Artist': John B. Fairbanks's Account of the Paris Art Mission." *BYU Studies* 50, no. 3 (2011): 133–59.

Dennison, Marie Caudill. "The American Girls' Club in Paris: The Propriety and Impudence of Art Students, 1890–1914." *Woman's Art Journal* 26, no. 1 (Spring/Summer 2005): 32–37.

DiMaggio, Paul. "Cultural Entrepreneurship in Nineteenth-Century Boston: The Creation of an Organizational Base for High Culture in America." *Media, Culture, and Society* 4, no. 1 (1982): 33–50.

Doss, Erika. "I *Must* Paint: Women Artists of the Rocky Mountain Region." In *Independent Spirits of the American West, 1890–1945*, edited by Patricia Trenton, 209–41. Los Angeles: University of California Press, 1995.

Douglas, Ann. *The Feminization of American Culture*. New York: Alfred A. Knopf, 1977.

Epstein, Barbara Leslie. *The Politics of Domesticity: Women, Evangelism, and Temperance in Nineteenth-Century America*. Middletown, CT: Wesleyan University Press, 1981.

Fehrer, Catherine. "Women at the Académie Julian." *Burlington Magazine* 136, no. 1100 (November 1994): 752–57.

Foster, Lawrence. *Women, Family, and Utopia: Communal Experiments of the Shakers, the Oneida Community, and the Mormons*. Syracuse, NY: Syracuse University Press, 1991.

Frazer, Mabel. "Art Appreciation." *Young Woman's Journal* 26, no. 12 (1915): 755.

———. "The Art Value of Bee-Hive Symbolism." *Young Woman's Journal* 31, no. 10 (1920): 559.

Garb, Tamar. "Revising the Revisionists: The Formation of the Union des Femmes Peintres et Sculpteurs." *Art Journal* 48, no. 1 (Spring 1989): 63–70.

———. *Sisters of the Brush: Women's Artistic Culture in Late Nineteenth-Century Paris* New Haven, CT: Yale University Press, 1994.

Gibbs, Linda Jones. *Harvesting the Light: The Paris Art Mission and Beginnings of Utah Impressionism.* Salt Lake City, UT: Church of Jesus Christ of Latter-day Saints, 1987.

Haseltine, James L. "Mormons and the Visual Arts." *Dialogue: A Journal of Mormon Thought* 1, no. 2 (1966): 17–34.

"Honors for Utah Artist: Her Painting Exhibited." *Salt Lake Tribune,* June 25, 1911.

Ichenhaeuser, Frau Eliza. *Bilder vom Internationalen Frauen-Kongress 1904.* Berlin: Druck und Verlag von August Scherl, n.d.

"In Memoriam—Alice Merrill Horne." *Relief Society Magazine* 35, no. 12 (1948): 816.

Kovinick, Phil. *The Woman Artist in the American West, 1860–1960.* North Orange County, CA: Muckenthaler Cultural Center, 1976.

Lambourne, Alfred. "Women in Art." *Young Woman's Journal* 32, no. 6 (1921): 347–53.

"Le Salon de la Société nationale des Beaux-Arts." *Journal des débats politiques et littéraires* 110 (April 10, 1912): n.p.

Levine, Lawrence W. *Highbrow/Lowbrow: The Emergence of Cultural Hierarchy in America.* Cambridge, MA: Harvard University Press, 1988.

Lloyd, Caro. "The Club for American Girls Studying in Paris." *Outlook* 50, no. 2 (July 14, 1894): 61.

McCarthy, Kathleen D. *Women's Culture: American Philanthropy and Art, 1830–1930.* Chicago: University of Chicago Press, 1991.

Merrill Horne, Alice. *Devotees and Their Shrines: A Hand Book of Utah Art.* Salt Lake City, UT: Deseret News, 1914.

———. "The Gospel of Beauty." *Relief Society Magazine* 7, no. 4 (1920): 202–3.

———. "Items about Art." *Woman's Exponent* 31, nos. 5–6 (August 1 and 15, 1902): 17.

———. "Mary Teasdel: The Utah Impressionistic Painter." *Young Woman's Journal* 21, no. 3 (March 1910):

———. "My Prayer." *Art Strands.* Ella Quayle Van Cott Memorial Number (1942): 13.

———. "Rose Hartwell—the Utah Colorist." *Young Woman's Journal* 22, no. 3 (1911): 127–32.

"Miss Sawyer Appointed." *Inter-Mountain Republican,* October 25, 1907.

"Miss Teasdel Returns: Salt Lake Young Lady Who Has Been Abroad." *Salt Lake Tribune,* October 15, 1900.

"Mother and Babe." *Young Woman's Journal* 13, no. 11 (November 1902): 522.

"Mrs. Alice Merrill Horne." *Relief Society Magazine* 4, no. 1 (1917): 10.

Mulvay, Jill. "Three Mormon Women in the Cultural Arts." *Sunstone* 1 (Spring 1976): 29–39.

Price, Raye. "Utah's Leading Ladies of the Arts." *Utah Historical Quarterly* 38, no. 1 (1970): 65–85.

Prieto, Laura R. *At Home in the Studio: The Professionalization of Women Artists in America.* Cambridge, MA: Harvard University Press, 2001.

Promey, Sally M. "Visible Liberalism: Liberal Protestant Taste Evangelism, 1850 and 1950." In *Religion in North America: American Religious Liberalism,* edited by Leigh E. Schmidt and Sally M. Promey, 76–96. Bloomington: Indiana University Press, 2012.

Pyne, Kathleen. "Whistler and the Religion of Art." In *Art and the Higher Life: Painting and Evolutionary Thought in Late Nineteenth-Century America.* Austin: University of Texas Press, 1996.

Roos, Jane Mayo. "Girls 'n' the 'Hood: Female Artists in Nineteenth-Century France." In *Artistic Brotherhoods in the Nineteenth Century,* edited by Laura Morowitz and William Vaughan, 154–84. Burlington, VT: Ashgate Press, 2000.

"Salt Lake Artists Form Association." *Salt Lake Telegram,* December 8, 1913.

"Salt Lake Painter Is Successful in Paris." *Salt Lake Tribune,* April 9, 1911.

Seifrit, William C. "Letters from Paris." *Utah Historical Quarterly* 54, no. 2 (Spring 1986): 179–202.

"Society." *Salt Lake Herald-Republican*, September 26, 1909.

Stokes, Claudia. *The Altar at Home: Sentimental Literature and Nineteenth-Century Religion.* Philadelphia: University of Pennsylvania Press, 2014.

Stritt, Marie. *Der Internationale Frauen-Kongress in Berlin 1904.* Berlin: Verlag von Carl Kabel, n.d.

"Successful Utah Artist." *Salt Lake Tribune*, March 4, 1900.

Swanson, Vern G., Richard S. Olpin, and William C. Seifrit. *Utah Painting and Sculpting.* Salt Lake City, UT: Gibbs Smith Publishers, 1997.

Swinth, Kirsten. "Illustrious Men and True Companionship: Parisian Study." In *Painting Professionals: Women Artists & the Development of Modern American Art, 1870–1930*, ed. Kirsten Swinth, 37–62. Chapel Hill: University of North Carolina Press, 2001.

Teasdel, Mary. "Michael [*sic*] Angelo's 'David.'" *Young Woman's Journal* 12, no. 3 (March 1901): 159–60.

———. "True Art: Harmony, Beauty and Eternal Fitness." *Young Woman's Journal* 15, no. 1 (January 1904): 14–17.

"Utah Artist's Success: Miss Mary Teasdel Has Work Accepted in Paris." *Salt Lake Tribune*, March 3, 1900.

Utah since Statehood: Historical and Biographical. Vol. 3. Salt Lake City, UT: S. J. Clarke Publishing, 1919.

Van Hook, Bailey. *Angels of Art: Women and Art in American Society, 1876–1914.* University Park: Pennsylvania State University Press, 1996.

Wein, Jo Ann. "The Parisian Training of American Women Artists." *Woman's Art Journal* 2, no. 1 (Spring/Summer 1981): 41–44.

Weisberg, Gabriel P., and Jane R. Becker, eds. *Overcoming All Obstacles: The Women of the Académie Julian.* New Brunswick, NJ: Rutgers University Press, 1999.

Wells, Emmeline B. "Thoughts and Remembrances." *Young Woman's Journal* 25, no. 10 (October 1914): 606.

"Western Clubs Group Appoints Salt Laker." *Salt Lake Telegram*, October 16, 1935.

CHAPTER SEVEN

Alexander, Thomas G. *Mormonism in Transition: A History of the Latter-day Saints, 1890–1930.* Urbana: University of Illinois Press, 1986.

Arrington, Harriet Horne. "Alice Merrill Horne: Art Promoter and Early Utah Legislator." In *Worth Their Salt: Notable but Often Unnoted Women of Utah*, edited by Colleen Whitley, 170–87. Logan: Utah State University Press, 1996.

Auslander, Leora. *Taste and Power: Furnishing Modern France.* Berkeley: University of California Press, 1996.

Beecher, Catherine E., and Harriet Beecher Stowe. *The American Woman's Home.* 1869. Facsimile of the first edition. Hartford, CT: Harriett Beecher Stowe Center, 1975.

Bourdieu, Pierre. *Distinction: A Critique of Social Taste.* Cambridge, MA: Harvard University Press, 1984.

Burrows, Edwin G., and Mike Wallace. *Gotham: A History of New York City to 1898.* New York: Oxford University Press, 1999.

Bushman, Richard Lyman. *The Refinement of America: Persons, Houses, Cities.* New York: Knopf, 1992.

Cutler, Virginia F. *A Twenty-One Gun Salute for Leah Dunford Widtsoe.* Logan: College of Family Life, Utah State University, n.d.

Damon-Moore, Helen. *Magazines for the Millions: Gender and Commerce in the* Ladies' Home Journal *and the* Saturday Evening Post, *1880–1910.* Albany: State University of New York Press, 1994.

Eastlake, Charles Locke. *Hints on Household Taste.* London: Longmans, Green and Co., 1868.

Ellis, Megan J. *Stir It Up: Home Economics in American Culture.* Philadelphia: University of Pennsylvania Press, 2010.

Erickson, Dan. *As a Thief in the Night: The Mormon Quest for Millennial Deliverance.* Salt Lake City, UT: Signature Books, 1998.

Gannett, William Channing. *The House Beautiful.* Boston: James H. West, 1895.

[Gates, Susa Young]. "Our Shopping Department." *Young Woman's Journal* 2, no. 8 (May 1891): 385–86.

Gates, Susa Young. "Hail and Farewell." *Young Woman's Journal* 40, no. 10 (October 1929): 675–78.

———. *Memorial to Elizabeth Claridge McCune, Missionary, Philanthropist, Architect.* Salt Lake City, UT, 1924.

Givens, Terryl L. *People of Paradox: A History of Mormon Culture.* New York: Oxford University Press, 2007.

Goldstein, Carolyn M. *Creating Consumers: Home Economists in the Twentieth Century.* Chapel Hill: University of North Carolina Press, 2012.

Gordon, Beverly. "Woman's Domestic Body: The Conceptual Conflation of Women and Interiors in the Industrial Age." *Winterthur Portfolio* 31, no. 4 (Winter 1996): 281–301.

Grier, Katherine C. *Culture and Comfort: People, Parlors, and Upholstery, 1850–1930.* Rochester, NY: Strong Museum, 1988.

Haber, Samuel. *Efficiency and Uplift: Scientific Management in the Progressive Era, 1890–1920.* Chicago: University of Chicago Press, 1964.

Horne, Alice Merrill. "Cyrus Edwin Dallin." *Young Woman's Journal* 21, no. 9 (September 1910): 491–97.

———. "James T. Harwood—the Strenuous Utah Artist." *Young Woman's Journal* 21, no. 1 (January 1910): 14–19.

———. "John Hafen, the Utah Landscapist." *Young Woman's Journal* 21, no. 2 (February 1910): 87–92.

———. "Mary Teasdel: The Utah Impressionistic Painter." *Young Woman's Journal* 21, no. 3 (March 1910): 130–37.

———. "Suggestions on Artistic Home Building." *Young Woman's Journal* 12, no. 3 (March 1901): 121–25.

———. "Suggestions on Artistic Home Building II." *Young Woman's Journal* 12, no. 4 (April 1901): 169–73.

———. "The Utah Painter—Lee Greene Richards." *Young Woman's Journal* 21, no. 5 (May 1910): 262–70.

———. "Utah's Sculptor, Mahonri M. Young." *Young Woman's Journal* 21, no. 4 (April 1910): 196–204.

Jones, Owen. *On the True and the False in the Decorative Arts: Lectures Delivered at Marlborough House, June 1852.* London, 1863.

Kaplan, Wendy. *The Arts and Crafts Movement in Europe and America.* London: Thames & Hudson, 2004.

Landow, George P. *The Aesthetic and Critical Theories of John Ruskin.* Princeton, NJ: Princeton University Press, 1971.

Lears, Jackson. "Beyond Veblen: Rethinking Consumer Culture in America." In *Consuming Visions: Accumulation and Display of Goods in America, 1880–1920*, edited by Simon J. Bronner, 73–97. New York: W. W. Norton, 1989.

Logan, Thad. *The Victorian Parlour: A Cultural Study*. Cambridge: Cambridge University Press, 2010.

Lynes, Russell. *The Tastemakers*. New York: Grosset and Dunlap, 1949.

Matthews, Glenna. *"Just a Housewife": The Rise and Fall of Domesticity in America*. New York: Oxford University Press, 1989.

McClaugherty, Martha Crabill. "Creating the Artistic Home, 1868–1893." *Winterthur Portfolio* 18, no. 1 (Spring 1983): 1–26.

Menlove, Robert L., ed. *Spring Lake, 1856–2000*. Spring Lake, 2000.

Merish, Lori. "'The Hand of Refined Taste' in the Frontier Landscape: Caroline Kirkland's 'A New Home, Who'll Follow?' and the Feminization of American Consumerism." *American Quarterly* 45, no. 4 (December 1993): 485–523.

National Register of Historic Places Inventory—Nomination Form, Alfred W. McCune Mansion, June 13, 1974.

Nelson, Daniel. *Frederick W. Taylor and the Rise of Scientific Management*. Madison: University of Wisconsin Press, 1980.

O'Brien, Kevin H. F. "'The House Beautiful': A Reconstruction of Oscar Wilde's American Lecture." *Victorian Studies* 17, no. 4 (June 1974): 395–418.

Peck, Amelia, and Carol Irish. *Candace Wheeler: The Art and Enterprise of American Design, 1875–1900*. New York: Metropolitan Museum of Art; New Haven, CT: Yale University Press, 2001.

Radke, Andrea G. "Refining Rural Spaces: Women and Vernacular Gentility in the Great Plains, 1880–1920." *Great Plains Quarterly* 24 (Fall 2004): 227–48.

Schuster, David G. *Neurasthenic Nation: America's Search for Health, Happiness, and Comfort, 1869–1920*. New Brunswick, NJ: Rutgers University Press, 2011.

Shriner, Larry. *The Invention of Art: A Cultural History*. Chicago: University of Chicago Press, 2001.

Smith, John Henry. Untitled address. *Conference Report* (April 1899): 101.

Snodin, Michael, and John Styles. *Design and the Decorative Arts, Victorian Britain, 1837–1901*. London: V&A Publications, 2004.

Stevenson, Louis L. *The Victorian Homefront: American Thought and Culture, 1860–1880*. New York: Twayne Publishers, 1991.

Tait, Lisa Olsen. "Between Two Economies: The Business Development of the *Young Woman's Journal*, 1889–1900." *Journal of Mormon History* 38, no. 4 (Fall 2012): 18–23.

Talbot, Christine. "The Church Family in Nineteenth-Century America: Mormonism and the Public/Private Divide." *Journal of Mormon History* 37, no. 4 (Fall 2011): 208–57.

Tiffany, Louis C. "The Gospel of Good Taste." *Country Life in America* 19, no. 2 (November Mid-Month, 1910): 105–6.

Tiffany Studios. *Portfolio of the Work of Tiffany Studios*. New York: Tiffany Studios, 1899.

Underwood, Grant. "Re-visioning Mormon History." *Pacific Historical Review* 55 (August 1986): 403–26.

Waggoner, Diane, ed. *The Beauty of Life: William Morris and the Art of Design*. New York: Thames & Hudson, 2003.

Welter, Barbara. "The Cult of True Womanhood, 1820–1860." *American Quarterly* 18, no. 2 (1966): 151–74.

Wharton, Edith, and Ogden Codman Jr. *The Decoration of Houses*. New York: Charles Scribner's Sons, 1898.

Wheeler, Candace. *Principles of Home Decoration*. New York: Doubleday, Page & Co., 1903.

Wilson, William H. *The City Beautiful Movement*. Baltimore: Johns Hopkins University Press, 1989.

Widtsoe, Leah Dunford. "Furnishing the Home." *Young Woman's Journal* 13, no. 1 (January 1902): 25–29.

——. "Furnishing the Home II: Basement, Cellar, Laundry." *Young Woman's Journal* 13, no. 2 (February 1902): 85–88.

——. "Furnishing the Home III: Color." *Young Woman's Journal* 13, no. 3 (March 1902): 124–27.

——. "Furnishing the Home IV: Color—(Continued)." *Young Woman's Journal* 13, no. 4 (April 1902): 179–81.

——. "Furnishing the Home V: About Carpets and Wall Papers." *Young Woman's Journal* 13, no. 5 (May 1902): 205–11.

——. "Furnishing the Home VI: About Curtains and Pictures." *Young Woman's Journal* 13, no. 6 (June 1902): 274–77.

——. "Furnishing the Home VII: Decoration and Furnishing in General." *Young Woman's Journal* 13, no. 7 (July 1902): 322–26.

——. "Furnishing the Home VIII: Kitchen and Pantry." *Young Woman's Journal* 13, no. 8 (August 1902): 367–72.

——. "Furnishing the Home IX: The Dining Room and Sitting Room." *Young Woman's Journal* 13, no. 9 (September 1902): 421–24.

——. "Furnishing the Home [X]: The Entrance Hall." *Young Woman's Journal* 13, no. 10 (October 1902): 467–72.

——. "Furnishing the Home [XI]: Bedrooms and Bathrooms." *Young Woman's Journal* 13, no. 11 (November 1902): 514–16.

——. "Furnishing the Home XII: The Two-Roomed House." *Young Woman's Journal* 13, no. 12 (December 1902): 566–73.

——. "The Home." *Young Woman's Journal* 10, no. 1 (January 1899): 37–41.

——. *Labor Saving Devices for the Farm Home*. Logan: Utah Agricultural Experiment Station, 1912.

——. "Studies in Household Art I: A Glance at the History of Architecture." *Young Woman's Journal* 10, no. 2 (February 1899): 132–37.

——. "Studies in Household Art II: Roman Architecture." *Young Woman's Journal* 10, no. 3 (March 1899): 87–91.

Woodger, Mary Jane. "Leah Widtsoe: Pioneer in Healthy Lifestyle Family Education." *Journal of Family and Consumer Sciences* 92, no. 1 (2000): 50–54.

Yorgason, Ethan R. *Transformation of the Mormon Culture Region*. Urbana: University of Illinois Press, 2003.

CHAPTER EIGHT

Abbott, Rachel Gianni. "The Scandinavian Immigrant Experience in Utah, 1850–1920: Using Material Culture to Interpret Cultural Adaptation." PhD diss., University of Alaska–Fairbanks, 2013.

Antrei, Albert C. T., and Allen D. Roberts. *A History of Sanpete County*. Salt Lake City: Utah State Historical Society, 1999.

Armstrong, Misty. "The Assimilation of Scandinavian Immigrants in Pleasant Grove, Utah, 1880–1900." *Genealogical Journal* 27, nos. 3–4 (1999): 116–30.

Attebery, Jennifer Eastman. *Up in the Rocky Mountains: Writing the Swedish Immigrant Experience*. Minneapolis: University of Minnesota Press, 2007.

Bitton, Davis. "A Reevaluation of the Turner Thesis and Mormon Beginnings." *Utah Historical Quarterly* 34, no. 4 (October 1966): 326–34.

"Charles Peter Warnick." In *Our Pioneer Heritage*, 20 vols., edited by Kate B. Carter, 10:58–63. Salt Lake City: Daughters of Utah Pioneers, 1958–1977.

Cheney, Thomas. "Scandinavian Immigrant Stories." *Western Folklore* 18, no. 2 (April 1959): 99–105.

Henrichsen, Lynn E., and George Bailey. "'No More Strangers and Foreigners': The Dual Focus of the LDS Church Language Program for Scandinavian Immigrants." *Mormon Historical Studies* 11 (Fall 2010): 23–53.

Homrighaus, Ruth Ellen. "Baby Farming: The Care of Illegitimate Children in England, 1860–1943." PhD diss., University of North Carolina at Chapel Hill, 2003.

Jenson, Andrew. *The Autobiography of Andrew Jenson.* Salt Lake City, UT: Deseret News Press, 1938.

——. *History of the Scandinavian Mission.* Salt Lake City, UT: Deseret News Press, 1927.

——. "Pleasant Grove First Ward Records, Utah Stake." Salt Lake City, UT: LDS Church Archives, 1900.

Jørgensen, Hans. *Daybook 1845–1883.* Salt Lake City, UT: privately printed, 1996.

Kent, Harald Jensen. *Danske Mormoner.* Copenhagen: Udvalget for Utahmissionen, 1913.

Kessler-Harris, Alice. *Out to Work: A History of Wage-Earning Women in the United States.* New York: Oxford University Press, 1982.

Lahlum, Lori Ann. "Women, Work, and Community in Rural Norwegian America." In *Norwegian American Women: Migration, Communities, and Identities*, edited by Betty A. Bergland and Lori Ann Lahlum, 79–117. Minneapolis: Minnesota Historical Society Press, 2011.

Lund, Jennifer. "Out of the Swan's Nest: The Ministry of Anthon H. Lund, Scandinavian Apostle." *Journal of Mormon History* 29, no. 2 (2003): 77–105.

Mulder, William. *Homeward to Zion: The Mormon Migration from Scandinavia.* Minneapolis: University of Minnesota Press, 1957.

Murphy, Miriam B. "Gainfully Employed Women, 1896–1950." In *Women in Utah History: Paradigm or Paradox?*, edited by Patricia Lyn Scott and Linda Thatcher, 183–222. Logan: Utah State University Press, 2005.

Olson, Beth R. "Chronological History of Pleasant Grove, Utah 1850–2000." In *Pleasant Grove Sesquicentennial History*, edited by Beth R. Olson and Mildred Sutch, 1:15–155. Provo, UT: Stevenson's Supply/Pleasant Grove City Corporation, 2000.

Sørensen, Jørgen Würtz. *Rejsen til Amerikas zion: den danske mormonudvandring før århundredeskiftet.* Aalborg, Denmark: Forlaget Fenre, 1985.

Warnick, Ruby Radmall. "The Life and Times of Coffee Oscar Olson." Typed manuscript, vertical file. Pleasant Grove, UT: Pleasant Grove City Library, n.d.

Wright, Rochelle, and Robert L. Wright. *Danish Emigrant Ballads and Songs.* Carbondale: Southern Illinois University Press, 1983.

CHAPTER NINE

Albanese, Catherine L. *A Republic of Mind and Spirit: A Cultural History of American Metaphysical Religion.* New Haven, CT: Yale University Press, 2008.

Alexander, Thomas G. *Mormonism in Transition: A History of the Latter-day Saints, 1890–1930.* Urbana: University of Illinois Press, 1986.

——. "The Reconstruction of Mormon Doctrine: From Joseph Smith to Progressive Theology." *Sunstone* 5, no. 4 (July–August 1980): 24–33.

Arrington, Leonard J. *Great Basin Kingdom: An Economic History of the Latter-day Saints, 1830–1900*. Cambridge, MA: Harvard University Press, 1958.

Beecher, Maureen Ursenbach. "Each in Her Own Time: Four Zinas." *Dialogue: A Journal of Mormon Thought* 26, no. 2 (Summer 1993): 119–35.

———. "The 'Leading Sisters': A Female Hierarchy in Nineteenth Century Mormon Society." *Journal of Mormon History* 9 (1982): 25–39.

———. "Three Women and the Life of the Mind." *Utah Historical Quarterly* 43, no. 1 (Winter 1975): 26–40.

Bigler, David L., and Will Bagley. *The Mormon Rebellion: America's First Civil War, 1857–1858*. Norman: University of Oklahoma Press, 2011.

"The Book of Abraham." *Times and Seasons*, March 15, 1842.

Bowman, Matthew B. "The Crisis of Mormon Christology: History, Progress, and Protestantism." *Fides et Historia* 40, no. 2 (Fall 2008): 1–27.

Bradford, Mary Lythgoe. "The Odyssey of Sonia Johnson." *Dialogue: A Journal of Mormon Thought* 14, no. 2 (Summer 1981): 14–26.

Braude, Ann. *Radical Spirits: Spiritualism and Women's Rights in Nineteenth-Century America*. 2nd ed. Bloomington: Indiana University Press, 2001.

———. "Women's History *Is* American Religious History." In *ReTelling U.S. Religious History*, edited by Thomas A. Tweed, 87–107. Berkeley: University of California Press, 1997.

Brekus, Catherine A. "Mormon Women and the Problem of Historical Agency." *Journal of Mormon History* 37, no. 2 (Spring 2011): 59–87.

———. *Sarah Osborn's World: The Rise of Evangelical Christianity in Early America*. New Haven, CT: Yale University Press, 2013.

Brooke, John L. *Refiner's Fire: The Making of Mormon Cosmology, 1644–1844*. New York: Cambridge University Press, 1994.

Brown, Samuel M. *In Heaven as It Is on Earth: Joseph Smith and the Early Mormon Conquest of Death*. New York: Oxford University Press, 2012.

Derr, Jill Mulvay. "The Significance of 'O My Father' in the Personal Journal of Eliza R. Snow." *BYU Studies* 36, no. 1 (1996–1997): 84–126.

Derr, Jill Mulvay, Janath Russell Cannon, and Maureen Ursenbach Beecher. *Women of Covenant: The Story of the Relief Society*. Salt Lake City, UT: Deseret Book, 1992.

Derr, Jill Mulvay, Carol Cornwall Madsen, Kate Holbrook, and Matthew J. Grow, eds. *The First Fifty Years of Relief Society: Key Documents in Latter-day Saint Women's History*. Salt Lake City, UT: Church Historian's Press, 2016.

Dinger, John S., ed. *The Nauvoo City and High Council Minutes*. Salt Lake City, UT: Signature Books, 2011.

Drake, Flora. Correspondence. LDS Church History Library, Salt Lake City, UT.

Easton-Flake, Amy. "Biblical Women in the *Woman's Exponent*: Nineteenth-Century Mormon Women Interpret the Bible." In *The Bible in Family Life*, edited by Philip Goff, Aruthru E. Farnsley II, and Peter J. Thuesen, 89–100. New York: Oxford University Press, 2017.

Felt, D. P. "A Man's Advice about Woman Suffrage." *Woman's Exponent*, November 15, 1891.

Flake, Kathleen. "Ordering Antinomy: An Analysis of Early Mormonism's Priestly Offices, Councils and Kinship." *Religion and American Culture* 26, no. 2 (Summer 2016): 139–83.

Follett, Louisa T. Diary. LDS Church History Library, Salt Lake City, UT.

Garvey, T. Gregory. *Creating the Culture of Reform in Antebellum America*. Athens: University of Georgia Press, 2006.

Ginzberg, Lori D. *Women and the Work of Benevolence: Morality, Politics, and Class in the Nineteenth-Century United States*. New Haven, CT: Yale University Press, 1990.

———. *Women in Antebellum Reform*. New York: Wiley-Blackwell, 2000.

Givens, Terryl L. *Wrestling the Angel: The Foundations of Mormon Thought: Cosmos, God, Humanity*. New York: Oxford University Press, 2015.

Givens, Terryl L., and Reid L. Neilson, eds. *The Columbia Sourcebook of Mormons in the United States*. New York: Columbia University Press, 2014.

Griffith, R. Marie. *God's Daughters: Evangelical Women and the Power of Submission*. Berkeley: University of California Press, 1997.

Hall, David D. "Backwards to the Future: The Cultural Turn and the Wisdom of Intellectual History." *Modern Intellectual History* 9, no. 1 (2012): 171–84.

Hanks, Maxine, ed. *Women and Authority: Re-emerging Mormon Feminism*. Salt Lake City, UT: Signature Books, 1992.

Harrell, Charles R. *"This Is My Doctrine": The Development of Mormon Theology*. Salt Lake City, UT: Greg Kofford Books, 2011.

Hedges, Andrew W., Alex D. Smith, and Richard Lloyd Anderson, eds. *Joseph Smith Papers: Journals*. Vol. 2, *December 1841–April 1843*. Salt Lake City, UT: Church Historian's Press, 2011.

Higginbotham, Evelyn Brooks. *Righteous Discontent: The Women's Movement in the Black Baptist Church, 1880–1920*. Cambridge, MA: Harvard University Press, 1994.

Holifield, E. Brooks. *Theology in America: Christian Thought from the Age of the Puritans to the Civil War*. New Haven, CT: Yale University Press, 2003.

Howe, Daniel Walker. *What Hath God Wrought: The Transformation of America, 1815–1848*. New York: Oxford University Press, 2007.

King, Hannah Tapfield. "Epistolary Fragment." *Woman's Exponent*, November 1, 1884.

———. "Silent Voices." *Woman's Exponent*, March 15, 1883.

"Ladies' Relief Society." *Times and Seasons*, April 1, 1842.

Madsen, Carol Cornwall. *An Advocate for Women: The Public Life of Emmeline B. Wells, 1870–1920*. Provo, UT: Brigham Young University Press, 2005.

Maffly-Kipp, Laurie F. "The Burdens of Church History." *Church History* 82, no. 2 (June 2013): 353–67.

Mason, Patrick Q. *The Mormon Menace: Violence and Anti-Mormonism in the Postbellum South*. New York: Oxford University Press, 2011.

Morrill, Susanna. *White Roses on the Floor of Heaven: Mormon Women's Popular Theology, 1880–1920*. New York: Routledge, 2006.

Nauvoo Relief Society Minute Book. LDS Church History Library, Salt Lake City, UT. Accessed May 2016. josephsmithpapers.org.

Noll, Mark A. *America's God: From Jonathan Edwards to Abraham Lincoln*. New York: Oxford University Press, 2002.

Park, Benjamin E. "'Reasonings Sufficient': Joseph Smith, Thomas Dick, and the Context(s) of Early Mormonism." *Journal of Mormon History* 38, no. 3 (Summer 2012): 210–24.

———. "(Re)Interpreting Early Mormon Thought: Synthesizing Joseph Smith's Theology and the Process of Religious Formation." *Dialogue* 44, no. 2 (Summer 2012): 59–88.

Peay, Ida S. "Taking a Stand for the Right." *Woman's Exponent*, June 1, 1913.

Perry, Seth. "A Mother Where?" *Los Angeles Review of Books*, April 29, 2015.

Peterson, Boyd Jay. "'Redeemed from the Curse Placed upon Her': Dialogic Discourse on Eve in the *Woman's Exponent*." *Journal of Mormon History* 40, no. 1 (2014): 135–74.

Proclamation of the Twelve Apostles of the Church of Jesus Christ, of Latter-day Saints. To All the Kings of the World. New York, 1845.

Quinn, D. Michael. *Early Mormonism and the Magic World View*. Salt Lake City, UT: Signature Books, 1987.

Schmidt, Leigh E. "Religious History and the Cultural Turn." In *A Companion to American Cultural History*, edited by Karen Halttunen, 406–15. Malden, MA: Blackwell Publishing, 2008.

Schultz, Kevin M., and Paul Harvey. "Everywhere and Nowhere: Recent Trends in American Religious History and Historiography." *Journal of the American Academy of Religion* 78, no. 1 (March 2010): 129–62.

Shipps, Jan. "The Reality of the Restoration and the Restoration Ideal in the Mormon Tradition." In *The American Quest for the Primitive Church*, edited by Richard T. Hughes, 181–95. Urbana: University of Illinois Press, 1988.

Smith, Ted A. "Redeeming Critique: Resignations to the Cultural Turn in Christian Theology and Ethics." *Journal of the Society of Christian Ethics* 24, no. 2 (Fall/Winter 2004): 89–113.

"Speech Delivered by Heber C. Kimball." *Times and Seasons*, July 15, 1845.

Stapley, Jonathan A. "Women and Mormon Authority." In *Women and Mormonism: Historical and Contemporary Perspectives*, edited by Kate Holbrook and Matt Bowman, 101–20. Salt Lake City: University of Utah Press, 2016.

Stapley, Jonathan A., and Kristine Wright. "Female Ritual Healing in Mormonism." *Journal of Mormon History* 37, no. 1 (Winter 2011): 1–85.

Stokes, Claudia. *The Altar at Home: Sentimental Literature and Nineteenth-Century American Religion*. Philadelphia: University of Pennsylvania Press, 2014.

Tait, Lisa Olsen. "The *Young Woman's Journal*: Gender and Generations in a Mormon Women's Magazine." *American Periodicals* 22, no. 1 (2012): 51–71.

Talbot, Christine. *A Foreign Kingdom: Mormons and Polygamy in American Political Culture, 1852–1890*. Urbana: University of Illinois Press, 2013.

Taysom, Stephen C. *Shakers, Mormons, and Religious Worlds: Conflicting Visions, Contested Boundaries*. Bloomington: Indiana University Press, 2010.

Tilly, Louise A. "Gender, Women's History, and Social History." *Social Science History* 13, no. 4 (Winter 1989): 439–62.

Ulrich, Laurel Thatcher. "An American Album, 1857." *American Historical Review* 115, no. 1 (February 2010): 1–25.

———. "Mormon Women in the History of Second-Wave Feminism." *Dialogue: A Journal of Mormon Thought* 43, no. 2 (Summer 2010): 45–63.

Walker, Ronald W., Richard E. Turley, and Glen W. Leonard. *Massacre at Mountain Meadows: An American Tragedy*. New York: Oxford University Press, 2008.

Wells, Emmeline B. "Why a Woman Should Desire to Be a Mormon." *Woman's Exponent*, December 1, 1907.

Wergland, Glendyne R. *Sisters in the Faith: Shaker Women and Equality of the Sexes*. Boston: University of Massachusetts Press, 2011.

CHAPTER TEN

Bendroth, Margaret Lamberts. *Fundamentalism and Gender, 1875 to the Present*. Rev. ed. Hartford, CT: Yale University Press, 1996.

Braude, Ann. *Radical Spirits: Spiritualism and Women's Rights in Nineteenth-Century America*. 2nd ed. Bloomington: Indiana University Press, 2001.

———. "Women's History *Is* American Religious History." In *Retelling U.S. Religious History*, edited by Thomas Tweed, 87–107. Berkeley: University of California Press, 1997.

Brooke, John L. *The Refiner's Fire: The Making of Mormon Cosmology, 1644–1844*. Cambridge: Cambridge University Press, 1996.

Brusco, Elizabeth E. *The Reformation of Machismo: Evangelical Conversion and Gender in Colombia*. Austin: University of Texas Press, 2011. First published in 1995.

Bushman, Richard Lyman. *Joseph Smith: Rough Stone Rolling*. New York: Vintage, 2007.

Bynum, Caroline Walker. *Holy Feast and Holy Fast: The Religious Significance of Food to Medieval Women.* Berkeley: University of California Press, 1988.

Cott, Nancy F. *The Bonds of Womanhood.* New Haven, CT: Yale University Press, 1997.

Darnton, Robert. *The Great Cat Massacre: And Other Episodes in French Cultural History.* New York: Basic Books, 2009.

Davis, Natalie Zemon. *The Return of Martin Guerre.* Cambridge, MA: Harvard University Press, 1983.

Derr, Jill Mulvay, Carol Cornwall Madsen, Kate Holbrook, and Matthew J. Grow, eds. *The First Fifty Years of Relief Society: Key Documents in Latter-day Saint Women's History.* Salt Lake City, UT: Church Historian's Press, 2016.

Flake, Kathleen. *The Politics of American Religious Identity: The Seating of Senator Reed Smoot, Mormon Apostle.* Charlotte: University of North Carolina Press, 2004.

Frederick, Marla F. *Between Sundays: Black Women and Everyday Struggles of Faith.* Berkeley: University of California Press, 2003.

Ginzburg, Carlo. *The Cheese and the Worms: The Cosmos of a Sixteenth-Century Miller.* Translated by Anne C. Tedeschi and John Tedeschi. Baltimore: Johns Hopkins University Press, 1992.

Givens, Terryl L. *The Viper on the Hearth: Mormons, Myths, and the Construction of Heresy.* Updated ed. Oxford: Oxford University Press, 2013.

Goldman, Karla. *Beyond the Synagogue Gallery: Finding a Place for Women in American Judaism.* Cambridge, MA: Harvard University Press, 2001.

Gordon, Sarah Barringer. *The Mormon Question: Polygamy and Constitutional Conflict in Nineteenth-Century America.* Charlotte: University of North Carolina Press, 2002.

Griffith, R. Marie. *God's Daughters: Evangelical Women and the Power of Submission.* Berkeley: University of California Press, 2000. First published in 1997.

Higginbotham, Evelyn Brooks. *Righteous Discontent: The Women's Movement in the Black Baptist Church, 1880–1920.* Cambridge, MA: Harvard University Press, 1993.

Jay, Martin. *The Dialectical Imagination: A History of the Frankfurt School and the Institute of Social Research, 1923–1950.* Berkeley: University of California Press, 1996.

Kern, Kathi. *Mrs. Stanton's Bible.* Ithaca, NY: Cornell University Press, 2001.

Kuhn, Thomas S. *The Structure of Scientific Revolutions: 50th Anniversary Edition.* Chicago: University of Chicago Press, 2016.

Mahmood, Saba. *Politics of Piety: The Islamic Revival and the Feminist Subject.* Reprinted with a new preface by Saba Mahmood. Princeton, NJ: Princeton University Press, 2011.

Mason, Patrick. *The Mormon Menace: Violence and Anti-Mormonism in the Postbellum South.* Oxford: Oxford University Press, 2011.

Orsi, Robert A. *The Madonna of 115th Street: Faith and Community in Italian Harlem, 1880–1950.* Hartford, CT: Yale University Press, 2010. First published in 1985.

———. *Thank You, St. Jude: Women's Devotion to the Patron Saint of Hopeless Causes.* Hartford, CT: Yale University Press, 1998. First published in 1996.

Painter, Nell Irvin. *Exodusters: Black Migration to Kansas after Reconstruction.* New York: W. W. Norton, 1992.

Raboteau, Albert J. *Slave Religion: The "Invisible Institution" in the Antebellum South.* Oxford: Oxford University Press, 2004.

Rouse, Carolyn. *Engaged Surrender: African American Women and Islam.* Berkeley: University of California Press, 2004.

Satter, Beryl. *Each Mind a Kingdom: American Women, Sexual Purity, and the New Thought Movement, 1875–1920.* Berkeley: University of California Press, 2001.

Schmidt, Leigh Eric. *Restless Souls: The Making of American Spirituality.* 2nd ed. Berkeley: University of California Press, 2012. First published in 2005 by HarperCollins.

Index

Page references for figures are italicized

205, 211. S*ee also* Edmunds-Tucker
Anti-Polygamy Act of 1887.
Pratt, Parley P., 54, 58–60, 62, 118, 210,
213–14
premortal existence, 133

Relief Society, xiii, 8, 117–18, 141,
218–20; charitable work by, 15;
Declaration, 8; Female Relief Society
of Nauvoo, 1; goals of, 121–22, 144,
159, 235; leadership of, viii, 69, 123,
154, 156, 158, 168; meetings, 13, 73,
158, 217; records of, 6–9; sisterhood,
xii–xiii, 13, 73
Relief Society Magazine, 141, 144, 158
Richards, Louisa Lula Greene, 117, 124
Richter, Daniel, 31–32
Rigdon, Athalia R., 60
Roberts, B. H., 2, 4, 11, 56–57

Sawyer, Myra Louise, 144, 149–50,
154; *French Landscape, 150*
Scandinavians in Utah, 195–203, 206;
See also Danish Mormons
Scott, Emily, x, 113–14, 134
Second Coming of Christ, 35, 168,
185n65
Selebak, Peter, 193, 194–95
Skandinaviens Stjerne (*Scandinavia's
Star*), 196–97, 202
Smith, Bathsheba W., 68, 69, 141, 156
Smith, Emma, 2, 5, 8, 72–73, 141; as
Relief Society President, 1, 219;
work with Book of Mormon, 1, 14
Smith, Hyrum, 55, 63, 71, 93
Smith, John Henry, 167
Smith, Joseph, 135n4, 183n65, 216–17,
219, 221; defense of women, xv,
54, 55, 58–62, 73; founder of LDS
Church, 1; on Heavenly Mother, 131;
history of, 5, 72, 228, 232; murder of,
63, 64, 71, 93; on temple work, 16–17,
84, 85, 91, 99, 218; writings of, 210
Smith, Lucy Mack, 1, 5, 8, 14
Snow, Eliza R., 3, 141, 210, 212;
biography, 5, 8, 158, 211; poetry,

118, 131, 132, 135n4; teachings of,
123, 124, 213, 214, 219; rape, 70–75
Snow, Lorenzo, 72, 178
Son, Elizabeth W., 53, 74–75
Stageman, Sarah, 16–17
Stone, Dorothy, 13
suffrage, women's, 2, 5, 7, 8, 118, 209,
218

Tanner, Mary J., 113–14, 134; "I'll Lay
by the Harp," 113
Taylor, John, 74, 189
Teasdel, Mary, x, xvi, 142, 144–50,
154, 156, 162n31; *Apple Blossoms,
148*; *Mother and Child*, 146, *147*,
148; "True Art: Harmony, Beauty,
and Eternal Fitness," 146
Teichert, Minerva, 8, 69
theology, Mormon female: male
domination of, 210–13, 216, 223;
redefining theology and context,
214–16, 222; and redemption, 216–
22; and Relief Society, 219–20
Turner, Frederick Jackson, 4

Ulrich, Laurel Thatcher, vii, 6, 13, 228
United Brethren, 88–89, 90, 92
Utah Art Institute, 146–47, 154, 161n14
Utah: Cache County, 196; Elsinore,
196, 203; Ephraim, 195–96; Logan,
196; Manti, 196; North Fields, 197;
Ogden, 28, 39, 40–41, 44n20, 47n65,
169, 185; Payson, 167–77; Pleasant
Grove, 185–86, 188, 192–201,
203–4; Pleasant Valley, 188; Salt
Lake City, 153, 156, 174, 176, 186,
188, 195–96, 200, 203–4; Salt Lake
Valley, 148, 159; Sanpete County,
195–97; Sevier County, 196; Spring
City, 196; Utah County, 195–96

Ward, Barney, 27–30, 34–36, 38, 39
Ward, Sally Exervier, x, xv, 27–28,
34; conflation with Sacagawea, 33;
daughters, 35, 40–41; marriage, 27,
31, 36–38; oral accounts of, 28–29,

Contributor Biographies

Julie K. Allen earned her PhD in Germanic languages and literatures from Harvard University, was the Paul and Renate Madsen Professor of Scandinavian Studies at the University of Wisconsin from 2006 to 2016, and has been a professor of comparative arts and letters at Brigham Young University since August 2016. She works on questions of national and cultural identity in northern Europe—particularly with regard to migration, gender, and religion—from the nineteenth to the twenty-first centuries. She is the author of *Icons of Danish Modernity* (2012) and *Danish but not Lutheran* (2017).

Rachel Cope is an associate professor of church history and doctrine at Brigham Young University. She has published several articles on American women's spirituality and conversion in the late eighteenth and early nineteenth centuries, which have appeared in various edited volumes and journals. She also coedited *Family Life in England and America, 1690–1820* (2015). Rachel is an assistant editor of *Wesley and Methodist Studies*, the managing editor of *Mormon Studies Review*, and one of the founding editors of the Transcribing Early American Manuscript Sermons project.

Amy Easton-Flake is an assistant professor of ancient scripture at Brigham Young University. Her research focuses on nineteenth-century women's reform literature and biblical hermeneutics. Her work may be found in the *New England Quarterly*, *Symbiosis: A Journal of Transatlantic Literary and Cultural Relations*, *Journal of Mormon History*, *Journal of Book of Mormon Studies*, and multiple edited volumes.

Keith A. Erekson is an internationally acclaimed writer, speaker, and public historian who currently serves as director of the Church History Library of the Church of Jesus Christ of Latter-day Saints. He earned a PhD in history from Indiana University and attained the rank of associate professor of history at the University of Texas at El Paso. He is the author of *Everybody's History: Indiana's Lincoln Inquiry and the Quest to Reclaim a President's Past* (2012) and the editor of *Politics and the History Curriculum: The Struggle over Standards in Texas and the Nation* (2012).

R. Marie Griffith, the John C. Danforth Distinguished Professor in the Humanities at Washington University in St. Louis, is currently the director of the John C. Danforth Center on Religion and Politics and the editor of the center's journal, *Religion & Politics*. Her first major publication was *God's Daughters: Evangelical Women and the Power of Submission* (1997), which examines the practices and perceptions of contemporary evangelical women. Her next book, *Born Again Bodies: Flesh and Spirit in American Christianity* (2004), explores the history of Christian-influenced attitudes and practices related to embodiment in modern America, culminating in the evangelical diet and fitness movement. These books, along with her three edited volumes—*Women and Religion in the African Diaspora: Knowledge, Power, and Performance* (coedited with Barbara Dianne Savage, 2006), *Religion and Politics in the Contemporary United States* (coedited with Melani McAlister, 2008), and *American Religions: A Documentary History* (2007)—exhibit Griffith's varied and thoughtful scholarship.

Amy Harris is an associate professor of history at Brigham Young University. She uses both her historical and genealogical training to study family relationships, particularly in eighteenth-century Britain. She is particularly interested in the way family and social relationships inform one another. She has published work on sibling relationships, childhood, and marriage in England as well as essays about genealogical methods and early Mormon women. She teaches courses on European history, genealogical methodology, and women's studies. She currently serves as the director for the Family History Program at Brigham Young University.

Heather Belnap Jensen is an associate professor of art history and the coordinator of the European Studies Program at Brigham Young University. While her primary research area involves women in post-Revolutionary French art and culture, on which she has presented and published extensively, she has recently turned her attention to transatlantic culture and Mormonism. Belnap Jensen has two book projects related to the latter area—one a coauthored text with Corry Cropper and Daryl Lee, *Marianne Meets the Mormons: Mormonism in the French Imaginary from 1830–1914*, and a monograph, from which the chapter in this volume draws, *Artistic Frontiers: Mormon Women Artists at Home and Abroad, c. 1880–1945*.

Benjamin E. Park is an assistant professor of history at Sam Houston State University. His articles have appeared in *Journal of the Early Republic*, *Early American Studies*, *American Nineteenth Century History*, *Journal of American Studies*, and *Journal of Mormon History*. His first book, *American Nationalisms: Imagining Union in an Age of Revolutions*, is forthcoming. He is currently an associate editor with *Mormon Studies Review*.

Josh E. Probert is a historian who specializes in the material culture of American religious and domestic history. He currently works as a historical consultant to the LDS Church Special Projects Department on projects related to nineteenth-century interiors. In 2005, he earned a master's in religion from the program in religion and the arts at the Yale Divinity School and Yale Institute of Sacred Music. In 2013, he earned a PhD in American history from the University of Delaware in cooperation with the Winterthur Museum.

Jenny Hale Pulsipher is an associate professor of history at Brigham Young University, specializing in early American and American Indian history. Her first book, *"Subjects unto the Same King": Indians, English, and the Contest for Authority in Colonial New England*, was published in 2005 and was selected as a Choice Magazine Outstanding Academic Title in 2006. Her second book, *John Wompas/John White: The Nipmuc Indian Who Sold His Birthright, Dropped out of Harvard, and Conned the King of England*, will be published in 2018. She has also published articles in the *William and Mary Quarterly*, *Early American Literature*, *New England Quarterly*, and *Massachusetts Historical Review*.

Andrea G. Radke-Moss is a professor of history at Brigham Young University–Idaho, where she teaches courses in American history, particularly US women's history and the history of the American West. She currently serves as the associate dean of faculty development for the College of Language and Letters at Brigham Young University–Idaho. Her book, *Bright Epoch: Women & Coeducation in the American West*, was published in 2008. Currently, Radke-Moss is researching a history of Western women's activism and participation at the Chicago World's Fair and Mormon women's experiences in the Mormon-Missouri War of 1838.

Lisa Olsen Tait is a historian and writer in the LDS Church History Department. She specializes in women's history and Mormon periodicals, focusing primarily on the late nineteenth and early twentieth centuries. Her PhD in American literature is from the University of Houston.